AGRICULTURAL MARKETING:
Systems, Coordination, Cash and Futures Prices

Wayne D. Purcell

Professor, Agricultural Economics,
Virginia Polytechnic Institute
and State University

61076

Reston Publishing Company, Inc.
A Prentice-Hall Company
Reston, Virginia

To my daughter, Tanya,
who likes to write

Library of Congress Cataloging in Publication Data

Purcell, Wayne D
  Agricultural marketing.
  Includes index.
  1. Farm produce—United States—Marketing.
2. Agriculture—Economic aspects—United States.
3. Marketing—United States. I. Title.
HD9004.P9   658.8'09'63   78-27889
ISBN 0-8359-0195-5

10 9 8 7 6 5 4 3 2 1

Printed in the United States of America

Contents

Preface

This book grew from a conviction that we need a treatment of agricultural marketing that focuses attention on the total marketing system and provides the analytical base to handle increasingly complex marketing problems. Filling that perceived need was and is my objective. The reader will decide whether I have succeeded.

In organization and in the choice of material, I have tried to keep the needs of the student and instructor in mind. After 12 years of classroom experience in this broad area of agricultural marketing, I have formed some perceptions of what will and will not work.

The book is organized in what I believe to be a logical sequence. It is written for the beginning student in marketing but offers material for the advanced undergraduate course or for a two-term marketing sequence. Upon examination, the instructor will find the more advanced coverage is positioned at the end of a chapter, in an appendix, or in a separate chapter. For example, Chapter 7 deals with techniques of price analysis. Coverage of model specification and simple quantitative models is included but is positioned at the end of the chapter. The instructor may prefer to not cover this material in the beginning course. Chapter 8 discusses the role of trade in commodity futures in general terms. Chapters 9 and 10 offer extensive coverage of trading techniques and hedging strategies. The materials in Chapters 9 and 10 are also suitable for the advanced course or the second term of a two-term sequence. By thumbing through the book, other such possibilities will be noted.

The book's coverage is not strictly conventional. Emphasis is placed on the market system and the concept of vertical coordination. As teachers, analysts, and students, we simply must make progress in moving toward increased awareness of the total system and how it functions. The coverage of price, pricing processes, and the techniques of pricing analysis is more extensive in this book than in many contemporary texts. Nothing is more important to the success of the marketing decision than the capacity to handle price. Coverage of commodity futures markets and hedging strategies is extensive and will, I hope, help to fill the void in the totally inadequate coverage in the available texts. This will be the growth area in the study of markets and marketing over the next 10 years. I hope the coverage in this text will help get us started on a solid foundation.

A course in economic principles or basic economic theory is a vital prerequisite to this book. Some formal training in statistics would help but is not essential. When statistical concepts are used, I have provided some basic coverage in appendices in terms the student can handle and understand. Every author gets a bit idealistic. Given a magic wand, I would have created a book that would transform the beginning student into an effective decision maker and problem solver where marketing is concerned. This is the reason for the many illustrations and the attention to contemporary problems. If I have come close to this goal, the writing will have been worthwhile.

Appreciation is extended to the Department of Agricultural Economics at Oklahoma State University. The book was written during my tenure there as a teacher and researcher in marketing. Leo Blakley, John Franzmann, John Goodwin, Jim Plaxico, and the rest of the faculty at Oklahoma State contributed more to the book than they realize. To Harold Breimyer, Richard King, John McCoy, and other reviewers, I extend a word of thanks. Thanks to Marilyn Wheeler who typed, proofed, and worried with the various drafts. To those close to me who both helped and were there when I was discouraged, thank you.

Wayne D. Purcell

part one

Introduction

Marketing has been defined in many ways. Most definitions have limited marketing to the economic activities performed after the product leaves the original point of production. But this is an overly restrictive approach. Marketing starts with production. The economic activities from production through consumption are a system. It is important that this perspective of a system be brought to the study of markets and marketing.

Chapter 1, Marketing in Perspective, sets the orientation for the text. A broad view of the total marketing system is encouraged. The interrelationships between stages of the system are stressed and presented as the important determinant of the level of vertical coordination that is achieved. The student of marketing will need to understand the total marketing system, the operational characteristics of the system, and why vertical coordination is important. The rewards take the form of more profitable marketing decisions and the capacity to contribute toward a more effective and more efficient total system.

The objective of Part I is to promote a systems orientation and a receptive and inquisitive frame of mind. If this is accomplished, the concepts and tools presented in later chapters will fall on more fertile ground.

chapter one

Marketing In Perspective

Establishing the proper perspective is necessary to the overall purpose of the text. Dealing with definitions is not usually productive but such will be essential in this case. Past definitions of marketing have served to constrain the scope and realism of what we have tried to understand and teach. This chapter will discuss what marketing is and is not, review some past approaches, stress the relative importance of marketing, and establish a base and an orientation for later chapters.

The Concept of Marketing

Many definitions of marketing exist in the literature but all definitions contain common threads. Most definitions that have either an agricultural or a food and fiber orientation refer to what happens *after* the product leaves the original point of production. This is the traditional "farm gate" approach. For example, Kohls and Downey define marketing as "the performance of all business activities involved in the flow of goods and services from the point of initial agricultural production until they are in the hands of the ultimate consumer."[1] Dahl and Hammond appear to follow the same theme and view marketing as a sequential series of functions that need to be performed as the input or product moves from its point of primary production to ultimate consumption.[2] The underlying idea is that production ends and marketing begins at the farm gate when the first transfer of ownership takes place.

Breimyer questions whether marketing as a concept can be distinguished from production. He correctly suggests the recombination of resources that takes place at each stage of marketing is production.[3] Other authors, aware of the difficulty in separating production and marketing, have tended to move toward a narrow concept of marketing. Bakken, writing in the early 1950s, suggested marketing should be confined to exchange.[4] Phillips has suggested limiting what we call marketing to information gathering and communication.[5]

The actual definition that is employed matters only insofar as it influences the orientation of the researcher, analyst, teacher, or student. Rather than define marketing in terms of highly restricted sets of economic activities, it appears that a broadening of what marketing is allowed to encompass would be more productive. It is difficult to separate, in a conceptual sense, production and marketing—so why try? The charge to marketing in an exchange system is to effect coordination between what is produced and what is demanded at the consumer level. Marketing is, therefore, nothing more than one dimension, an ongoing process, within the exchange system that serves to bridge the gap between producer and consumer.

Being a bit more specific, marketing might be defined as the set of economic and behavioral activities that are involved in coordinating the various stages of economic activity from production to consumption. Accepting this definition means no effort will be made in this textbook to formally separate production and marketing. Instead, production is viewed as a part of an interrelated set of economic activities, and emphasis is placed on the workings of the marketing system as the means of achieving coordination between production and consumer demands.

Figure 1.1 presents this concept of marketing in a simple but useful format. Starting with production, there is a set of economic stages of activity that constitute building blocks in establishing the bridge between production and consumption. Each stage is a link in the chain of activities that is being completed as the product moves toward the consumer. And each stage produces either form, place, or time utility to contribute to the final product that is made available to the consumer.

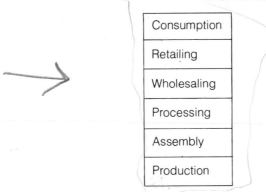

| Consumption |
| Retailing |
| Wholesaling |
| Processing |
| Assembly |
| Production |

FIGURE 1.1   ECONOMIC STAGES OF ACTIVITY IN A MARKETING SYSTEM[a]

[a]Not all marketing systems are comprised of this simple set of economic activities. In some systems, the wholesaling function has been essentially eliminated and the processor has taken over the brokerage, storage, and distribution functions the wholesaler once performed. Some systems have no organized assembly function and the product flows directly from producer to processor. What functions are performed by identifiable system participants changes over time with economic pressures, economic incentives, policy decisions, and changes in the way the system is organized.

Importance of Marketing

The study of marketing is important to both the individual and to society. To the individual, an understanding of marketing is important primarily because of the economic gains that understanding can bring. To society, benefits accruing to a better informed public include lower costs, more output per dollar of expenditure, or a better quality product.

TO THE INDIVIDUAL

From top to bottom in the marketing system, the individual decision maker faces marketing problems—and opportunities. The wheat producer must decide whether to sell his wheat or store it. All the expertise he has as a producer does him little good at this point. To make an effective marketing decision—that is, a decision that will be correct a high percentage of the time—requires knowledge of price patterns within the storage year. It costs money to store wheat. Will the price increase this year be enough to cover those costs and make storage profitable? How does the producer decide whether to store?

Table 1.1 illustrates the outcome of selling at harvest versus storing for several alternative price patterns. Clearly, there is much potential here. *The benefits of a year-long and outstanding job of production can be wiped out with a single poorly informed marketing decision.* Knowledge of prices, of pricing patterns, and the capacity to analyze the economic forces that cause and

Table 1.1
Illustration of the Outcome From Sell-Store Decisions
for Different Price Levels

Date	Cash Price of Wheat ($ per bu.)	Action Taken [a]	Net to Storage ($ per bu.)
June 10	$3.50	Estimate cost of storage to March @ $.25 per bu.	NA
March 10	3.00	Sell stored wheat	−.75
March 10	3.25	Sell stored wheat	−.50
March 10	3.50	Sell stored wheat	−.25
March 10	3.75	Sell stored wheat	0
March 10	4.00	Sell stored wheat	+.25
March 10	4.25	Sell stored wheat	+.50

[a]The action taken reflects the decision that was made. Note the sell or store decision can be made without regard to the costs of producing and harvesting the wheat since these costs are fixed and do not affect the profitability of the sell-store decision. In later chapters we will develop the tools needed to effectively analyze this decision situation and to make a decision with a high probability of being right.

change those prices will be a necessary condition to effective marketing decisions.

There exists a parallel to the decision situation confronting our wheat producer at all levels in all marketing systems. The manager of the breaking plant for beef carcasses must decide which carcasses he should buy and what combination of cuts he should prepare. Technical knowledge surrounding the breaking process is important, but the price relationship between the final beef cuts is the critical variable in determining which type of carcass and array of cuts will be most profitable.

At the retail level, the marketing decision is critically important. Consumer buying habits change over time. Habits and preferences differ across various socio-economic categories. The manager of the retail outlet must coordinate his offerings, his pricing policies, and his advertising campaigns to his particular market. Knowledge and understanding of consumer behavior is crucial—and this is part of marketing.

TO SOCIETY

The interest of society in marketing revolves around two related considerations:

1. The efficiency with which activities along the continuum from producer to consumer are performed; and

2. The efficiency of the marketing system in effecting change and adjustment when such is needed to insure or restore alignment between what is produced and consumer demands.

Figure 1.2 demonstrates why efficiency is important. The "marketing bill," defined as the cost of all economic activities after the original production, takes a high percentage of the consumer's dollar spent on food and fiber products and related services. Inefficiency, which is defined here as a smaller ratio of $ output/$ input than is possible given available technology, proves costly to society in terms of high consumer prices. The level of utility is constantly changing throughout the marketing system as the product is changed in form, transported, and moved toward the point of contact with the final consumer. Since utility is roughly equivalent to consumer satisfaction, increasing the efficiency with which the various economic activities are performed is desired by society.

The efficiency of the marketing system as a mechanism to maintain coordination between production and consumer demands is more difficult

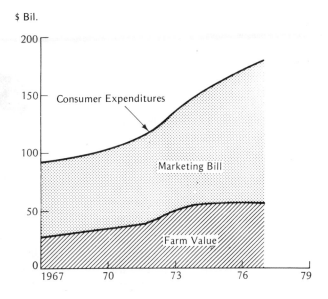

Source: *1977 Handbook of Agricultural Charts,*
Ag. Handbook No. 524, USDA.

FIGURE 1.2   FARM-FOOD MARKETING BILL AND CONSUMER FOOD EXPENDITURES

to monitor and measure. But this dimension of efficiency is important to society. Consumer preferences change over time and with a change in preferences comes a change in demand. Production costs and capabilities change with technology and resource availability. When demand or production possibilities change, an adjustment is needed. Failure to make an adjustment or delays in completing the adjustments mean lack of alignment between what is produced and consumer demands. The level of consumer satisfaction is therefore below levels that could be realized had the adjustments been made.

Marketing Efficiency

In our food and fiber marketing systems, we are concerned with two types of efficiency: technical efficiency and pricing efficiency. Both types were involved in our discussion on the importance of marketing.

Technical efficiency, as noted earlier, refers to the input-output relationships involved in the task of producing utility throughout the marketing system. Product forms are changed, storage and transportation functions are performed, all the necessary economic activities are financed, and the product eventually reaches the point of contact with the consumer. Traditionally, the efficiency with which these activities and functions are performed has been considered to be largely a function of the available technology. At the production level, a given level of technology dictates the combination of land, capital, fertilizer, feed, water, etc., to produce a particular product most efficiently. At the processing level, the available technology sets constraints on how things are to be done. The efficiency with which the total marketing task is performed varies with how effectively the various activities, when put together, merge into a total marketing system.

A perspective of technical efficiency that puts more emphasis on the total system is needed. Combining economic activities that are being performed efficiently when viewed independently *does not* guarantee a technically efficient total system.

Figure 1.3 illustrates what is at stake here. Without worrying just yet about what economic function is being performed at each level, average total cost curves (ATC) are shown for two states of economic activity. In a technical sense, the activity at stage I is most efficient (product produced at minimum ATC) for a volume of OQ_1 per unit of time. But the situation at stage II is different. Needs are for a different quantity, OQ_2, to realize the minimum cost of production. When the costs at both stages are considered and added, the total per unit cost of performing all the needed economic functions increases significantly when the weekly flow of output falls outside the ranges of quantities determined by OQ_x and OQ_y.

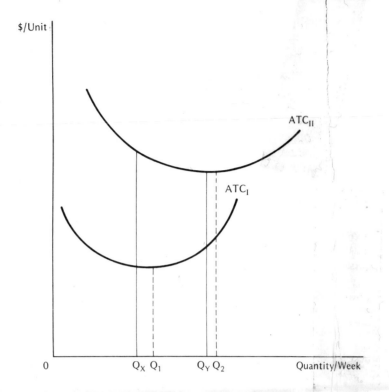

FIGURE 1.3   ILLUSTRATION OF THE IMPORTANCE OF COORDINATING RAW
MATERIAL AND PRODUCT FLOWS

Extending the concept of technical efficiency to cover the relative
efficiency of the total system effort is important, and places emphasis
where it appears to belong—on the degree of interstage or interlevel coordination that is achieved. Examining the simple graphics in Figure 1.3
suggests the cost of producing this product or service and making it ready
for the consumer will depend upon the extent to which weekly operating
levels are coordinated across all the stages of activity.

Pricing efficiency is certainly a related concept. It refers to the capacity
of the system to effect change and to prompt a reallocation of resources to
maintain consistency between what is produced and what is demanded by
consumers. In effect, the price mechanism serves as a communication system to relay the wishes of the consuming public to the producing segment.

Price signals become the messages. When a product or particular
quality of a product is in strong demand by consumers, the price is "bid
up" relative to the price of competing products or qualities. This price
signal is passed down through the system to the producer level where the
producer, given time to make adjustments he feels are economically jus-

tified, shifts resources toward production of the product or quality favored by the consumers. When a product falls out of favor with the consumer, the process is reversed—the price signal is a lower price and, at the producer level, resources are shifted away from the particular product.

The process is deceiving in its simplicity. The price signal has a long and potentially treacherous path to follow between the consumer and the producer. At every stage where decision makers of two identifiable economic stages of activity interact, a price is negotiated and a product changes hands. Several conditions must be met if the price signal is to be transferred through the negotiations, reach the producer, and motivate the desired response. Among the more important of these are:

1. The value of the product must be described and categorized by grades or other descriptive terminology so that both buyer and seller have a common or comparable interpretation of value;

2. The bargaining power, defined as the capacity to influence price or other terms of trade, must be comparable for buyer and seller; and

3. Prices must not be so volatile at the producer or any other level in the marketing system that the price signal is distorted or concealed.

Again, the need for interstage coordination is apparent. Analyzing the degree of "pricing efficiency" achieved by any particular marketing system will require considering the level of interstage coordination that is achieved. When defining pricing efficiency, then, it needs to be defined within the context of the total system. The level of pricing efficiency can be high only if the level of interstage coordination is high.

Approaches to Study and Analysis

Several references describe in some detail the traditional approaches to the study of marketing and analysis of marketing problems.[6,7] Emphasis has traditionally been placed on the commodity involved, the economic functions performed, or the institutions that are involved in performing the various functions.

THE COMMODITY APPROACH

The commodity approach focuses on what is done to the product after it leaves the original point of production. The approach follows the commodity along the path between producer and consumer and is concerned with describing what is done and how the commodity could be handled more efficiently. Historically, many of the marketing courses at the land grant universities dealt with a particular commodity or group of commodities. Often, courses in livestock marketing, dairy marketing, or fruit and vegetable marketing were taught.

The simplicity of the approach is its primary advantage. Focusing on the commodity cuts through the complexity of the situation and allows clear, definitive descriptions of what happens. Problems relating to spoilage, mishandling, poor quality control, multiple and unnecessary handlings, duplication of transportation, etc., are readily observed when the commodity is followed through the market channels.

But the disadvantages of the approach are apparent. Focusing attention on the commodity suppresses concern for the behavioral dimension of the activities throughout the system. Consideration of the stages of economic activity is forced to the background. Little or no attention is focused on the concept of interstage coordination and the importance of such coordination to the efficiency of the total marketing system.

THE INSTITUTIONAL APPROACH

Focusing attention on the institutions involved in handling the commodity or providing the marketing service is another approach to the study of marketing.[8] The institutions are important. They are the base of the behavioral decision processes and are the center of change. There can be no change and no adjustment without action by the institutions.

But emphasis on the institutions is not sufficient. In the final analysis, it will be the interaction of the institutions along the marketing continuum from producer to consumer that determines the degree of coordination and total system efficiency achieved. Neither detailed descriptions of the institutions involved, nor in-depth analysis of the actions of the institutions, will contribute in any significant way toward increased efficiency in marketing unless the focus of attention is extended to include the interstage actions and interactions.

THE FUNCTIONAL APPROACH

The efficiency with which the various economic functions are performed is important. And regardless of how the marketing system is organized, the economic functions necessary to the production of form, time, and place utilities must be performed. Since focus on the functions performed usually leads to consideration of institutions and a particular commodity, the functional approach provides the skeletal framework for a more encompassing approach to the study of marketing. Most contemporary marketing texts follow to varying degrees a functional approach.

The functional approach evolved because it offers one very strong advantage in study and analysis—specialization of attention. Focusing on a particular function such as processing, retailing, transportation, or consumption permits the careful scrutiny and detailed analysis needed to uncover and correct problems. A useful analogy is provided by the assembly line in any assembly plant. When the entire process is considered, it is difficult to recognize small but potentially significant inefficiencies at any one station along the line. A slight change in the speed of a conveyor belt, raising or lowering a work table, etc., might improve operations at a particular work station and eliminate a bottleneck that slows down the entire line.

But the specialization of attention gives rise to the disadvantage of the functional approach. If carried too far, specialization can treat the particular function as if it were independent of other functions to which it is technically related. The thread of continuity is severed when a function is "pulled out" for special attention and analysis. When refined and changed, the function may or may not "fit" the needs of the rest of the system. The synthesis of several functions, each of which is efficient when operated in isolation, in no way guarantees an efficient total system.

THE SYSTEMS APPROACH

A systems approach to marketing can range from the simple to the very complex. Where perception and orientation are important, the "systems approach" need be no more complex than a concern for the total system and a concurrect awareness of the importance of interstage coordination to the efficiency of the total system. If detailed analysis is needed, the systems approach may involve construction, testing, and application of complex mathematical models of a particular marketing system.

But awareness of the essential attributes of a total system must underlie all the approaches from simple to sophisticated. Among these attributes are:

1. An ongoing and continuous process of economic activity. In a marketing system, flows of the product and related flows of information are continuous and potentially reversible processes.

2. Control centers to act on or control the identifiable activities. The decision centers at the stages of economic activity in the marketing system function as control centers at each stage or level.

3. A control mechanism to integrate the identifiable activities into an ongoing process and a system. In marketing systems, the control mechanism varies with the organizational structure of the system. In an exchange system, activity at the various stages is controlled by identifiable management centers and price becomes the

mechanism to effect interstage coordination. When all stages are owned and controlled by a single management entity, the system is said to be integrated vertically. Management directive replaces price as the coordinating mechanism.

Adopting a systems approach means emphasis is placed on the total system, its efficiency, and the ongoing, continuous processes that make up that system. When the economic functions at any stage of activity are discussed, the discussion revolves around the role of that function in the total system. When group activities are discussed, these activities are discussed within the context of the total system. Attention is paid to the level of coordination achieved at the interface of any two or more stages that are technically related. The entire continuum, from producer to consumer, becomes the focal point of attention and this "systems orientation" influences the way marketing is described and analyzed.

Current Issues and Needs

Implicit in the discussion to this point is the need for a broader perspective in the study of marketing and in the analysis of marketing problems. Adopting a systems approach in this text recognizes that need.

Recognizing the need for a systems approach is not new. Kohls was calling for a systems approach in the 1950s.[9] Shaffer echoed the theme in the 1960s and called for a change in orientation in our study of marketing and in the analysis of marketing problems.[10] Godwin and Jones, writing in the 1970s, bemoaned the lack of progress in moving toward a systems approach.[11] Purcell argued the same point and offered suggestions for how the research orientation should be changed.[12]

Change in the way we study marketing must precede, or at least come concurrently with, change in the way marketing analysis is conducted. The idea of a system is abstract; the idea of systems analysis is both abstract and complex. This is why progress in moving toward a systems approach has been slow.

In the classroom, more attention will have to be focused on the concept of interstage coordination. Better understanding of what goes on at the interface of any two stages and how it relates to overall system efficiency will prove to be essential. But these concepts are difficult to show on a blackboard. They are difficult to illustrate. And from the student's viewpoint, there is a tendency to view the activity of the system as yet another step removed from reality. The teaching function becomes more difficult.

In the research and analysis arena, we find an analogous barrier to change. The economic activity at any particular stage is easily identified, easily described, and is usually amenable to measurement. These are the conditions for the type of analysis that is rather straightforward, manageable—and relatively easy. Moving to a systems approach brings a significant change in complexity. Product transformations are involved as the product form is changed in moving from stage to stage. Time lags emerge and the behavioral reactions of the decision centers start to exert influence on what is done and how it is done. Marketing research and analysis becomes more complex and more difficult. But the task is certainly not a hopeless one. Progress is being made and the outlook is encouraging.

Purcell describes an approach that may have potential.[13] To focus attention on the interfaces of the beef marketing system, the traditional approach to field interviews was altered. Subsystems of the total marketing system were identified. Questions probing goals and operating procedures were posed to decision makers in one stage. Then the "mirror image" of those questions was presented to decision makers at the interrelated stage of activity.

To illustrate, consider the producer-cattle feeder subsystem of the beef marketing system. In simple terms, the task of the producers is to produce an output (feeder cattle) that becomes an input to the cattle feeder. To establish the extent to which the output is consistent with input needs, a battery of questions and a series of pictures were presented to the producers. The questions dealt with the type of feeder cattle the producers wanted to produce and the type of feeder cattle the producers felt would meet the input needs of the cattle feeder. The pictures were selected to show cattle representative of the range of types that pass through the market place. Response patterns of the producers were recorded. The "mirror image" questions and the same series of pictures were then presented to cattle feeders. Again, the response pattern was recorded.

The recorded preferences of the two groups were significantly different. The hypothesis that interstage activity in this particular subsystem of the total beef marketing system is not coordinated was confirmed. And the results raise questions for the teacher, student, and analyst alike. Why does the inconsistency prevail? Why is there little evidence of interstage coordination? If the price mechanism is to effect change and insure interstage coordination, what has happened in this particular case? We will come back to consideration of these and related difficult and thought provoking questions throughout the remainder of the text. More detailed examination of approaches to systems analysis will be presented in later chapters.

Orientation Of The Text

Examining the shortcomings in past approaches to the study of marketing and analyzing marketing problems dictates that we attempt to understand the total marketing system. This text is dedicated to that purpose and proceeds on the premise that broad and in-depth understanding of the total system is prerequisite to specialized and sophisticated analysis. The refinement in analytical procedure must come *after* the basic understanding has been developed.

The objective of the text is to foster and nurture the problem-solving ability of the marketing student of all ages who is or will be charged with making marketing decisions. In this chapter, the need for a broad "systems approach" has been discussed in some detail. Once the perspective of a system and the need to operate within the broad confines of that system have been established, attention can then be turned to developing the analytical tools necessary to cope with the complex problems the marketing system can bring.

Chapters 2, 3, and 4 emphasize developing and describing the marketing system and the economic and public policy environments within which the system must operate. Special attention is paid to price and pricing processes in subsequent chapters since the price mechanism is charged with the task of coordination. A change in scope is then made and more attention is focused on the individual marketing firm within the total system. It is here that the marketing decision must be made. Special attention is paid to price as the primary source of risk and uncertainty confronting the maker of marketing decisions. Strategies to cope with the risks and uncertainties of the market place are developed, analyzed, and applied as we move toward developing the student as a problem solver.

Summary

Worrying too much about exactly how marketing should be defined is unproductive and potentially misleading. Viewing marketing as the total system of economic activities that handles the necessary physical functions, transmits the related information, and coordinates production with consumer demand puts us on the right path. Such a perspective encourages looking at the total system and prompts concern about interstage coordination as the key ingredient of overall system efficiency. More importantly, it influences the thought processes of the teacher, analyst, and student of marketing and increases the level of understanding of the total marketing system.

Footnotes

1. Richard L. Kohls and W. David Downey, *Marketing of Agricultural Products* (New York, N.Y.: Macmillan, 1972), pp. 8–9.

2. Dale C. Dahl and Jerome W. Hammond, *Market and Price Analysis* (New York, N.Y.: McGraw-Hill, 1977), Chapter 1.

3. Harold F. Breimyer, *Economics of the Product Markets of Agriculture* (Ames, Iowa: Iowa State Univ. Press, 1976), Chapter 1.

4. Henry H. Bakken, *Theory of Markets and Marketing* (Madison, Wisc.: Mimir, 1953), p. 34.

5. John Phillips, "A Revised Approach to Marketing", *Rev. Marketing and Agr. Econ.*, Vol. 36, pp. 28–36, 1968.

6. Edward A. Duddy and David A. Revzan, *Marketing, An Institutional Approach* (New York, N.Y.: McGraw Hill, 1953), Chapter 1.

7. Max E. Brunk and L. B. Darrah, *Marketing of Agricultural Products* (New York, N.Y.: Ronald Press, 1955), Chapters 1, 2.

8. As used in this text, the term "institutions" refers to the aggregate of the firms or behavioral systems that operate at the different stages of the marketing system. For example, central markets or processors, taken as an aggregate or a group, are a type of institution. Similarly, market advisory services or farm organizations such as Farm Bureau and Farmers Union are institutions. Whether there is an organized trade group varies from stage to stage and across commodities.

9. Richard L. Kohls, "A Critical Evaluation of Agricultural Marketing Research", *J. Farm Econ.*, Vol. 39, pp. 1600–1609, Dec. 1957.

10. James D. Shaffer, "Changing Orientations of Marketing Research", *J. Agr. Econ.*, Vol. 50, pp. 1437–1449, Dec. 1958.

11. Marshall R. Godwin and L. L. Jones, "The Emerging Food and Fiber System: Implications for Agriculture." *Am. J. of Agr. Econ.*, Vol. 53, pp. 806–816. Dec. 1971.

12. Wayne D. Purcell, "An Approach to Research on Vertical Coordination: The Beef System in Oklahoma", *Am. J. of Agr. Econ.*, Vol. 55, pp. 65–68, Feb. 1973.

13. Ibid.

Questions

1. What distinguishes a system from a group of unrelated activities?

2. Students of systems talk about control centers. What do you think the control center might be in our food and fiber marketing systems? How does it work?

3. Why do most traditional approaches to the study of marketing (commodity, functional) fail to provide a completely viable and effective approach?

4. How does technical efficiency differ from pricing efficiency? Can you see how a higher level of pricing efficiency could lead to higher levels of technical efficiency over time?

5. As a consumer, can you see any reason to be concerned about the level of technical efficiency being achieved in our food and fiber marketing systems?

Selected References

Breimyer, Harold F., *Economics of the Product Markets of Agriculture.* Ames, Iowa: Iowa State Univ. Press, 1976.

Dahl, Dale C. and Jerome W. Hammond, *Market and Price Analysis.* New York, N.Y.: McGraw-Hill, 1977.

Godwin, Marshall R. and L. L. Jones, "The Emerging Food and Fiber System: Implications for Agriculture," *Am. J. of Agr. Econ.,* Vol. 53, Dec. 1971.

Kohls, Richard L. and W. David Downey, *Marketing of Agricultural Products.* New York, N.Y.: Macmillan, 1972.

McCoy, John, *Livestock and Meat Marketing.* Westport, Conn.: Avi, 1972.

Purcell, Wayne D., "An Approach to Research on Vertical Coordination: The Beef System in Oklahoma," *Am. J. of Agr. Econ.,* Vol. 55, Feb. 1973.

Shaffer, James D., "Changing Orientations of Marketing Research," *J. Agr. Econ.,* Vol. 50, Dec. 1958.

Shepherd, Geoffrey S. and Gene A. Futrell, *Marketing Farm Products.* Ames, Iowa: Iowa State Univ. Press, 1969.

Sorenson, Vernon L. (ed.), *Agricultural Market Analysis.* East Lansing, Mich.: Michigan State Univ. Business Studies, 1964.

part two

The Market System and the Operating Environment

A marketing system is a viable and interactive set of economic functions with the potential for change. What we see emerge in terms of system performance is the net result of decisions made by individual decision makers operating as part of particular subsystems. The nature of that performance depends on the extent to which those decisions reflect understanding of the system and the implications of coordinated activity.

Marketing decisions are not made in a vacuum. The economic environment in which he operates determines what the decision maker can do. Policies set by federal and state governments often constrain the actions that could be taken and influence the outcomes of the actions that are taken. Some subsystems operate in an environment approaching pure competition. Others are oligopolistic in nature. The government is a factor in the market for all subsystems.

The objective of Part II is to foster understanding of the environment within which the decision is made and how that environment can exert influence. Goals for the individual firm, the subsystem, and the total system must be set with the operating environment in mind. The decision models that are adopted and the analytical tools that are employed must reflect awareness of that same operating environment. If the objective of Part II is reached, the important concepts and tools developed in Part III will increase the decision maker's ability to cope successfully with complex marketing problems.

chapter two

Market Systems

Developing a definition of "system" will help us understand our marketing systems. Ackoff discusses a system in terms of any entity, conceptual or physical, which consists of interdependent parts. He goes on to add that those who trade or work in the social services (such as economics) are interested primarily in *behavioral* systems or those systems which can exhibit action and interaction.[1]

Rabow presents a useful definition of a system and talks about systems analysis as follows:

> A system is an assembly of components that perform together in an organized manner. A component of a system may itself be a smaller system, sometimes called a subsystem. The systems approach is a method of dealing with complicated systems. It consists essentially of breaking up a systems problem into a number of component or subsystem problems.[2]

In these simple definitions, the concept of interdependence stands out. And interdependence is the key distinguishing feature of a system. If the activity or activities being considered are so simple that only one activity and one control center can be identified, there is no system. Pursuing this line of reasoning suggests the simplest system is comprised of two identifiable and interdependent functions and a single control center.

That our food and fiber marketing systems extend far beyond this simple type of system is apparent from the most casual observation. Many stages of economic activity are observable for any and all commodities along the continuum from producer to consumer. Specialization has become a way of life in our marketing systems. Each time a new specialty emerges, the system becomes more complex and another interface joins those that already exist. The change is particularly noticeable at the producer stage. The producer now specializes in production and leaves the transporting, storing, processing, and related functions to other specialists.

All the necessary ingredients of a viable and functional system are to be found in our marketing systems. The technical interrelationships guarantee the existence of interdependence. But we need to push our perception of a marketing system beyond just recognizing the interstage interdependence. In Chapter 1, mention was made of the role of our marketing systems as a coordinating mechanism. Change and adjustment over time must be possible if coordination between production and demand at the consumer level is to be maintained. Technical interdependence, which takes the form of input-output interrelations between stages of economic activity, tends to be static and resistant to change. It is the operational dimensions that can change.

The seat of adjustment and change is found in the other necessary conditions for a system. Paraphrasing Ackoff, three additional conditions can be identified:

1. There must be an opportunity to choose from sets of possible courses of action with two or more decision centers to make these choices;

2. The distinct and identifiable decision centers are aware of each other's behavior and actions either through communication or observation; and

3. There exists, within the system, some freedom of choice of both courses of action and desired outcomes.

Merge these three conditions with the existing technical interdependence and we have a workable picture of a marketing system. Whatever the product or service, the conditions are met. There are distinct decision centers along the production-consumption continuum that are aware of each other, work with each other, struggle and compete with each other, and, economically speaking, live and die with each other.

Interstage Interfaces

Activity along the interface[3] is the primary determinant of the degree to which technically related stages of economic activity are effectively coordinated. To further advance understanding of the system, therefore, requires attention to what goes on along those interfaces.

Along the interface, exchange is negotiated, price and other terms of trade are bargained, and the product changes hands. A legitimate buyer-seller conflict evolves. The seller comes seeking the highest possible price subject to any constraints he feels are necessary to guarantee a viable position in the market over time. The buyer comes seeking the lowest possible price subject to the pressures of needing the seller's product as input to his own operation. Emphasis is placed on price and other important terms of trade—quantity, timing of product flow, when title changes hands, liability for loss, and quality considerations or restraints.

Procedurally, the buyer-seller interaction along the interface of any two related stages of economic activity serves to merge the two stages, provide the needed services, and continue the ongoing processes of product preparation and information flows that are a part of any system. The two technically related functions must be brought together in an operational sense. Timing and coordination of effort between two stages of activity is a necessary condition to coordinated and efficient activity. What is needed is similar to the coordinating of two work stations in an assembly line.

But the market system is complex and coordination is more difficult to achieve. In Chapter 1, we introduced the issue of coordination and briefly discussed the role of price. In an exchange system, price signals are relied upon to transmit the needed messages and see that the needed coordination is there. But the message initiated at the retail level must be passed through not one but many price negotiations. In an assembly line, an overseer or foreman can watch over the entire line and correct any malfunctions. Work stations that become bottlenecks and hold down the output of the entire line because they are not properly coordinated with the adjoining stations on the line can be identified and changed as needed. In a market exchange system, there is no single control center to watch over the workings of the system, and the price signals often face a rough and perilous path.

Implicit Systems

In describing a market system, our attention has been focused on stages of economic activity and product flows. Brief reference has been made to technical interrelationships. But internal or implicit to the marketing system are other identifiable systems.

THE TECHNICAL SYSTEM

The technical or input-output system is the obvious physical backbone of the marketing system. Input-output relationships provide interstage linkages throughout the system. Technical coefficients control the input-output relationships and constitute one of the sources of gradual change in the system over time. For example, the cotton that leaves the producing areas of the South is transformed into clothing in factories around the country. But man-made fabrics now offer serious competition. The input-output relationships in cotton production and processing have changed over time as new and more efficient technology has evolved and competition has intensified. The Choice steer that leaves the feedlots of the Midwest and Southwest produces around 43 percent of its live weight in the form of lean, boneless cuts of beef. The move toward more grain-fed beef since the 1960s has increased this percentage. And selective breeding, employing new technology and knowledge of genetic structure, is producing beef cattle that will yield higher percentages of lean cuts of beef for given feeding programs. The technical system can change over time, does tend to react to the economic pressures of competition, price, and cost, and is a source of possible improvement in overall system performance.

THE POWER SYSTEM

Alderson popularized the idea of a power system in each of our marketing systems.[4] Power struggles are characteristic of any marketing system and occur each time exchange is negotiated. In general, the power held by any one of the identifiable decision centers is a function of the economic structure within which the decision center operates.

At the level at which most food and fiber products are produced, the economic structure approaches the theoretical conditions of pure competition. There are many small sellers, the product is largely homogeneous, and the only restraint to entry into the industry is the increasingly large capital requirements. The wheat farmer in Kansas hauls his wheat to the elevator and accepts the posted price that is an industry-determined price adjusted for differences in location. Generally the same situation faces the cotton farmer in Oklahoma, the peanut farmer in Georgia, and the truck crop farmer in California. The New York dairy farmer faces a slightly different situation with federal market orders influencing price, but there remains the characteristic feature—there is no price negotiation.

Moving higher into the system moves away from the conditions of pure competition. The processor changes the form of the product, attaches a brand name, creates an image for the product through a merchandising program, and negotiates a price. Even wheat, a homogeneous product in the unprocessed state, becomes something different when it is processed and becomes an identifiable brand of flour.

With the change in economic structure comes a change in the market power position of the decision center. At the farm level, the producer is a price taker. Above the farm level, the situation is different. Market power, the capacity and ability to influence price and/or other terms of trade, becomes a reality. As a general rule, the larger firms are usually able to wield more market power. Regardless of size, the financial strength of the firm, the nature of the product (perishable or non-perishable), the degree of product differentiation achieved, and the degree of diversification in product lines and raw material needs all influence the market power of the firm. We will come back to these issues in later chapters and deal with the different economic structures in more detail. The concept of a power system within the various structures helps us to understand the interactions between and among decision makers at the various stages.

THE COMMUNICATION SYSTEM

In any system of interdependent activities a communication system is an integral and important dimension of the total system. Communication is an ongoing, continuous, and potentially reversible process that largely controls the behavioral procedures at the decision centers in the marketing system.

The price mechanism has been identified as an important means of communication in our marketing systems. Price signals become the primary messages. But the key requirements for an effective communication system must be met if communication is to effect coordination.

A basic requirement is comparable knowledge on the part of all involved in the communication process. In communication theory, the message is encoded by an entity called a "source." After passing over some "channel," the message is accepted and decoded by another entity called a "receiver." If the receiver is to give the message the interpretation desired by the source, a level of knowledge comparable to that used by the source in encoding the message must be available and employed.[5]

Consider what this means in a marketing system. Price is charged with the task of carrying the message. Price is negotiated by buyer and seller—but price for what? How is the product described? If by grades or other indication of quality, do the grades receive common interpretation by buyer and seller? If interpretations applied to the grades are different, or if value or quality differences within the grades allow for vagueness in interpretation, the probability is small that the price mechanism can serve as an effective communication system. If the exchange system is not effective as a communication system, the probability of coordination between what is produced and the demands of consumers is low.

Inadequate communication in the exchange system can help motivate change to improve communication. Contracts can be brought into use to correct some of the communication shortcomings. Not only price but other important terms of trade, such as the timing of the exchange, can be specified. Quality restraints and conditions which clarify exactly what is being traded can be written in to help control quality. If no other benefits accrue from the contractual arrangement, describing the product and writing down the details of the trade are likely to improve communication.

An alternative to the negotiated cash contract is to enter into contractual arrangements and tie price by a formula to some market indicator either in the current time period or on the date of delivery. This "formula pricing" is important for several commodities and is a source of increasing concern to many market analysts. Some feel the only competitive price is the negotiated price. Others argue formula pricing is more efficient because it eliminates the need for every buyer or seller to get involved in the negotiation process. We will look at this question in Chapter 6. But the key to whether formula pricing or any other approach is effective or efficient is the level of communication that is achieved.

Another alternative is to completely eliminate the need for communication along the interfaces of the marketing system.[6] The organizational structure of the system can be changed to bring two or more of the economic stages of activity under the control of a single decision center. This is called vertical integration. The stages of activity can then be managed to insure the desired coordination. The timing of product flows is controlled, quality is controlled, and the entire process is fine-tuned and synchronized like the assembly line used in the earlier analogies. The only limits to the level of vertical coordination achieved are the available technology and the extent to which the decision maker(s) can effectively control the interstage processes. Coordination by management directive can be used when coordination via communication is difficult to achieve.

Vertical Coordination

Knowledge of the economic environment and effective communication have been identified as requisites of coordinated activity along the vertical continuum from producer to consumer. A related and very important requirement is the existence of economic incentive.

If interstage coordination is to be achieved in an exchange system, the decision maker must see some possibility of economic gain. It could be reduced costs, increased profits, more stability in the profit stream, firm growth, a stable supply of raw materials, or any one of many possible sources of economic gain. But to work with others in the system requires a capacity to look beyond the obvious buyer-seller conflict and into the complexities of the system—and to see a possibility of economic gain through coordination.

Consider the situation facing a processor. The processor depends on the producing subsystem for raw materials. Consistent quality, a consistent quantity per unit of time (day, week, etc.), and the time at which the raw material is made available are all important to the processor.

The problems evolving from a variable flow of raw materials demonstrate both the need for coordination and the potential gains from coordination. A daily flow of output outside Q_1Q_2 in Figure 2.1 because of a variable flow of raw materials increases the per unit cost of processing. But coordination is required to stabilize the raw material flow. If the producer-processor interaction is viewed as nothing but an adversary relationship, the coordination is not likely to be forthcoming. The potential reductions in cost are missed.

To get a simple measure of the potential, let the per unit cost at a quantity OQ_m be \$.20 per unit. If the raw material flow declines and daily output drops to OQ_1 on half the working days, the average cost over time would then be \$.225 per unit. The cost of "no coordination" or failure to hold output at OQ_m is \$.025 per unit. This \$.025 per unit savings could be shared between the two stages of activity if they recognized the potential and worked together. Just how the savings would be allocated between the two will always be an unknown but the opportunity is there.

The obstacles to vertical coordination are implicit in the preceding discussion. Lack of knowledge, which extends to an understanding of

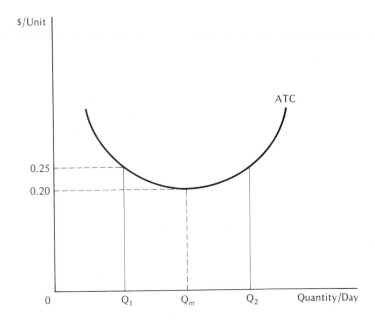

FIGURE 2.1   ILLUSTRATION OF THE POTENTIAL COST SAVINGS THROUGH INTER-STAGE COORDINATION

systems and how they operate, is a basic problem. Without understanding, there is a tendency to view cooperation or coordination as a zero sum game—that is, each participant believes the buyer or seller can benefit only at the expense of the other party to the transaction. And with this attitude, there will be no coordination and the adversary relationship will prevail. The effectiveness of the total market system falls short of its potential.

Related to lack of understanding is the problem of goal conflicts. When there is no clear understanding of the technical input-output relationships, the goals of system participants often conflict. What a particular decision center tries to accomplish in terms of product quality, timing of product flows, etc., may or may not coincide with the goal-related actions of other system participants.

As noted earlier, effective communication is of key importance. To a significant extent, the degree of vertical coordination achieved will vary directly with the effectiveness of communication along the vertical continuum from producer to consumer: If the price mechanism serves as the base for an effective communication system, the set of price signals will cut through the barriers, provide the necessary economic incentives, and help to offset the tendency toward an adversary relationship.

This concept of vertical coordination will be referred to often in later chapters. Technical interrelationships provide the physical structure of a marketing system. Vertical coordination is required to convert the physical structure into a viable system capable of change and adjustment. There is no concept more important when we are concerned about the performance of our marketing systems.

Alternative Vertical Structures

There are essentially no limits to the different ways of organizing the stages of economic activity within the total system. The alternatives range between the following polar extremes:

1. An exchange system that features ownership and control of each stage by a separate and identifiable management or control center. Important dimensions of this type of organizational structure include price negotiation along the interface between any two adjoining stages, and reliance on the price mechanism as a communicating and coordinating mechanism.

2. A totally integrated or closed structure that features ownership of all stages of activity by a single management or control center. Coordination is achieved by management directive. There is no price negotiation and the only visible pricing point is usually at the consumer level.[7]

Alternatives between the two extremes feature either lesser degrees of integration, a combination of integrated subsystems with non-integrated subsystems, or alternative ways of achieving coordination such as contractual arrangements.

As implied earlier, the trend is toward vertically integrated structures. Contracting is often an intermediate step. Integration is most likely in these commodity areas amenable to something approaching assembly line production and processing. The economic motivations are:

1. The ability to control the rate and timing of raw material and product flows;

2. The ability to control quality;

3. The direct contact with the consumer market, which can help to eliminate or reduce the time lag in adjusting production to changes in consumer buying patterns;

4. The elimination of part of the moving, hauling, handling, and transferring that occurs in an exchange system; and

5. The reduced costs, due to increases in both technical efficiency and communication, which can accompany a move to integrated structures.

Barriers to integration come in the form of large financial requirements, legislation that blocks mergers and acquisitions, the attitude of the public toward large corporate giants, and the absence of sufficient management ability to visualize and manage the integrated operation. But the barriers are obviously not sufficient to stop the move toward integrated structures. Vertical integration has made rapid strides in several commodity areas in recent years. A noteworthy example is broilers. Almost all broiler production is now under the control of completely integrated operations.

Comparisons of the overall effectiveness and efficiency of the alternative structures is of interest and is important. Firm management is interested because of the need to evaluate the potential payoffs (profits, firm growth, large market share, etc.) against the risks of failure that always accompany a significant change in structure. Policy makers are concerned because of their interest in overall system performance (as measured by price levels, price variability, profit margins, etc.) and because the legislation and advisory positions taken in the policy arena will influence, if not control, the extent to which our marketing systems become integrated. The consuming public is always interested if there is potential impact on the cost of products and services they must buy.

Budgets can be used to compare alternative structures. Research at Texas A & M University used the budgeting approach in estimating the cost of alternative structures in the beef marketing system.[8] The overall conclusion noted a significant cost saving under the integrated system as compared to the exchange system. Research at Nebraska employed a different approach, which included budgeting, and reported the possibility of large savings if market structures were altered to permit the use of electronic teleauctions in buying and selling livestock and related products.[9]

At Oklahoma State University, sophisticated models were constructed to evaluate the relative effectiveness of alternative structures.[10] The results proved interesting. The costs of producing the final product were reduced significantly by the integrated system. To check the importance of lack of coordination in an exchange system, all stages of activity above the producer level were restricted to the type of raw material (type and breed of cattle) the producer preferred to offer. Costs of producing beef increased significantly, profits to all stages decreased, and the rate of return on total system investment dropped. These and other approaches to analyzing alternative systems will be treated in more detail in Chapter 12.

Summary

The concept of a "marketing system" is nebulous and proves difficult for most students, teachers, and market analysts. But it is a crucially important concept to this text. Unless we can get the perspective of a total system firmly in mind, much of what is to come in later chapters will miss its mark. Without the perspective of a system and a systems orientation in thinking about marketing, what is taught and what is learned will fall short of the level needed to prepare the student to be an effective decision maker and problem solver in the systems of the real world.

When we look at the composite of all the economic activities in marketing as a system, interdependence is both recognized and emphasized. This is a significant departure from the more traditional approaches to the study of marketing. In the past, the most popular approach has been to "pull out" for study and analysis the economic activity at one particular stage. Such an approach permits specialization of attention but it also permits, perhaps even encourages, treating activity at that stage as if it were independent of the rest of the system. This implicit assumption of independence impedes understanding of the technical interrelationships that tie the stages together and blocks concern for the behavioral interrelationships. After careful study of activity at the particular stage, the student or the analyst still does not understand the intricate and complex workings of the total system.

Once the importance of interdependence is recognized, the focus of attention shifts to the interface or the interactions between the stages, not the stages themselves. The behavioral dimension becomes important as study reveals that it is how the decision centers at each stage react to, and interact with, each other that determines the level of coordination achieved. The level of coordination, in turn, exerts direct influence on the efficiency of the system. Technical efficiency is affected because the technical input-output relationships vary with the level of interstage coordination. The cost of doing the total job, from production through consumption, is therefore affected. Pricing efficiency is largely synonymous with vertical coordination. By definition, pricing efficiency is a measure of the capacity of the system to maintain coordination between what is produced and what is demanded by consumers. If high levels of vertical coordination are achieved, there will be coordination between production and demand.

To make the system complete, more than one course of action must be available to the decision centers within the system. If this condition is met and if the various decision centers are at least aware of the existence and actions of other centers, we have a behavioral system that is capable of change, adjustment, competition, error, needless competition, improvement, confusion, mistrust, inefficiency, and efficiency. All these possibilities argue well for study and understanding of the total system.

Footnotes

1. Russell L. Ackoff, "Systems, Organizations, and Interdisciplinary Research," *Organizations: Systems Control and Adaptation Vol. II* (New York, N.Y.: John Wiley and Sons, 1969), pp. 120–126.

2. Gerald Rabow, *The Era of the System* (New York, N.Y.: Philosophical Library, 1969), p. 2.

3. The interface is the point at which any two technically related stages of economic activity come together in an operational sense. In Chapter 1, the marketing system was visualized as a set of building blocks. In this context, the interface is the junction of two building blocks. There will be such an interface whenever and wherever any two stages require behavioral interaction to allow the technical tasks of product preparation and product transfer.

4. Wroe Alderson, *Marketing Behavior and Executive Action* (Homewood, Ill.: Richard D. Irwin, 1957), Chapters 1–3.

5. An excellent and straightforward approach to communication is provided by Berlo in the book listed in the references at the end of this chapter. The reference by Purcell reports an effort to conceptualize and view marketing as a process of communication. Increased understanding of communication processes appears to offer insight into what goes on in a marketing system and helps to isolate barriers to communication, coordination, and higher levels of efficiency.

6. The term "eliminate" may be a bit strong. There will always be a need for communication. What vertical integration does is replace the need for communication *between different management centers* with a need for communication between those directing various functions *within a single management center*.

7. This is typically referred to as a "vertically integrated" system. Thus, vertical integration refers to a method of vertical coordination which features control by ownership of two or more related stages of economic activity.

8. Ed Williams and Donald E. Farris, *Economics of Beef Cattle Systems* (College Station, Texas: Dept. of Ag. Econ. Rep. No. 74-3, 1974).

9. Ralph Johnson, *An Economic Evaluation of Alternative Marketing Methods for Fed Cattle* (Lincoln, Nebr.: Nebraska Agr. Exp. Sta. Bul. 520, 1972).

10. Kenneth E. Nelson, *A System Analysis of Information and Communication in Beef Marketing* (Stillwater, Okla.: Unpublished PhD Dissertation, Dept. Agr. Econ. 1976).

Questions

1. What is a "system interface" and why is activity along an interface important to the overall efficiency of a marketing system?

2. Do you think the type of technical system that prevails at any time will influence the type of communication system that will be needed within the overall marketing system? If the technical system changes, would you expect the communication system to change? Why or why not?

3. List and describe as many potential gains from interstage coordination as you can. Can you visualize any situation where coordination could possibly be a zero-sum game?

4. If the costs of performing the functions in a total marketing system are lower when the system is integrated, why have we not seen more moves to vertically integrated systems?

5. Try to put yourself in the position of an individual decision maker operating as part of one stage of economic activity in a marketing system. What steps would you take if your objective was to maximize your contribution to the total system effort?

Selected References

Ackoff, Russell L., "Systems, Organization, and Interdisciplinary Research", *Organizations: Systems Control and Adaptation Vol. II.* New York, N.Y.: John Wiley and Sons, 1969.

Alderson, Wroe, *Market Behavior and Executive Action.* Homewood, Ill.: Richard D. Irwin, 1957.

Berlo, David K., *The Process of Communication.* New York, N.Y.: Holt, Rinehart and Winston, 1960.

Collins, Norman R., "The Changing Role of Price in Agricultural Marketing", *J. of Farm Econ.*, Vol. 41, pp. 528–534, Aug. 1959.

Purcell, Wayne D., *An Appraisal of the Information System in Beef Marketing.* East Lansing, Mich.: Mich. State Univ. Agr. Econ. Rep. No. 151, 1969.

Rabow, Gerald, *The Era of the System.* New York, N.Y.: Philosophical Library, 1969.

chapter three

Economic Environment

The marketing decision must always be made within the constraints imposed by the economic environment within which the marketing firm operates. The flexibility of the decision maker, the alternatives he can consider, the power to influence price or other terms of trade, and whether he has any discretionary power in the market place are all a direct function of the economic environment.

There are an infinite number of possible organizational structures in any economic system. In the literature and in the development of economic theory, four structures have been identified and given extensive treatment:

1. Pure competition,

2. Monopolistic competition,

3. Oligopoly, and

4. Monopoly.

Numerous references treat this area in detail and several are listed at the end of this chapter. Our coverage here will focus on the implications of these competitive structures to the marketing decision.

Pure Competition

The primary feature of importance in the pure competition structure is the large number of firms. Many small firms comprise this structure and the individual firm, by its production and marketing decisions, can have no influence on price. Consequently, the individual firm faces a demand curve that is horizontal at the industry-determined price level.[1] This is illustrated in Figure 3.1.

Given this economic structure, the individual firm has no pricing decision to make. Once production, storage, and "when to sell" decisions are made, the decision maker must look to the industry-determined price. He cannot and does not "set" a price for his product. But this does not mean an individual decision maker should ignore analyzing and understanding the discovery and behavior of price. In fact, the opposite is true. If the capacity to influence price is denied the firm, the ability to anticipate and react to moves in the industry-determined price is even more important.

In practice, however, the individual decision maker faces real limitations on what he can do to improve his situation even if he understands the implications of the environment within which he operates. The individual firm in a purely competitive structure is caught up in what we might call a "micro-macro paradox."

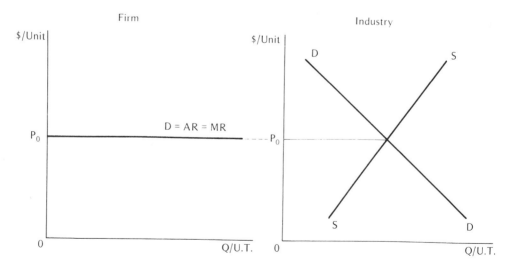

FIGURE 3.1   FIRM LEVEL DEMAND UNDER CONDITIONS OF PURE COMPETITION

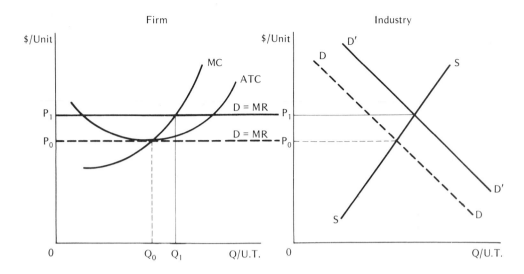

FIGURE 3.2   **ILLUSTRATION OF THE REACTION OF THE FIRM TO AN INCREASE IN INDUSTRY PRICE**

Production agriculture is the best example of a sector of the economy that approaches the conditions of pure competition. Within production agriculture, the wheat farmer is probably the best example of an individual decision maker who is confronted with the micro-macro paradox. Look at Figure 3.2. Assume the industry price rises from OP_0 to OP_1 because of an increase in industry demand from DD to D'D'. This increases the demand at the farm level. The individual farmer responds by increasing the quantity produced in the next crop year from OQ_0 to OQ_1.[2] This is consistent with economic theory that calls for the individual firm to maximize profits by equating MC and MR. In the short run, the portion of the MC curve above AVC is the supply curve for the individual firm.

Figure 3.3. illustrates the macro result. New firms enter and add to the production by each existing firm. Industry supply increases from SS to S'S' and industry price falls—back to OP_0 in Figure 3.3. At this point, we see the beginnings of a long-run problem for the wheat farmer, and, in the process, see the consequences of a competitive structure approaching pure competition. The response at the firm level is not an irrational response. Even if the individual farmer predicts the implications of the aggregate response, it is still rational to respond and increase production. Other firms *will* enter and the price *will* fall. The individual firm, if it did not increase output, would simply have fewer units of product to sell at the lower price. By his own actions, he cannot prevent the decline in price. Unless he has alternative uses for his resources, he faces the price problems that will come when the increase in supply hits the market.

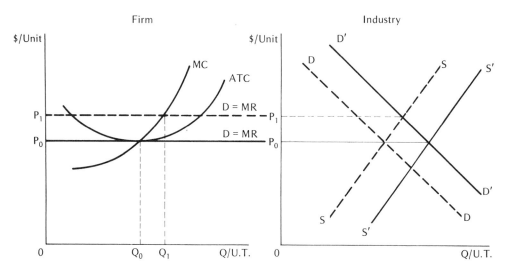

FIGURE 3.3   ILLUSTRATION OF THE MACRO RESULTS OF INCREASED OUTPUT BY
EXISTING FIRMS AND NEW FIRMS THAT ENTER THE INDUSTRY

Let's recap what has been discussed to this point:

1. Starting from an equilibrium position, industry demand increases, which increases the price to the individual firm;

2. The individual firm responds to the higher price by increasing production and new firms enter the industry; and

3. The aggregate or macro response from the many small firms increases industry supply and forces a decline in industry price (back to OP_0 in Figure 3.3). New resources have been brought in by the new firms and by existing firms that expanded their production capabilities.

Let's discuss more fully this last point because it is here that the long-run problems begin. Many of the resources brought into production during the short-run period of higher prices will stay in production after the prices fall for two primary reasons:

1. The alternative uses for the land resources are often limited. Through much of the winter wheat belt from Texas northward through Nebraska, the acreage is best suited to wheat production. Also, because all grains are to some extent substitutes, the prices of other grains—such as barley—tend to be down when wheat prices are down.

2. Capital equipment, such as combines and tractors, will usually be worth more in use even at relatively low product prices. Figure 3.4 illustrates this point. P_{acq} is the acquisition or purchase price of a combine. P_{salv} is the salvage price of the combine after it has been used. There is typically a large difference between the two prices. The MVP curve is the demand curve for the combine—a "value in use" schedule. Since MVP = MPP · $P_{product}$, the MVP curve shifts up when the price of the product increases and shifts down when the price of the product decreases. The product price must decrease enough to shift the MVP curve back through point A before P_{salv} > MVP—and the combine or other piece of equipment is taken out of production.[3]

This usually requires very low product prices. Given the tendency for equipment to stay in use when prices fall after a production increase, we see something other than the typical textbook supply response. Figure 3.5 illustrates some of the many possible "response paths" the individual firm might follow. The move from A to B is in response to an industry-wide increase in price. But once the expanded production swells the market pipelines, prices tend to fall. If we assume for purposes of illustration prices return to the original level, the next point on the supply response function for the individual firm may be a point such as point C—or D, or E. Output can be well above that at point A even though price is the same.

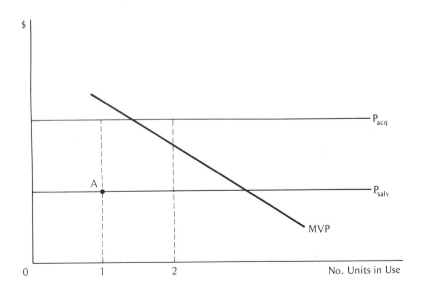

FIGURE 3.4   **ILLUSTRATION OF THE ECONOMIC FORCES THAT KEEP EQUIPMENT IN PRODUCTION**

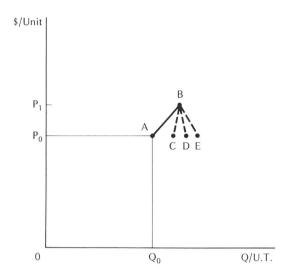

FIGURE 3.5   THE SUPPLY RESPONSE OF THE INDIVIDUAL FIRM WHEN INDUSTRY
PRICE FALLS

Output will tend to stay up until land and capital equipment are shifted out
of production or into other uses. And for reasons explained above, this
tends to be slow in coming.

The "micro-macro paradox" was very much in evidence in the wheat
market during the 1970s. During 1972, world supplies of wheat were
down. The USSR harvested a poor crop due to bad weather and bought
heavily from the U.S. Prices for wheat moved higher in dramatic fashion
accompanied by a great deal of publicity. Consumer groups grew concerned about the short supplies and high prices. In 1973, legislation removed the prior restraints on production and the wheat farmers responded
to the high prices by increasing acreage and bringing new equipment into
use. There was a waiting period of 6–10 months on new combines, tractors,
and related equipment. Production increased rapidly and surged to record
levels in 1976 and again in 1977. The 1977 crop of more than 2.0 billion
bushels was added to stocks of more than 1.0 billion bushels left over from
the 1976 crop—and prices tumbled to levels less than one-half the high
prices seen in 1972–73. But the resources bid into use during the period of
high prices were kept in production. To start the industry on a path toward
price recovery, the government returned to the marketplace with a program
involving set-aside possibilities for the crop seeded in 1977.

Other sectors of production agriculture face a similar problem. Most
individual firms producing cattle, hogs, soybeans, cotton, grain, or any
crop that is widely produced by many relatively small firms face something
very close to a horizontal or completely elastic demand curve. The micro-

macro paradox is a very real problem. Feedlot facilities constructed during periods of strong fed cattle prices still exist and are usually in use when prices fall. The grass, forage, fences, and equipment of the cow-calf operator and the farrowing and finishing facilities of the hog producer tend to stay in production when price moves down.

In summarizing the influences of a competitive structure approximating pure competition on the decisions of the individual firm we could list:

1. The individual firm is a price taker because it must sell its product(s) at an industry-determined price.

2. The tendency to "bid" resources into use during short-run periods of high prices proves to be self-defeating since the aggregate result is an increase in supply, which drives prices back down.

3. Resources brought into use by short-run high prices tend to stay in use if prices subsequently fall because their value in use exceeds their salvage price for all but the extremely low levels of product prices. There are exceptions but the tendency is there.

4. Product prices paid the individual firm can and do fall below the short-run ATC of production. Only for a time span long enough to allow the resources used in production to become variable so that they could be taken out of production, can we be sure product prices will move to a level equal to or greater than ATC.

Given the environment within which he must operate, the manager of the individual firm in a structure approaching pure competition clearly faces limitations on what he can do in terms of marketing decisions. But he must cope with the situation.

The first need is to understand the environment within which the firm is operating. Once the firm manager understands he is a price taker, he then realizes he cannot (1) set price on his product above the ATC of production, or (2) expect the price to stay above the ATC of production in the short run. Accepting this information, he can then move to a more positive approach to the problem.

The astute manager might then decide he will not blindly "follow the crowd." Expanding output in response to higher prices is economically rational. But the response must be prompt, efficient, and completed while there is a high probability of moving the expanded production to market before the price breaks. Continuing to expand wheat production in the year after price has been pushed below ATC of production is not a rational decision. Holding back gilts to expand hog production when every other producer has already started along the same response path is not rational. The weight of cyclical increases in production will force price to low levels by the time the expanded output of slaughter hogs is ready for the market. The individual manager does not have to be a "follower"—he can be a leader. But to do this requires perception and an understanding of what is going on in the market—and a set of signals to give a warning in time. The individual will want to watch such things as:

1. Stocks of wheat or other grains in both the U.S. and around the world. Year to year increases in stocks mean production is exceeding consumption, and, as stocks accumulate, pressure on price will surely follow.

2. In cattle, the cow-calf operator can watch such indicators as the rate of growth in the cow herd, the ratio of steer to heifer slaughter, the percentage of female slaughter, etc. We will treat this topic in detail in Chapters 6 and 7.

3. In hogs, hog-corn ratios that approach or exceed 20:1 will almost guarantee holding of gilts and a breeding herd expansion. A subsequent break in price, after time for the larger pig crops to be fed to market weights, is also essentially guaranteed. The astute producer does not have to play this game and could react by (a) culling his herd to the most efficient sows before the price breaks sharply, and (b) timing any expansion in his breeding herd so he will have more slaughter hogs during the periods of cyclically higher prices. This topic will also receive more attention in Chapters 6 and 7.

A third requirement in coping with the markets is the capacity to use the analytical tools available to the decision maker. Among those of value are:[4]

1. The seasonal index that indicates the normal seasonal pattern in prices. For example, the seasonal index for wheat starts to peak and level off in December. This raises questions about the advisability of storing wheat past the end of December.

2. Isolation and analysis of any cyclical production and price patterns. Establishing just where the industry is in the cycle allows the progressive manager to plan his production to minimize the damage from, or even take advantage of, the cycle.

3. Models to predict the level and direction of change in cash prices are important aids to the marketing decision. Whether the model is a graphical analysis, a balance sheet approach, or a more sophisticated quantitative approach, the ability to develop or adopt an outlook model is a necessary correlation to effective production and marketing decisions.

4. Technical analysis of the futures markets can help place and manage effective hedges. When combined with cash price outlook (to determine whether to hedge), technical analysis (to determine when to place and lift hedges) can make an important contribution to the decision maker's efforts to protect himself against cash price variability and uncertainty.

Monopolistic Competition

In this competitive structure, we are still dealing with many small producers and sellers but the condition of a homogeneous product across all sellers is missing. When there is product differentiation or any reason for a potential buyer to prefer one seller's product over another seller's product, the individual seller no longer faces a horizontal demand curve.[5] Therefore, marginal revenue is below demand at all quantity levels.

Figure 3.6 illustrates with a short-run equilibrium position for the individual firm. Profits are maximized where MR = MC at a quantity OQ_0 and price OP_0. The short-run supply function is the schedule of price-quantity combinations that would be generated by equating MC and MR for varying levels of MR. In the short run, the cost structure for the individual firm will not change and the MC curve shown in Figure 3.6 would

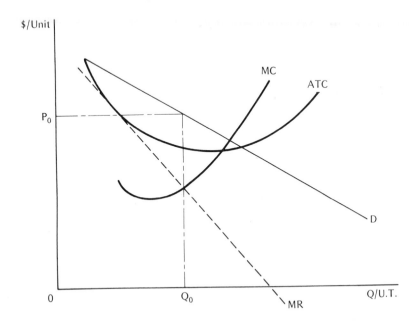

FIGURE 3.6   PROFIT   MAXIMIZING   POSITION   FOR   INDIVIDUAL   FIRM: MONOPOLISTIC COMPETITION

remain in effect. The demand curve facing the individual firm will shift with a change in industry demand for the general product grouping. How much change will occur depends on the degree of product differentiation at the firm level.

Within production agriculture are examples of conditions approaching monopolistic competition. The producer of seed wheat or seed corn offers a product that is different. Quality becomes a factor. Quality is also a factor in the production of cotton where staple length is important or in cattle where quality grade, dressing percentage, and yield grade are all potentially variable determinants of value. In practice, most producers have very little success in differentiating their product. But the key point is that the producer does not *have* to be strictly a price taker. He can bring information about the value of his product into the pricing process and *attempt* to establish a differential in price relative to his competitors in production.

Higher in the marketing system, the structure tends to move farther from the pure competition end of the continuum. In the grains, in the livestock industry, in the oilseeds, in the fibers, and in fruits and vegetables the number of firms decreases and the average firm size increases as we move to consideration of the processing sector. Both the level and the nature (the elasticity) of the demand curve facing the firm is partly a function of the efforts of the firm to differentiate their product-service offerings.

Live hogs may be essentially the same but individual brands of bacon can be significantly different as meat packers pass their product into distribution channels. Part of the difference can be physical, given different processing procedures, different additive packages, etc. But part of the difference can be a perceived difference. Brand X may be essentially the same as Brand Y but if the brand name under which X is sold has been effectively promoted via advertising, it may be perceived as different by consumers. To the extent the customer can be convinced Brand X is the "only brand to buy" both the level and the nature of the demand for Brand X are affected.

The ability to differentiate a product gives the individual firm flexibility in its pricing policy. In general, the firm moves away from a price taker status if it can do an effective job of differentiating its product or brand name. For a given price-quantity combination the demand curve becomes steeper, and, therefore, less elastic or perhaps inelastic. Given this set of circumstances, the quantity offered may be controlled by the manager to take advantage of the higher price for a smaller quantity. But the potential is limited. Each supplier is still sufficiently small that actions of any individual supplier will not exert significant influence on the general price level for the product. There is a higher price at which Brand X bacon will lose essentially all its buyers. Conversely, there is little reason to lower the price significantly below the price of competitive products. If price is lowered, the individual firm will simply sell its supply at a price below the level that could have been realized.

The marketing strategy and related pricing policies of the firm operating in an environment of monopolistic competition will stress efforts to differentiate the product and/or services in a relatively small market area. A pricing policy is then designed to conform with the overall marketing effort and the level of differentiation achieved. Because the capacity to effect product differentiation will be limited, the firm will use price competition as an important part of its overall marketing strategy. Price specials and price changes will be important parts of the program. Because the interfirm price competition is usually intense, any cost reduction coming from new technology or from an abundant supply of raw materials usually gets passed on to the buyer with very little time lag.

Oligopoly

The structure labeled "oligopoly" moves still further from the pure competition end of the continuum and is a significant move beyond monopolistic competition. Each firm is large enough for its actions to influence the market. Therefore, the firms are interdependent and this interdependence becomes the key determinant of marketing strategies and pricing policies.

Product differentiation is the primary means of competition in an oligopolistic market structure. And this typically means huge sums of money spent on advertising. Price competition is avoided.

Figure 3.7 illustrates why price competition is not usually a part of the marketing strategy of the oligopolistic firm. The firm cannot be sure of the location or level of the demand curve it faces because it can never be sure of the intensity of the reaction of competitive firms to a price change. If a particular firm has produced quantity OQ_0 and offered it at a price OP_0 for some time, the firm can generally expect the following reactions to a price change:

1. If price is increased, competing firms will not raise their price. The quantitative response (decrease in quantity sold) to the higher price will be a function of the extent to which the firm has been able to differentiate its product. Unless the efforts at differentiation have been highly successful, the portion of the demand curve at prices above OP_0 will be elastic—which means a percentage decrease in quantity greater than the percentage increase in price and a decrease in total revenue.

2. If price is decreased, competing firms will tend to retaliate by lowering their price. This will curtail the quantitative response to the

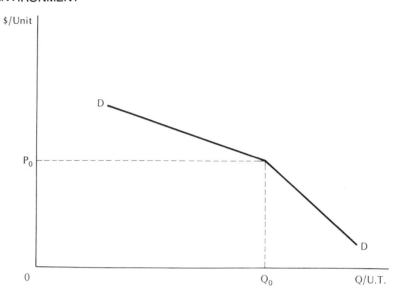

FIGURE 3.7   THE UNCERTAIN DEMAND STRUCTURE OF THE OLIGOPOLISTIC
FIRM

price decline and make the portion of the demand curve below OP_0 inelastic—which means a decline in total revenue if price is lowered.

Because of this interdependence, prices in an oligopolistic structure tend to be stable. Once an array of prices is established, it tends to stay the same. The difference between prices of various firms is a function of the comparative success at product differentiation. This gives the "kinked" demand curve shown in Figure 3.7. Each firm faces a demand curve like this. The quantity and price the firm selects is a function of the cost structure of the firm and the ability of the firm to differentiate its product.

The flour milling industry approaches oligopolistic status. Wheat is wheat but the flour produced by each firm is advertised as if it were a unique product. Processors in the fruit and vegetable sectors constitute another example. In the meat industry, the situation is a bit different. There are a few large national firms with many smaller firms active at the state or regional level. This particular industry might be labeled an oligopoly with a monopolistic competition fringe.

An oligopolistic industry in its purest theoretical form is difficult to find. There are sectors of our agricultural processing industry that offer the key characteristics of an oligopoly—heavy reliance on non-price competition (advertising, unique services, packaging, etc.) and a virtual absence of price competition. Because of the reluctance to compete on a price basis, the impact of a change in costs due to technology, change in raw material supplies, etc., may be absorbed for some time by the processor before it is passed on to their buyer or to the final consumer.

Given the setting within which the oligopolistic firm operates, there is a strong tendency for price leaders to emerge.[6] There are two primary types of price leaders:

1. The dominant firm price leader. One firm is dominant by virtue of either its relatively large share of the market and/or advantages in terms of lower costs of production.

2. The barometric price leader. A particular firm is essentially given the role of price leader by other firms because of demonstrated efficiency in operation, low cost of operation, proficiency in analyzing the market, setting effective prices, etc.

Figure 3.8 demonstrates the situation when there is a dominant firm price leader. The dominant firm determines its profit maximizing output of OQ_d and the other firms "fill in" the rest of the market. General Motors is an acknowledged price leader in the auto industry. U.S. Steel typically sets the pace in the steel industry. In the agriculture or agri-business sector, the

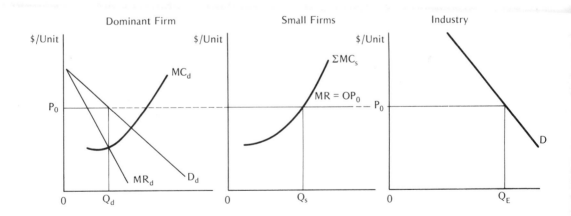

FIGURE 3.8   DOMINANT FIRM PRICE LEADERSHIP[a]

[a]The dominant firm equates MR and MC and maximizes profit at quantity OQ_d and price OP_0. The small firms equate MC to their MR (which is equal to price OP_0) and "fill in" the rest of the total industry demand. Note that $OQ_d + OQ_s = OQ_E$

dominant firm price leader is a bit more difficult to isolate. The actions of Pillsbury are watched by other firms in the milling and baking area. Iowa Beef Processors exerts significant influence by its pricing actions in the carcass beef market. In practice, we often see a "watered down" version of the dominant firm price leader where other firms watch the particular firm but do not fit the description of just filling in the rest of the market.

Figure 3.9 illustrates the barometric price leader. In the agricultural sector, a mixture of the dominant firm and barometric price leader is probably most typical. In the beef industry, for example, Iowa Beef Processors is the largest in terms of cattle slaughter. But IBP has also been an industry leader in developing and adopting new technology and new cost-reducing procedures in production and distribution. Consequently, at least part of the influence IBP wields in the market is related to its operating efficiency—an element of the barometric price leader.

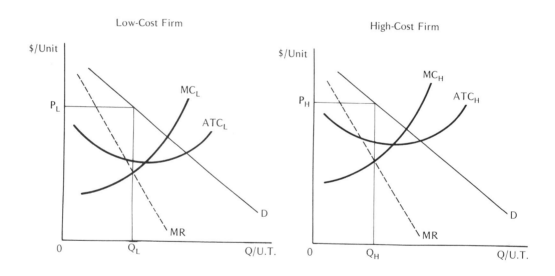

FIGURE 3.9   BAROMETRIC PRICE LEADERSHIP: LOW-COST FIRM WITH TWO FIRMS IN THE INDUSTRY[a]

[a]The low-cost firm maximizes profit at OQ_L and price OP_L. The high-cost firm would like to produce OQ_H and charge a price of OP_H but has no choice but to "match" the low-cost firm and produce OP_L at a price of OP_L. Total industry output at price OP_L is therefore $2OQ$. Over time, the high-cost firm will either accept a lower profit margin or, if OP_L is below long-run ATC, be forced to reduce costs or exit from the industry.

Monopoly

A monopoly is the opposite of pure competition. Instead of many small firms there is a single large firm. In its purest form, the monopoly firm faces the equivalent of an industry demand curve. Figure 3.10 illustrates the profit maximizing and equilibrium position of the monopoly firm. Profit is maximized where MC = MR at quantity OQ_E and price OP_E.

In the real world, the concept of a monopoly must be discussed within the context of a defined geographical area or market. Given delineation of a market or geographical area, there exists the so-called natural monopolies such as the utility companies. The ATC curve continues to show declines in per unit cost up to extremely large volumes and the most efficient economic structure to provide the services is a single firm monopoly. Figure 3.11 illustrates the type of ATC curve that dictates this approach.

In the agricultural sector, monopolies come close to being realized on a localized basis. In a particular rural community, the seller of farm machinery, fertilizer, or other input may be the only supplier in town. For all practical purposes the firm has a "sheltered market" and will be able to fill most of the local needs at a price that is a function of prices in surrounding markets, plus the costs of buyers going to those surrounding markets. With an aggressive program of product differentiation and after-the-sale service programs, the local firm may face a demand function that is gener-

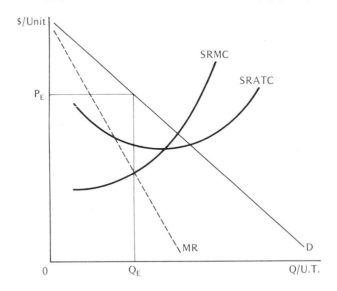

FIGURE 3.10   SHORT-RUN PROFIT MAXIMIZING POSITION FOR THE MONOPOLY FIRM

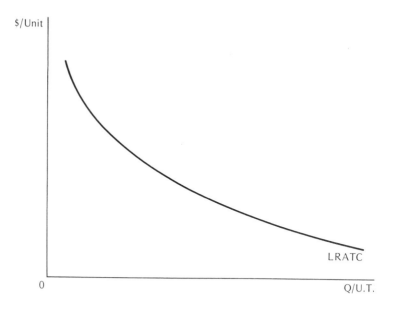

FIGURE 3.11   AVERAGE COST CURVE FOR THE NATURAL MONOPOLY[a]

[a]The long-run ATC continues to decline over all reasonable levels of operation. Under these cost conditions, consumers can be served most efficiently (at lowest cost) by a single firm.

ally inelastic. Given this situation, the firm can move up its demand curve into the elastic portion by controlling output.

Study of the monopoly is useful not only because monopoly situations are encountered at the local level but also because of the use of performance in a monopoly as a standard of comparison. In general, the monopolist will tend to restrict output and sell at higher prices than would be the case under a purely competitive structure—if pure competition or something approaching pure competition could in fact exist. If there are significant economies of size in producing the product or providing a needed service, using pure competition as a norm may not be realistic.

Overall, monopoly positions are approached in the agricultural sector primarily on a localized basis and on the input side. When these conditions exist, there will be a tendency toward emphasis on non-price competition—especially advertising—to help perpetuate the monopoly position. Pricing policies will be designed to secure pure profits but price levels will often be held down in order to discourage entry of competing firms. In production agriculture, the closest approximation would be a producer who sells certified seed, a purebred breeder in cattle or hogs, etc. A monopoly is not an important structure where the seller of agricultural products is concerned.

The Entire System

When the entire system is considered, one feature that stands out in importance is the sharp differences in the role the decision makers play in the pricing process. In general, as attention moves up through the system from the producer level, the ability of the decision maker to influence price or other terms of trade increases. The role of price taker is restricted primarily to the original production level.

Illustrations help to clarify this point and it is an important point to the maker of market decisions. In the beef sector, price is determined at the various levels as follows:

1. The retail chains evaluate the yes-no decisions of consumers at particular price levels for the various cuts of beef. These decisions or "votes" are interpreted and formulated as price bids to the firm engaged in breaking the beef carcass and selling primal and subprimal cuts. Over time, the array of bids is planned to realize a goal specified in terms of a return to the meat department of the retail chain.

2. The carcass breaker considers the bids from the retail chain and calculates what price can be offered for carcasses of a specified quality to realize an operating margin per carcass.

3. The slaughtering firm converts the price it can get for dressed carcasses of various qualities into bids for live cattle with the bids planned to realize a gross operating margin per head.

4. The cattle feeder "takes" the bid for live cattle with little or no capacity to influence price on a given quantity of cattle.

5. The producer of stocker and feeder cattle "takes" the market price on any particular day he sells with little or no redress. He is a price taker with, as a rule, no one below him in the production-marketing chain to allow him to realize some operating margin by adjusting buying prices. His "buying price" is essentially his cost of production.

Figure 3.12 illustrates the interstage interactions in a simple schematic framework. On any particular day, the supply of slaughter cattle made available for slaughter is largely fixed—the daily supply is for all practical

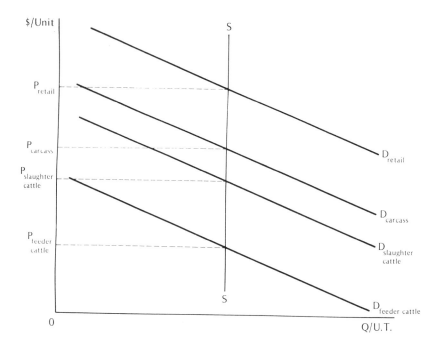

FIGURE 3.12   ILLUSTRATION OF DERIVED DEMAND AND DERIVED PRICES FOR A
FIXED SUPPLY AND CONSTANT MARKETING MARGINS[a]

[a] All prices must be converted to a common-product base such as carcass equivalent to make
this type of presentation consistent. As shown, a lower price for feeder cattle is "derived." This is
not always the case when grain is at a low price and the costs of grain in the feedlot are below the
expected selling price for the slaughter animal at the end of the feeding period. Under these
circumstances, the feeder steer will often command a premium over the price of the slaughter
animal.

purposes totally inelastic. Below the retail level, the demand function facing the decision maker is essentially a "derived demand"—a direct function of price at the next higher level and the operating margin requirements
of the firms one step higher in the system. At the breaking and slaughtering levels, the firm has the option of ceasing operations if the margins
being realized mean a loss. Flexibility at the feeding level is more limited.
Once cattle are placed on feed, it is seldom rational to take them off feed or
move them to slaughter at unusually light weights. So the feeding program

tends to be completed. The cow-calf operator has little or no flexibility. So long as the cow herd is maintained, calves will be produced. This can mean production well below the ATC of production.

The process of passing a "derived price" back down through the system is not free of problems and frictions. On any particular day, for example, the slaughtering firm may send its buyers into the field with instructions to buy a particular type and quality of cattle at or below a specific price. The bid price has been set to allow a prescribed gross operating margin per head given the price at which the finished carcass can be sold. If the quantity of cattle in the marketing channels and available for direct movement into slaughter is low on that particular day, the buyers may not be able to meet their price guidelines. With a high ratio of fixed to variable costs, the slaughterer must have cattle. Most large plants are unionized and even labor becomes a fixed cost.[7] Prices may be bid up in the short run to insure at least a minimum flow of cattle into the plant. But if cattle flow to market in larger quantities the following week, the packer-buyers will try to "even up" by pushing price down. The net result, over time, is the realization of an operating margin at every level in the system above the cattle feeder and a price structure that dictates there will be a "derived price" at the producer level.

Much the same thing happens in the grain market. Exporters calculate their bids to local and regional elevators based on price in the world market and a per bushel operating margin. Elevators take these bids, deduct the margin they need to cover their costs and risk, and "derive" a bid to the local producer. At every level above the producer, the transaction is typically protected by a cash contract or a hedge using the grain futures.

If the exporter or domestic processor needs grain, he may be forced to adjust the basis to encourage producers or other holders of grain to sell. This can come under a supply-demand balance or picture that features relatively low supplies, upward trending prices, and producer expectations for still higher prices. Alternatively, adjustments in the basis may be required to move grain when the supply is very heavy, prices are relatively low, and producer expectations are for improvement in prices. This latter situation may be short-lived but it can and does occur in the short run.[8] These and other situations do preclude a direct or 1:1 transfer of changes at the top level down through the system. But over time, the operating margins will be realized, will be set to cover costs at all levels above the producer, and the price at the producer level will be a "derived" price.

Summary

The economic environment within which the marketing firm operates is an important influence on marketing decisions. If we look along the continuum from producer to consumer in our marketing systems, we see a broad range of economic structures.

At the producer stage, the structure approaches the conditions of pure competition. There are many small producers. Each producer tends to be a price taker. The firm-industry interrelationships create problems since the individual firms respond to short-run higher prices by increasing output. New firms enter the industry and the resulting increase in industry supply forces prices down. Output tends to stay up, however, because new equipment and other resources brought into production tend to stay in use. Any profits over and above ATC will be short-lived since entry is not blocked and competitive pressures eliminate any pure profits.

Moving up through the marketing system from the producer level tends to bring other economic structures. Where the firm is able to realize at least limited product differentiation, there is some slope to the demand curve. We call this monopolistic competition. There are still many small firms. Decisions on price and price negotiation are possible, however. Competition tends to be on a price basis since the opportunities to differentiate the product are limited. Pure profits or profits over and above ATC of production will be eliminated by the ease of entry and competitive pressures unless significant product differentiation is achieved.

At the processing and retailing stages, an economic structure called oligopoly is frequently seen. Characterized by a few large firms, each firm in the oligopolistic industry is large enough to influence price. Because of the uncertainty as to how the competition will react, prices tend to be stable. Most competition is on a non-price basis and heavy expenditures on advertising are typical in an attempt to differentiate a particular product or brand name. The large size of firms, the emphasis on product differentiation, and the uncertainty in the demand picture creates barriers to entry into the industry. The benefits of cost-reducing technology are not automatically passed on to the final consumer in the short run. Some form of price leadership is typical.

Where a single firm dominates a market or market area, we have conditions approaching a monopoly. The firm is the industry and faces the industry demand curve. Pricing decisions are important. Non-price competition is used to help protect the monopoly position. Pure profits (price above ATC) are possible so long as the monopoly situation is maintained. The benefits of cost-reducing technology or increased efficiency will be slow to move to the consumer. Potential entry of other firms, policy moves by the government to eliminate the monopoly position, and the firm's concern for its public image preclude maximum exploitation of the monopoly situation.

Footnotes

1. Such a demand curve is infinitely elastic. The individual firm can sell all its products or none of its products and the decision maker's actions will have no influence on price.

2. Note the increase is a movement along the MC or supply curve. This is a rational response to the price increase and keeps the producer in a flexible position. No new combine, tractor, or other equipment was brought into use in expanding output and the cost structure did not change. As we will see a bit later, increased production that comes from bringing new equipment and land into use creates a problem and tends to keep production up even if the price of the product later falls.

3. Examination of the graph reveals what happens. When product prices increase, the MVP curve shifts up and to the right until $MVP > P_{acq}$—and the piece of equipment is purchased. Because there does tend to be a large difference between P_{acq} and P_{salv}, the product price has to fall a great deal for MVP to be below P_{salv}. This seldom happens in the short run so the equipment stays in use until wear and tear plus obsolescence reduces the MPP part of the equation $MVP = MPP \cdot P_{product}$. This, combined with a declining product price, eventually takes the equipment out of production.

4. All the tools mentioned here will be treated in later chapters. In this chapter, there is a need to recognize the importance of appropriate tools in trying to cope with the risk and uncertainty to which the decision maker is exposed.

5. A product is "differentiated" in the mind of the consumer when it is *perceived* as being different from competing products. The difference may not be real, it may not be significant, and it may be totally a product of the consumer's imagination. But if the consumer *believes* there is a difference, product differentiation has taken place.

6. The price leadership type of oligopolies is an example of imperfect collusion. Where perfect collusion exists, some type of cartel will emerge. The centralized cartel involves an agreement by the firms to turn over decisions on output and price to a central agency. The central authority will typically seek the same price and output the pure monopolist would select. Market-sharing cartels take many forms. There is some type of agreement on price and market shares. When the product is essentially homogeneous (oil, wheat, cement) we have a "pure" or "homogeneous" oligopoly and the price in different markets might be essentially the same.

7. Most union contracts require a worker to be paid for a 36-hour work week if he or she reports for work on Monday morning. Notice must be given by a prescribed time on Friday afternoon if workers are to be "laid off" for the following week. This means the plant will operate except under extremely negative circumstances, and means it must have cattle even if prices have to be "bid up" to the point the pre-determined operating margin cannot be met on this particular day.

8. In the corn belt, the cash bids are X cents below the nearby corn futures contract on the Chicago Board of Trade where "X" is the basis (cash minus futures). During any particular crop year, this basis may vary from −20¢ to −60¢ as the supply-demand picture changes. If the basis narrows to −20¢, this means the cash bid to the producer is improved relative to the futures quotes. At least some of this improved price to the producer will come from decreases in the operating margin of the eleva-tor, exporter, or other firm in the system between the producer and the final sale of the corn.

ted References

Chamberlin, Edward H., *The Theory of Monopolistic Competition*. Cambridge, Mass.: Harvard Univ. Press, 1962.

Leftwich, Richard H., *The Price System and Resource Allocation*. Hinsdale, Ill.: The Dryden Press, 1976.

Robinson, Joan, *The Economics of Imperfect Competition*. London, England: Macmillan and Co., Ltd., 1933.

Scitovsky, Tibor, *Welfare and Competition*. Homewood, Ill.: Richard D. Irwin, 1971.

Stigler, George J., *The Theory of Price*. New York, N.Y.: Crowell-Collier and Macmillan, 1966.

1. At the producer level, the decision maker is a price ta
   no ability to negotiate a price. Given these condition:
   prices and price behavior important to the produce

2. One of the problems facing the agricultural produce
   the economic environment is the "micro-macro parac
   firm responds to higher industry prices by increasi
   response plus entry of new firms gives an increase
   that drives prices back down. As a producer and de
   would you handle this problem?

3. Given the economic structure of our food and fiber in
   for the farm product is a "derived price." Explain wh
   producer from making plans based on the assumptic
   fall below ATC in the short run.

4. Why would the manager of an oligopolistic firm pre
   stable prices?

5. In general, there is a tendency to argue for publicly
   and product development (R&D) at the producer l
   processing, fabricating, wholesaling, and retailing
   their own R & D. Why do you think this is true? What
   economic structure make?

chapter four

Public Policy and the Marketing System

The marketing system and the individual firm within that system must operate within the bounds and guidelines set by the prevailing public policy. As used here, public policy refers to that body of statutes, legislation, laws, rules, and programs at the federal and state level that have impact on the economic system in general and on our food and fiber marketing system in particular.

Public policy can be divided, quite arbitrarily, into *regulatory* and *facilitative* dimensions. The regulatory part deals with the regulatory and restraining policies. The antitrust legislation is the most important part of the regulatory policy. Ad hoc or one-time policy moves, such as a temporary ban on exports of grain, constitute examples of policies which restrain. As used here, facilitative public policy is quite different. Included are publicly supported research, market news activities, the activities of the statistical reporting services to report crop and livestock data, and other related programs as part of the USDA, Department of Labor, or other governmental agencies. These efforts are designed to inform and otherwise help the producer and other buyers and sellers who are not in a position to do these things for themselves.

Regulatory Policy[1]

The set of antitrust laws that now prevails has grown in something of an "add on" fashion over time. First came the Sherman Antitrust Act of 1890. The primary intent behind this particular law was to declare restraint of trade illegal. Some years later, in 1914, the Clayton Act was passed to strengthen weak spots in the Sherman Act. Just what constituted "restraint of trade" was established in a more definitive manner. The Clayton Act also declared price discrimination to be illegal. Later, in 1936, the Robinson-Patman Act clarified just what was meant by price discrimination.

And so it goes. The body of antitrust legislation has grown on an "as needed" basis. Within the policy, the marriage of the legal and the economic has not always been a comfortable one. Such scholars as Low, in his thorough exposition of the legal-economic dimension of our modern economic organizations, are critical of the lack of economic content in much of the court action. Low's concerns appear to be justified. There is a significant difference, for example, in the *legal* versus the *economic* definition of price discrimination. In the legal arena, price discrimination refers solely to charging different prices to different customers where the price inequalities do not reflect different costs of serving the customers. Most economists would include under the heading of price discrimination (1) charging different prices for the same product to different customers when the different prices do not reflect cost differences, and (2) charging the same price to all customers when the costs of servicing the customers are different.[2]

The question of just what norm or criterion underlies modern regulatory policy is both an interesting and an important one. The concern for firm size and the heavy emphasis on price competition as being desirable suggests an underlying norm of pure competition. Perhaps it would be more accurate to suggest the current concern is to halt, or restrain, the current and pending moves away from pure competition.

Figure 4.1 illustrates the point. As we have seen in earlier chapters, economic structures vary from pure competition on one end of the continuum to pure monopoly at the other extreme. The pressures from economies of size in procurement, production, distribution, and merchandising tend to prompt increases in firm size. Increases in firm size tend to push the structure of industry groups further from the pure competition end of the continuum. Chapter 3 covered the types of economic structures in more detail. But it should be emphasized here that with larger and fewer

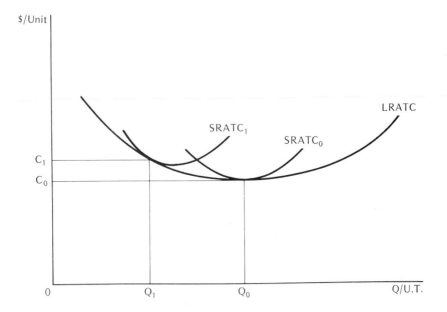

FIGURE 4.1   ILLUSTRATION OF THE TRADE-OFF BETWEEN THE PRESSURES OF
ECONOMIES OF SIZE AND THE POLICY TO RESTRICT FIRM SIZE[a]

[a] Output OQ_0 could be produced by a single firm at a cost of OC_0. If policy forces at least two firms to produce OQ_0 the cost will be some higher cost such as OC_1.

firms, there *is* a tendency to move toward non-price competition. Economic theory gives solid support to this tendency. Fully aware of the situation, the Justice Department and the Federal Trade Commission often block mergers and acquisitions that would increase firm size.

Others have also concluded the norm is pure competition and argue such a norm is not appropriate. A group of scholars have argued for what they call "workable competition."[3] There would be less concern over firm size and more willingness to allow a relatively high level of profit because profits are believed to be necessary to support research and development activities in the private sector of the economy. This argument has appeal in those sectors where risk associated with research and development is high or where the public monies to finance activities are not available.

The controversy over just what norm should be employed will continue. But the difference is one of degree. Most analysts would agree the general goals of antitrust and regulatory policy include:

1. Preventing restraint of trade due to collusive action by a group of firms;

2. Preventing price fixing where the forces of price competition are blocked by inter-firm arrangements;

3. Preventing price discrimination where there is no economic justification for the price differences; and

4. Preventing the adoption and use of pricing arrangements that impose rigidities on the workings of the price mechanism.

Typical of the policy is explicit and implicit opposition to most types of group action as being collusive and monopolistic in nature.

PRODUCTION AGRICULTURE

For many years, however, production agriculture has been treated differently insofar as group action is concerned. Recognizing the unique economic structure of production agriculture, a structure which *does* approach the conditions of pure competition, the policy positions have generally allowed and even promoted group action by agricultural producers.

The Capper-Volstead Act of 1922 became enabling legislation for the cooperative movement. Agricultural producers are allowed to act in groups and, when certain conditions are met, are protected from prosecution under the antitrust laws and are given differential treatment in terms of taxes. Lauded by some as the panacea for agricultural producers facing income and price problems, the number of cooperatives peaked in the 1920s and 1930s. Though still important in both the input markets and the farm product markets, cooperatives have not been the answer to the producers' continuing problem of lack of bargaining power.

Over time, there has continued to be evidence that policy makers subscribe to a need for group action in agriculture. The National Commission on Food Marketing said it best in the mid-1960s.[4] Having examined the operations and relative efficiency of our food marketing systems, the Commission expressed doubt about the ability or inclination of the individual producer to coordinate his efforts with the rest of the marketing system. A recommendation was made for legislation to encourage more group action by agricultural producers. The Commission also recommended the extension of marketing agreements and marketing orders to more of the basic commodities. If these alternatives failed, the Commission suggested a Federal Marketing Board be established to make decisions on how much of a particular product to produce and how it should be marketed.

The request for legislation was apparently heard. In the late 1960s, the

Agricultural Fair Practices Act was passed. The primary feature of the Act was a provision that made it illegal for a processor or handler to discriminate against an individual producer because he is part of a producers' association. Another giant step was attempted with the introduction of the National Agricultural Marketing and Bargaining Act of 1971, popularly known as the "Sisk Bill." This piece of proposed legislation had the potential to put bargaining power in the hands of the producer.

The primary provisions of the Sisk Bill can be paraphrased as follows:

1. A group of producers could organize under the provisions of the legislation and select agents or representatives to bargain on behalf of the group.

2. Any processor or handler to whom members of the producer group have sold products within any 2 of the most recent 5 years would be required to bargain with the legal representatives of the producer group.

3. While bargaining was proceeding, the processor or handler could not bargain with other producers who were not members of the producer group.

4. Once an agreement was reached with the producer group, the processor or handler could not negotiate more favorable terms with other producers who were not members of the group.

There were other provisions in the proposed legislation but these were the key points. They would have essentially eliminated the "free rider" problem[5] that has always plagued voluntary group action by agricultural producers. A National Agricultural Bargaining Board would have been established to administer the provisions of the legislation. Members of the Board would have been appointed by the President with the advice and consent of the Senate.

But the Sisk Bill never made it to the floor of the U.S. House of Representatives. And it is highly unlikely that any such bargaining legislation for the agricultural producer will be passed. It appears the philosophy has changed. There is increasing concern over the implications of placing a powerful bargaining tool in the hands of a producer group. Some politicians are now beginning to view the Capper-Volstead Act as an umbrella of protection for monopolistic activity by the well organized producer group.

Increasingly, the political arena and the policy makers are adopting a consumeristic orientation. The price ceilings of 1973, the embargo on soybean exports in 1974, the modification of import quotas on beef in 1978—all these actions are oriented toward the consumer and show a concern for high food prices. More detailed coverage of such issues will be delayed until Chapter 5 but the general tone of these actions is important to our discussion here. The price ceilings of 1973 were the first such moves in the U.S. since the war years of the 1940s. The embargo on soybean shipments came after official denials that any such action would be taken. The relaxing of import quotas on beef in June of 1978 came in the face of cattle prices recovering from a record liquidation of beef cattle numbers that lasted almost four years. The prices had surged after it became clear the cycle in prices had bottomed. After four years of losses, the beef industry was treated to the change in imports after only six months of improving prices.

There are clear signs the policy orientation toward production agriculture is beginning to change. If this is the case, it is important that producers, producer groups, trade associations, market analysts, and students of marketing at all levels recognize what is happening and reflect it in their analyses, studies, and deliberations.

THE STRUCTURE-CONDUCT-PERFORMANCE MODEL

We have suggested to this point that an implicit goal of public policy has been to protect and promote a setting that approaches the conditions of pure competition. Consistent with this position is the Structure-Conduct-Performance model (S-C-P), which appears to provide a significant part of the theoretical support for our policy positions.

Presented by Joe Bain in his book *Industrial Organization,*[6] the S-C-P model postulates a predictable relationship between the structure of the industry, the conduct (behavior) of firms within that industry, and the performance of the firms or industry subsystem. For our purposes, it will suffice to define structure as the organizational characteristics of the industry or economic subsystem in which we are interested.

Several characteristics of market structure could be identified. Easily, the most widely used is *seller concentration*, which refers to the extent to which the economic activity is concentrated in the hands of a few large firms. The literature has popularized concentration ratios for the four and 10 largest firms. A concentration ratio of 82 for the four largest firms means the four firms control 82 percent of the economic activity (such as dollar sales) in the industry.

Among other characteristics of structure are *buyer concentration, barriers to entry,* and the *degree of product differentiation.* Buyer concentration refers to the extent to which buying volume is concentrated in the hands of a few large firms. Barriers to entry include those forces that make entry into an industry difficult—patents, copyrights, control of a key input, differentiated products, and established brand names. Generally, these barriers are the non-natural barriers; capital requirements or economies of size could well be formidable barriers but may be simply economic facts of life.

The degree of product differentiation, which can be a barrier to entry, is often identified separately because of the attention paid to expenditures on advertising in creating the differentiation in the minds of the consumer.

Conduct refers to the behavior and action program by firms given the structure within which they operate. Pricing policies, non-price competition, expenditures on advertising, actions to change market share, etc., are examples of firm "conduct" that are frequently mentioned.

Performance refers to the end result of the pattern of conduct that evolves. The consuming public is generally concerned with performance since this is the observable part—price levels, pricing patterns, profit margins, investment and reinvestment of profits, research and product development, etc.

According to the supporters of the S-C-P model, there is a predictable relationship among the three components of the model. Given a structure, a pattern of conduct can be predicted which, in turn, leads to a predictable pattern of performance. This flow can be illustrated by placing arrows in the schematic of the model to demonstrate the flow of causal influence:

$$S \rightarrow C \rightarrow P$$

Much of the regulatory part of our public policy has been designed to exert influence on or control structure to effect a desirable conduct and resulting performance. If high levels of concentration (structure) cause collusion among the firms (conduct) which, in turn, causes inflexible and high prices (performance), then it follows that the level of concentration should be reduced or at least kept in check. For example, forcing the major oil companies to divide into several smaller operations and concentrate on activity in one dimension of the energy business would reduce concentration. Theoretically, this would lead to more competition on a price basis and more acceptable performance indicators (such as lower profit margins). Blocking the attempted merger of two or more firms would tend to hold the level of concentration where it is or keep it from increasing.

There is a time lag that varies across industries between changes in structure and changes in performance. When an immediate impact is desired, the policy makers have turned to direct control of performance. This happened when the price ceilings and embargoes were employed. The policy makers were unwilling to wait for market forces to work out the problems or issues.

The willingness to control performance directly stems in part from an increasingly powerful and relatively new force in the policy arena—the consumer activist groups. Concern over rising food costs surfaced in a vocal and visible fashion starting in late 1972 when the food price index moved above the all-items consumer price index (CPI). The food index led the CPI, widely used as a measure of inflation, higher through 1973. We will show in Chapter 13 that consumers did feel pressure from the rising food prices. But that is not the issue here. The issue is that the political arena exhibits a sensitive ear to the pleas of the consumer groups. This tendency gives every appearance of becoming a permanent part of the overall policy orientation.

THE ECONOMIC ISSUES

From the S→C→P model comes increased concern for large size and related high levels of concentration. Efforts to change or control structure have generally taken the form of opposition to increasing levels of concentration and larger firm size. But there can be a cost associated with reducing or restraining increases in concentration ratios.

The economies of size can be very important in many sectors of the economy. In Figure 4.2, the curve labeled ATC_1 typifies the cost structure in an industry that we called a "natural monopoly." Per unit costs continue to decrease for very large volumes. Public utility firms are examples.

Most firms do not face a cost structure like ATC_1 in Figure 4.2. But many face the traditional U-shaped ATC curves such as ATC_2 where the "bottom" of the curve occurs at large levels of output per unit of time. Preventing firms from growing to large size or creating several smaller firms from one large one can cause the per unit cost of producing a product or providing a service to increase.

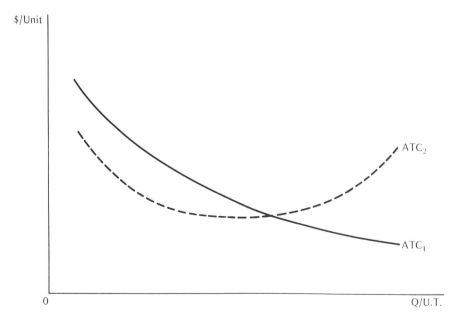

FIGURE 4.2   COST STRUCTURES REFLECTING SIGNIFICANT ECONOMIES OF SIZE

The empirical evidence on the relationship between structure and performance is mixed. Greig found statistically significant positive correlations between levels of concentration and performance indicators such as profit margins.[7] But Greig's work was based on national data. Concentration ratios, and the economic significance of varying levels of concentration, may be considerably different when it is regional instead of national data. Mori and Gorman found no relationship between price levels and levels of concentration for retail supermarkets in several large midwestern cities.[8]

Other evidence can be found on both sides of the issue. High levels of concentration do not, it appears, necessarily mean an undesirable pattern of conduct and subsequent performance. On the other hand, extremely large size is not always needed to capture most of the potential economies of size. The National Commission on Food Marketing concluded many firms in our food marketing systems are larger than they would need to be to capture most of the economies of size.

What is needed is a broader base of information and analysis to establish the tradeoffs between the possible benefits of controlling structure and the impact of varying firm sizes on per unit costs. We also need to know more about the relationship between structure, conduct, and performance.[9] Analysis for each industry or sub-industry grouping is needed to guide the particular policy extended to that particular industry. Currently available research results suggest no one policy should be extended to all industry groups, to all geographical markets, or to all subsystems of the total marketing system.

Facilitative Policy

Much of the publicly supported activity that would fall under the "facilitative" label is directed at firms or individuals who would experience difficulty in coping with the environment in which they must operate without assistance. Included are agricultural producers who could not afford to develop new grain varieties, conduct their own research on how to more effectively market their product, or gather their own market information. Also included is the low-income consumer whose income is subsidized to permit a nutritionally adequate diet.

Publicly supported research is very much a part of the ongoing public policy. Research at the land grant universities, the USDA, and various other federal and state agencies generates the scientific knowledge the individual or small firm could not provide for themselves.

Exerting more direct influence on the market system are the various publicly supported activities in the collection and dissemination of basic production and price data. The Statistical Reporting Service is a joint venture of the USDA and the various state Statistical Reporting Services. Planting intentions, production estimates, stocks, livestock inventory data, cattle on feed data, etc., are all part of this broad spectrum of activity. Published information is used by farmers, market analysts for private firms, university researchers, and others. Discussion of the impact of the information, how it is used, and related issues is found in Chapters 5, 6, 7, and 8.

Public activity in research and development of grades is an important input. In Chapter 6, the role of the price system as a coordinating mechanism is stressed. If the price system is to be effective, there must be an adequate and effective set of grades. "Effective" means a set of grades that facilitates a set of sharp and clear price signals. Such price signals require a set of grades that identify and categorize all significant variations in value in terms understood and recognized by buyers and sellers. Over time, the relative value of product attributes changes. Adjustments in grades may be required to meet changing needs and facilitate the coordinative role of the price mechanism. The USDA maintains a constant program of research and analysis on grades and periodically proposes changes.

The grades are used in another important dimension of publicly supported activity, the reporting of market news. The Federal-State Market News Service is again an example of federal and state cooperation. Trade in all important food and fiber commodities is reported by the Market News Service in special releases picked up and disseminated by the newspapers, radio and TV, or mailed directly to users. In many market centers, toll free phone numbers are provided. Users can call day or night to listen to recordings of the day's trading activity. Given the importance of well informed decision makers, the importance of market news activities is apparent. The collection and analysis of information is time consuming and expensive. Most individuals and many firms could not afford to gather and analyze the raw data that is available. Many lack the analytical expertise. In this instance, publicly supported activity is the equalizer that permits the small operator to compete in an arena where large and well-informed firms would otherwise reap benefits from their superior base of information.

A number of government programs are designed to supplement the diets of low-income families.[10] For example, the School Lunch Program is designed to provide free meals or meals at reduced rates to children of families in certain income categories. The Food Stamp Program is a significant influence in boosting the demand for food products. Consumers are allowed to buy food stamps at part of their face value and use the stamps to buy foods or other products on an approved product list. Differential impacts on demand accompany the addition of foods to an expanding list of approved foods and products. For example, beef was added to the list of approved foods in the early 1970s. The net impact on the demand for beef is difficult to analyze but most analysts feel the influence was significant.

Impact on Market Systems

Coverage of public policy in this chapter has been brief.[11] It is a broad and complex area. The references listed at the end of the chapter will guide those who wish to pursue the area in more detail. Selected aspects of the policy, which exert significant influence on the workings of the marketing systems and the decision processes of the marketing firm, will be given more detailed coverage in later chapters. The purpose here was to establish awareness of public policy and begin to build a base of understanding on how it has impact on our food and fiber marketing systems.

A major purpose of the regulatory policy is to influence or control the types of organizational structures that evolve over time. Various types of marketing systems are usually identified by differences in their organizational structure. The concept of an open exchange system has been introduced and discussed. An exchange system is organized around separate ownership and control of the various stages of economic activity. At the other extreme is the vertically integrated system. Total integration implies that ownership and control of all stages of economic activity rest with a single management entity. Essentially the same economic activities or economic functions must be performed regardless of the organizational structure as the product moves from producer to consumer. But the way in which the system is organized to perform this task can be different.

Various aspects of the regulatory policy exert influence on the type of organizational structure. The concern over large firm size and high concentration ratios may block any single firm from accumulating the capital and size needed to integrate across all stages.

The fear of prosecution under the antitrust laws restrains firm growth. Some processors of agricultural products establish policies that prevent the construction of a processing facility in a certain area or expansion of existing facilities. If a significant percentage of the raw materials in a defined producing area around the plant site would be required to keep the plant operating, the processors will avoid the site. They fear problems of raw material availability and they fear both the legal possibilities and the public reaction if they dominate the buying in the area.

Actions taken under the umbrella of the antitrust laws can directly influence organizational structure. In the 1910–1920 era, the level of concentration in meat packing was very high. The five largest meat packers, to avoid more stringent prosecution under the antitrust laws, entered into a consent decree with the Justice Department in 1920. Among the major provisions of the decree was agreement by the packers that they would never get involved in retailing of meats. The level of concentration in this particular industry has decreased since that time but the decree remains in effect. Any ambitions toward vertical integration by the five companies across the years have been blocked by the consent decree. Other firms have moved past the five in size and are now much larger and more important in meat processing.

The vast expenditures of public monies on facilitative types of policies exert influence on the type of organizational structure that will evolve and survive. Research and market news activities financed by public funds have largely precluded the necessity of research and accumulation of market news at the farm level. This has tended to protect and perpetuate a structure characterized by many small firms at the producer level. And in the process, the publicly financed effort has permitted and even encouraged separate ownership and control of the economic activities at the producer level.

Activities to gather and disseminate basic information and market news keep the small producer informed so that he can survive and compete. Without these publicly supported programs, the efforts at the producer level would have been operated from a less well informed position, would not have achieved the degree of coordination with the rest of the marketing system that has been achieved, and the pressures for integration backward from the processing levels would have been more intense.

The organizational structures and the type of marketing systems that exist at any point in time are a function of past and prevailing public policy. Changes in policy orientations or goals can and will, given time for the influence to be felt, change the types of system that will be economically viable. Awareness of these influences is critically important to decision makers throughout the marketing system.

Summary

Both regulatory and facilitative types of public policy are important in our marketing systems. Regulatory policies constrain, prohibit, and lay out the rules of the game. In a sense, regulatory policy is preventive medicine in that it attempts to keep problems from developing. For example, the advocates of the S→C→P model would argue that controlling structure is the way to prevent the "ills" of undesirable conduct and performance.

If regulatory policy is preventive medicine, then facilitative policy is get-well medicine. Publicly financed research contributes to the well being of the firm, the individual decision maker, and to society. Data collection and dissemination, in conjunction with grading and market news activities, help keep the decision maker informed and eliminate the need for individual efforts in collecting original information. Programs such as the food stamp program subsidize the income and buying power of consumers and influence the demand for food and fiber products.

Public policy influences the type of economic structure and marketing systems we see. Regulatory policies affect firm size and often serve to discourage integration. Facilitative policies, by financing research and information-related activities, influence the ability of the small firm to compete and thus affect the type of structure that evolves over time. We can repeat the key point of this chapter: public policy exerts significant influence on the operating environment of the marketing firm.

Footnotes

1. The coverage here will necessarily be brief. For an excellent treatment of this topic, refer to Part V. Antitrust and Government in Richard E. Low, *Modern Economic Organization* (Homewood, Ill.: Richard D. Irwin, 1970). Low discusses the development and application of the antitrust statutes and develops some of the legal-economic issues and inconsistencies in the regulatory dimension of public policy.

2. Richard E. Low, *Modern Economic Organization* (Homewood, Ill.: Richard D. Irwin, 1970), p. 396.

3. The idea was apparently originated by the late Columbia University economist John Maurice Clark as early as 1940. It was during the 1950s and 1960s that the concept was developed in more detail by authors such as Clark, Markham, Edwards, and Stocking. Some of the writings of these authors are listed in the selected references at the end of the chapter.

4. The National Commission on Food Marketing was established by Congress in 1964. The Commission was organized to make a comprehensive study of the food industry in the U.S. Comprised of politicians, industry representatives, and agricultural economists the Commission released the popular version of its report *Food From Farmer to Consumer* in June 1966. Numerous technical and analytical studies were conducted and published in support of the Commission's investigation.

5. The free rider problem is another characteristic of the economic structure of production agriculture. Any benefits that come from group action to secure a higher price or more favorable terms of trade accrue to all producers, both participant and non-participant. There is always a tendency for some to get a "free ride" without paying their part of the advertising program, committing their supply to the group bargaining effort, or otherwise making a contribution.

6. Joe S. Bain, *Industrial Organization* (New York, N.Y.: Wiley, 1968). This reference provides detailed discussion of the structure, conduct and performance concepts, and their theoretical relationships. The reference by Low referred to earlier, *Modern Economic Organization*, provides excellent coverage of the economic and legal dimensions of the S—C—P theory.

7. W. Smith Greig, *Profitability and Other Financial Operating Ratios by*

Firm Size in the Food Processing Industry (Washington Agr. Exp. Bul. 778, July 1973.).

8. Hiroshi Mori and Wm. D. Gorman, "An Empirical Investigation Into the Relationship Between Market Structure and Peformance as Measured by Prices", *J. Farm Econ.*, Vol. 48, (Aug. 1966), pp. 162–171.

9. An excellent compilation of the issues is found in Bruce W. Marion and Charles R. Handy, *Market Performance: Concepts and Measures*, Agr. Econ. Rep. No. 244, ERS, USDA, 1973. As the authors note, it is often difficult to find statistically significant measures of relationships between structure and performance. But this does not prove the relationships are not there. Economic theory generally supports the position that large size gives market power and market power usually means higher prices and larger profit margins.

10. The school lunch program and the food stamp program are two of the more important. Examination of USDA data indicates over 10 million school children were receiving free meals or meals at a reduced price in the late 1970s. The number of persons participating in food stamp programs was around 20 million.

11. Much more could be written here. For example, we have bypassed the impact of such governmental agencies as the Environmental Protection Agency (EPA), the Food and Drug Administration (FDA), the Packers and Stockyards Administration (P&S). The activities of the EPA are primarily restrictive as the agency seeks to protect the environment from pollution. The FDA often exerts direct influence. The banning of DES, a growth promotant in cattle feeding, received much news attention in the mid 1970s. A bit later came FDA action involving the use of nitrites as preservatives in bacon. All these activities have impact on the market and keep the decision maker on his toes—uncertain and agitated.

Questions

1. If you had the opportunity to provide input, what type of norm would you suggest for the antitrust dimension of our regulatory policy? Why?

2. In recent years, policy makers have moved to direct controls over the performance part in the S→C→P model. Why do you feel this was done? List pros and cons of direct control via price ceilings or price freezes on food prices.

3. Briefly critique the position adopted in this chapter that public policy and the political arena are becoming increasingly consumeristic. List any recent governmental policy actions of which you are aware and try to analyze the change to see what subsystem of the food and fiber marketing systems will be most influenced by the actions.

4. Describe the strengths and weaknesses of the S→C→P model as a base for public policy.

5. Discuss the role of economies of size in public policy actions that influence firm size and concentration ratios. Based on your discussion, what is the "correct" size firm?

Selected References

Bain, Joe S., *Industrial Organization*. New York, N.Y.: John Wiley & Sons, 1968.

Breimyer, Harold F., *Economics of the Product Markets of Agriculture*. Ames, Iowa: Iowa State Univ. Press, 1976.

Clark, John Maurice, "Toward a Concept of Workable Competition," *Amer. Econ. Rev. Supl.*, Vol. 30, 1940.

Clodius, Robert L. and Williard F. Mueller, "Market Structure Analysis as an Orientation for Research in Agricultural Economics," *J. Farm Econ.*, Vol. 43, 1961.

Edwards, Corin D., *Maintaining Competition*. New York, N.Y.: McGraw-Hill, 1949.

Low, Richard E., *Modern Economic Organization*. Homewood, Ill.: Richard D. Irwin, 1970.

Markham, Jesse W., "An Alternative Approach to the Concepts of Workable Competition," *Amer. Econ. Rev.*, Vol. 40, 1950.

National Commission on Food Marketing, *Food From Farmer to Consumer*. Washington, D.C.: U.S. Govt. Printing Office, 1966.

Sosnick, Stephen H., "Toward a Concrete Concept of Effective Competition," *Am. J. Agr. Econ.*, Vol. 50, 1968.

Stocking, George W., "The Rule of Reason, Workable Competition and the Legality of Trade Association Activities," *Univ. of Chi. Law Rev.*, Vol. 21, 1954.

chapter five

Government Programs
and Their Influence

In Chapter 4, we looked at the area of public policy in a broad sense. There are policies that regulate and control, policies that provide information and assistance, and a wide range of government programs that has direct influence on the agricultural sector. In this chapter, we look briefly at government programs in the market place and emphasize their impact on price and on marketing decisions. Continuing the established orientation, most coverage will be at the producer level.

Programs Influencing Price

Prices can be influenced by government programs either directly or indirectly. A price freeze or a price ceiling has direct impact. A price support has direct impact if set above the equilibrium price. Other actions by the government influence price indirectly by exerting influence on supply, demand, or both. Examples include production controls that influence supply, embargoes on exports that influence total demand for the product, and loan rates if they are established above the equilibrium price.

PRODUCTION CONTROLS AND PRICE SUPPORTS

The two concepts must be treated together. A price support set above the equilibrium price will prompt increased production if the guaranteed minimum price is above the average variable cost of production. Each unit produced will contribute something to fixed costs, and, with no price risk involved, the producer will expand production. Theoretically, to maximize profits the producer will equate marginal cost and marginal revenue. In this case, marginal revenue equals the support price if the price is set above the equilibrium price. Figure 5.1 illustrates. Demand at the industry level becomes DED' not DD. The quantity produced at a price OP_S will be OQ_T, not the equilibrium quantity OQ_E. A surplus quantity in the amount Q_SQ_T will be produced.

If price is to be supported in such a fashion, controls will be needed to keep production from running at levels that continually add to the surplus stocks the government or some outside party will be required to hold. With price supports at OP_S, quantity supplied would be matched with quantity demanded at quantity OQ_S. If production controls hold the quantity produced at OQ_S, the relevant supply curve becomes SAS' as shown in

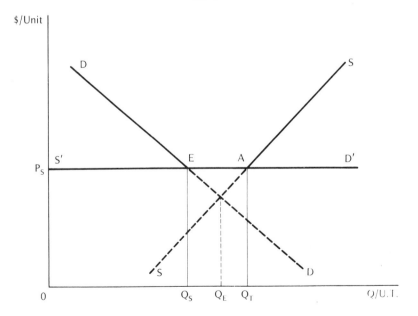

FIGURE 5.1   THE IMPACT OF PRICE SUPPORTS ON PRICE, DEMAND, SUPPLY, AND THE QUANTITY AVAILABLE TO CONSUMERS

Figure 5.1 and not SS. If the quantity that would be taken at the support price OP_s can be accurately estimated and if production can be controlled to hold the quantity produced at or near the quantity OQ_s, the situation is stable and the level of stocks will remain relatively constant. But if demand shifts, the situation is out of equilibrium and another round of adjustments will be required.[1]

Price supports are essentially a method of income transfer to the farm sector. Production agriculture is the only sector of the economy that approaches the conditions of pure competition. As such, it is vulnerable to the problems of price variability, to overproduction, is hurt by periodic droughts, and is prone to financially ruinous cyclical swings in production and price. Price supports have reflected a concern for the well-being and stability of the farm sector and have periodically been part of farm policy. Production controls have typically accompanied the supports.

Price supports set above equilibrium prices interfere with the resource allocation and reallocation roles of the price system. Resources that would otherwise be transferred to alternative uses are held in production of the commodity with the support price. The short-run benefits of the price support and production control programs are bid into the value of fixed assets—especially land. The market value of land is increased because of the programs. But if the programs are then discontinued, land prices will fall accordingly and this becomes disruptive. Because of such problems, the higher prices and stronger markets of the early 1970s were used as an opportunity to move away from policies of price supports and acreage controls.

LOAN AND TARGET PRICES

When production controls were removed in the early 1970s, a wave of expanded production brought record crops in wheat, corn, soybeans, feed grains, and increases in cotton. By the mid 1970s, prices had been driven below most estimates of the per unit cost of production and the farm sector was in financial trouble again. With this cost-price squeeze came government policies that featured loan and target prices.

The target price is a price set by the political process using administration or USDA recommendations as a point of departure. Its sole purpose is to establish one end of a price range that indicates the magnitude of direct payments or subsidies that will be paid to farmers if prices are below levels considered appropriate by the policy makers. In general, the procedure works as follows:

1. The target price is set by Congressional action;

2. The average market price for the first 5 months of the crop year is calculated; and

3. Farmers are paid the difference between the target price and 5-month average (if the average is lower) per bushel for the farmer's proven yield or production taken from ASCS records.[2]

This amounts to a direct payment during periods of low prices without interfering with the market price.

Loan programs have typically been used with target prices. The loan rate is set by Congressional and administration action as part of legislation dealing with issues at the farm level. The producer can place his crop in storage under the provisions of the loan program. Later, he can remove the product from the program, pay the prescribed storage fees, and sell the product in the cash market or hold the product as a cash speculator. If market prices do not rise enough to encourage pulling the crop out of loan, the producer can leave it in the program and accept the net from the program after paying holding charges. Therefore, when prices drop below the loan rate, minus the cost of holding the product in the program, the grain or other product tends to move into or stay in the loan program. This places some support under the market at or near the price equal to the loan rate minus the cost of holding the grain in the program. A part of the supply is removed at least temporarily from the cash market. But when the downward pressure on price is intense, such as during the harvest period, the cash price can and often does fall well below the apparent "floor" price based on the loan rate. Lack of knowledge of the program, reluctance to take part in government programs, and other factors prevent the loan price from becoming a more important factor in the market in the short run. Once the short-run pressure subsides, the market price tends to move back toward a price level equal to or above that which the producer could net from the loan program.

To clarify these points, let's illustrate the loan rate and target price and show how they are used together. Assume the following:

1. The loan rate is $2.75 per bushel;

2. The cost of holding the grain in the loan program (storage, interest, insurance, etc.) is $.25 per bushel;

3. The target price is set at $3.50 per bushel; and

4. The average market price for the first five months of the crop year (June through October for wheat) is $2.65 per bushel.

The payment to participating farmers would be $.75 per bushel. The difference between the target price and the five-month average is $.85 but the underlying legislation has typically set the difference between the target price and the loan rate as a maximum payment. The "net" from the loan would be $2.50 or the $2.75 minus the "holding costs." Price at the local market level for which the $.25 holding costs are valid would find some support at $2.50. If pushed below this level due to weak demand or excessive short-run supplies, there would be some tendency for price to move back to the $2.50 level and remain at this price or higher.

RESERVE PROGRAMS

Policies including a loan program that extends beyond a single crop year take on the appearance of a reserve program. The reserve program employed by the USDA in 1978 as part of a farm program was designed to boost farm prices of wheat in the short-run by taking supplies off the market. The program established threshold price levels, tied to the 1978 target price, which would be required before the wheat could be taken out of the three-year loan program.[3]

In terms of economic analysis, what we have is a transfer of supply from the current to a later marketing year. Figure 5.2 illustrates. Let DD and SS represent the short-run demand and supply schedules before the program is enacted. Expectations of supply and demand for a later period are represented by D'D' and S'S'. Given enactment of the program and assuming significant participation, we see the supply curve for the current period shift to S_aS_a and for the later period to $S_a'S_a'$. Price is pushed higher in the current period at the expense of larger supplies and lower prices in the later period.

The long-run impact of the reserve policy may be even more important. If the short-run result is to bring higher and more stable prices than

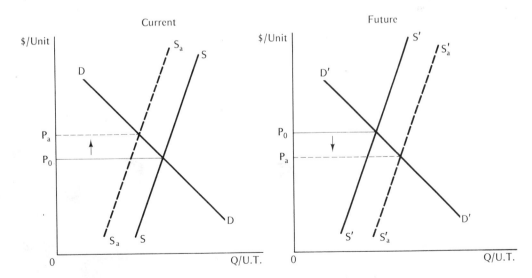

FIGURE 5.2   IMPACT OF A MULTI-YEAR RESERVE PROGRAM ON PRICE FOR A STORABLE GRAIN IN CURRENT AND FUTURE TIME PERIODS

would have been the case without the program, this could influence expectations at the producer level and prompt an increase in planted acreage the following year. There is considerable research evidence to show producers base expectations for the future and production plans on current prices. If such does happen, this means even more downward pressure on price in the later years because of an increase in supply that could be attributed to the reserve program.

Overall, the impact of the reserve program depends on the particular price levels in the program and the length of run we are considering. In general, there will be a tendency to remove supply pressure in the short run but this pressure will be transferred to later marketing years. Whether prices in later years are actually lower than current period prices depends on many other economic forces but, assuming other things equal, the reserve program could tend to make them lower.

IMPORT-EXPORT POLICIES

Increasingly, all products produced in the U.S. are affected by the world market and world trade. The impact of government policies and programs on the markets for food and fiber products takes both direct and indirect forms. The impact of policies to influence export demand in general or specific policies to control or influence quantities moving into export is quite direct. Policies to encourage or discourage imports of products that compete directly with products produced in the U.S. will also have direct impact on domestic markets and prices. But policy positions regarding the general level of food and fiber prices in the U.S. market will have a less obvious effect.

A short-run embargo on exports of a product such as wheat or soybeans, which depend heavily upon export outlets, usually brings a highly visible reaction in price. Figure 5.3 illustrates what happens. With supply for the year essentially fixed and therefore highly inelastic, a decrease in demand from DD to D'D' brings with it a sharp reduction in price from OP_0 to OP_a. If the embargo is in effect for 60 days, it essentially takes the equivalent of two months of exports out of the total demand for the market year. With transportation and handling facilities typically at or near capacity, it is difficult to "make up" a significant portion of the exports when the embargo is lifted. And potential buyers turn to other exporters both in the short run during the embargo and in the long run because of concern over the availability of U.S. supplies.[4]

On the import side, policies that limit the quantities of imports for a product that is a substitute for U.S. products help to hold U.S. prices up. For example, legislation passed in 1964 limits the volume of beef imports. Quantities that can be impoted vary with U.S. production and have run around seven to eight percent of domestic production. Such policies in-

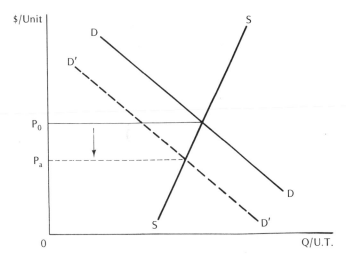

FIGURE 5.3   PRICE EFFECT OF SHORT-RUN EMBARGO ON A COMMODITY THAT DEPENDS HEAVILY ON EXPORT DEMAND

variably come under pressure from consumer groups when prices move higher in the U.S. The higher beef prices in 1978 brought administrative action to allow more imports.[5] Efforts continue in Congress to revise the 1964 law to allow more, not fewer, imports when U.S. production is down and prices are high.

Among the general economic policies that indirectly influence the level of food and fiber prices in the U.S. are the policies relating to the balance of payments problem. In general, a negative balance of trade (dollar imports greater than dollar exports) is taken as a sign of weakness in the domestic economy and tends to devalue the dollar compared to other currencies in the world market and finance centers. If the tendency is toward deficits because of heavy use of imported oil or heavy imports of other foreign produced products, any administration will be most reluctant to support farm programs that boost U.S. farm product prices relative to world prices. Agricultural products constitute a very important part of total exports from the U.S. A declining dollar in the world markets tends to increase exports and decrease imports. Both improve the balance of trade. Supporting U.S. prices above world prices would eliminate any chance of improving the trade balance via increased agricultural exports. Export subsidies would be required to get U.S. products into export channels.

PRICE FREEZES OR PRICE CEILINGS

When prices are frozen by governmental action at a specific level or when price ceilings are imposed, the workings of the entire price mechanism come to a halt. In terms of impact on the market demand schedule, freezing the price reduces demand to a single price-quantity point on the schedule. If the underlying demand shifts, we simply get other points at a lower or higher quantity for decreases and increases in demand respectively. What impact the freeze will have on product availability depends on where the price is frozen relative to the equilibrium price. Since price freezes normally come during periods of high prices, the freeze level will typically be below the equilibrium price. If this is the case, the quantity demanded will exceed the quantity supplied at that price level and a shortage will result.

Figure 5.4 illustrates. If price is frozen at a level OP_F, a shortage in the amount Q_1Q_2 will develop. Buyers will want quantity OQ_2 but suppliers will only offer OQ_1. A price ceiling set at level OP_F would have exactly the same impact—a shortage would develop in the magnitude Q_1Q_2.

The impact of the price controls is not easy to assess. If the mechanisms underlying supply were sufficiently flexible, the quantity offered would be reduced to the quantity OQ_1 shown in Figure 5.4. A shortage would result, and the complaints coming from consumers unable to buy the product at any price would probably prompt eventual removal of the price ceiling. But the production process in the food and fiber sectors is not that flexible. The fruits, vegetables, or soybeans keep growing. The cattle keep eating and the sows that were bred will farrow. The production

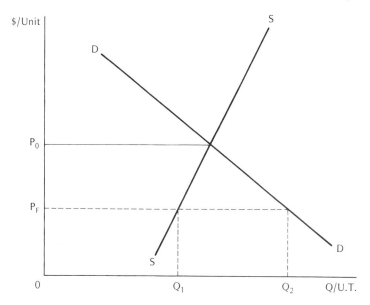

FIGURE 5.4   ILLUSTRATION OF THE IMPACT OF A PRICE FREEZE OR PRICE CEILING BELOW THE EQUILIBRIUM PRICE

process rolls on. What we have is the accumulation of an output planned with expectations of higher prices, and, in all probability, reflecting a cost of production consistent with the higher prices. Producers tend to hold, refuse to sell, and hope for a higher price when the ceilings are lifted. Eventually, however, the product must come to market. If the accumulated production is large enough, the result can be the prompting of a price break and extremely volatile markets.

The price ceilings placed on beef, pork, and other important food items in the first half of 1973 can be used to illustrate. We will set the background for the ceiling action and use a bit of basic economic analysis to trace the implications of the price ceilings.

Inflation as measured by the Consumer Price Index (CPI) ran high in 1972 reaching levels deemed unacceptable by the administration. In mid-1972, the percent of income spent on food reversed a long-term downward trend and began to move higher. The food component of the CPI (there is a separate index for food) moved up and became a force in pulling the CPI to higher levels. Beef prices at retail surged to record levels and consumers, feeling the pressure of the rapidly rising food prices, staged vocal protests and boycotts. Beef was singled out for much of the attention. Reacting to the urgings of the consumer groups and to the widespread concerns over inflation, price ceilings were imposed by the administration in March of 1973.

To understand what impact the price ceilings had on the cattle industry requires an understanding of what was going on internal to the industry at that time. In the 1971–73 period, the industry was approaching the end of the herd building phase of its production cycle that had started in 1965–66. Annual rates of growth in the cow herd pushed above three percent. Growth rates at these levels were being accomplished by holding cows in the herd to more advanced ages than normal, and by holding back heifers to enter the breeding herd. The ability to produce for some later time period was being increased at an almost frantic pace but this was taking its toll in the form of holding down daily or weekly slaughter and beef production—and pushing beef prices higher.

By early 1973, the industry was on the verge of moving into a period of cyclical liquidation. The herd-building years were ready to bear fruit in the form of increased marketings from several years of large calf crops and cattle on feed numbers that had pushed to record levels near 13 million head in late 1972. With the industry in this stage of its cyclical development, increased production and lower prices were imminent. But the public was not willing to wait. Neither the consumer groups nor the government's Cost of Living Council demonstrated an understanding of what was happening in the cattle industry. The price ceilings were imposed.[6]

During the late spring and summer of 1973 while the beef price ceilings were in effect, the following developments could be observed:

1. The concept of derived demand came into play. The ceiling at retail was quickly reflected in the form of unofficial "ceilings" on carcass beef prices, fed cattle prices, and feeder cattle prices. Retail chains plugged the ceiling price at retail into their calculations on how much they could pay for carcass beef. This process of covering operating margins was continued down through the system with effective but unannounced ceilings evolving at each level.

2. Grain costs, the cost of protein supplement, and other costs increased rapidly during 1973. With selling prices on live cattle limited to the derived ceiling prices, the cattle producer was caught in a cost-price squeeze. In attempting to avoid losses, producers held cattle off the markets waiting for the price ceiling to be lifted. The ceiling price on beef was continued for several weeks after action was taken to lift the ceiling on other commodities and was eventually removed in early September of 1973.

3. When the price ceiling was lifted, the cattle that had been "held back" came to market in a rush. Instead of prices moving higher, a major price break began.[7] Fueled by the cyclical liquidation that was beginning to emerge, and a tendency to hold cattle to excessive weights waiting for price to recover, prices trended lower through the late spring and early summer months of 1974. Losses on cattle coming out of feedlots in 1974 ran as high as $200 per head. Feedlots that had hedged neither slaughter cattle nor feed costs moved toward insolvency and a significant number never recovered.

Looking back and analyzing the situation, it would appear the economic implications of the price ceilings rest primarily in the impact on the intensity and magnitude of the price break. Whether the ceilings hastened the start of the cyclical break is less clear.

There is a great deal of support for the position that the ceilings brought a bigger break in prices than would have occurred without them. Cattle numbers were building rapidly in the early 1970s and slaughter was also moving higher each year. But commercial cattle slaughter dropped significantly in 1973 when cattle were held off the market during the price freeze. These "held back" cattle came to market in late 1973 and early 1974 and came carrying so much weight and finish they were undesirable— putting more downward pressure on price. Whether the ceilings accomplished their intended purpose of helping to slow the inflationary spiral is open to conjecture. But there can be little doubt that the cyclical liquidation was more violent than would have been the case without the ceilings.

Programs Influencing Availability of Information

The level and quality of information at the disposal of buyers and sellers influence price and the pricing processes. Price determination, price discovery, and techniques of price analysis will be covered in Chapters 6 and 7. Here, we add to the brief coverage of this topic in Chapter 4 and look at why we have publicly financed collection and dissemination of information. Emphasis is placed on the implications of such activities in the market place.

When we look at the stages of activity above production agriculture, we find relatively large firms with the financial capacity and analytical ability to gather and analyze information. But the individual producer is not in a similar position. He is too small and lacks the capital that would be necessary to collect the data and conduct the analysis he needs. To prevent the producer from operating at a disadvantage in his price-related decisions, both the federal and state governments are active in the business of gathering and publishing information. The information affects both the long- and short-run decisions of the producers.

Information on planted acreage, estimated production, stocks, exports, estimated carryout at the end of the crop year, and related information is available as the producer makes his planting, selling, holding, and hedging decisions. For the livestock producer, we see cattle inventory reports, periodic reports of cattle on feed (which include placements, marketings, and on-feed numbers), quarterly hog and pig reports, and reports on related products such as egg and poultry production.[8] All this has an influence on how many cattle will be placed on feed, how many sows will be farrowed, etc.

To illustrate, let's trace out a crop year for a hypothetical corn producer to see what information he has available as he makes his decisions. In January, the USDA releases results of the first survey they take of planting intentions. This is the first indication our producer has of nationwide tendencies toward corn, soybeans, or other crops that compete for corn acreage. These estimates are updated in April and estimates of planted acreages are released in late June.

The estimates, especially the planting intentions, should always be used with care. They *are* intentions. Producers can and do change their minds. But the intentions give a useful reflection of overall tendencies. If the intentions reveal a wholesale shift to soybeans, for example, because soybean prices last year were good compared to corn, the producer can see the red flags waving. Can the shift to soybeans be so pronounced that corn ends up being the best alternative this particular year? It can and certainly has been in the past. Instead of playing "follow the crowd," our producer might at least analyze the situation and decide between corn and soybeans in an objective manner based on the best outlook information he can get.

Periodically during the year, the USDA releases stock reports that show the amount of corn in storage. Since stocks plus production give the total supply that must be consumed, the information on stocks is important. And there is also help on the production figure. After the late June report on planted acreage is released, an estimate of production is released.

In 1972 huge purchases of wheat and other grains by the USSR brought sharply higher prices of wheat and prompted concern about the adequacy of U.S. stocks. The USDA reacted to those concerns and since that time has published their *Agricultural Supply and Demand Estimates* after each major report on plantings, production, or stocks. With information on beginning stocks and an estimate of production, the producer has a total supply figure with which to work. Also provided in the Supply and Demand reports are estimates of all major components of demand—domestic use for seed and industrial, domestic use for feed, and exports. Throughout the year the producer has a flow of information as he first makes planting and hedging decisions and then, later in the year, sell or store and possibly hedging decisions.

As the volatility of grain and livestock markets increased through the 1970s, the reporting activities of the USDA increasingly came under attack from producers and producer groups. Producers watched prices react downward on the occasions when the USDA estimates gave unexpectedly high planted acreages, stocks, or production estimates. And on these occasions, there was a tendency to assign causality—the release of the USDA report *caused* the break in price. As concern over these occurrences grew, the credibility extended to other USDA reports and activities was affected. Some producers refused to respond to the USDA's questionnaires; other producers have been heard to say they distort the data which they submit to the USDA.

It is difficult to see how producers can be better off with less information. For this to be true, the information released by the USDA would have to be so inaccurate that it is not useful or better information would have to be available from other sources. But such has not been the case. For those critics who have chosen to follow up on a report that was a surprise, they typically find that what happens in the market confirms the accuracy of the report.

To illustrate how the market can confirm a report, suppose a quarterly *Hog and Pigs* report shows a surprisingly small inventory of hogs given expectations based on the numbers and farrowing intentions of the previous quarterly report. Watching hog slaughter data in the weeks and months following the report will allow the analyst to "check" on the accuracy of the report. And there is another way. The majority of the corn used for feed in the U.S. is fed to hogs. If the corn used for feed calculations run lower than expected, and this can be learned by reading the grain stocks reports, this statistic also tends to confirm the *Hog and Pigs* report.

We do need to remember that most of the data that has an impact on the market are estimates. By definition, estimates will be subject to variation and a recognized probability of error that is built into the estimating procedure. During the growing season for the food and fiber crops, weather indications will influence the estimates and will bring fluctuations during the year.

Figure 5.5. illustrates. During this particular crop year, estimates of the final crop to be harvested were revised upward as the growing season progressed. In general, the price level will tend to drop either in anticipation of the higher estimate or after it is released. This process continues until the final estimate is made. And it is during these years that the criticism emerges. There is a tendency to feel the price would not have dropped if the estimates had not been released.

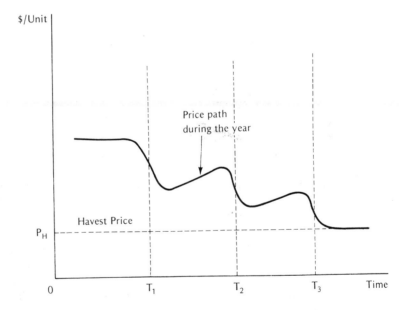

FIGURE 5.5   **PRICE IMPACT OF PROGRESSIVELY LARGER ESTIMATES OF NEW-CROP PRODUCTION**[a]

[a] If estimates at T_1, T_2 and T_3 during the growing season show larger and larger estimates, price levels tend to work down in a "stair step" fashion. Typically, there is an over reaction to the report and then some recovery in the weeks following the report.

But let's examine what is happening during the year. *If* the crop is to be large, *then* consumption and use need to be increased during the year to decrease the stocks at the end of the crop year. Increased usage will only come at a lower price. As the price works lower during the year, increased usage is prompted and the stocks that will be carried to the harvest period and be added to by the new crop are reduced.

What would the situation be like if price did not respond to expectations and drop during the year? Too little "getting ready" would be accomplished and the total supply—stocks plus harvest—during the new-crop harvest period would be especially burdensome. We would expect to see a hard and potentially ruinous price break at harvest time and low prices throughout the year because of the large total supply. Overall, we would expect to see the following if the periodic reports during the year were not there:

1. More extreme year-to-year volatility in prices;

2. Dramatic price breaks during the harvest period when the crop is large and equally dramatic surges in price when the crop is small;

3. Increased difficulty for the producer who is trying to decide which crop to produce;

4. Wider operating margins (and therefore lower prices to producers) by processors and handlers because of the increased uncertainty; and

5. Loss of markets in the U.S. and at the world level because of the increased instability in the U.S. market.

The list could go on but the point is made—everyone in the system should benefit from information that helps the price mechanism do its job of rationing available supplies, allocating across years, and guiding the allocation of resources at the producer level.

Governmental activities in reporting market news affect short-run marketing decisions but are motivated by similar reasons and are equally important. The producer does not have the time or the communication network to develop his own market news. To be able to stay informed and compete effectively, he must have help.

Market news is essentially equivalent to communication. In a broad sense, the prices at the consumer level provide the ingredients for a message to the producer. By "bidding up" the price of a product or a particular quality they like, consumers send a message to producers in the form of a price premium. If the premium gets to the producer and is recognized as a premium (and therefore a message), the producer can consider shifting more resources and production emphasis to this product. Market news becomes an integral and important part of this message.

To be effective, market news activities must meet certain necessary conditions for effective communication. Among the more important are:

1. Market news must be timely. Old news is no news in a fast moving market. The producer needs information daily and even knowledge of developing changes in price direction within the day.

2. Market news must accurately represent the mainstream of trading activity and respond to changes in the way in which trade is carried out.

3. Market news releases must use grades or other descriptive terminology that identifies important value-related attributes in a manner that allows the receiver and user of the message to accurately relate the message to his own product.

Because the situation is constantly changing, it is difficult to discuss in great detail what is needed to make market news more effective. But there are some additional generalizations. Where possible, quantities traded should be reported. This helps protect the user against putting too much reliance on a price report that is based on small quantities or unusual circumstances.

Indication of buyer representation can help supplement information on quantities, on the pace of activity, and on the general direction of price movement. Where auction markets are involved, an indication of buyer representation relative to some norm will help the user visualize what went on in the market. Where the report covers direct sales, an indication of how many (or what proportion) of the buyers normally active in the market are active on a particular day would help.

Grades are tremendously important to effective market news. Therefore, input from the market news branches of the USDA should be a factor in any grade change. Remember, we rely on the price mechanism to communicate needed changes from consumer to producer. Price signals are the specific medium used. It is obvious that a particular value-related attribute can have a price signal attached if and only if that attribute is identified and brought into the price negotiation process. If the desires of consumers for leaner beef are to get through the maze to the producer, there must be some way to communicate those desires. Yield grades for beef carcasses and live cattle have been presented as the answer.[9] Prices are quoted in terms of quality grade and yield grade combinations and at least the mechanism for development of price signals is there. In similar fashion, if high protein wheat or cotton of a particular staple length is worth more to the processor, grades must include these characteristics so a price differential—premium or discount—can be attached in an attempt to guide the efforts of producers.

It is also apparent that the terminology used in reporting market activity needs to be consistent with the terminology used by buyers and sellers in day to day trading activity. For many years, feeder cattle sales were reported by the USDA in terms of Choice, Good, etc.—grades theoretically consistent with grades on slaughter cattle. But the trade did not use the official grades. Terminology such as Okie 1, Okie 2, etc., emerged and was used by buyers and sellers in placing orders for feeder cattle and in discussing feeder cattle prices. It was not until 1978 and 1979 that the USDA moved to announce a new set of feeder cattle grades based on frame size and muscling potential. These two criteria were related to performance in the feedlot and carcass characteristics and were thus a move to facilitate pricing feeder cattle more nearly consistent with their potential. This was what the "Okie 1" terminology had been designed to do in a rough fashion for many years.

Publicly supported activities to provide planning information to the individual producer and keep him abreast of the market are there because of the competitive structure of production agriculture. So long as there are many relatively small producers, each so small they cannot influence the market by their actions, the need for public assistance will be present. But the situation and setting will continue to evolve. Toward the end of the 1970s, new forces were emerging in the market. Government reporting activities were being watched more closely by more people. Widespread awareness of commodity futures markets meant more producers watched the occasional dramatic price reaction to a USDA report when the report contained unexpected numbers on planting intentions, production estimates, placements of cattle on feed, etc. The credibility extended the reports became a more important issue and alternative sources of information and analysis began to emerge.

Gradually, information bases are being developed that do not rely directly on USDA data series. For example, a service called Cattle Fax was developed by a division of the American National Cattlemens Association. The service provides weekly information on the number of cattle moving into feedlots owned by reporting subscribers to Cattle Fax, the number of cattle moving out, weights of cattle moving in, weights of cattle moving out, prices by areas of the country, etc. In the grains and oilseeds, the Leslie Report, which is typically issued before the USDA report, provides the results of privately collected information on estimates of planted acreage for the grains and soybeans, estimates of production, etc. Other information is being offered either as a service of a national trade association, a state trade association, or a privately owned concern that sells its services to subscribers.

In the reporting of trade in wholesale meats, the commercial service offered by the *National Provisioner* (The "Yellow Sheet") has long been the series used by the trade.[10] But there are few such examples of widely used private sources and the coverage is far from complete. To the extent the private services are based on original information that is collected in a scientific fashion, the overall informational base should be improved as the private services expand.

Development of advisory services in the private sector is expanding more rapidly. Advisory services are conducting the analyses and offering the outlook information that once was handled almost totally by the USDA and outlook specialists at the land grant universities. Some of the work is being sponsored by commodity brokerage firms as a service to their clients but the commercial advisory services with no brokerage affiliation are expanding rapidly. The subscriber can "buy" weekly market letters, charts, access to a recorded message giving buy-sell recommendations, direct access to an analyst or a combination of these and other services depending on how much money he is willing to spend. With volatile prices and increasing levels of uncertainty, more market assistance is needed. As this need is recognized, the advisory services are emerging and presenting themselves as the answer. This trend toward moving at least part of the analytical and advisory burden from the public to the private sector will continue as more management time is allocated to the increasingly important marketing function. Information will always be needed.

Summary

Government programs are an important influence in the market. The market of the 1970s has been volatile for all grain, fiber, and livestock commodities. With increasingly active participation in the world market and with the trend away from direct price supports and production controls, the markets of the 1980s will also be volatile.

The market is extremely sensitive to government action that influences supply, demand, or both. Governmental moves to allow more imports or discourage exports are very visible actions. As a general rule, we can expect to see price reactions to such policy moves in excess of the price adjustment that can be justified using fundamental supply-demand analyses. With the ongoing concern for inflation, for balance of payment problems, and given an increasingly sensitive ear to the wishes of the organized consumer groups, we can expect to see governmental action in the import, export, and price control arenas.

In relative terms, the government will play a less important role in providing information in the future. Decision makers are becoming more sophisticated, more aware of what goes on around them, and much more aware of the problems relating to risk and uncertainty. The demand for the detailed help that the commercial advisory service can provide is growing and will continue to grow. As membership in these services gets larger, the base for survey information to supplement the USDA's efforts is being developed. We can expect to see the decision maker turn to the commercial service for information, analysis, and advice.

Footnotes

1. The process of reaching and maintaining a stable position is difficult. First, the quantity demanded at the price support level must be accurately projected. Second, the quantity produced must be matched to the quantity demanded. Both are difficult to do. Demand can and will change over time. Weather, insects, disease, and other unknowns affect the level of production. Historically, supporting price above the equilibrium level has created surpluses when acreage controls were in effect.

2. The Agricultural Stabilization and Conservation Service (ASCS) has been the federal agency charged with the responsibility of accumulating data and establishing a representative yield for farms. These yields have been used in establishing payments for crop insurance, for disaster payments by the federal government, and are now used in the target and loan price programs.

3. The three-year loan program was separate from the short-term loan program in the 1977 farm act. The purpose of the 3-year reserve was to take wheat and feed grains out of the market channels in the short run to boost the depressed price levels of 1977 and early 1978.

4. This tendency deserves special attention because of its lasting impact. Within weeks after the embargo on soybean exports in 1974, Japan was busy trying to negotiate a long-range deal with Brazil. Heavily dependent on imported beans, meal and oil, the Japanese were concerned about the reliability of the U.S. as a supplier. This type of response decreases the demand for U.S. beans and encourages other producing countries, such as Brazil, to increase their level of production.

5. The import quotas were increased by 200 million pounds in early June, 1978. During the 10 days before the announcement and for about 10 days after the announcement, we saw a dramatic turnaround in the psychology of the market. Choice steer prices at Omaha in early March were around $46.00. Prices moved sharply higher to the $62 level by early June. In anticipation of the announcement that came on June 8, prices moved lower. By the end of June, Omaha prices were around $52. Carcass beef dropped from $95 to $83 in the midwestern trading region during the same period. Without question, the market had moved too high too soon. But the price moves correlated with the time period before and after the announcement provide vivid evidence of the impact that government action and the anticipation of more stringent action can have in the market.

6. Some members of the Senate and the House contacted industry analysts and agricultural economists at the land grant universities. The overwhelming recommendation was against any move to impose price ceilings. But the voices of the consumer groups were louder, and the Cost of Living Council, with little representation from those who understood the cattle industry, decided price ceilings were needed to hold down inflation. Five years later, in 1978, we are hearing the rumblings for price controls again. By 1979 and 1980 when this book is in print, we will in all probability have seen price controls again.

7. Some analysts have suggested this price break indicates the ceiling price was above the equilibrium price. But this position is difficult to support. During the period from March to early September, there were shortages of beef. The stream of weekly or monthly market-clearing prices would have been higher without the price ceilings. It was the expectations of cattlemen that prompted the price break. Most cattle coming from the feedlots and marketed off pastures during the March-September period lost money at the "derived" ceiling prices. The result was predictable—producers as individuals held cattle expecting price to surge after the ceiling was lifted just as hog prices had done. It was the micro-macro problem at work again.

8. Almost all the information that is not of the market news type is released by the Crop Reporting Board of the USDA. An annual catalog of what reports are prepared and released is available from the USDA. Write to:
   > Crop Reporting Board
   > Room 0005
   > USDA
   > Washington, D.C. 20250

9. Grades will be discussed in more detail in later chapters. The USDA's yield grades, announced in 1965, attempt to identify the value differentials within beef carcasses of a particular quality grade. The yield grades are numbered 1—5 with 1 indicating a high percentage of lean in the carcass.

10. The yellow sheet has been the source of some controversy for many years. It is often used as the price base in formula pricing—a practice of concern to many analysts. In mid-1978, government hearings were conducted concerning the way the *Provisioner* accumulates and reports prices. A competitor, called the "Meat Sheet" has recently emerged and the USDA continues to report trading activity in carcass beef. Over time, these issues will be resolved and a still better information base will be the result.

Questions

1. Assume you are in a position of market analyst for an advisory committee to the President. The rate of inflation is approaching 10 percent on an annual rate basis and food prices are leading the increase. You are asked whether price controls on food prices at retail should be instigated. How would you respond? Why? Can you defend your position using supply-demand analysis?

2. Under what conditions would an individual decision maker be in a better bargaining position if USDA reports were not released?

3. In the 1960s, farm policy was dominated by an approach that involved price supports and acreage controls. In the early 1970s, the approach was switched to a target price-loan price program. Describe the key differences between the two types of policies in terms of (a) impact on market price, (b) the ability of the U.S. to compete in the world market, and (c) impact on price in its role of allocating resources.

4. List several reasons why the importance of commercial market advisory services is increasing relative to the USDA and market analysts at the land grant universities. Do you agree these services will continue to increase in importance? Why or why not?

5. List and defend several reasons on both the positive and negative side of the debate topic:

   Resolved that the USDA should continue and improve its efforts in gathering and reporting news of market activity.

Selected References

Breimyer, Harold F., *Economics of the Product Markets of Agriculture.* Ames, Iowa: Iowa State Univ. Press, 1976.

Dahl, Dale C., and Jerome W. Hammond, *Market and Price Analysis.* New York, N.Y.: McGraw-Hill, 1977.

Hightower, Jim, *Hard Tomatoes, Hard Times.* Cambridge, Mass.: Schenkman Publishing Co., 1973.

National Commission on Food Marketing, *Food From Farmer to Consumer.* Washington, D.C.: U.S. Govt. Printing Office, 1966.

Purcell, Wayne D., "USDA Reports: More Help Than Hurt," *Beef*, Vol. 12, Feb. 1976.

Rhodes, V. James, *The Agricultural Marketing System.* Columbus, Ohio: Grid Publishing, 1978.

Rogers, George B., "Pricing Systems and Agricultural Marketing Research," *Agr. Econ., Res.*, USDA, ERS, Jan. 1970.

part three

Prices and Price Analysis

No single variable is a more important part of the markets than price. No single variable is subjected to more varying interpretation and to more misunderstanding than price and pricing processes.

Chapter 6 develops the concepts of price determination and price discovery with an eye toward the needs of the decision maker and the student of market systems. Attention is focused on the economic forces that have the potential to inject uncertainty into the system: new information, the government, and developments in the world market. The behavioral dimension of the price discovery process is given special attention. This dimension is difficult for most decision makers, students, and analysts to see and handle—but it is important. Timing is often the critical element in market decisions and the behavioral dimension affects the timing of price moves.

The objective of Chapter 7 is to describe and illustrate the tools needed in analyzing price and price movements. On a base of understanding of the market system, the operating environment, and the basics of pricing processes, the material in Chapter 7 should move the student toward a capacity to cope effectively with price as the volatile dimension of the market. Handling price and the techniques of price analysis is a necessary condition to successful marketing decisions.

chapter six

Price and Pricing Processes

Pricing processes involve the interaction of supply and demand. The level of supply and demand is in turn determined by the level of certain economic forces or variables that influence them. Among the important "demand shifters" are changes in income, in tastes and preferences, or in the price of related goods or services in the consumption pattern. Aggregate demand changes with changing levels of population. Among the important "supply shifters" are changes in technology, in the price of significant inputs, or in the price of related goods in the production process.

Price Determination

A distinction is often made between price determination and price discovery. Price is *determined* by a balance between given levels of demand and supply. Since the levels of demand and supply are known only after the fact, we must talk about price determination primarily in an ex post facto sense. Alternatively, price can be viewed as being determined over time in a comparative statics context. That is, price can be "determined" initially for a given level of demand and supply. If a shift in demand develops because of a change in the level of one of the demand shifters—such as income— price has been "determined" again after the adjustment to the new level of demand has run its course. Figure 6.1 pictures the process. For a given supply function S_1S_1, price is determined at a level OP_1 for a demand D_1D_1. If demand shifts to a higher level such as D_2D_2, a new price is determined at OP_2 after the adjustment process is completed. Both OP_1 and OP_2 are equilibrium or market-clearing prices. The original equilibrium price OP_1 was disturbed by the change in the level of demand and OP_2 is the new equilibrium price.

In a comparative statics approach, interest is in the level of prices determined by the different supply-demand combinations. The price levels are analyzed and possibly compared after the adjustment processes are completed or projected. We see, then, that interest in price determination will evolve in those situations in which there is reason to be concerned about different or potential levels of price. In the illustration above, the exact level of price OP_2 may be an important input into a production, marketing, or investment decision. The decision maker must therefore sharpen his or her abilities to analyze the impact of demand and supply shifters.

The impact of changes in the level of population can be eliminated by

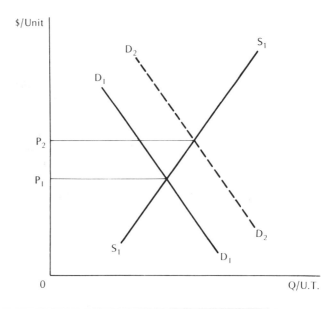

FIGURE 6.1   ILLUSTRATION OF PRICE DETERMINATION AFTER A SHIFT IN DE-
MAND

considering demand on a per capita basis. Attention can then be focused on taste and preferences, on income, and on prices of related goods in consumption.

DEMAND SHIFTERS

A consumer's tastes and preferences change slowly and over time. Since most marketing decisions are made within a fairly short time period, the shifting influence of changes in tastes and preferences often is not of primary importance. For some commodities there is a significant seasonal pattern to tastes and preferences, however, and this seasonality should be considered. For example, the "preference" for turkeys is highly seasonal and surfaces around Thanksgiving and Christmas. The preference for hams shows a seasonal tendency, reaching its peak around Christmas. Seasonal patterns in the preference for perishable fruits and vegetables are literally forced by highly seasonal production patterns and related seasonal availability. Such seasonal patterns in preferences for certain products are important but are also stable and largely predictable. Once the decision maker is aware of the patterns and takes them into consideration, there is little reason to spend time and effort in analyzing this particular demand shifter.

There is more potential in analyzing the impact of changes in income and changes in the prices of related goods and services in the consumption pattern. And with these shifters, several analytical techniques can be helpful.

Income elasticity[1] coefficients are effective gauges of the demand shifting influence of changes in income. If the coefficient is positive and relatively large, an increase in demand for the product or service can be anticipated if per capita disposable income increases significantly. Conversely, if the income elasticity coefficient is negative, an increase in income will reduce the quantity of the good taken. Table 6.1 lists several popular food items and available estimates of income elasticity coefficients. In general, the meats, the fresh fruits and vegetables, and products with time saving features such as extensive processing and precooking have positive income elasticity coefficients. Foods such as potatoes, wheat flour, and corn meal, which require more preparation time and provide fewer built-in services, have small positive or negative coefficients.

The cross elasticity coefficient[2] is a gauge of the strength of the demand relationship between two different products. If the coefficient is positive and relatively large (significantly different from 0) the products are substitutes and compete for the consumer's limited food dollars. For negative coefficients, the products are complements and tend to be used together. Most products tend to be substitutes. Table 6.2 records estimates of cross elasticity coefficients for some important food products.[3]

Given understanding of the important demand shifters and an ability

Table 6.1
Estimates of Income Elasticity Coefficients for Selected Commodities

Commodity	Income Elasticity	Commodity	Income Elasticity
Beef	.290	Lettuce	.446
Pork	.009	Dry vegetables	−.914
Chicken	−.037	Frozen vegetables	.616
Fish	−.036	Wheat flour	−.685
Eggs	−.076	Corn meal	−1.143
Fresh milk	.377	Soup	.236
Cheese	.249	Fresh beans	−.495
Potatoes	.008	Oranges	.260
Apples	.140	Breakfast cereals	.058

Source: P. S. George and G. A. King, "Consumer Demand for Food Commodities in the United States With Projections for 1980," *Giannini Foundation Monograph Number 26,* California Agr. Exp. Sta., March 1971.

to use the elasticity concepts, the decision maker is in a position to formulate a useful expectation of the equilibrium price that will eventually be "determined" in some future time period. This price expectation can then be incorporated into a decision model.

To illustrate, consider the position of the cattle feeder who would like to have a useful estimate of the average price of Choice 900–1100 lb. steers during the coming year. By studying the research publications and outlook materials of the USDA, university outlook specialists, and the publications and releases of the advisory service to which he subscribes, the following information is gathered:

1. Per capita disposable incomes for the next year are expected to increase by four percent;

2. The income elasticity coefficient for cattle at the live cattle level is .5;

3. Slaughter hog prices are expected to increase by 10 percent in the next year due to a cyclical reduction in pork production; and

4. The cross elasticity coefficient between hog prices and the quantity of live cattle purchased is .25.

Looking only at the demand side for the moment and holding the quantity of slaughter cattle constant, the feeder anticipates a 4.5 percent increase in price of cattle for the next year. Two percent of this comes from the "income shifter" and 2.5 percent comes from the "price of related product" shifter. Figure 6.2 records the expected change. If a quantity of Choice

Table 6.2
Estimates of Cross Elasticity Coefficients
for Selected Commodity Combinations

Commodity	Commodity for Which Price Changes and Cross Elasticity Coefficient	
	Pork	.0826
	Chicken	.0675
	Fish	.0031
Beef	Cheese	.0008
	Eggs	.0013
	Fresh Milk	.0028
	Potatoes	.0004
	Beef	.0763
	Chicken	.0352
	Fish	.0046
Pork	Cheese	.0015
	Eggs	.0026
	Fresh Milk	.0053
	Potatoes	.0007
	Beef	.0082
	Pork	.0121
	Chicken	.0026
Potatoes	Fish	.0664
	Cheese	.0065
	Eggs	.0131
	Fresh Milk	.0047

Source: P. S. George and G. A. King, "Consumer Demand for Food Commodities in the United States with Projections for 1980," *Giannini Foundation Monograph Number 26*, Calif. Agr. Exp. Sta., March 1971.

steers OQ_1 sold for an average price of $50 in the current year, the price expectation for the coming year would be $52.25.[4] If these estimates of the shift in demand prove to be accurate and the quantity offered for sale is OQ_1, a new yearly average equilibrium price will be "determined" at or near the $52.25 level.

SUPPLY SHIFTERS

Changes in the technology of production shift the supply of food and fiber products over comparatively long periods of time. A significant development such as hybrid seed corn has immense potential but requires many years for widespread adoption. Because of the time lags involved,

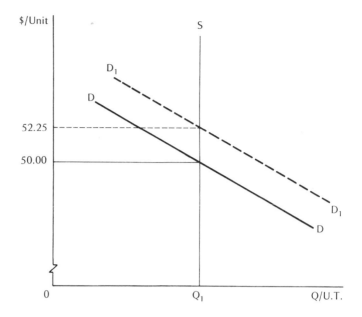

FIGURE 6.2 INFLUENCE ON PRICE OF A GIVEN SHIFT IN DEMAND WITH SUPPLY HELD CONSTANT

changes in technology are not usually very important price determining influences within the marketing year.

The theory of production dictates a profit maximizing level of usage for inputs at particular prices. When the prices of the inputs change, either in absolute value or relative to each other, the profit-maximizing level of usage changes. Given time for the biological processes of production to be completed, the level of production offered at a particular product price will change—the supply function will shift—as a result of the change in input prices.

Some of the more graphic examples of changes in supply evolving from changes in input prices are seen in the livestock sector. In the swine industry, for example, changes in corn prices can prompt a shift in the supply of market hogs. Since corn is the primary input, changes in corn prices can lead to changes in the potential profitability of hog production. The hog-corn ratio has long been used as a barometer of the profitability of hog production. Relatively high levels of the ratio usually prompt expansion in hog production.[5]

Changes in product prices are also important supply shifters in the short run. Where inputs are flexible or mobile, they tend to flow toward production of the product where the marginal productivity of the inputs is greatest. In equilibrium, particular inputs are allocated so as to equate the marginal return from the last dollar spent in producing each alternative product. In algebraic terms, the equilibrium position is as follows:

$$\frac{MVPx_1y_1}{MFCx_1} = \frac{MVPx_1y_2}{MFCx_1} = \cdots = \frac{MVPx_1y_n}{MFCx_1}$$

Where:

$MVPx_1y_1$ = Marginal value product of input x_1 in producing product y_1; and

$MFCx_1$ = Marginal factor cost of input x_1 (equal to the price of the input x_1 if bought in a purely competitive market).

A reduction in the price of wheat, for example, tends to shift land and capital inputs to alternative uses such as barley or other grains.[6]

Another illustration is available from the livestock sector. The corn belt farmer-feeder can sell his corn as a cash crop, feed it to cattle or feed it to hogs. In general, low-priced corn is marketed by feeding it to livestock, especially when cattle or hog prices are relatively high. The relationship between these variables is clear if price series for slaughter steers and for corn are matched with placements of cattle on feed. Placements tend to increase when steer prices move up and/or corn prices move down.

Whatever the time period considered, the workings of the demand and supply shifters generate a particular level of demand and supply and a price for that time period is determined. The level at which those prices are determined will dictate whether producing and selling the particular product or service will be profitable. It is apparent, therefore, that an ability to predict the level at which prices will be determined is important to the success of the production-marketing decision.

Price Discovery

Price determination refers to the price levels that evolve given the impact of supply and demand shifters. Emphasis is on the level of price which evolves after the forces of demand and supply have made themselves felt. Price discovery differs in that emphasis is placed on buyer and seller interaction and price negotiations that are based on estimates or expectations of supply and demand. When considering price discovery, we are therefore concerned with the actions of buyers and sellers as they interact in the market place on the basis of something less than perfect information concerning the level of supply and demand.

Consider, for example, what happens when the manager of a feedlot begins to negotiate the sale of cattle to a packer-buyer who calls at his office. The feedlot manager must bring to the negotiation process an estimate of the effective demand for a particular pen of cattle—just what will the buyer pay on this particular day? The feedlot manager has such information as the following at his disposal:

> Last week, the buyer bought cattle of comparable quality and value at $50.00 per cwt. But the feedlot manager knows the carcass beef market has declined by $2.00 per cwt. within the past week. Since the packer tries to operate on the basis of a gross margin per head, the buyer's price bids will be lower since the carcass market has declined. Also, the feedlot manager knows the inventory of cattle on feed is relatively large and that the supply of market-ready cattle is higher than it was a week earlier. The feedlot manager decides that the buyer's maximum bid will be $48.50.

On the other side of the bargaining table, the packer-buyer has formulated expectations with regard to the possible offer prices of the feedlot manager. He has at his disposal such information as the following:

> Demand for carcass beef has faltered as the movement through retail outlets has slowed. Packers have responded by cutting back on daily slaughter and the movement of cattle from feedlots has declined accordingly. But the cattle he has inspected at various feedlots have not been on feed so long that the feedlots are in trouble. With the recent union contract in the packing plant, even

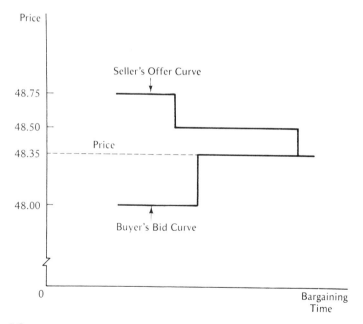

FIGURE 6.3   ILLUSTRATION OF THE PRICE BARGAINING PROCESS BETWEEN BUYER AND SELLER

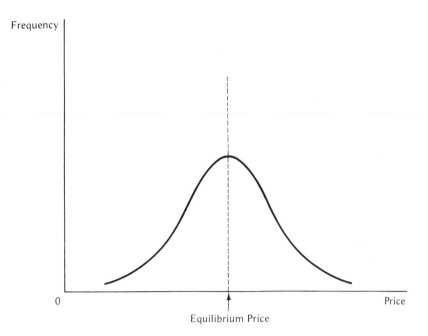

FIGURE 6.4   FREQUENCY DISTRIBUTION OF PRICES AROUND THE EQUILIBRIUM
PRICE

the labor has become a fixed cost and they must have cattle. The
buyer has been authorized to pay up to $48.75 for the cattle but
believes the feedlot manager's minimum to be as low as $48.25.

Figure 6.3 pictures the negotiation process. The buyer's "bid curve"
shows an initial bid of $48.00 and a move during the negotiation period up
to the purchase price of $48.35. The seller's "offer curve" starts with an
offer of $48.75 and then a fairly quick dip to the $48.50 level. He holds here
for some time before accepting the $48.35 bid.

The simple framework shown in Figure 6.3 can be used to illustrate
several important points. Consider, for example, the implications if one of
the two parties to the negotiation process is poorly informed. Suppose the
feedlot manager as seller underestimates the strength of demand and expects the buyer's maximum bid would be $48.00. His "offer curve" may
start well below the price the buyer would be willing to pay—and the final
price is sure to be below the $48.35 negotiated when the two parties were
both well informed.

What we begin to see, therefore, is that the process of price discovery
is something less than an exact process. During any particular trading day
there will be prices around the equilibrium or market-clearing price that
will ultimately be "determined" for the day. Figure 6.4 illustrates the

process by showing a frequency distribution of prices around the unknown but underlying equilibrium price. In general, we can conclude the prices that are farthest from the equilibrium price are generated by either poor or inaccurate information on the part of both buyer and seller, an imbalance in the levels of information available to buyer and seller, or signficant differences in the bargaining power of the buyer and seller. If the pricing errors above the equilibrium price match the pricing errors below the equilibrium price in both magnitude and frequency of occurrence, the realized prices form a normal distribution, and the equilibrium price would be the average price for the day.[7]

What occurs during a particular market session is therefore a process that reflects the underlying expectation of supply and demand relationships by competing buyers and sellers. Since these expectations can and do change over time and with new information, both time and new information play major roles in the price discovery process.

ROLE OF INFORMATION

In discussing price determination, emphasis was placed on a comparative statics approach. An equilibrium or market-clearing price was visualized in a theoretical sense for a given set of supply-demand relationships. But when the demand or supply (or both) changes, a new equilibrium price must be determined. This recurring pattern of change and adjustment has been noted as the essence of price discovery processes.

Changes in the available body of information often effect a shift in demand or supply and thus become important factors in the price discovery process. This is particularly true when the new piece of information comes as a "surprise" to the trade—that is, it brings a significant shift in the expectations of supply or demand.

To illustrate, consider the impact of a forecast released by the USDA that calls for a significant increase in production of winter wheat compared to earlier forecasts. The earlier and smaller forecast was an important part of the base of information upon which prices were being established prior to release of the new forecast. But with the report, a new base of information is available. Such a development can have impact on the demand for old-crop wheat in storage during the months prior to the new harvest (in June and July). Figure 6.5 illustrates what can happen. Since old-crop and new-crop wheat are essentially perfect substitutes, a decrease in the price expectation for the new-crop wheat (caused by an increase in supply to S'S') changes one of the economic forces influencing the level of demand for old-crop wheat. The demand for old-crop wheat shifts down to D'D' reflecting the change in expectations and prices fall on the wheat in storage to some lower price such as OP_2.[8]

Anyone who has ever plotted the path traced out by cash price

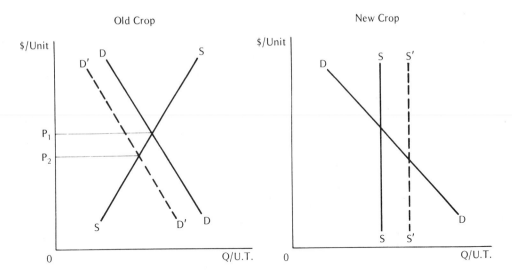

FIGURE 6.5   IMPACT OF AN INCREASE IN EXPECTATIONS FOR NEW-CROP WHEAT ON DEMAND FOR OLD-CROP WHEAT IN STORAGE

movements over time is well aware of this endless and continuing process of adjustment and readjustment to changes in the body of information available to buyers and sellers. At any one point along the time continuum prices are being discovered, and negotiated prices are a function of the available information. When the information changes, prices will change—and we see the pattern of variable prices which draws the attention of decision maker, market analyst, and policy maker.

ROLE OF TIME

Time records the ongoing price discovery processes and serves as a barometer of pricing accuracy. In general, prices tend to focus in on what will be the equilibrium price for a particular point "t" in the future as "t" approaches.

This process is evident on the central markets for livestock. When the buyers and sellers arrive early in the morning, they come reflecting a particular, if then unknown, set of supply and demand relationships. The supply is essentially fixed for the day when all the livestock are unloaded. When private treaty[9] negotiations or the auction process begins, the first indication of the strength of demand on this particular market is available. As the day proceeds, the "true" demand comes out of hiding. Buyers who need cattle or hogs to keep slaughter operations going compete for the available supply of livestock. Prices may move as much as $1.00 per cwt.

up or down during the day compared to the early sales as the competitive bidding acts to "discover" the market-clearing price given the essentially fixed supply and the aggregate demand of buyers.

The process of price discovery across time is most apparent in the futures markets.[10] Trade in a distant commodity futures on any particular day is based at least in part on the expectations of cash prices in the future month. Across time, trading levels react to new information and start to focus in on the equilibrium price for the month as expectations are adjusted and refined. Figure 6.6 illustrates. In the encircled area, a *Hogs and Pigs* report was released by the USDA which revealed hog numbers well below the levels expected by buyers and sellers of the futures contract. Prices traded higher in response to this new information. The impact of the positive news continued to exert influence in the weeks that followed as prices trended higher at least partially on the strength of lower hog numbers and lower pork supplies than had been expected prior to the report. Each day that passed reflected efforts of buyers and sellers to discover the correct price for the April live hog futures. On April 20 (the last trading day for this futures contract), the futures prices continued to focus in on the cash price. On the last day of trading, the futures closed at $.90 per cwt. above the cash.[11] This "trading path" in the months prior to April provides a graphic illustration of the process of price discovery at work along the time continuum.

ROLE OF GOVERNMENT PROGRAMS

In discussing price discovery processes, we referred briefly to both the role and impact of new information. The adequacy of the information base on which buyers and sellers are acting is of critical importance to the timeliness and efficiency of price discovery processes.

Publicly supported efforts to provide information, especially price information, reflect a concern over the possibility of an imbalance in the availability of information to buyers and sellers. Most of the monies and efforts are directed toward the farming sector. With many relatively small farms, the individual farmer can seldom afford to develop his own original sources of information. But the buyers, dealers, and processors with whom the producer must deal have the benefits of an often complex private communication system and skilled analysts to decipher the messages in price and price movements.

Statistical Reporting Service.   Active at the federal and state level, the Statistical Reporting Service (SRS) assimilates and distributes most of the basic data dealing with production, stocks, and prices.[12] Most market analysts view the efforts of the SRS in this area as indispensable—and usually find a need for still more data. But as we noted in Chapter 5, not all producer and

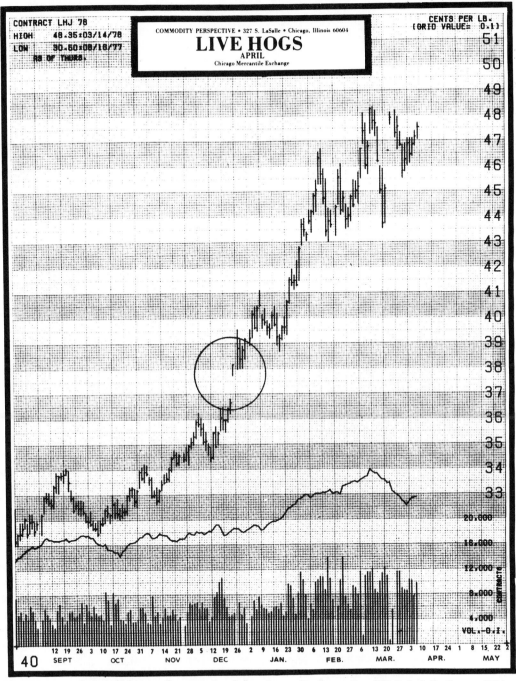

Chart reprinted with permission from: *Commodity Perspective*, 327 S. LaSalle Street, #536, Chicago, Ill. 60604.

FIGURE 6.6   THE RESPONSE IN PRICE LEVELS OF APRIL LIVE HOG FUTURES TO A DECEMBER *HOGS AND PIGS* REPORT

113

trade groups share the positive attitude of the analyst. They see prices fall on some occasions after a report is released and they blame the release of the information.

Much of the skepticism and negative attitude on the part of producers and producer groups can be traced to lack of understanding of the price discovery process. When price reacts dramatically to the release of a new statistical report, it is because the report is a surprise—it has a high informational value. We expect a reaction as a step in the process of discovering the market-clearing price, and price levels are expected to change with changes in information.

Assuming resonable accuracy of the reports, it is difficult to build a case to show how the many small producers would be in a better position without the reports. In Chapter 5, we discussed briefly how the release of reports calling for a large grain crop helps the market "get ready" by encouraging increased consumption through lower prices. There are obvious parallels in the livestock. A cattle on feed report that shows unexpectedly heavy placements of cattle on feed during a particular month dampens the enthusiasm for still more placements. Expectations change and the market adjusts to this new piece of information through lower prices. How could we argue that a particular cattle feeder would be better off if he did not know about the increased placements? If a lower price does follow the report, is this not protecting him against the possibility of even greater losses by discouraging placements?

And there are other important reasons for the collection dissemination of information. The theory of bargaining power continues to evolve and grow but there is little question of the need for equality of information to help balance the ability of buyer and seller to influence terms of trade. The emergence and rapid growth of commercial advisory services in recent years provide tangible evidence of a need on the part of many producers. Advisory services develop the communication networks, establish the market contacts, employ the analysts, and provide a service that is beyond the financial capacity and analytical abilities of most individual producers. They become a factor in the price discovery process. Some of the information advisory services use in developing their advisory positions is gathered from their own surveys. But much of their information base comes from the federal and state statistical reporting services.

The techniques and procedures of price analysis are presented in Chapter 7. Price analysts in the USDA, in the land grant colleges, in other universities and colleges, in private consulting firms, and in commercial firms rely heavily on the body of information provided by the governmental agencies. Seasonal indices, estimates of the price elasticity of demand, analysis of price cycles—all these require a data base. These and other guides become factors in price discovery processes and are made possible by the efforts of governmental agencies such as SRS.

Market News Services.   The Federal-State Market News Service is the short-run counterpart of the SRS efforts. Reporting market prices is the key charge of this agency. Daily prices and even intra-day price movements are reported for a vast array of markets around the country. The efforts of these reporting stations are at the base of TV, newspaper, radio, and other reports of price levels and market activity.

Market news services are in the communication business. The effectiveness of their efforts will determine their effectiveness in informing potential buyers and sellers. If the communication effort is effective, the process of price discovery is made more efficient.

Effective communication has many requisites but none is more important than the symbols that are used in the communication process. Meaning is not inherent in the symbols employed. Meaning is in the interpretation of the user or receiver of the message. For any communicated message to be effective, therefore, the interpretation attached to the symbols by the receiver must be the same as that intended by the sender.

Grades are the symbols that are often an important part of market news releases. Prices are reported in terms of grades and if a particular grade effects the same product picture or mental image in the minds of all readers, the message "communicates." Thus, a producer who reads or hears a message such as "No. 2 yellow corn at Chicago traded from 3.10–3.12½" or "Choice 600–700 lb. steers sold for $49.00–51.50" can attach a reasonably accurate price expectation to his corn or his cattle of a similar grade.[13]

The important role that grades play in market news releases explains why grades are constantly being reviewed, analyzed, and sometimes changed. As a general rule, a grade is needed for each product category that identifies a significant and recognizable difference in product value. When there is a significant variation in value *within* a grade, price messages are not sharp—and the communication effort of market news services is not as effective as it could be.

The refinement over time in grades for live slaughter cattle illustrates the problems that can occur. For several decades, slaughter cattle were graded for quality (Prime, Choice, Good, etc.). But it became increasingly apparent beef carcasses of the same quality grade could vary significantly in value because of differences in cut-out or yield of lean meat. In the 1960s, the USDA introduced "yield grades" to account for the differences in value due to differences in the ratio of lean cuts to total carcass weight. Figure 6.7 illustrates. Within each quality grade such as Choice, there are five yield grades with number one representing the carcass with the highest yield of lean cuts. According to the official USDA releases, lean cuts as a percent of carcass weight vary 4.6 percent per yield grade.

Consider the potential impact of the introduction of yield grades on

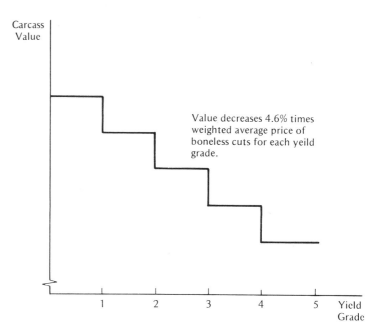

FIGURE 6.7   ILLUSTRATION OF THE DIFFERENCES IN BEEF CARCASS VALUES
ASSOCIATED WITH YIELD GRADE

market news messages. Prior to yield grades, a market news release reporting trade in beef carcasses might have read as follows:

> Choice 600–700 lb. beef carcasses sold in a price range of $75.00–
> 78.50.

If the trade referred to above included carcasses with yield grades ranging
from two to four, the message using yield grades might read as follows:

> Choice 600–700 lb. yield grade 2–3 carcasses sold in a range of
> $77.00–78.50 with yield grade 4 carcasses trading in a price range
> of $75.00–77.00.

The reader of this second message should be able to formulate a more exact
price expectation for beef carcasses of a particular yield grade.

Market news activities play a significant role in pricing processes.
Potential buyers and sellers rely upon market news releases to help them
formulate price expectations for a particular product they are planning to
buy or sell. The effectiveness of these messages in terms of motivating a
mental picture or interpretation consistent with that intended by the sender of the message is an important determinant of how well the buyer or

seller is prepared when he enters the bargaining arena. If the message is "noisy" and subject to varying interpretation, the range of possible prices for a given product of a given quality is expanded, and the price discovery process is less efficient and subject to more variation.

ISSUES IN PRICE DISCOVERY

To this point, we have discussed price discovery without getting into some of the issues that are causing concern among market analysts, private decision makers, and governmental policy makers. Historically, the arena within which price discovery took place was the organized market. Livestock, fruits and vegetables, tobacco, cotton—all these and other commodities were assembled at a market center. Buyers came, inspected the product, and bid on a competitive basis. The process was characterized by physical proximity of buyer and seller and the ability to physically inspect the product. Price was discovered through competitive bidding or direct negotiation between buyer and seller.

Direct movement from producer to processor or handler bypasses the organized market. With better grades and better communication technology, products are now routinely sold without physical inspection. As these changes have occurred, new and different procedures in pricing have developed. Among the more widely discussed are:

1. Formula pricing,

2. Committee pricing, and

3. Administered pricing.

Prices are discovered using *formula pricing* when the price at which product transfer will occur, either now or in the future, is tied to some market report or other indicator by a formula. The most widespread use of formula pricing occurs in the trade of wholesale beef. A market news report prepared by the *National Provisioner,* called the "yellow sheet" in the trade, is the base for widespread application of formula pricing. The meat packer in Boston, Omaha, Houston, or San Francisco prices beef carcasses or primal cuts to potential buyers on the basis of the yellow sheet quote for a particular day plus or minus some margin reflecting his location and the size and quality of the shipment being sold.

In Chapter 5, we noted the practice of formula pricing is of concern to many analysts. It received a great deal of attention by the National Commission on Food Marketing in the 1960s and was the subject of government hearings in the late 1970s. The concern was and is whether prices can be "correct" or "fair" when most of the trade is based on formula pricing and very little on negotiated prices. What percent of the volume must be based on negotiated trade to provide an acceptable pricing base? Would 50 percent, 20 percent, or even five percent be enough? This is a tough set of questions to answer and the answers are not apparent.

Committee pricing involves price discovery by a committee comprised of representatives for buyers and sellers. Efforts are made to estimate the relevant supply and demand levels and report a market-clearing price based on the supply-demand estimates. The reported price is changed daily or whenever supply or demand is judged to have changed. The price reported for major markets in cotton is essentially a committee determined price. Attempts have been made to establish a committee pricing system in eggs.

When a buyer or seller announces a price at which he will buy or sell, we have *administered pricing*. Most finished products sold at retail are sold this way. Further down in the marketing system, some buying is done via administered prices. Managers of a wheat elevator or cotton gin will often quote a price at which they will buy for that particular day. The firm employing this approach to pricing must accept the level of sales or purchases that results.

Authors such as Breimyer and Rogers[14] provide more detailed coverage of this topic area. Here, we will leave the topic by listing a few observations that are designed to shed at least limited light on the pertinent issues and motivate some thought by the student:

1. The "protection" of the competitive bidding process in the organized markets may be more apparent than real. Some analysts have long argued this is the only competitive way to price and the only way the producer or other seller is guaranteed a fair price. But what is a "fair" price? Most shipments to the organized market are on a non-recourse basis. On any particular day, the supply can be in excess of the needs of the buyers represented on the market. The market-clearing price that is discovered on this particular day may be significantly below the price of the previous day for product of the same quality. And other problems can crop up. An important buyer may not get to a particular market center on a particular day. Demand could be lower simply because his buying power is missing from the market.

2. Formula pricing has both strengths and weaknesses. Clearly, we would like to be assured that at least some of the buyers and sellers are committed to being informed on the changing levels of supply and demand that are present in the market. But does every buyer and seller need to spend time and money working on this? It could be that the small operator in an outlying market comes much closer to

getting a fair price given his location, the quality of his product, etc., if he prices on a formula basis using a price reported from a larger and more active market area. And negotiation is typically still involved in the process of setting the plus or minus margin compared to the market report that is being used as the price base.

3. The arguments that say a majority of the product must move by negotiated price to have the necessary degree of competition for the correct price to be discovered have some loopholes in theory and in fact. Most economic analysis is completed at the margin—marginal cost, marginal returns, marginal value product, marginal revenue product, etc. Does the marginal concept apply in price discovery? Which transaction in any particular market on any particular day merits the most weight or attention? Is it the first sale, the middle sale, or is it the marginal or last sale? If we wanted one transaction to represent the market-clearing price for the day, we could argue the last sale is the one. At any rate, there is little reason to argue that the distribution of prices—if five percent of the volume is based on negotiated sales—would be any different than the distribution if 95 percent of the volume is based on negotiated sales.

4. Committee prices or administered prices can certainly be effective prices if a good job of analyzing supply and demand is done in establishing the announced price level. Truly competitive prices in the open market are vulnerable to day-to-day fluctuations in supply and demand, to the weather and "weather scares," to rumor, and to the tendency to overreact to any perceived change in supply or demand. The resulting price variability decreases the level of pricing efficiency that is achieved and brings a high level of risk to all participants.

There are as yet no guidelines to tell us which is the "best" way to discover price. An open-minded approach to the issue is needed. Blind allegiance to any system is not the answer. Some systems will work for some products with their particular economic structure but might not work as well for other products. We must keep in mind that the bargaining position of the seller is important, that other terms of trade have price implications, that the costs of selling are increasing, that the modern decision maker is better informed than in past years, and that new technology and analytical capacity to estimate supply and demand are being developed. Taking a dogmatic stand on the way price is discovered can and will have an influence on the capacity to recognize the possibilities of progressive change throughout the marketing system.

Behavioral Considerations in Pricing

The behavioral dimension is important in all pricing processes. But it is in the cyclical and seasonal price patterns that the behavioral dimension is most apparent and very important.

Chapter 7 treats the cyclical and seasonal price movements in an analytical sense. Techniques and procedures are developed there that are designed to quantify important dimensions of the long recognized and much discussed price cycle. Methods to isolate the normal or typical seasonal pattern are also presented. But true understanding of the nature of cyclical price patterns and why they occur requires looking behind the mechanics into the decision processes that prompt these recurring behavioral patterns.

BEHAVIORAL DIMENSIONS OF THE PRICE CYCLE

Price cycles are most evident in the livestock commodities. Figure 6.8 shows a plot of cattle prices over several decades. Note the "troughs" that occur in the 1950s, 1960s, and again in the 1970s. Also shown in Figure 6.8 are inventory numbers—the total number of cattle and calves on farms on January 1 of each year. The cycle in numbers is also apparent with the peak in cattle numbers tending to occur two to three years after the prices start to turn down from their cyclical peaks. The reason for the time lag is apparent when we examine Figure 6.9. Cattle slaughter, and therefore beef production, tends to show a significant increase before cattle numbers peak. This is logical since it is the increased slaughter that precipitates a break in price and the eventual decline in cattle numbers.

With this picture of numbers, slaughter, and price we have the base we need to understand how the behavioral dimension becomes a factor. As prices start to climb from the bottom of the price trough, producers start to look to the future with a more optimistic attitude. Each producer is influenced by the rising prices and he starts to think about expanding. To do this, he cuts down on the cows he culls each year by keeping older cows for another year. And more importantly, he starts to buy or hold back his own heifers to put them into the cow herd. This takes cows and heifers out of the slaughter channels, which reduces beef production and tends to push prices higher. As prices climb, the holding and herd-building tendencies are intensified, beef production is constrained even more, and prices climb still higher. Eventually, this process of herd building moves the cow herd and total cattle numbers to a level with the potential for sharply higher slaughter.

As slaughter levels climb, beef production begins to increase and downward pressure on price starts to build. Within two to three years, prices have declined enough that the psychology of the producer starts to change from a herd-building orientation to one of liquidation. Often, the

FIGURE 6.8 CATTLE AND CALVES ON FARMS JANUARY 1 AND PRICE OF 500–700
POUND FEEDER STEERS AT KANSAS CITY, 1925–78

first reaction is to "hold" and wait for prices to improve. But the pressure
on price from increased slaughter will not be denied. The next emotion
may then be one of panic as prices not only fail to improve but continue to
decline. Cattle flood the market and the cows from an expanded herd begin
to show up in the slaughter channels in increasing numbers. Heifers are no
longer being held for the cow herd and also enter the slaughter channels in
increasing numbers. The price break is underway.

     Cycles in cattle prices are a consequence of the competitive structure
of the beef industry. There are many small producers and each producer,
acting as an individual, contributes to an aggregate pattern of action that

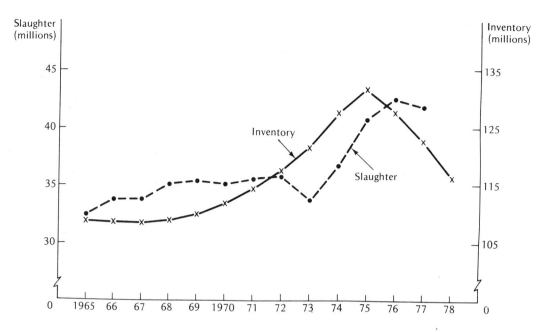

FIGURE 6.9   CATTLE AND CALVES ON FARMS JANUARY 1 AND COMMERCIAL CATTLE SLAUGHTER 1965–78

results in the cycle. For any particular producer, the best strategy is to understand the cycle and minimize the problems it causes him. With this in mind, we point to the following key indicators of when to be prepared to take action:

1. During the herd-building phase of the cycle, the ratio of male to female slaughter continues to increase. A "be alert" signal emerges the first year this ratio fails to show a year-to-year increase. The price break is usually not far behind.

2. Cow slaughter drops to less than 20 percent of total slaughter during the building phase of the cycle. Any year-to-year increase in this percentage is a warning sign that a price break is on the way.

3. Later in the building phase of the cycle, year-to-year increases in the cow herd reach the three to four percent level. Historically, an annual rate of increase of around two percent gives slaughter levels that can be moved without dramatic decreases in price. When annual increases exceed three percent for two consecutive years, this usually spells trouble ahead.

Watching these indicators keeps the astute producer in a position to minimize losses from a price break. Before the break occurs, the herd can be culled down to an efficient number. Older cows and poor producers are moved to market while the prices are still high. Since the liquidation phase of the cycle usually runs its course within three to four years, the herd with young and productive cows can span the liquidation phase and be largely intact when prices turn higher again.

Behavioral considerations influence the length of the beef cattle cycle. The biological process of production places a minimum on the time between peaks or troughs. It takes time to hold back heifers, to get them to breeding age, have them calve, and then raise their progeny to slaughter weights. But these biological processes are shorter than the typical 10 to 12 year length of the cattle cycle. It is the behavioral dimension that adds time to the biological dimension.

During all phases of the cycle, there is a lag in the producer's response. As the liquidation phase runs its course and prices show signs of having reached a bottom, the astute producer may begin to build his cow herd back toward capacity levels. But not all producers respond this quickly. The pain of the price break is still there and the producer is wary. The producer's financial agent may contribute to this wariness by hesitating to loan money. Slowly, the attitude changes and this group of producers starts to build again. Still later, another group of producers finally decides "things look better" and starts to buy cows and hold back heifers. The "in-and-out" individual, often a part-time farmer, may climb aboard the band wagon here. These response lags explain why the building phase of the cycle can last six to eight years.

On the downside, the order of response is essentially reversed. The astute producer monitors warning flags such as those we noted earlier and culls his herd early. Another wave of producer reaction follows. Then comes the group who follows a "wait until price recovers" philosophy—but price does not recover. The break continues and panicky liquidation follows. The lag prolongs the liquidation phase.

In hogs, the cycle is much shorter—usually about three and one-half to four years. The lags in response are still evident but the biological processes are shorter—and the breeding herd can be built to "break" levels much quicker. The signals to monitor are similar.

Forward Pricing

Cash contracts and commodity futures are the two commonly used means of forward pricing. Both typically present the same underlying reasoning—the need to reduce or eliminate the risk of cash price fluctuations. With a cash contract, the producer intends to deliver the physical product on or by some future date specified in the contract. But with commodity futures, no actual physical delivery is usually intended. The futures are used to provide protection against the risk of cash price variability. Both approaches deserve more discussion.

Forward pricing via a cash contract provides for delivery in some future time period with price or a basis for determining price and other terms of trade being established in the current time period. For example, a cotton producer might work out a contract with the local processor in the spring that calls for delivery of cotton on or before a certain date the following fall. Appendix A lists the factors that should be considered in the contract. This lists makes the process look complex but these and possibly other variables demand consideration. Anything that can significantly affect the economic position of either buyer or seller should be covered. *The other terms of trade can often be more important than the level of price.*

Futures contracts can also be used by the producer as a means of forward pricing. Users talk about a "guaranteed price" using the futures but this is not technically correct. It is more nearly correct to talk about a guaranteed margin that could then be converted to a price equivalent. But whatever it is called, the hedged position does become a form of forward pricing.

To illustrate use of the futures, let's assume a cotton producer wants to protect against low or declining prices on his growing cotton crop. He estimates his yield, his costs, and generates a break-even cost of 53 cents per pound. Early in the production season he has a chance to sell December cotton futures at 65 cents per pound. Because his local prices typically run 3 cents below the futures quote in New York, he deducts the 3 cents and gets a net futures quote of 62 cents. Subtracting, this gives him a 9 cent margin over his cost estimate. By selling enough December futures contracts (each contract is for 50,000 pounds) to cover the part of his crop he wants to protect, the producer "locks in" the 9 cent profit margin. If cash cotton goes to 45 cents, he would expect to be able to buy the futures back at around 48 cents. He loses 8 cents in the cash market, makes 17 cents in the futures (65 cents minus 48 cents) and nets 9 cents. For those who want to talk about this in terms of a guaranteed price equivalent, it would be 62 cents.[15]

Often, the two mechanisms are combined. In the grain trade, for example, the local elevator will offer the producer a cash contract for future delivery at a specific price. The price offered reflects the current quote on a distant futures contract minus an operating margin. A similar procedure is used in the livestock industry. A meat packer may offer a cash contract to a cattle feeder at the current quote for a live cattle futures contract minus a margin to cover the packer's cost of trading the futures. The packer will often maintain his only purpose is to schedule a more stable flow of cattle into his plant.

The pros and cons of cash contracts versus using the futures market to hedge are often discussed. Both can be viewed as forward pricing. Both can provide protection against the risks of cash price fluctuations. Among the differences which merit attention are:

1. A position in the futures offers flexibility. The producer can be "locked in" to a cash contract if he suffers a crop failure. The futures position is easier to offset. Too, if the price outlook changes and prices move higher, the producer can remove his commitment in the futures. The commitment in the cash market cannot be readily offset.

2. Most cash contracts are hedged by someone. The grain elevator will hedge the position he takes when he extends a cash contract to the producer. The producer who argues he would not be involved in hedging his position pays someone else to do it for him when he accepts a cash contract. And we could argue the elevator manager charges, via the operating margin he sets, a price for services the producer could perform for himself.

In general, we can expect to see a continued increase in contractual arrangements between closely related stages in our marketing systems. Both seller and buyer have an interest in offsetting the price risk to which they are exposed. And there is interest in stabilizing raw material or product flows by contracting and establishing a delivery schedule.

Price As A Rationing Mechanism

Among the functions of price that influence marketing systems directly is price as a rationing mechanism. The rationing function is important for any product that is produced on a seasonal basis. For example, corn in the U.S. is harvested in the September-November period. But the need for corn as a food and as a livestock and poultry feed lasts throughout the year. Price is asked to ration the disappearance of the product and make it available through the year.

What we have is a stock of corn that is available during one quarter of the year. In theory, price will be at its low for the year during the harvest period and increase during the market year reflecting cumulative storage costs. The exact pattern we see within the year will depend on price expectations of producers, buyers, and others who are in a position to store corn. Unusually low prices during the harvest period provide an incentive for producers to store corn instead of selling it immediately. Such "holding action" limits the volume of corn moving into export channels or into processing and precludes more downward pressure on price during harvest.

If exporters and processors need corn, they use price to attract an increased volume of movement. They increase their bids and corn begins to move as the net cash price to the potential seller improves. How much will be "turned loose" by those in control of the stocks depends on their price expectations. If stocks are large, expectations for price increases during the year are dampened. Movements of corn out of storage may be "price responsive" and quantities sold will show a significant increase for each five to 10 cents increase in price.

Figure 6.10 illustrates the normal seasonal pattern in prices for a commodity produced and harvested in one part of the year. The pattern is one of rising prices reflecting cumulative storage costs through much of the year followed by a period of adjustment prior to the next harvest. Several forces can distort the expected pattern. Unexpected developments in the export arena can change the picture. For example, strong export buying during any quarter of the year can push prices during that quarter above the normal seasonal pattern.

Years in which monthly prices show a downward trend during much of the year are not uncommon. Overly optimistic price expectations early in the year can create such a pattern. Low prices at harvest prompt holding in anticipation of higher prices later in the year. But if stocks are large, the

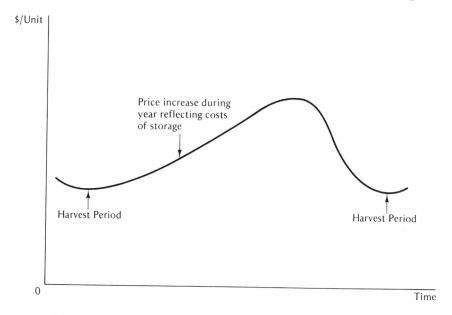

FIGURE 6.10   TYPICAL SEASONAL PRICE PATTERN FOR THE COMMODITY HARVESTED DURING ONE PERIOD OF THE YEAR

better prices may not materialize. Too much grain is held into the second half of the year and when it comes to market, still lower prices are the result.

Extremely short supplies can sometimes lead to a price pattern within the crop year which is called an "inverted carrying charge." Competition among buyers for a limited supply pushes current cash prices higher. The futures market may present a picture with the nearby contracts trading above contracts for later in the year. In these instances, price truly becomes a rationing device. The limited supply of product moves to the most critical areas of need and to those for which the demand is most inelastic. Later in the crop year, as the new harvest period approaches, prices may falter as buyers decide to wait until the new harvest is completed.

Summary

In a study of markets and marketing, nothing is more important than price. In this chapter, the discussion has focused on pricing processes, on the importance of price, and on other selected topics. Chapter 7 focuses on the analytical tools that are valuable in explaining and/or predicting price. In later chapters price will be the focal point of concern as we develop an understanding of futures prices, hedging, hedging strategies and move toward the building of decision models. To the individual decision maker, to the analyst concerned with the effectiveness and efficiency of our marketing systems, and to society in general, price will continue to be a topic of interest and concern.

Key dimensions of price include price determination and price discovery. A price is "determined" for given or known levels of supply and demand. Price is "discovered" by the interactions of buyers and sellers acting on something less than perfect knowledge of supply and demand forces. Such controversial practices as formula pricing, committee pricing, and administered pricing become part of the price discovery process.

Price functions as a director of economic activity, serves as a rationing mechanism for products produced during one period of the year, and becomes a barometer and measure of the behavioral dimensions at work in the marketplace. With the increased volatility in prices during the 1970s, more attention is being paid to forward pricing whether by cash contract or by using the futures market. Decision makers who never worried much about the marketing decision are increasingly concerned as the risk associated with price movements increases. With that risk comes potential. This potential is the motivating factor behind increased interest in price, pricing processes, and analytical processes to help in efforts to cope with the volatile markets.

Footnotes

1. Income elasticity is a measure of the quantitative response to a change in income. For a hypothetical commodity or service A, income elasticity can be defined conceptually as

$$I_{E(A)} = \frac{\% \text{ change in quantity of A taken}}{\% \text{ change in income}}$$

with all prices held constant. Stated in terms of a simple calculating formula, income elasticity can be defined as

$$I_{E(A)} = \frac{\dfrac{Q'_A - Q_A}{Q'_A + Q_A}}{\dfrac{I' - I}{I' + I}}$$

Where: Q'_A = quantity of A taken after the income change;
   Q_A = quantity of A taken before the income change;
   I' = income level after the change; and
   I = income level before the change.

2. Cross elasticity is a measure of the quantitative response in one product to a price change in a related product. For two hypothetical products B and C, cross elasticity can be defined conceptually as

$$X_{E(B,C)} = \frac{\% \text{ change in quantity of B taken}}{\% \text{ change in price of C}}$$

with income and all prices except the price of product C held constant. In terms of a calculating formula, the cross elasticity between B and C *for price changes in C* is

$$X_{E(B,C)} = \frac{\dfrac{Q'_B - Q_B}{Q'_B + Q_B}}{\dfrac{P'_C - P_C}{P'_C + P_C}}$$

Where: Q'_B = quantity of B taken after the price change in C;
   Q_B = quantity of B taken before the price change in C;
   P'_C = price of C after the change; and
   P_C = price of C before the change.

3. Note the cross elasticity coefficients are not "symmetrical." When pork prices increase (decrease) by 1.0%, the quantity of beef taken

increases (decreases) .0826%. But when the price change is in beef, the relationship is slightly different. Each 1.0% increase (decrease) in beef prices increases (decreases) the quantity of pork taken .0763%. Consumers are a bit more reluctant to leave beef and go to pork than vice versa.

4. We arrive at the $52.25 as follows:

$$\text{Impact of the income increase} = 4\% \times .5 = 2\%$$
$$\text{Impact of the change in hog price} = 10\% \times .25 = 2.5\%$$
$$\text{Total influence on demand} = 2\% + 2.5\% = 4.5\%$$

Therefore, we get $50 + .045(\$50) = \$52.25$ per cwt. looking only at the demand side. If supply is not fixed at OQ_1, there would also be an influence from the supply side to consider.

5. The hog-corn ratio is the number of bushels of corn equal in value to one cwt. of live hogs. For example, suppose that for a particular week in Omaha we get the following weekly average prices:

$$\text{No. 2 yellow corn} = \$3.00 \text{ per bushel}$$
$$\text{U.S. No. 1–3 barrows and gilts} = \$60.00 \text{ per cwt.}$$

The hog-corn ratio would be 20:1. Historically, corn belt farmers have tended to feed their corn to hogs and expand hog numbers when the ratio moves to the 18:1 or 20:1 level. Liquidation of sows and an eventual decrease in hog production have typically occurred when the ratio drops to the 12:1 or 10:1 level.

6. To illustrate, let y_1 = wheat, y_2 = barley and x_1 = irrigation water. $MVPx_1y_1 = MPPx_1y_1 \cdot Py_1$ or the marginal physical product of x_1 in producing y_1 times the price of y_1. When the price of wheat or Py_1 drops, the following inequality exists

$$\frac{MVPx_1y_1}{MFCx_1} < \frac{MVPx_1y_2}{MFCx_1}$$

Since the producer has no control over price, he restores the equality and equilibrium by shifting x_1 from wheat to barley. Shifting water from wheat to barley tends to increase $MPPx_1y_1$ and decrease $MPPx_1y_2$ since $MPPx_1y_2$ and $MPPx_1y_2$ are both declining throughout the rational range of usage of x_1 (stage II of the production function). The equality is restored.

7. A normal distribution is characterized by symmetry around the mean. For example, if seven different prices and frequencies with which they occurred were as shown below on a particular market on a particular day, the observed prices form a normal distribution, the mean

is the midpoint of the price range, and we could argue the mean is the best estimate of the market-clearing price.

Price	Frequency
$60.75	5
60.50	10
60.25	15
60.00	20
59.75	15
59.50	10
59.05	5

8. An alternative way to look at this is to say the demand for storage falls with the lower expectations. If the demand for storage decreases, this means the wheat in storage has lower value and this gets reflected in the form of a lower price for old-crop wheat.

9. On many central markets, the product is consigned to a commission agency who acts as the agent of the seller. Price negotiations between this agent and the buyer are often on a 1:1 basis and are referred to as "private treaty" sales by the trade. This approach is most prominent in the large central markets for livestock.

10. Trade in commodity futures will be discussed in detail in later chapters. The concept is introduced here because trade in commodity futures is justified at least in part by its role in price discovery processes.

11. The trading level of the futures contract is expected to close above cash by an amount reflecting the cost of delivery of the product under the provisions of the futures contract. We will find in Chapter 9 there are no forces in the market place that can guarantee the two prices will come still closer together, because when futures = cash + delivery costs, this is a break-even position for the few marginal buyers and sellers who use the futures as a mechanism for delivery of the physical product.

12. The Statistical Reporting Service is the organization that prepares the many reports released by the USDA's Crop Reporting Board referred to in Chapter 5. As a rule, data are gathered by a cooperating state SRS agency. The various states send their reports in to Washington where they are combined, and the report is prepared and released at a particular time on a previously scheduled day.

13. An adjustment is needed to form a price expectation at the producer's local market. The corn producer in Iowa must adjust the Chicago quote by the normal difference between Chicago and his local market. This difference is the "basis" we have talked about. More attention will be paid this important concept in later chapters.

14. Refer to Harold F. Breimyer, *Economics of the Product Markets of Agriculture* (Ames, Iowa: Iowa State University Press, 1976) and George B. Rogers, "Pricing Systems and Agricultural Marketing Research", *Agr. Econ. Res.*, USDA, ERS, Jan. 1970.

15. The guaranteed price equivalent will always be the price at which the futures are sold minus the adjustment factor to convert to local market conditions. Cotton futures are traded on the New York Exchange. The cotton producer in Mississippi or Louisiana must know the relationship between the New York futures and his local cash market. If the futures average three cents a pound over local cash, then the adjustment factor or "local basis" is three cents—and the futures minus the three cents gives the price equivalent of the hedge. In later chapters, we will come back to this concept of basis and discuss ways to use variability in the basis to advantage.

Questions

1. What is the difference between price determination and price discovery?

2. Discuss the economic strengths and weaknesses of the following procedures as part of the price discovery process:
    a. Competitive bidding in an auction,
    b. Formula pricing, and
    c. Committee pricing.

3. Using graphs and related descriptions, illustrate the role of information in the price discovery process. Then list pros and cons of publicly supported activities to gather and report information such as planting intentions, estimates of production, stocks of grains, cattle on feed, etc.

4. Describe how the behavioral reactions of decision makers affect the length of the price cycle in livestock. Do you see any such influence of the behavioral dimension in the grains? Why or why not?

5. List the advantages and disadvantages of a cash contract vs. hedging as a means of forward pricing. Which would you recommend for the decision maker with little expertise in the analysis of markets and prices? Why?

Selected References

Breimyer, Harold F., *Economics of the Product Markets of Agriculture*. Ames, Iowa: Iowa State Univ. Press, 1976.

Collins, Norman R., "The Changing Role of Price in Agricultural Marketing," *J. of Farm Econ.*, Vol. 41, Aug. 1959.

Dahl, Dale C. and Jerome W. Hammond, *Market and Price Analysis*. New York, N.Y.: McGraw-Hill, 1977.

Leftwich, Richard H., *The Price System and Resource Allocation*. Hinsdale, Ill.: The Dryden Press, 1976.

Purcell, Wayne D., *An Appraisal of the Information System in Beef Marketing*. East Lansing, Mich.: Mich. State Univ. Agr. Econ. Rep. No. 151, 1969.

Rhodes, V. James, *The Agricultural Marketing System*. Columbus, Ohio: Grid Publishing, Inc., 1978.

Stout, Thomas T. and Paul R. Thomas, "Implementing Improved Pricing Accuracy for Cattle and Beef," *Long-Run Adjustments in the Livestock and Meat Industry: Implications and Alternatives*, Ohio Agr. Res. and Dev. Center Res. Bul. 1037, 1970.

Tomek, William G. and Kenneth L. Robinson, *Agricultural Product Prices*. Ithaca, N.Y.: Cornell University Press, 1972.

Appendix 6.A

Cash Contracts: Issues and Procedure

Most decision makers are familiar with the notion of a cash contract. Grain elevators, cotton gins, vegetable processors, and other buyers have offered contracts across the years in attempts to tie down raw material needs. Price usually receives the bulk of the seller's attention but other provisions of the contract are often more important. In this appendix, we look at some of the provisions that should be included in a contract and why they are important.

Provision	Reason Important
Names and addresses of buyer and seller.	To expedite handling of the contract and meet legal requirements.
Date the contract is established.	To meet legal requirements.
Signatures of all parties to the contract, witnesses or notary public.	Contract is not legal until signed. Signing before a notary public is recommended.
Price or the basis upon which price will be determined.	Very important. Price should either be set in clear and specific terms or detailed indications of how price will be determined should be included. If the price is to be tied to some market indicator, exactly which price, which market, and which date should be included.
Quality specifications with a schedule of premiums and discounts for departures from the quality specified in the contract.	Very important. This provision is needed to insure payment in accordance with value. If the product is a superior product, a premium is justified. If the product is of inferior quality, the buyer deserves the discount. Both parties need to know exactly what quality was delivered.
Time and conditions of weighing, transfer, storage, etc.	Detailed specifications are needed here. What might appear to be minimal variations in procedure can

have significant price implications. If an allowance for shrink is to be used, the seller needs to know what shrink can be expected. If a discount for moisture, foreign matter, etc., is to be included, the seller must know what a reasonable discount would be. What appears to be an attractive price offer can sometimes lose its appeal if the price implications of the terms of the contract are calculated.

Specifications of when title transfer and liability are to change from seller to buyer.	The liability is especially important. If the time of transfer is clear, the responsible party can get appropriate insurance or otherwise prepare for an emergency or loss.
Penalties for default.	A contract is a business proposition and should be treated that way. Too often, parties to a cash contract default with little or no penalty because the time and expense of court action is so great. A clear statement of actions expected of each party with related penalties in the event of default will expedite legal deliberations.

Obtaining the services of a lawyer is advisable since legal advice on drafting and handling a contract is very important. But a word of caution is in order. Most lawyers cannot recognize the subtleties of the weighing conditions, premiums and discounts, etc. because they're not familiar with the business and the commodity that is being bought and sold. The buyer or seller must use his own expertise in working with the lawyer.

chapter seven

Price Analysis:
Concepts and Tools

Price and changes in price are of key importance to marketing decisions. Whether to sell or store, when to sell, whether to maintain ownership through processing, whether and when to liquidate breeding stock or take land out of production—all these and other market-related decisions require an ability to analyze price movements and project future prices with a useful degree of accuracy. In Chapter 6, price and pricing processes were discussed in general terms. In this chapter, the primary purpose is to develop and illustrate the analytical tools that are important in dealing with price in a decision framework.

Time Dimensions

Most analyses of price deal with the time dimension. It is over time that the demand and supply shifters operate and it is over time that the behavioral dimensions of the market place make themselves felt. For purposes of

137

simplicity and ease of analysis, it is convenient to talk about trends, cyclical moves, and seasonal moves in price.

TREND

Trend is the long-run movement in price levels. The question of how short the planning period can be and still be called "trend" is difficult. Here, trend will be used to refer to moves in cash prices that span at least two sets of production decisions when no cyclical patterns are present or span at least one complete cycle when a cycle is evident. For grains, then, we can talk about price trends when we have prices for at least two crop years.[1] For livestock, covering a complete cycle means 10 to 12 years in cattle and three to four years in hogs.

In terms of analytics, several techniques are commonly used to describe and measure trend. Among the most common are moving averages and single equation regression models.

Moving averages can be used over an extended period of years to record the long-term movement of prices. Figure 7.1 shows an 11-year moving average plotted across utility cow prices from 1924 through 1977.[2] Note the tendency to "fill the valleys" and "cut the peaks." This is characteristic of any moving average—it tends to smooth the data.

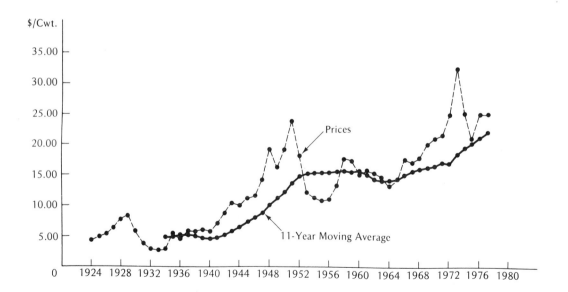

Source: *Livestock and Meat Statistics*, ERS, USDA.

FIGURE 7.1   ELEVEN-YEAR MOVING AVERAGE TREND LINE FOR UTILITY GRADE COWS: CHICAGO, 1924–50, AND OMAHA, 1951–77

The advantages of a moving average approach to analyzing trend are the following:

1. Moving averages are easy to calculate, and

2. Moving averages are flexible and capable of changing directions. A change in direction of the moving average is often a signal the direction of trend has changed and this can have important implications to the decision maker.

A primary disadvantage of the moving average approach to analyzing trend is the absence of any base for projections. The moving average describes what is going on but has no analytical or statistical base to allow prediction of future price levels.

Regression or other single equation models are often used to analyze price trends over time. The simple linear regression model[3] describes price movements as a linear function of time:

$$Y = a + bX + e$$

where: Y = price such as an annual average price;
   a = a parameter, the intercept term;
   b = a parameter, the slope of the regression line;
   X = time in years (actual years or coded so that X = 1 for first year, etc.), and
   e = an error term.

In many price series, there is a tendency for the long-run trend in prices to be up or down and to continue that same pattern over time. Figure 7.2 records annual cattle prices across a 20-year period from 1958 to 1977. A simple linear regression line fitted to this data is

$$Y = -41.240 + 1.066X$$

This regression line is shown on Figure 7.2.

Not all price series trend in the same direction in a linear fashion. Yearly average wheat prices are shown in Figure 7.3. Note the tendency toward a slight downward trend in prices from the 1950s through 1972 and then the move to higher prices starting in 1973. A linear regression line does not give a good "fit" to this data. Note the straight line marked $Y = .403 + .025X$ is actually a compromise that is influenced and turned up by the higher prices of the 1970s. The trend in wheat prices appears to have changed directions starting in 1973. Here, some other approach is needed.

Sticking with a single equation model, a regression model of the following general form would be expected to work better for the wheat data:

$$Y = a + b_1X + b_2X^2 + e$$

The quadratic form of the single equation regression model will allow the

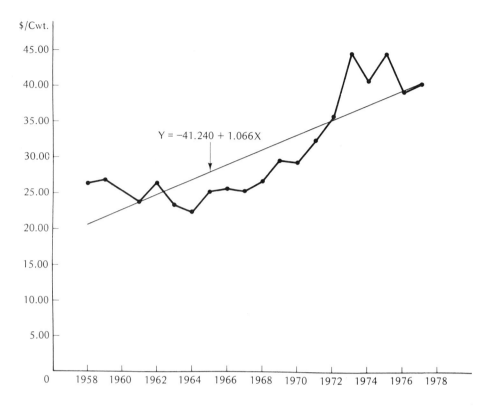

Source: *Livestock and Meat Statistics*, ERS, USDA.

FIGURE 7.2 PRICES AND LEAST-SQUARES TREND LINE FOR CHOICE SLAUGHTER STEERS, OMAHA, 1958–77

fitted curve to turn back up and thus "fit" the data better. The fitted form of this model as shown in Figure 7.4 is

$$Y \times 31.128 - 0.959X + 0.008X^2$$

The more complex form of the single equation model brings with it a shortcoming, however. The model is incapable of changing direction again after it turns up in response to rising prices late in the period. It would take a function with an X^3 component or term to turn the curve back down. The procedure starts getting complex and difficult to use.

A reasonable compromise is to use a straight-line trend so long as the data plot approximates a straight line. If the direction of the trend appears to be changing due to changes in the fundamental supply-demand picture, because of changes in production technology or for other reasons, a new straight-line trend can be fitted with a slope more representative of the new

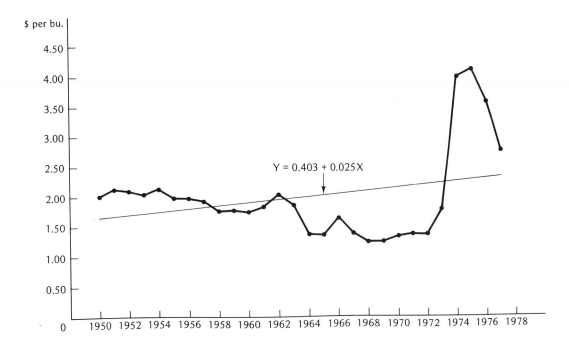

Source: *Wheat Situation*, ERS, USDA.

FIGURE 7.3   PRICES AND LEAST-SQUARES TREND LINE FOR WHEAT, PRICES RE-
CEIVED BY FARMERS, U.S., 1950–77

price path. But there will be a time lag before enough observations are generated to allow calculation of a new trend. During the transition, we have very little basis for projecting trend.

Knowing the direction of price trends is important to the decision maker in several ways. Price trends are important inputs into decisions that reallocate resources within a firm. The farmer who can produce both corn and soybeans is interested in the long-run price trends in the two crops that compete for his land and other resources. With the continuing move by American consumers toward eating away from home, the price of processing beef may trend higher at a more rapid rate than the price of Choice beef of a table-cut quality. The cattle producer needs to know this. Faced by intense price competition from synthetic fibers, the price of cotton may falter compared to other products. If such a trend is developing and shows no signs of being reversed, everyone in the cotton industry—from the farmer to the mill to the local clothing store—needs to know it. A change in the direction of price trend will usually require some adjustment throughout the marketing system for the commodity being considered.

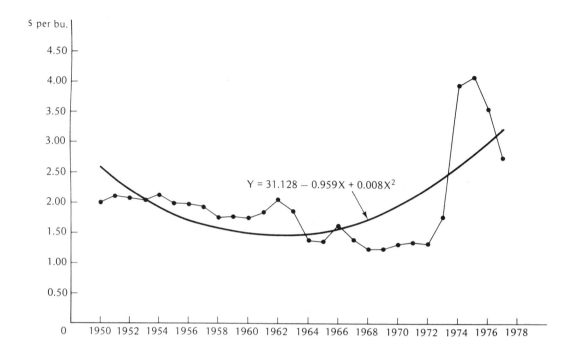

Source: *Wheat Situation*, ERS, USDA.

FIGURE 7.4   PRICES AND LEAST-SQUARES FIT FOR SECOND DEGREE POLYNO-
MIAL FOR WHEAT, PRICES RECEIVED BY FARMERS, U.S., 1950–77

In terms of price analysis, knowing the trend in price data is also important for analytical reasons. If the purpose of the analyst is to isolate any existing price cycle, he may wish to eliminate price trend from a series of yearly prices. Figure 7.5 shows price data for slaughter hogs for a 20-year period 1955–1974. The period was selected to allow illustration of five complete four-year cycles. Figure 7.6 shows the same prices after the effect of price trend is removed. A simple linear regression model of the general form $Y = a + bX$ was fitted to the price data. The slope estimate, $\hat{b}$ or .843, was subtracted from the second price in the series, $2\hat{b}$ from the third price, etc. The cyclical nature of the prices is clear in Figure 7.5 and Figure 7.6. The year 1956 was a second year of liquidation. From that year forward, there is a pattern of "two years up, two years down"—at least in relative terms.

If the purpose is to remove the effect of trend, the first need is for a test to see whether significant trend is present in the data. A recommended procedure is as follows:

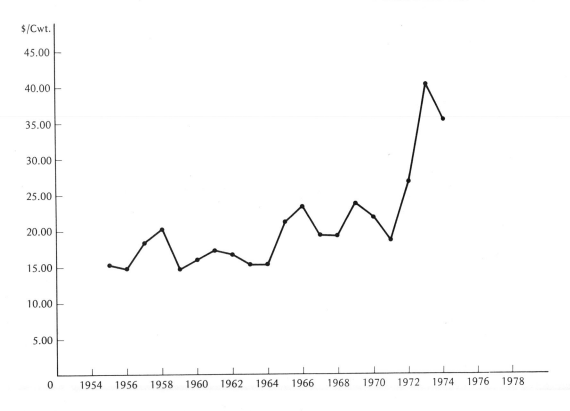

Source: *Livestock and Meat Situation*, ERS, USDA.

FIGURE 7.5   YEARLY AVERAGE PRICES FOR BARROWS AND GILTS, 7 MARKETS, SELECTED YEARS, 1954–74

1. Deflate the price data before testing for trend.[4] If general price inflation is the only reason prices are trending upward, it is important to know this. Upward trending real prices suggests increasing demand, decreasing supply, or some combination of the two.

2. Plot the deflated price series against time. Visual examination should tell you whether any trend that appears to be present approximates a linear relationship. Fit a simple linear regression model to the data and test for statistical significance of the estimated slope parameter. (Appendix A illustrates procedure).

3. If significant trend is found, eliminate the trend by removing (subtracting for positive trend, adding for negative) its influence from the deflated price series. A plot of the resulting data series will

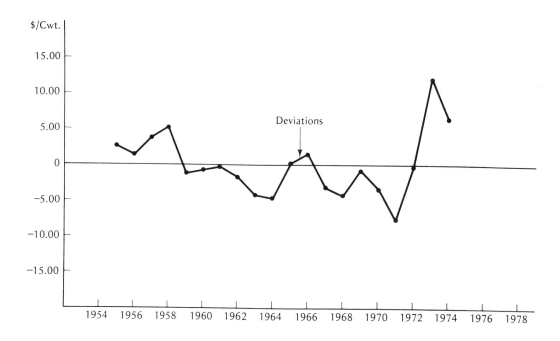

Source: *Livestock and Meat Situation*, ERS, USDA.

FIGURE 7.6   YEARLY AVERAGE PRICES FOR BARROWS AND GILTS, 7 MARKETS, AS DEVIATIONS FROM TREND LINE, SELECTED YEARS, 1954–74

show any cyclical pattern in yearly data without the influence of trend. Note this is equivalent to plotting the original prices as deviations from the trend.

CYCLICAL

With cyclical moves in prices come both problems and opportunities. The long-run economic success of the firm often rests squarely on how well the decision maker understands and handles the cyclical moves in price. Since the problem is most acute in the livestock sectors, the beef and pork subsectors are used as bases for illustrations.

Figure 7.7 paints the picture. Hog slaughter and hog prices show an inverse relationship. Every three and one-half to four years, the industry moves faithfully and predictably through the cycle. The behavioral dimensions are similar to those discussed for the cattle cycle in Chapter 6. To review briefly, the phases of the cycle are:

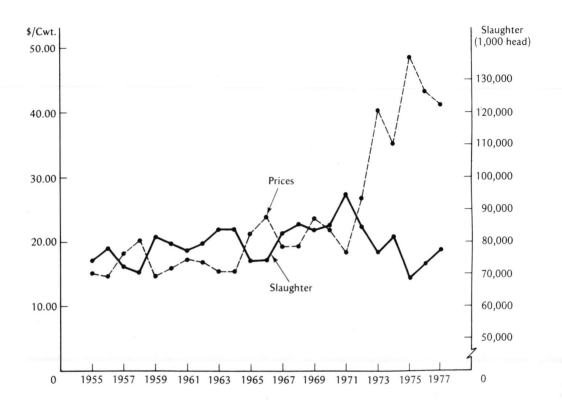

Source: *Livestock and Meat Situation*, ERS, USDA.

FIGURE 7.7   COMMERCIAL HOG SLAUGHTER AND PRICES OF BARROWS AND
GILTS, 7 MARKETS, 1955–77

1. Starting at the price lows, sows are moving to slaughter and gilts are being fed for slaughter instead of being held back to go in the brood sow herd.

2. With a time lag of six to 12 months, the influence of the liquidation of females starts to show in the market in the form of reduced marketings of slaughter hogs. Prices begin to rise as a result of the reduced slaughter.

3. The increase in prices changes the outlook of producers, makes hogs look more profitable, and renewed interest in expanding production begins to emerge.

4. Gilts begin to be held out of slaughter channels and placed in the breeding herd. This "holding action" reduces slaughter even more and gives prices another boost, which prompts more holding of gilts and expansion of production. The process feeds on itself as prices are forced higher.

5. The pigs from increased farrowings of sows and gilts start to hit the market as slaughter hogs some six to 10 months later. Pressure builds again on prices as slaughter levels climb and pork production increases. Within a few months, prices are pressured downward to a level that prompts the start of female liquidation and the process starts over again.

Economic forces outside the pork industry often serve to either dampen or accentuate the cyclical swings in hog prices. Cattle prices are always a factor. The cycle in cattle prices is 11 to 12 years in length but when the cyclical lows in cattle and hogs occur together, the downward pressure on hog prices is intensified. Table 7.1 shows what happened for selected years in the first half of the 1970s as both the cattle and hog sectors moved into the liquidation phases of their respective cycles. Hog prices broke to levels that imposed heavy losses on producers and the result was a massive liquidation that lasted into 1974. By mid-1975, the results of the liquidation were apparent. Per capita pork availability and consumption dropped to the lowest level since the 1950s and hog prices zoomed to record levels in September of 1975.

Developments in the feed complex can also be important. Significant changes in the level of corn prices can help to start certain phases of the cycle and, without question, can accentuate the cyclical moves in price. In May of 1974, the hog-corn ratio dropped to near the 10:1 level. For the year, it averaged only 11.7:1. Historically, herd liquidation has always developed when the hog-corn ratio drops below 12:1. Table 7.2 records what happened as hog prices moved lower into 1974 and corn prices increased relative to earlier years. During 1975 as hog prices moved higher, corn prices dropped. The result was a move in the hog-corn ratio above 20:1 in late 1975. This prompted another wave of expanded production and a decline in hog prices a few months later. By September of 1976, hog prices were more than $20 below the record $61.23 of September, 1975, and were still falling.

In analyzing the price cycle, the first need is to identify economic variables that can indicate or possibly predict what is coming in terms of cyclical developments.[5] Let's review some of those identified in Chapter 6 and analyze them in more detail:

1. The percent of female slaughter. In cattle, cow slaughter as a percentage of the total will drop to 15–17 percent toward the end of

Table 7.1
Prices, Estimated Net Margins, Per Capita Consumption of Beef and Pork by Quarters, 1972–1975

Year and Quarter		Cattle			Hogs		
		Choice Slaughter Steers @ Omaha	Estimated Net Margins [a]	Per Capita Consumption Beef	Barrows and Gilts @ 7 Markets	Estimated Net Margins [a]	Per Capita Consumption Pork
		($ per cwt.)		(lbs.)	($ per cwt.)		(lbs.)
1972	I	35.71	+1.34	28.2	24.67	− 2.19	17.7
	II	36.04	+ .27	28.9	25.00	− 2.51	16.6
	III	36.26	−1.06	29.4	28.85	+ .60	15.8
	IV	35.12	−4.05	29.6	28.89	− .55	17.3
1973	I	43.28	− .98	28.0	35.63	− .71	16.0
	II	45.84	−2.36	26.2	36.82	− 2.22	15.4
	III	48.57	−5.56	26.8	49.04	+ 2.85	14.0
	IV	40.47	−8.67	28.6	40.96	− .53	16.2
1974	I	45.46	−5.67	28.3	38.40	− 4.20	16.7
	II	40.01	−9.61	28.8	28.00	−14.13	17.2
	III	43.91	−6.90	29.4	36.59	− 1.84	16.1
	IV	38.19	−6.40	30.3	39.06	+ 2.95	16.6
1975	I	35.72	−9.97	30.3	39.53	− .62	15.1
	II	48.03	+4.18	28.4	46.11	+ 3.56	14.0
	III	48.64	+8.36	30.2	58.83	+13.17	12.3
	IV	46.05	+2.60	31.2	52.20	+ 4.40	13.4

[a] The estimated net margins show the difference between the average cost of finishing cattle or hogs during the calendar quarters compared to the selling prices shown. For example, the 1.34 for quarter 1 of 1972 indicates the $35.71 average price was $1.34 above the average break-even price for the quarter.
Source: *Livestock and Meat Situation*, ERS, USDA. The net margins from Quarter II of 1974 through 1975 are calculated as simple averages of monthly data.

Table 7.2
Hog Prices, Corn Prices, and the Hog-Corn Ratio by Months, 1974–1975

Year and Month		Barrows and Gilts, 7 Markets	No. 2 Yellow Corn, Omaha	Hog-Corn Ratio
		($ per cwt.)	($ per bu.)	
1974	Jan.	40.59	2.71	15.0:1
	Feb.	39.73	2.95	13.5:1
	Mar.	34.88	2.76	12.6:1
	Apr.	30.52	2.49	12.3:1
	May	26.09	2.51	10.4:1
	June	27.40	2.68	10.2:1
	July	36.31	3.19	11.4:1
	Aug.	37.67	3.55	10.6:1
	Sept.	35.79	3.46	10.3:1
	Oct.	38.90	3.63	10.7:1
	Nov.	38.34	3.46	11.1:1
	Dec.	39.93	3.36	11.9:1
1975	Jan.	38.93	3.07	12.7:1
	Feb.	39.61	2.79	14.2:1
	Mar.	39.52	2.75	14.4:1
	Apr.	40.69	2.85	14.3:1
	May	46.44	2.81	16.5:1
	June	51.19	2.84	18.0:1
	July	57.17	2.92	19.6:1
	Aug.	58.10	3.12	18.6:1
	Sept.	61.23	2.95	20.8:1
	Oct.	58.52	2.75	21.3:1
	Nov.	49.74	2.55	19.5:1
	Dec.	48.33	2.56	18.9:1

the building phases of the cycle. During the liquidation phases, cow slaughter increases sharply as a percent of total slaughter. *Any year-to-year increase in cow slaughter after several years of herd building should be a warning the cyclical break in prices is not far away.* Table 7.3 records pertinent data prior to and during the cattle liquidation that occurred in the 1970s. Note the increases in 1973 and 1974.

2. The rate at which the cow herd is being increased is important. Two to three successive years of building the cow herd at the 3–4 percent level usually spells trouble. Annual rates of increase in the cow herd were 3.9 and 3.1 percent during 1973 and 1974. The average rate of increase was 0.5 percent from 1965 through 1972.

3. Profit indicators such as the hog-corn or steer-corn ratio should be watched. With the stage set for a price break—after a sustained period of herd-building activity—a dramatic change in grain prices can initiate a course of events that leads into liquidation. For example, if the hog sector is poised for a cyclical break, developments in the corn market such as reduced plantings, drought, or increased exports that increase corn prices can bring a change in producers' outlook and initiate actions to increase marketings of hogs.

Moving to a more analytical approach to the issue, the first need is to isolate the cycle so it can be studied. Plotting the yearly (or monthly) observations after the trend has been removed, or as deviations from trend as we did in Figure 7.6, is a first step. Simple arithmetic measures of the properties of the cycle can then be used. The cycle shown appears to be four years in length. In Figure 7.6, the patterns are not as symmetrical as they would normally be in a "text example." But real-world data are seldom that nice to us. The first "up" year averages $3.05 above trend, the second $1.58. The first and second "down" years average $2.81 and $1.88 respectively below the trend line. A quick glance at the plot of Figure 7.6 tells us the pattern is subject to considerable variability around these averages.

Table 7.3
Cow Slaughter as a Percent of Federally Inspected Slaughter, 1950–1977

Year	Federally Inspected Cow Slaughter (1,000 head)	As % of Federally Inspected Slaughter (%)	Year	Federally Inspected Cow Slaughter (1,000 head)	As % of Federally Inspected Slaughter (%)
1950	4,267	32.6	1964	5,322	21.1
1951	4,008	33.7	1965	6,646	25.0
1952	4,090	31.1	1966	6,120	22.4
1953	5,591	31.7	1967	5,540	20.0
1954	6,236	33.8	1968	5,785	19.5
1955	6,656	34.9	1969	5,998	19.6
1956	6,624	32.8	1970	5,373	17.4
1957	6,051	31.1	1971	5,627	17.9
1958	4,558	25.8	1972	5,402	16.7
1959	3,836	22.0	1973	5,659	18.5
1960	4,441	22.9	1974	6,794	20.4
1961	4,033	20.2	1975	10,421	28.2
1962	4,250	20.9	1976	9,704	24.9
1963	4,157	19.2	1977	9,131	23.6

For decision purposes, the trend can be calculated and projected to the future by adding the slope of the regression line for each year being projected. Given the trend projection, an adjustment can be made for the cycle. If the next year will be the first "down" year in the cycle, the price estimated using the trend line can be adjusted by subtracting the average deviation from trend of the first down year in the cycle. This gives a useful estimate of what the average price will be for the next year and decisions can be made accordingly.[6]

Once the cycle has been isolated and the decision maker forms an opinion as to what phase of the cycle he is in (and what phase he is going into), decisions can then be made to minimize the damage from the price cycle or even to take advantage of the cycle. Timing is important. To illustrate the actions that can be taken, assume the second "up year" is being completed and the hog producer sees the possibility of a price break coming within a few months. Possible courses of action are:

1. Sell feeder pigs instead of feeding to slaughter weights. During the late stages of expansion, feeder pigs are often "bid up" to price levels that make the profitability of feeding programs questionable.

2. Sell sows, especially the marginal producers, before the break in prices. This is simply a matter of selling sows or gilts that are not expected to wean enough pigs to pay their way during the trough of the price cycle.

3. Try to schedule slaughter hogs so they will go to market either before or after any cyclical break in prices that appears to be on the horizon. But it is important to stay current—that is, sell slaughter hogs as soon as they reach market grade and weight. Holding hogs during a downward moving market never seems to work. Other producers do the same thing and as weights climb, tonnage increases, and prices fall even more.

It is important to recognize the large-scale producer must continue to operate throughout the cycle. Seldom will price fall to a level it does not cover variable costs, and economic theory tells us production will continue so long as the variable costs are covered. What happens is a fine-tuning of the operation to move it toward its most efficient level of operation. Figure 7.8 illustrates a typical U-shaped average total cost (ATC) curve. If production has been pushed to OQ_3 beyond the level at which the system was designed to operate at minimum ATC, cutting back on the level of operation to OQ_2 will clearly reduce ATC. But if the production level is decreased even more, to a level such as OQ_1, then ATC will start to increase. What we have, then, is a situation requiring marginal analysis. If the sows that are culled would lose money if carried through the cyclical price break, then

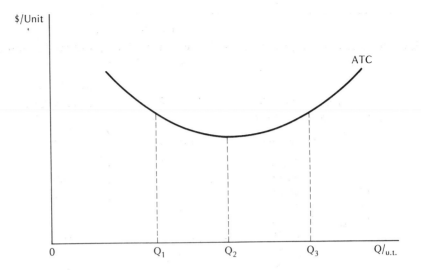

$/Unit

ATC

0   Q_1 Q_2 Q_3 $Q/_{u.t.}$

FIGURE 7.8   COST STRUCTURE FOR A HOG OPERATION SHOWING COST IMPLICA-
TIONS OF OPERATING LEVELS ABOVE AND BELOW THE POINT OF MINIMUM ATC

there is a positive marginal increase in the profit stream for each "loser"
that is sent to slaughter. But there is a change in cost at the margin for each
sow eliminated and ATC, for the remaining sows, increases if the level of
output moves back below the least-cost output of OQ_2.

Much the same observation would be in order where the beef industry is concerned. The cycle is longer but the same patterns are there. In the
bottom of the price cycle, cows may sell for only 30 to 40 percent of the
price they will command just before the price break. The percentage break
in prices of light cattle is often even larger. And the impact of grain prices is
there. Table 7.4 records prices of Choice fed steers, feeder steers, and corn
during the early 1970s. As grain prices climbed and fed cattle prices faltered, price on the 600–700 feeder steers dropped dramatically. Clearly,
the producers of feeder cattle were feeling the pressure from the higher
grain prices that were increasing the break-even prices on the finished
steers.[7]

In the grains and fiber crops, the idea of price cycles is a bit more
difficult to grasp. For livestock, the length of the cycle is a function of the
length of the biological growth process and the reaction time of decision
makers who can change the level of production. In the grains and fibers,
more attention has to be turned to the reactions of producers. A cobweb
type phenomenon is there but it is usually built of the following developments:

1. A shock in the market that changes prices significantly. For example, a short crop in the USSR can increase the export demand for

Table 7.4
Monthly Prices of Slaughter Cattle, Feeder Cattle, Corn, and the Slaughter-Feeder Margin, 1973–1975

Year, Month		Choice 900–1100 lb. Steers, Omaha	No. 2 Yellow Corn, Omaha	Choice 600–700 lb. Feeder Steers, Kansas City	Slaughter-Feeder Steer Margin
		($ per cwt.)	($ per bu.)	($ per cwt.)	($ per cwt.)
1973	J	40.65	1.50	47.33	− 6.68
	F	43.54	1.55	50.98	− 7.44
	M	45.65	1.49	54.01	− 8.36
	A	45.03	1.51	51.82	− 6.79
	M	45.74	1.84	54.55	− 8.81
	J	46.76	2.25	54.85	− 8.09
	J	47.66	2.32	56.49	− 8.83
	A	52.94	2.71	62.40	− 9.40
	S	45.12	2.37	55.06	− 9.94
	O	41.92	2.34	51.86	− 9.94
	N	40.14	2.40	51.02	−10.88
	D	39.36	2.49	47.71	− 8.35
1974	J	47.14	2.71	50.58	− 3.44
	F	46.38	2.95	47.95	− 1.57
	M	42.85	2.76	44.81	− 1.96
	A	41.53	2.49	44.15	− 2.62
	M	40.52	2.51	40.14	.38
	J	37.98	2.68	35.10	2.88
	J	43.72	3.19	36.72	7.00
	A	46.62	3.55	36.70	9.92
	S	41.38	3.46	30.49	10.89
	O	39.64	3.63	30.94	8.70
	N	37.72	3.46	28.71	9.01
	D	37.20	3.36	28.27	8.93
1975	J	36.34	3.07	26.45	9.89
	F	34.74	2.79	26.96	7.78
	M	36.08	2.75	28.75	7.33
	A	42.80	2.85	31.69	11.11
	M	49.48	2.81	35.50	13.98
	J	51.82	2.84	36.81	15.01
	J	50.21	2.92	34.70	15.51
	A	46.80	3.12	34.34	12.46
	S	48.91	2.95	37.59	11.32
	O	47.90	2.75	38.09	9.81
	N	45.23	2.55	38.26	6.97
	D	45.01	2.56	37.83	7.18

Source: Computed from data in *Livestock and Meat Situation*, ERS, USDA and *Feed Situation*, Economics, Statistics, and Cooperative Services, USDA.

wheat. During the year this occurs, prices can be bid above the price that could normally be expected based on price trends.

2. Decisions are made by individual producers in the U.S. to increase production in response to the higher prices. Often, new land or other capital equipment is brought into use.

3. The expanded output by existing firms and entry of new firms tend to increase supply to the level that prices come under pressure and are forced lower. As explained in Chapter 3, the assets "bid into" production during the period of higher prices tend to become "trapped" in production and stay in use.

4. Given time for some of the resources to become variable and be shifted to alternative uses or to be taken out of production, output declines and the reduced supply tends to move prices back to higher levels.

5. A new upward surge in prices can then start the process over again.

Whether this recurring process of expansion and contraction in the grain, fibers and food products can be called a cycle may be open to some debate. But the patterns are there in the grains, fibers, and products such as potatoes and the fruits. The cycles can be isolated with essentially the same analytical tools as those used in the livestock commodities and the same need for informed decisions is present. Remembering that the individual producer is a price taker, the following guidelines can be offered to help cope with the "cyclical" moves in prices of these nonlivestock commodities:

1. Analyze the situation carefully to determine whether any higher prices are likely to be temporary. Is the price increase based on economic forces of a long-run nature (shift in demand that is not likely to be reversed) or is the increase based on a short-run development (drought in one major importing country)?

2. If there is reason to expect the higher prices to be temporary, the producer should restrict any increase in output to the increase possible with the given production plant. This means moving up the MC curve (the supply curve to the firm) and equating MC and MR at the higher price and increased level of output *without changing the cost structure of the firm*. If prices later move back toward their pre-increase level, output can be adjusted downward more easily because no new capital equipment is involved.[8]

3. Move to expand output by bringing in new assets only if there is a reasonable expectation the higher prices will be there for a plan-

ning period long enough to justify the new capital expenditures. Be careful not to make long-run investment decisions on the basis of cyclical moves in price.

SEASONAL

Seasonal price patterns are important in marketing decisions. When to sell and when to store grain, whether to sell or hold livestock, etc., are all decisions that are made within the year. And regardless of the trend and irrespective of what phase of the cycle is developing, the seasonal moves in price will be key determinants of the success of the decisions within the marketing year.

Fortunately, the analytical techniques needed to handle the seasonal patterns are well established and relatively simple. Plotting monthly prices across recent years and examining what is occurring gives a useful picture and a place to start. But more analytical rigor is needed in approaching the making of actual decisions.

A first approximation to the seasonal pattern of prices can be made by removing the effects of trend and then calculating the average price by months. Table 7.5 illustrates the procedure assuming trend (if any) has already been taken out. By expressing the average price for each month as a percent of the overall average, a useful approximation of the seasonal pattern can be generated. This approach suggests prices in August have averaged 3.3 percent above the yearly average price, prices in December have averaged 2.8 percent below the yearly average price, etc.

Most analysts prefer to use a moving average approach and calculate a seasonal index. A ratio to a centered 12-month moving average is a popular choice in terms of technique. The monthly prices are arranged in a chronological array and a 12-month moving average is calculated. Each monthly price is then expressed as a percentage of this moving average to form an index value for the particular months. By averaging across the N index values generated for each month, the monthly entries in a seasonal index can be calculated.[9] A seasonal index has been calculated for the data shown in Table 7.5 and is shown for purposes of comparisons. Figure 7.9 is a plot of the seasonal index to demonstrate the correct plotting procedure.

Each monthly index expresses the relationship between the price for that month and the yearly average price in a normal or typical year. For example, an index value of 102.4 for June would suggest that price in June will be 2.4 percent above the yearly average price. An index value of 96.6 for November would suggest that price for November will be 3.4 percent below the yearly average price. In this normal pattern, the price move from June to November could be expressed as

$$P_J - \left[\frac{(I_J - I_n)}{I_J} \right] P_J = EP_N$$

Table 7.5
Monthly Prices for Choice 600–700 lb. Steers Kansas City, 1970–1977, Monthly Seasonal Pattern and Seasonal Index

($ per cwt.)

Year	J	F	M	A	M	J	J	A	S	O	N	D
1970	32.83	34.44	35.85	35.01	35.00	34.92	34.54	33.28	32.86	32.66	31.79	31.28
1971	32.20	34.24	34.26	34.46	34.52	34.52	34.36	35.18	34.97	35.64	36.88	37.20
1972	37.92	38.86	38.64	38.54	40.43	41.94	42.02	42.07	43.29	44.15	43.17	45.77
1973	47.33	50.98	54.01	51.82	54.55	54.85	56.49	62.40	55.06	51.86	51.02	47.71
1974	50.58	47.95	44.81	44.15	40.14	35.10	36.72	36.70	30.49	30.94	28.71	28.27
1975	26.45	26.96	28.75	31.69	35.50	36.81	34.70	34.34	37.59	38.09	38.26	37.83
1976	37.46	40.42	39.69	44.62	44.21	42.83	39.18	38.94	36.18	36.72	36.26	36.23
1977	36.49	37.86	38.95	41.81	41.72	39.90	40.64	41.99	40.85	40.82	39.94	41.33
Monthly Average Across Years	37.66	38.96	39.37	40.26	40.76	40.11	39.83	40.61	38.91	38.86	38.25	38.20
Monthly Average as % Overall Average[a]	95.8	99.1	100.1	102.4	103.7	102.0	101.3	103.3	99.0	98.8	97.3	97.2
Seasonal Index[b]	96.7	99.8	100.2	103.3	104.6	102.4	101.3	102.5	98.3	98.3	96.6	95.8

[a]Calculated by dividing each monthly average by the overall mean of $39.315. For example, $37.66 ÷ 39.315 = .9579 or 95.8% for January.
[b]Calculated from the data in the table using the centered 12-month moving average procedure explained in Appendix C.

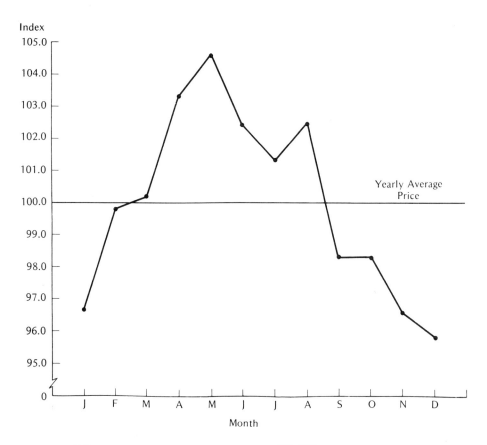

FIGURE 7.9   SEASONAL INDEX FOR CHOICE 600–700 LB. STEERS, KANSAS CITY, BASED ON 1970–77

where: P_J = price in June
   I_J = index value for June
   I_N = index value for N number, and
   EP_N = estimated price for November.

Alternatively, the estimated price for November could be expressed as

$$\frac{I_J}{P_J} = \frac{I_N}{X}$$

where: X = estimated price for November,
   I_J, P_J, I_N are as described above

In addition to its relative simplicity, there are other advantages to the 12-month moving average as a means of calculating a seasonal index:

1. A 12-month moving average calculated over a series of monthly prices tends to remove any cyclical components in the data series. The moving average follows the cyclical ups and downs and is not therefore significantly influenced by the cycle unless cyclical forces exert much or all of their influence within a 12-month period. Trend in the monthly data is eliminated for the same reasons.

2. Using a 12-month moving average serves to isolate the seasonal pattern. It is characteristic of a moving average that it will follow recurring undulations in data if the length of the moving average (here 12 months) is consistent with the length of time between successive highs (or lows) in the data. Since grains, foods, and fibers are typically produced once in a 12-month period, it follows that the seasonal pattern will tend to be 12 months from high to high or low to low. The livestock sector tends to get a 12-month seasonal pattern imposed on it because (a) the grazing season begins (and ends) only once during the year, (b) grain producers buy and place animals on feed primarily during or just after the grain harvest, and (c) there is some seasonality in demand for livestock products.

Knowledge of the normal seasonal pattern in prices is a good place to start in establishing a base upon which to make a decision. A few illustrations should help.

In the grains, the producer is always faced with a question of whether to sell or store, and, if he decides to store, how long to store the grain. Table 7.6 lists seasonal indices for several commodities including hard red winter wheat. Examination of those data indicate that in the normal seasonal pattern, prices tend to peak for the year in January. Holding wheat beyond January is not an economically sound decision unless economic forces at work during a particular year indicate otherwise. With storage costs two to three cents per bushel per month, storage beyond January has a very low probability of being profitable.

The cowman faces a decision when he has yearling steers on grass late in the grazing season. The seasonal index for 600–700 lb. steers in Table 7.6 indicates prices will normally fall significantly from August into October. Should the cattle be sold in August? The end of the grazing season really does not come until October. Why not hold the cattle and get the added weight gain? Looking at this decision in some detail, the comparative costs and returns are shown in Table 7.7 for a typical illustration.

Note that costs of carrying the cattle until August 15 are ignored. This becomes a fixed cost on August 15 and does not affect the decision on whether to hold or sell. In this particular situation, the calculations suggest holding the cattle. But the decision is not that easy for the cowman. The

Table 7.6
Seasonal Indices for Selected Commodities[a]

Index Value

Month	Wheat	Peanuts	Cotton Lint	G. Sorghum	Choice Feeder Steers 600–700 lbs.	Choice 900–1100 lb. Slaughter Steers	Utility Cows	Hogs B&G U.S. 1–3	Milk
Jan.	105.9	100.1	96.4	97.3	98.3	99.9	96.9	99.7	104.2
Feb.	103.4	99.5	96.0	98.0	99.5	98.0	103.2	103.2	102.7
March	100.4	99.0	98.4	99.9	100.3	94.8	106.7	96.2	99.7
April	96.6	98.4	101.8	103.9	102.8	102.0	108.1	93.0	95.7
May	93.9	98.4	100.9	100.8	102.2	103.6	106.2	98.6	94.3
June	91.9	101.8	103.5	99.7	102.0	103.1	102.9	104.4	93.7
July	93.7	101.3	105.5	98.7	102.1	105.0	98.8	110.4	94.8
Aug.	99.6	99.6	104.6	100.2	102.3	105.0	100.1	108.3	96.9
Sept.	103.1	101.2	104.0	100.4	98.9	99.3	97.1	100.6	102.3
Oct.	103.9	100.3	97.9	101.1	97.0	97.1	93.5	96.1	104.5
Nov.	102.2	99.7	95.8	100.9	96.7	94.5	91.8	92.7	106.1
Dec.	105.3	100.7	95.3	99.1	97.8	97.7	94.8	96.8	105.1

[a] All commodities except Choice slaughter steers are based on Oklahoma prices for the 10-year period ending with 1977. Choice slaughter steer prices are based on Amarillo prices for the 5-year period ending in 1977.

Table 7.7
Illustration of an Analytical Approach to the Hold-Sell Decision

Date	*Actions*
August 10	Checks markets and estimates current selling price at $60 per cwt. for estimated weight of 600 lbs. average per animal.

Estimates cost of keeping cattle until October 10 at $15 per head (includes vet, feed, interest on the $360 the cattle would bring in August, insurance, 1% death loss, labor, etc.). Expects marketing and selling costs to be the same in October as in August.

Estimates gain from August 10 to October 10 at 90 lbs. per animal

Projects price for October using the seasonal index:

$$\frac{\$60}{102.8} = \frac{X}{97.0} = \$56.61$$

Estimates net from keeping cattle until October 10:

$$\text{Gross returns} = 6.9 (56.61) = \$390.61$$
$$\text{Subtract carrying costs} \quad \underline{15.00}$$
$$\$375.61$$

Net to holding is $375.61 − 360 = $15.61 per head higher given the estimates used.

---

calculations are based on expectations of "normal" price movements between August and October 15. Are there economic forces at work that suggest the price decline in this particular year will be greater than normal? What about the added risk associated with holding the cattle? Death loss must be considered along with the possibility of vet or other health-related costs. These concerns are added to the uncertainty with regard to price. To cover these uncertainties and risks, the cowman might well decide to discount his expected weight gains, his price expectation for October, or in some other way reflect his concern. Such "discounting for uncertainty" is a logical approach and should be used when hold-sell decisions are made for cattle, grains, foods, or fibers.

COMBINING THE TIME DIMENSIONS

The trend, cyclical and seasonal components, once isolated and measured, can be put back together again for decision making and price forecasting purposes. Steps are as follows:

1. Project the trend into the next year or the year for which a price forecast is needed, call it year t + k;

2. Adjust the preliminary forecast based on trend for the cyclical influence you would expect in year t + k; and

3. If a monthly price is needed, apply the seasonal index for the commodity to the price in step 2 to generate an estimate of the monthly price.

To illustrate, consider the following set of information under the assumption t + k is 2 years from the current year:

1. Trend as measured by the slope coefficient on a least-squares trend line indicates price is increasing by $.75 per cwt. per year.

2. Two years from now should put prices in the second "up" year of a four-year cycle and this phase of the cycle has shown a price $1.25, on average, above the trend line.

3. Average price for last year, the most recent year for which we have data, was $50.00 per cwt.

4. An estimate of the yearly price in t + k would therefore be $50.00 + 3($.75) + 1.25 = $53.50.

For planning both marketing and production-related activities, this is a useful way to approach the price outlook for a period two years later. If for any reason a monthly price estimate were needed, it could be generated by multiplying the $53.50 estimate by the index value for the particular month of interest.

The question of reliability and accuracy of the "forecast" is obviously of concern. Remember the sources of possible error:

1. The trend could change direction, could change to a non-linear pattern, or otherwise change relative to the period of time across which the trend was estimated. Even if no underlying change occurs, the projection is with a least-squares function that inherently allows for deviation from the line. As we will see later in this chapter, the accuracy and reliability of the estimates will decline as the year for which we are forecasting moves farther into the future.

2. There is variability in the cyclical pattern. The adjustment for the second up year has all the mathematical shortcomings of an average adjustment—there could be wide variability across previous cycles which is masked by using an average.

3. The seasonal pattern could change or be distorted by economic forces at work within the year t + k.

But the mechanism and conceptual framework are valuable. For most marketing decisions, the *direction* of price moves and *when* the price moves are

likely to develop are more important than accuracy in projecting the level
to which prices will go once the move has begun. And this approach forces
the decision maker to look at the data, provides a picture of the cycle so its
length and amplitude are there to be examined, and requires consideration
of all the time elements at work on prices. Working through an approach
that encourages looking at the trend, cyclical moves and seasonal patterns
is half the battle.

Quantitative Models

Discussions of trend and of cyclical and seasonal movements in price have
focused on the time dimensions of price movements. That underlying economic forces cause the recurring patterns or dictate the direction of the
trend is recognized, but these economic forces have not to this point been
made a part of the analytical process. An approach that offers more theoretical and analytical rigor involves models to incorporate the impact of the
economic forces at work in the marketplace.

FUNCTIONAL FORMS

Time trends were introduced in the previous section. A simple linear
regression model of the form $Y = a + bX + e$ will estimate trend. Least-
squares estimates of the parameters a and b are calculated as follows:

$$\hat{b} = \frac{\sum_{i=1}^{n}(Y_i - \bar{Y})(X_i - \bar{X})}{\sum_{i=1}^{n}(X_i - \bar{X})^2}$$

$$\hat{a} = \bar{Y} - \hat{b}\bar{X}$$

The least-squares estimates identify the *one* linear relationship from the
family of possible linear relationships denoted by $Y = a + bX$, which has
the following characteristics:

1. The line will always pass through the coordinates of $\bar{X}$, $\bar{Y}$, and

2. It is the "line of best fit" in that it best represents the observations
   in the data set.

Linear regression analysis is not limited to the simple linear two-
dimensional case. More complex functional forms can be employed to
bring in more variables or to use different mathematical forms of the same

variable. Earlier, for the data plotted in Figure 7.3, we found we would have to use the more complex functional form

$$Y = a + b_1X + b_2X^2 + e$$

This is still "linear regression" even though the X^2 term is included as what we would call an *explanatory* or *independent* variable (with Y the *dependent* variable). And we can still show this somewhat more complex form since there are still only two variables, X and Y, and we are plotting on a two-dimensional graph.

When several variables are involved, the techniques are still available but the ease of graphical representation disappears. For example, suppose there are three different explanatory variables and the general functional form is

$$Y = a + b_1X_1 + b_2X_2 + b_3X_3 + e$$

This equation includes more than two dimensions so simple graphics don't help. Think about a rubber ball through which you can pass a needle with thread attached. As the needle passes through the ball, it is subjected to the influences of forces from all directions that we can picture as the forces of the explanatory variables. The direction of the needle can and will change during its travel because the *net* influence from X_1, X_2 and X_3 will change as the levels of X_1, X_2 and X_3 change. The path moves through the ball in a manner that registers the net influence of the X_1, X_2 and X_3 variables taken together.

A least-squares fit would therefore give you the estimate of Y which best represents the net influence of the X variables. The estimates of the parameters, such as b_1, must be interpreted accordingly. It will register the estimate of the relationship between X_1 and Y given that the influence of X_2 and X_3 is also present. Single equation models that employ more than one explanatory variable and take on the general form described here are widely used in analysis of economic data. To fully understand how they are used requires discussion of models and model specification.

MODELS AND MODEL SPECIFICATION

Analysts use models in an attempt to approximate the real world. In a model dealing with prices, for example, an attempt is made to build the model in such a way that it provides a useful approximation of the real world without being so complex and cumbersome that it is overly difficult or time consuming to use. Based on this, two requirements to be met by a "good" model are (1) it serves the function for which it is intended, and (2) it is as simple as possible.

Careful attention needs to be paid to model specification as an important first step in building a model. Both the functional form of the model and the choice of what variables to include are important. Given its flexibility and widespread use, we will focus on the single equation multiple linear regression model. Even though the functional form is determined, the question of which variables to include is important and requires a look at both economic and statistical considerations.

Economic Considerations.   Variables should be included if economic theory indicates an important economic relationship. Whatever the dependent variable, the analyst should draw on his knowledge of economic theory and ask "what variables should have influence on the dependent variable?"

Suppose, for example, we are specifying a model to predict the price of No. 2 yellow corn. Drawing on theory, we could list such economic forces as the following that would be expected to exert influence on corn prices:

1. Stocks of corn in storage facilities across the U.S.;

2. Planting intentions if the crop is not yet planted or planted acreage if the crop has been planted;

3. Expected per acre yields;

4. Weather or weather expectations;

5. Usage of corn for domestic food, industrial, seed purposes;

6. Quantity of corn fed to livestock;

7. Exports of corn;

8. World stocks of corn and other feed grains; and

9. U.S. stocks and production of feed grains other than corn.

Variables 1–4 are general measures of the available supply of corn. Stocks of any storable grain are always an important determinant of price levels. The available stocks are there for release into market channels and are therefore a very "liquid" form of supply. Planting intentions, planted acreages, expected yields, and weather are the necessary ingredients in estimates of new-crop production. The estimates indicate "potential supply" from new-crop corn and become a factor in setting price. Late in the growing season, buyers can wait for the harvest instead of buying old-crop corn.

Variables 5–9 are general measures of the demand for corn. Domestic use of corn, for feed and non-feed purposes, is the most important type of "disappearance" and the largest component of total demand. Domestic stocks of feed grains (including wheat) other than corn will affect the demand for corn since they are substitutes for corn. The world stocks of corn and feed grains (often referred to as "coarse grains" in the literature) are important determinants of the export demand for corn. Most buying countries appear to buy on a "need" basis. For example, if the USSR has a relatively poor crop, the demand for corn may increase as she buys to prevent liquidation of livestock and poultry numbers. Other countries including the People's Republic of China and the Eastern European countries buy on a similar basis. Countries such as Japan and Mexico are consistently major buyers because of a lack of domestic production.

To continue the illustration, assume the model is specified in general form

$$P_c = a + b_1 S_t + b_2 P_r + b_3 D_o + b_4 L_f + b_5 E_x + b_6 S_{fg} + e$$

where:

P_c = yearly average price of No. 2 yellow corn in Chicago ($ per bu.);

S_t = estimated year-end stocks of corn at the end of the current crop year (million bu.);

P_r = projected or estimated U.S. production of corn in the next crop year (million bu.);

D_o = domestic use of corn for feed, seed, and industrial purposes in the most recent crop year (million bu.);

L_f = quantity of corn fed to livestock in the most recent crop year (million bu.);

E_x = estimated corn exports for the current crop year (million bu.); and

S_{fg} = estimated year-end feed grain stocks other than corn in the current market year (million bu.).

Drawing on economic theory, we can discuss what sign we would expect on the estimated coefficient for each variable as follows:

b_1: negative; increasing levels of ending stocks indicate increased supply. Therefore, the sign on this estimate should be negative since an increase in supply, other factors the same, would tend to decrease price.[10]

b_2: negative; increasing the expected crop production will, by increasing the total supply from stocks and expected production, increase the available supply of corn.

b_3: positive; increased domestic usage will increase the total demand for corn and should push price higher.

b_4: positive; the quantity of corn fed to livestock in the most recent year would be expected to indicate roughly the level at which feed use will be during the current year. If this variable is increasing over time, it would tend to increase demand and cause higher prices.

b_5: positive; increased estimates of exports will tend to push price higher. Of all the explanatory variables, exports may have the most potential to change price levels since it is potentially the most volatile and unpredictable from year to year.

b_6: negative; increasing stocks of substitute or competing grains would tend to decrease the demand for corn and decrease price.

If any one of the explanatory variables has an incorrect sign given the theoretical expectations, there is reason to question whether the model is correctly specified. This is especially true if the estimate of the parameter for the explanatory variable under question is statistically significant. There are both economical and statistical reasons for an "incorrect" sign. Often, the relationship between an explanatory variable and the dependent variable is a lagged relationship. If the correct lag is not incorporated into the model, the sign may be unexpected. This and other reasons for unexpected signs, such as the statistical problem of multicollinearity, will be treated in more detail later in the chapter.

Statistical Considerations.   Introducing the notion of statistical significance brings in the second criterion that is used in deciding on the final model. Economic theory helps in choosing potential explanatory variables. Once the variables are selected based on economic criteria, statistical measures can help make the final determination of which variables to use. As implied, there are typically several "preliminary" fits of the model before deciding on the final model.

In general terms, statistical significance deals with the question of whether the estimated relationship between an explanatory variable and the dependent variable is a valid relationship or whether it is just a chance occurrence. The statistical measure that is employed is the t-test that tests, for a particular estimate such as b_1, the following set of hypotheses:

$$H_0: b_1 = 0$$
$$H_1: b_1 \neq 0$$

The null hypothesis, H_0, indicates the estimate of b_1 is actually zero. The alternative hypothesis, H_1, specifies that b_1 is not zero. Since the analyst has carefully selected the variable—in this case S_t—he would hope to be able to reject H_0 and accept H_1.

The hypotheses are tested by employing the so-called "t-test"—a test widely used in statistics and quantitative analyses. For an estimate of b_1 such as $\hat{b}_1$, the t-statistic is defined as follows:

$$t = \frac{\hat{b}_1 - 0}{S\hat{b}_1}$$

The denominator, $S\hat{b}_1$, is the standard error of the estimate of $\hat{b}_1$. The standard error is the square root of S^2 which is an estimate, based on the sample of data being used, of σ^2 or the variance of the estimates of b_1. The variance and therefore the standard error are measures of dispersion or variability. The larger the standard error, the more variable the array of estimates of b_1 would be if we took repeated samples of the data and generated numerous estimates of b_1. Logically, this would raise questions about the validity of our particular estimate of b_1 and this is really how it works. Since the t-statistic is a ratio of the estimate of b_1 and its standard error, the size of the statistic would increase with a larger $\hat{b}_1$ or a smaller $S\hat{b}_1$, or both.

The estimated t-statistic is compared to tabled values of Student's t distribution.[11] For a given combination of degrees of freedom and pre-selected levels of significance, H_o should be rejected and H_1 accepted if the estimated t-statistic is larger than the table value of t. For example, the table value for an extremely large sample size and a significance level of .05 is 1.96. If the t-statistic is greater than 1.96, reject H_o and accept H_1. This means that in statistical terms, the relationship is valid—the probability the observed relationship is just random chance is less than .05.

There is a t-test for each of the parameters. The test can be used to help decide whether to keep the particular variable in the model.

Another statistical criterion which is widely used to evaluate regression models is the coefficient of determination or R^2. It is defined as

$$R^2 = \frac{\% \text{ of variation explained by the model}}{\text{total variation in the data set}}.$$

Returning to the two-variable case, the concept of R^2 can be explained graphically. Figure 7.10 partitions the variation in Y for a particular value of X or X_k. In general terms, these relationships are:

$$\sum_{i=1}^{N}(Y_i - \bar{Y})^2 \equiv \text{ the total sum of squared deviations,}$$

$$\sum_{i=1}^{n}(\hat{Y}_i - \bar{Y})^2 \equiv \text{ the sum of squared deviations explained by the model, and}$$

$$\sum_{i=1}^{n}(Y_i - \hat{Y}_i)^2 \equiv \text{ the error sum of squares.}$$

Given these relationships, R^2 can be defined in algebraic terms as

$$R^2 = \frac{\sum\limits_{i=1}^{n} (\hat{Y}_i - \bar{Y})^2}{\sum\limits_{i=1}^{n} (Y_i - \bar{Y})^2}.$$

The least-squares fit, by definition, minimizes the error sum of squares. It follows that the least-squares fit also gives a larger R^2 than any other straight line.

For a given set of variables, therefore, we would look for a large value of R^2 and explanatory variables that have a significant statistical relationship with the dependent variable. But there are dangers in letting either of these statistical criteria become all-important. There are times when economic theory says a particular variable should stay in the model even though the t-test does not measure up to popular levels. And just trying to increase R^2 is not the answer. Adding explanatory variables to the model will always increase R^2 or leave it the same—it is mathematically impossible for R^2 to decrease when variables are added.

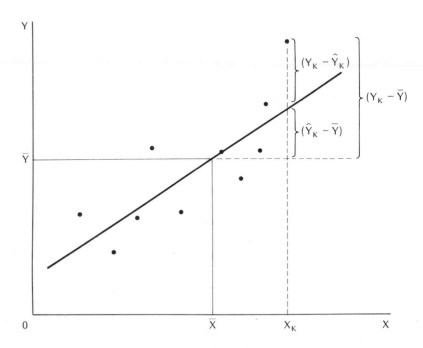

FIGURE 7.10   PARTITIONING OF THE TOTAL VARIATION IN Y FOR THE X_K VALUE OF X

SOME COMMON PROBLEMS

There are several statistical problems that crop up and trouble the analyst. Two of the most frequent are multicollinearity and autocorrelation. Multicollinearity is a problem in many models and we will examine it here because it is relevant to selection and retention of explanatory variables. Autocorrelation is a problem that runs deeper and often requires some other type of model specification.

Multicollinearity means dependent or explanatory variables are correlated. Since most economic phenomena are related, it is not surprising to find that explanatory variables have influence on each other. And this causes problems when deciding on the variables to use in the model.

In the corn price model, for example, several of the explanatory variables are sure to be correlated. Some of the more apparent "problems" are summarized as follows:

1. World production or world stocks of grain will be negatively correlated with exports;

2. Domestic production will be positively correlated over time with ending stocks; and

3. Feed use in the U.S. will be negatively correlated with ending stocks.

If we move to consideration of models dealing with other variables, the problem crops up again. In a model explaining cattle prices, cattle slaughter and beef tonnage are both variables that theory says would be important determinants of supply. But they are so highly correlated they are essentially the same variable.

Two or more explanatory variables that are highly correlated cause special problems for a least-squares regression model. The least-squares procedure is not capable of correctly and consistently allocating the "explanatory power" between the two correlated variables. If t-tests are used, one variable may "pick up" much or all of the statistical significance—but they might be equally important in terms of the underlying economic theory. If another slightly different data set is used and the model fitted again, the apparent importance of the two correlated variables might switch. Both the size of the estimated parameters and the t-tests are simply not stable across repeated estimates.

Before turning to possible solutions to the problem, we must recognize that the importance of the problem is a function of the purpose of the model. The purposes of price models are twofold: (1) to predict price, and (2) to estimate parameters.

When the purpose is to predict price, the correlation need not present insurmountable problems. If the set of explanatory variables is chosen using solid economic theory, a particular variable is often kept in the model in spite of a poor t-test brought on by multicollinearity. The need is to get explanatory power into the model, and this explanatory power can contribute to the capacity of the model to accurately predict price regardless of how it is allocated across the variables. When prediction is the objective, the following rules of thumb will help:

1. Use only explanatory variables that are sound based on economic theory.

2. Don't discard any variable just because the t-statistic is relatively poor. If the variable appears to help the predictive accuracy of the model, consider keeping it so long as the t-statistic is greater than 1.0 in absolute value.[12]

3. Use the R^2 to help decide on which model to use. Choose the model that is fairly simple so long as R^2 does not decrease significantly. For example, a model with four explanatory variables and $R_2 = .9011$ would be preferred to a model with seven or eight explanatory variables and an R_2 of .915 or less.

If the purpose is to estimate a parameter, the situation is different. Here, the size and sign of the parameter estimate are important. The model must be "cleaned up" to remove the effects of multicollinearity. Among the possibilities are the following:

1. Remove one of the correlated variables. Any two or more variables that are highly correlated are, statistically speaking, essentially the same variable. If two variables show a simple correlation of greater than .5 in absolute value, consideration should be given to deleting one of the two.

2. Use a ratio of the correlated variables. One way to keep both of two correlated variables in the model is to put them in as a ratio. But the parameter of a ratio is often difficult to interpret and a ratio may not be what is needed if the purpose is to estimate an elasticity coefficient.

Autocorrelation presents a somewhat different but rather common problem. One of the assumptions that clears the way to use least-squares procedures is that the values of the error term in one time period are not influenced by the values of the error term in a previous time period. If this assumption is not met, it shows up in the form of a correlation between the error term in period t and the error term in time period t–l, or t–k where k takes the value from l to n.

A statistical test called the Durbin-Watson test can be used to test whether such correlation exists and whether it is negative or postive. Without getting into too much detail here, one of two approaches is usually adopted when autocorrelation is found to exist in the data and a least-squares model has been fitted:

1. Assume the correlation between time periods such as t and t–l is stable as time passes, and don't worry about it. The least-squares estimates are then used. In practice, this assumption is often made. Unless significant changes in the economic structure of the industry or the way decision makers operate within that industry have occurred, there is no reason to argue the relationship between the error terms from one time period to the next has changed.

2. Estimate the correlation between the time periods and incorporate it into the model. The direct use of least-squares estimation procedures is not valid, however, and the estimation procedures become too complex to be involved here. The statistical references listed at the end of the chapter treat the topic area in detail.

EMPIRICAL CONSIDERATIONS

The step from textbook coverage of model building to actual application is a long one. Real-world use of a model requires some additional insight.

Assume we are building a model to predict a monthly price three months into the future. How can this be done? There is no place to find values of the explanatory variables three months into the future. The secret is to specify the model so that prediction is possible. There are two basic ways to do this.

One approach is to specify the model in terms of lagged relationships between the dependent and the explanatory variables. If we let t be the current month, then the model is specified as

$$Y_t = f(X_{1_{t-3}}, X_{2_{t-3}}, \ldots, X_{n_{t-3}})$$

In other words, the data set used in fitting the model is not a set that matches values of the dependent and the explanatory variables in the same month. It is a data set created by matching the dependent variable for a particular month with values of the explanatory variables three months earlier. After the model is fitted, it can be used to predict three months into the future by inserting current values of the explanatory variables and calculating a forecast of the dependent variable.[13]

If time lags are used, it is important to remember this when specifying the model. The variables that theory suggests have an immediate influence on price are not necessarily the same variables that have a lagged influence on price. For example, suppose you were trying to predict the prices of Choice slaughter steers for next month. The number of steers on feed in the 900–1100 pound range would be a logical indicator of supply since most cattle are sold at 1100 pounds or less. But if the interest is in price predictions for three months into the future, the 700–900 pound group would be more important. These are the steers that will be finishing three months from now.

Another approach involves building separate models to predict the future values of explanatory variables. In a model to predict corn prices, we have suggested exports or expectations of the export level is an important determinant of overall demand. A separate model could be specified to predict exports two quarters into the future. The predicted level of exports could then be used as an explanatory variable in a model to predict corn prices two quarters into the future.

It is of course possible to use both approaches in the same model. Variables with a time lag that appears stable can be specified with a time lag. Other variables might not show such stability or they might be relatively easy to predict and these explanatory variables could be predicted. Per capita disposable incomes constitute an example. A very simple trend model will do a good job of predicting the income variable.

Which approach is best? There is no simple answer. The analyst worries about the added error component built into a statistical model when the explanatory variables are predicted. But concern over the stability of the time lag relationships is also legitimate.

Regardless of the way the model is specified, the reliability of the forecasts decreases as the explanatory variables move away from their mean values in either direction. Figure 7.11 illustrates using the two-dimensional case. As the fixed values of X for which Y is being predicted move away from the mean, the predicted values of Y become much more variable. A 90 percent confidence interval,[14] for example, "balloons out" for values of X away from $\bar{X}$.[15] In particular, a forecast of Y for a value of X, which falls outside the range of X from which the model was estimated, would be subject to a great deal of variation.

A second important use of the single equation model is to estimate parameters that represent important economic relationships. Among the relationships of interest are price elasticity of demand, income elasticity, and cross elasticity.

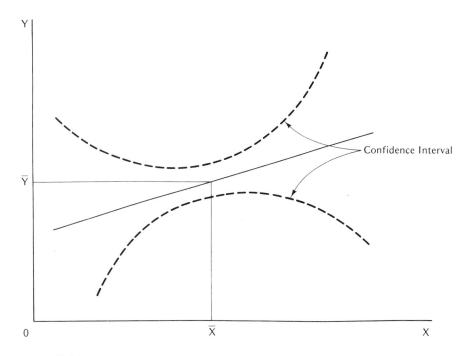

FIGURE 7.11   ILLUSTRATION OF THE DECLINING CONFIDENCE IN ESTIMATES OR PREDICTIONS OF Y FOR VALUES OF X SIGNIFICANTLY DIFFERENT FROM X̄

Both price elasticity and cross elasticity are often calculated from parameter estimates in single equation models where quantity is specified as the dependent variable. Consider the following model:

$$Q_p = a + b_1P_p + b_2P_B + b_3I + e$$

where:

Q_p = yearly per capita consumption of pork (lbs., carcass equivalent);

P_p = yearly average price of pork ($ per lb. converted to carcass equivalent);

P_B = yearly average price of beef ($ per lb. converted to carcass equivalent); and

I = per capita disposable income per year ($).

The coefficient of the explanatory variable P_p can be defined or interpreted as

$$\hat{b}_1 = \frac{\Delta Q_p}{\Delta P_p}.$$

The ratio can be combined with selected price-quantity combinations to estimate the price elasticity of demand for pork. For the mean values of Q_p and P_p, we get the following:

$$P_{\epsilon_{pork}} = \frac{\Delta Q_p}{\Delta P_p} \cdot \frac{\bar{P}_p}{\bar{Q}_p} = \acute{b}_1 \cdot \frac{\bar{P}_p}{\bar{Q}_p}$$

This expression estimates the price elasticity of demand for pork at the mean values of Q_p and P_p.

In similar fashion, the coefficient for P_B or $\acute{b}_2$ can be used in calculating an estimate of the cross elasticity:

$$\acute{b}_2 = \frac{\Delta Q_p}{\Delta P_B}$$

$$X_{\epsilon_{P,B}} = \frac{\Delta Q_p}{\Delta P_B} \cdot \frac{\bar{P}_B}{\bar{Q}_p} = \acute{b}_2 \cdot \frac{\bar{P}_B}{\bar{Q}_p}.$$

This expression estimates the cross elasticity coefficient between pork and beef, for price changes in beef, at the mean levels of P_B and Q_p.

By working with b_3, the estimated parameter for I, an estimate of the income elasticity coefficient for pork can be generated. The procedure uses $\acute{b}_3$ since

$$\acute{b}_3 = \frac{\Delta Q_p}{\Delta I}.$$

Income elasticity is defined as

$$I_{\epsilon_{pork}} = \frac{\Delta Q_p}{\Delta I} \cdot \frac{\bar{I}}{\bar{Q}_p} = \acute{b}_3 \cdot \frac{\bar{I}}{\bar{Q}_p}.$$

An alternative approach is possible. Because of the impact of changing prices on real income, analysts may choose to work with "cross section" data. By recording income and quantity data at a particular point in time across selected levels of income, the relationship between quantity taken for a particular good or service and income level can be estimated. Prices are thus held constant. The implicit assumption is that persons who move to higher (or lower) levels of income will behave like members of their new income group in terms of buying the product or service.[16]

OTHER FUNCTIONAL FORMS

The single equation model is appropriate in situations where the direction of causality is apparent and one variable (the dependent) is determined by the others (the explanatory variables). For example, the number of barrows and gilts going to slaughter in the second and third quarter of a particular year is determined by the pig crop from the December–February farrowing period. The price of corn in the first and second quarters of a particular year is determined by the size of the harvest in the preceding year. It is obvious in these simple illustrations which variable is the dependent variable. But in many cases the line of causality is not so apparent and some other approach is needed.

When two variables are *jointly* determined, a single equation model is not sufficient. If the price being considered is the price of turkeys, the quantity of turkeys produced within the year can be influenced by the price. As the corn belt farmer approaches planting time, the price of corn relative to soybeans can influence which he plants and therefore the quantity of each produced. When production is affected by price but not vice versa, a plot of price-quantity combinations over time would yield a supply curve. When price is affected by production but not vice versa, we would get a demand curve. But if price and production influence each other, any plot of price-quantity coordinates would yield neither a supply curve nor a demand curve but a mixture of the two. A set of two or more equations would be required to handle such interaction or simultaneity.

The simplest set of equations is the two-equation set that shows a demand curve and a supply curve such as

$$Q = b_1 + b_2P + e \quad \text{(demand curve)}$$
$$Q = b_1' + b_2'P + e \quad \text{(supply curve)}$$

By adding to each equation a predetermined variable[17] and carrying through certain transformations, it is possible to estimate both equations together. In the process a set of equations is generated from which predictions are possible and the structural parameters (b_1, b_2, b_1', b_2') can be estimated. A simple discussion of these procedures is presented by Shepherd[18] in his book on price analysis.

Discussion on which type of model does the best job of prediction continues. The single-equation model is often preferred because of its simplicity and because it is usually as accurate as a more complex set of equations. When estimation of parameters is the purpose, however, the set of equations can be the better approach if it enables the analyst to control some of the problems of multicollinearity.

Summary

Price analysis is a broad and complex area. Entire books have been written on the subject—and the authors usually complain about all the material they did not have an opportunity to cover. The treatment in this chapter must therefore be considered as a capsule treatment of the complex area of price analysis. More specifically, the coverage is designed to stress the topic areas that are important in terms of their actual and potential contribution to making marketing decisions.

Price movements over time can be conveniently divided into price trends and into cyclical and seasonal price patterns. Trend deals with long-run moves in price that span two or more production seasons or, when price cycles are evident, at least one complete cycle. Price cycles reflect the inverse relationship between production and price, and occur because of a seemingly inherent tendency for agricultural producers to overreact in terms of production. Seasonal price patterns reflect the intra-year price movements built around once-a-year production of grains and fibers or the tendency for marketings of livestock, production of milk, etc., to increase during a particular period of the year.

Price trends are important in long-run investment decisions, in deciding between alternatives that compete for limited resources (such as land), and in projecting price movements and forecasting prices. Single equation regression models, which express price as a function of time, are widely used as a means of estimating price trend.

Cyclical moves in price can become real problems—or real opportunities— to the marketing program. Being aware of what is going on and where the industry is in terms of phases of the cycle is an important first step. Plotting the price data helps. Fitting a trend line to the data and removing trend, or plotting prices as deviations from the trend, isolates the cycle. The objective is to sharpen understanding of the cycle's time dimensions. Knowing when the cyclical turning points are coming creates the opportunity to adjust production levels or reallocate resources to prevent being badly hurt by the cycle.

Most marketing decisions within the year are decisions on when to hold or sell livestock, whether to store or sell grains, cotton, and soybeans, and whether and when to forward price. Understanding the seasonal price pattern is a necessary condition to effective intra-year marketing decisions. Seasonal price patterns can be seen by plotting monthly prices on either a calendar or crop-year basis. A more sophisticated and more effective approach in analytical terms is to calculate a seasonal index, which eliminates the influence of trend and cycles and presents each month as a percentage of the yearly average price. Even when the normal seasonal pattern will not prevail because other economic forces are at work during the year, knowing the normal pattern gives a base upon which to build a decision model. The impact of other economic forces can be analyzed in terms of their probable impact on the normal seasonal pattern.

In analytical terms, the trend, cyclical and seasonal forces can be combined to develop useful projections of price. The trend line can be projected to give a first approximation of price in the year for which a forecast is needed. This initial estimate can be adjusted by extending the cyclical pattern that has been isolated and adjusting the trend price for the appropriate phase of the cycle. If a monthly price forecast is needed, the cyclically adjusted yearly forecast can be multiplied by the index value for the particular month in question.

An alternative to looking at price as a function of time is to conceptualize a model that presents price or some other dependent variable as a function of selected explanatory variables. The linear regression procedure is widely used. Initial selection of explanatory variables is made on the basis of economic theory. Statistical criteria are then employed to help decide on the final model. The statistical properties that are considered acceptable can vary slightly if the intended use of the model is to predict versus estimate some particular parameter or economic relationship.

The importance of price has been stressed earlier in this text. We are stressing price again in this chapter. The ability to effectively analyze price and price movements will not guarantee successful marketing decisions. But the *inability* to analyze prices will make successful marketing decisions much, much more difficult.

Footnotes

1. When trend is defined this way, either annual or monthly data can be used. If only two or three crop years are being considered, either monthly or quarterly data would need to be employed in the analysis. As a general rule, yearly data over a number of years are considered. When a cycle is involved, I would prefer that the term "trend" not be used to refer to intra-cyclical price moves. In cattle, for example, price cycles are 10 to 12 years in length and the increasing prices during the herd-building phase of the cycle are often described as an upward price trend. I would prefer to relate these price moves to the cycle and not call this a price trend.

2. An 11-year moving average, for example, is calculated by adding the 11 most recent yearly prices and dividing by 11. The process is repeated each year to get a new moving average value for that particular year.

3. For those students with little or no exposure to regression, Appendix A to this chapter offers a brief exposition. Additional help will be available from any introductory treatment of statistical methods.

4. Divide the prices by the Index of Prices Received by Farmers. This deflates the data and removes the influence of inflation. The references by Shepherd (Chapter 8, pp. 121–134) and by Tomek and Robinson (p. 210 and pp. 330–332) listed at the end of the chapter discuss deflation in more detail.

5. The traditional "cobweb theorem" is one way of describing cyclical developments. A description of the theorem, its graphical framework, and the way it operates is shown in Appendix B to this chapter. I think this is a useful way to describe cyclical developments but because of the importance of the decisions that must be made as the price cycle runs its course, I have chosen to focus attention on the behavioral dimension and on the marketing decisions made during the cyclical price moves.

6. If the trend data were deflated and projected in real terms, multiply the trend value by the price index used in deflating to get the price back to real-world terms. Note you would have to predict the future value of the index to allow this. The most simple approach is to fit the trend line without deflating the data, and project the future trend value directly.

7. This is a vivid illustration of the concept of derived demand at work. The cattle feeder has no control over selling price for his finished cattle. He must formulate some expectation as to value of the finished animal and then estimate the costs of getting a particular feeder steer to finished weights. If he subtracts the feeding costs from the projected value of the finished animal, he gets the total dollars he could pay for the feeder steer and break even. Since he wants a profit and since there is uncertainty in his estimates of value of the finished cattle and in costs of feeding, he is likely to discount (lower) his bid price on the feeder steer to protect against uncertainty and try to insure a profit to his feeding program.

8. Adjustment will still be difficult. If the increase in output was accomplished by more fertilizer, more irrigated acreage, etc., these moves can be reversed. But if the increase required hiring more labor or establishing crop-share lease arrangements, adjustments may be difficult to make even though no new capital equipment—or land—was brought into use.

9. Appendix C to this chapter provides more detail on calculation procedures and offers a brief illustration. The question of how many years to include in the monthly data set is always a difficult one. To gain statistical significance, there is a tendency to increase the sample size and go back across more years. But the benefits of added statistical significance may be questionable if the longer time period spans a transition period or structural change in the industry. For example, I would question the wisdom of including years before about 1965 in calculating a seasonal index for slaughter cattle. The feedlot industry and year-round feeding were just beginning to develop in the early 1960s. Similarly, I would wonder about extending the data set on wheat back beyond 1972. Prior to that year, the government had regulated production and supported price. And it was in 1972 that the USSR policy makers decided to go into the world market and buy wheat and feed grains instead of just "tightening their belts" the way they had in past years when they had a short crop. The seasonal patterns look different since 1972.

10. To review, the estimate of the parameter, b_1, shows how much the price of corn would change for a 1 unit increase in S_t. Since an increase in S_t would indicate increasing stocks and an increasing supply, the sign would be expected to be negative. For example, if $b_1 = -.1000$ this would indicate the yearly average price of corn would be expected to *decrease* $.10 per bu. for each 1.0 million bushel *increase* in ending stocks.

11. Reference is to the table values of Student's t distribution found in the

back of all references on statistics and statistical methods. The calculated t-statistic can be compared to the table value for the correct degrees of freedom and for a selected probability level. Appendix A illustrates the test.

12. Whether the variable helps can be checked by going back in the data set, using the model to predict values of the dependent variable, and plotting the predicted values against the actual prices. If deleting a variable that has a poor t-test results in poorer performance of the model when predictions are checked against actual values of the dependent variable, then consider keeping the variable in the model. When the t-statistic is less than $|1.0|$, the standard error of the estimated parameter is larger than the estimated parameter and it will be most difficult to justify keeping the variable in the model.

13. For a single model with two explanatory variables that has been fitted using the lagged relationships we would proceed as follows:

$$Y_t = 32.500 + 0.500X_{1(t-3)} - 0.002X_{2(T-3)}$$

Assume we observe the following in month t (the current month):

$$X_{1(t)} = 30$$
$$X_{2(t)} = 4000$$

We calculate a forecast for $Y_{(t+3)}$ or Y three months into the future as follows:

$$Y_{(t+3)} = 32.5 + .500(30) - .002(4000)$$
$$= 32.5 + 15 - 8$$
$$= 39.5$$

14. A 90 pcercent confidence interval for forecasts of Y is the interval in which we would expect 90 of 100 forecasts of Y to fall if we took repeated samples of XY pairs, fitted the models, and calculated forecasts of Y for given or fixed values of X.

15. The reason for the ballooning effect is found in the variance of an estimate of Y for a particular value of X. If we are predicting Y for a particular value of X, say X_K, the estimated variance of $\hat{Y}_K$ is defined as follows:

$$\hat{\sigma}^2_{Y_k} = S^2_{Y_k} \left(1 + \frac{1}{n} + \frac{(X_K - \bar{X})^2}{\sum\limits_{i=1}^{n}(X_i - X)^2}\right)$$

The numerator of the ratio $\dfrac{(X_K - \bar{X})^2}{\sum\limits_{i=1}^{n}(X_i - X)^2}$ increases sharply as the value of X for which Y is being forecast moves away from $\bar{X}$.

16. Some analysts argue the lag in adjusting consumption levels means this assumption is not valid. They would prefer to estimate income elasticity from models fitted across time series data such as the pork model discussed above. If price is in the model, this should allow for the influence of price and hold price constant insofar as the income elasticity is concerned.

17. By "predetermined variable" is meant either an exogeneous variable (one determined outside the model) or a lagged version of an endogenous variable (one determined inside the model). Interested students should check references such as the Hu and the Pindyck-Rubinfeld references at the end of the chapter.

18. Geoffrey S. Shepherd, *Agricultural Price Analysis* (Ames, Iowa: Iowa State University Press, 1963). Another much used reference in this area is Richard J. Foote, *Analytical Tools for Studying Demand and Price Structures*, Ag. Handbook No. 146, Ag. Mkt. Ser. USDA, August 1958.

Questions

1. Do you agree that knowing when cyclical turns in price are coming is more important to the decision maker than being able to project how far the price move will go? Why or why not?

2. As a decision maker, would you rely solely on a seasonal index to formulate expectations of intra-year price patterns? Why or why not? What other factors could be considered?

3. One approach to predicting a monthly price for a commodity in some future year is to
   a. Project a trend line to get the trend estimate of price;
   b. Adjust the trend price for cyclical influences; and
   c. Multiply the value in step b by the seasonal index for the particular month of interest.
   Critique this approach. In developing your answer, list all the important sources of error that could influence your estimate. Can you develop a better approach?

4. Describe how economic and statistical considerations can be effectively used together in deciding on a model to be used for prediction purposes.

5. What is meant by an "incorrect sign" in a least-squares model? List and describe all the forces you can—economic and statistical—that might lead to an incorrect sign.

Selected References

Dahl, Dale C. and Jerome W. Hammond, *Market and Price Analysis,* New York, N.Y.: McGraw-Hill, 1977.

Foote, Richard J., *Analytical Tools for Studying Demand and Price Structures,* Ag. Handbook No. 146, USDA. Washington, D.C.: U.S. Govt. Printing Office, Aug. 1958.

Hu, Teh-wei, *Econometrics: An Introductory Analysis.* Baltimore, Md.: University Park Press, 1973.

Keith, Kendell and Wayne D. Purcell, *The Beef Cycle of the 1970s: Analysis, Behavioral Dimensions, Outlook and Projections,* Okla. Agr. Exp. Sta. Bul B-721, Stillwater, March 1976.

Pindyck, Robert S. and Daniel L. Rubinfeld, *Econometric Models and Economic Forecasts.* New York, N.Y.: McGraw-Hill, 1976.

Shepherd, Geoffrey, S., *Agricultural Price Analysis.* Ames, Iowa: Iowa State Univ. Press, 1963.

Tomek, William G. and Kenneth L. Robinson, *Agricultural Product Prices.* Ithaca, N.Y.: Cornell Univ. Press, 1972.

Appendix 7.A

Least-Squares Regression Procedures

The simplest form of linear regression is the expression $Y = \alpha + \beta X$. This is the general form for a family of straight lines that can be plotted on a two-dimensional graph. Y is the *dependent* variable and X is the single *independent* or *explanatory* variable. The term α is the intercept—the value of Y when $X = 0$. The term β is the slope that shows how Y changes with a one-unit change in X.

Starting with a plot of data, let's assume there is a need for a model to express in quantitative terms the relationship between two variables. What we need is the single model that does the best job of expressing that relationship. The least-squares line is the answer. Let's look at why and then illustrate.

Algebraically, the estimates of α and β are

$$\hat{\beta} = \frac{\sum_{i=1}^{n} (X_i - \bar{X})(Y_i - \bar{Y})}{\sum_{i=1}^{n} (X_i - \bar{X})^2}$$

$$\hat{\alpha} = \bar{Y} - \hat{\beta}\bar{X}$$

It can be shown mathematically that these estimates minimize

$$\sum_{i=1}^{n} (Y_i - \hat{Y}_i)^2 = \sum_{i=1}^{n} e_i^2$$

where e_i is defined

$$e_i = (Y_i - \hat{Y}_i)$$

In other words, if Y_i is the actual value of Y for the ith observation of X, then $\hat{Y}_i$ is the estimate from the model of the ith value of Y. Therefore, e_i is the *deviation* or the extent to which the estimated value "misses" the actual value. It seems logical that we would prefer *the* model from the family of models $Y = \alpha + \beta X$ which minimizes these deviations or errors. The least-squares model does this.

Graphically, we can identify the general components as shown in Figure 7A.1 and define them as follows:

$Y_i - \bar{Y}_i$ = the total deviation of Y_i or the ith value of Y around the mean value of Y;

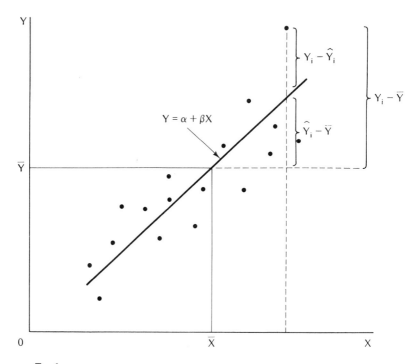

**FIGURE 7A.1   PARTITIONING OF THE TOTAL VARIATION OF Y AND THE FITTED
MODEL Y = α + βX**

$Y_i - \hat{Y}_i$ = the part of the total deviation of Y_i *not* explained by the model;
and

$\hat{Y}_i - \bar{Y}$ = the part of the total deviation of Y_i that *is* explained by the
model.

Using these terms, we can define a measure called the coefficient of determination (R^2 in popular language) as follows:

$$R^2 = \frac{\sum\limits_{i=1}^{n} (\hat{Y}_i - \bar{Y})^2}{\sum\limits_{i=1}^{n} (Y_i - \bar{Y})^2}$$

Thus, R^2 is the proportion of the total variation in Y explained by the
model. Other things equal (number of observations, e.g.) we would like for
R^2 to be relatively large. Values above .5 (or 50 percent) and closer to the .9
level would certainly be preferred.

One criterion in evaluating a model is therefore R^2. But we would also be interested in knowing whether the relationship we are measuring, as measured by β, is a significant and important quantitative relationship or whether what we are measuring is likely to be due to chance. A widely used test of significance is

$$t = \frac{\hat{\beta} - 0}{SE_{\hat{\beta}}}.$$

where $SE_{\hat{\beta}}$ is the standard error of $\hat{\beta}$. The standard error of β is the square root of the variance of $\hat{\beta}$. The variance is a measure of dispersion or "spread" in estimates of $\hat{\beta}$ if we were to take repeated samples of X and Y and estimate β many times. When this value is large, this means the estimates show no strong tendency to cluster around any particular value but fall throughout a wide range of values. A large variance means a large standard error that is undesirable. We feel more confident in our particular estimate of β if we know we would be likely to get estimates of a comparable level if we went back and estimated it again.

Let's look at the t-statistic again

$$t = \frac{\hat{\beta} - 0}{SE_{\hat{\beta}}}.$$

This ratio will be large when (1) $\hat{\beta}$ is large, (2) $SE_{\hat{\beta}}$ is small, or (3) $\hat{\beta}$ is large *and* $SE_{\hat{\beta}}$ is small. We hope β is *not* zero since we have formulated the relationship. And we would prefer $SE_{\hat{\beta}}$, since it measures the variability in our estimates, to be small. Putting these together means large values of the t-statistic are to be preferred. But what size t-statistic is large enough for us to decide $\hat{\beta}$ is estimating a significant relationship?

The statisticians have helped us here. In the back of every statistics text is a table of values of t-statistics and probabilities. The table gives the probability of observing a larger value of calculated t-statistics than those shown if there is no relationship and the estimate of β or $\hat{\beta}$ is just a chance occurrence. The larger the calculated t-statistic, the smaller the probability it is due to chance. When n or the number of XY pairs in the sample is very large, the probability of finding a calculated value of t, which is due to chance, larger than $|1.96|$ is .05. For small samples, the value associated with the .05 probability of getting a larger t by chance is larger. For a sample of 10, the t-value associated with the .05 probability is 2.306 for 8 degrees of freedom.*

To illustrate, we will fit a model to the data shown in Table 7A.1. The dependent variable will be commercial hog slaughter during the

---

* The degrees of freedom (df) will be n or the sample size minus the number of sample statistics used in calculating the values used in the t-statistic. Since $\bar{X}$ and $\bar{Y}$ must be calculated to get estimates of β and the standard error of $\hat{\beta}$, the degrees of freedom will be n-2 or 8.

Table 7A.1
Commercial Hog Slaughter January–March and Hogs
and Pigs on Farms, U.S., in 60–180 lb. Range
December 1 of Previous Year

Year	Hogs and Pigs December 1 60–180 lbs.	Commercial Hog Slaughter January–March
	(1,000 head)	(1,000 head)
1968	24,426	—
69	22,597	22,234
70	27,046	19,949
71	25,285	24,256
72	23,685	22,260
73	24,076	20,224
74	22,367	20,149
75	19,096	18,759
76	21,239	17,431
77	21,763	19,768
78	—	19,398

Source: *Livestock Slaughter* and *Hogs and Pigs*, ERS, USDA.

January–March quarter. The explanatory variable is the number of hogs on feed in the 60–119 lb. plus 120–179 lb. weight ranges in the December 1 *Hogs and Pigs* report released by the USDA. In other words, the number of hogs on feed between 60 and 180 lbs. on December 1 will, according to our model, be an important determinant of hog slaughter in the subsequent January–March period. The model we will demonstrate is of the form

$$Y = \alpha + \beta X$$

where Y = commercial hog slaughter January–March (1,000 head), and
X = hogs on feed in the 60–180 lb. range December 1 of the previous year (1,000 head).

The data are plotted in Figure 7A.2. Also shown is the fitted least squares regression line which is

$$Y = 2287.128 + 0.784X.$$
$$(0.295)$$

For this model, $\hat{\beta} = 0.784$ and $\hat{\alpha} = 2287.128$. The intercept term is meaningless. The estimate of 0.784 indicates commercial hog slaughter will increase

784 head in January–March for each 1,000 head increase in the number of hogs on feed in the 60–180 lb. range on the previous December 1. The 0.295 value shown under $\hat{\beta}$ is SE$_{\hat{\beta}}$. The calculated t-statistic to test whether $\beta = 0$ would be

$$t = \frac{0.784 - 0}{0.295} = 2.658$$

The probability of observing a calculated value of t this large by chance is less than .05—meaning the estimate of β *is* different from zero and *is* measuring a legitimate relationship.

The R^2 for the model is .884, which is about what the experienced

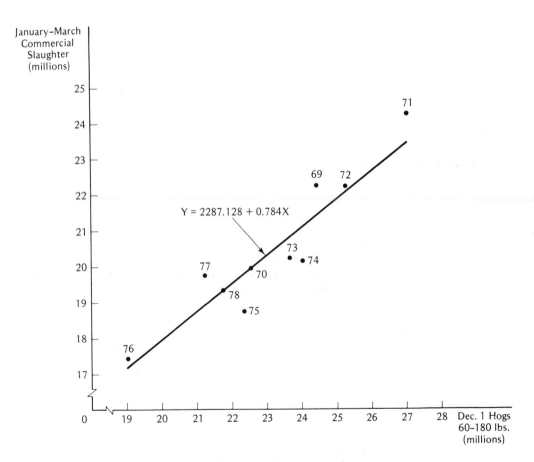

FIGURE 7A.2   RELATIONSHIP   BETWEEN   COMMERCIAL   HOG   SLAUGHTER JANUARY–MARCH AND NUMBER HOGS 60–180 LBS. PREVIOUS DECEMBER 1

analyst would expect.* Visual examination of the plot in Figure 7A.2 suggests there is a rather strong linear relationship. X and Y increase together and show something other than a random pattern.

The most obvious use of this little model is to predict commercial hog slaughter. To the hog farmer who recognizes price moves inversely with slaughter, this prediction could be very useful as he decides whether to hold gilts for farrowing, whether to buy more feeder pigs or cut back, etc. Using the above model, a *Hogs and Pigs* report that shows 24 million hogs on feed in the 60–180 lb. range would suggest a commercial slaughter in the following January–March as follows:

$$
\begin{aligned}
Y &= 2287.128 + 0.784X \\
&= 2287.128 + 0.784\ (24{,}000) \\
&= 2287.128 + 18816 \\
&= 21{,}103.128 \text{ units of 1,000 head or slightly} \\
&\quad \text{over 21 million.}
\end{aligned}
$$

Appendix 7.B

The Cobweb Theorem and Price Cycles

The cobweb theorem was presented by Mordecai Ezekiel in 1938.† Cyclical moves in prices, especially for farm products, do not fit the simple version of supply-demand analysis. Because of the biological and behavioral lags in production, supply in time period t is not a function of price in

* R^2 is calculated as

$$
R^2 = \frac{\left[\sum_{i=1}^{n} (X_i - \bar{X})(Y_i - \bar{Y})\right]^2}{\sum_{i=1}^{n} (X_i - \bar{X})^2}{\sum_{i=1}^{n} (Y_i - \bar{Y})^2}
$$

$$
= \frac{\text{reduction of sum of squares of Y attributable to X}}{\text{total sum of squares of Y}}
$$

† Mordecai Ezekiel, "The Cobweb Theorem," *Quarterly Journal of Economics*, Vol. 52, No. 2, February 1938.

t. Supply in t is a function of price in t-l or t-k where k = 1,2, . . . , n and possibly some *expectation* of price for time period t. This leads to an adjustment pattern around the equilibrium price, which resembles a cobweb in appearance.

Figure 7B.1 illustrates the *converging* cobweb. Starting with a quantity OQ_1, buyers would be willing to pay a price OP_1. Producers observe this price and respond by producing a quantity OQ_2—and price drops to OP_2. Producers then produce a quantity OQ_3, price jumps to OP_3, and more adjustments are needed as price converges on the equilibrium price. While the converging cobweb is illustrated in Figure 7B.1, there are three types of cobweb patterns:

1. Converging. If neither demand nor supply shifts, price will converge on the equilibrium price because the price elasticity of supply is less elastic than is the price elasticity of demand.

2. Diverging. Price elasticity of supply is greater than price elasticity of demand in absolute value, and each pair of supply-demand reactions carries price farther away from the equilibrium price. Figure 7B.2 illustrates.

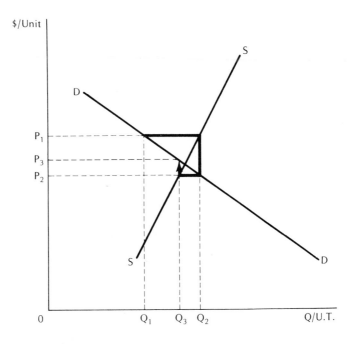

FIGURE 7B.1   THE CONVERGING COBWEB: ELASTICITY OF DEMAND GREATER THAN ELASTICITY OF SUPPLY

3. Stable. The price elasticity of supply is equal to the price elasticity of demand in absolute value and the path of adjustment is repeated over and over again. Figure 7B.3 illustrates.

In the real world, something will change, demand or supply will shift, and the cobweb adjustment pattern is disturbed. We cannot find, for example, a situation that parallels the stable cobweb. And we certainly don't see the completion of the converging cobweb that goes to an equilibrium price and stays. But it is easy to find examples of what appears to be a diverging cobweb.

The diverging cobweb crops up in production agriculture where, in the short run, the price elasticity of supply exceeds the price elasticity of demand. Producers overreact to a higher price signal, produce more than is demanded except at sharply lower prices, and the diverging pattern begins. In theory this type of cobweb pattern will "explode." Prices will move around the equilibrium price at increasing high or low levels. In practice, the pattern is halted by either a policy move or the reallocation of resources. In the livestock commodities where government policy has not been used, the forced exit of resources usually limits the supply response and allows the demand side to catch up. The liquidation of brood sows in

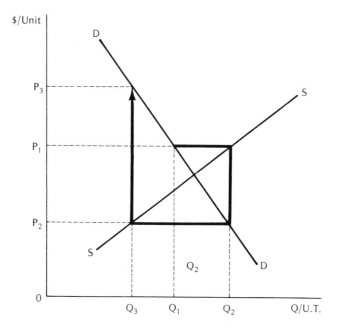

FIGURE 7B.2   THE DIVERGING COBWEB: ELASTICITY OF SUPPLY GREATER THAN ELASTICITY OF DEMAND

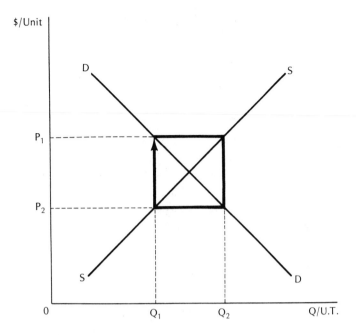

$/Unit

P₁

P₂

0   Q₁   Q₂   Q/U.T.

FIGURE 7B.3   THE STABLE COBWEB: ELASTICITY OF DEMAND EQUALS THE ELAS-
TICITY OF SUPPLY

1974 as prices dropped below the cost of production brought on a sharp reduction in supply and record hog prices in mid-1975. But the divergence was curtailed in the months and years that followed as producers, working with a reduced sow herd and reduced production potential, did not over-react to the extent the divergence was continued.

Appendix 7.C

Calculation of a Seasonal Index

A seasonal index is a valuable marketing tool. Increasingly, calculations are completed by a computer. Here, we will explain and then illustrate a hand-calculated procedure to help insure understanding.

In preparing to calculate a seasonal index using a centered 12-month moving average, complete the following steps in order:

1. List the monthly prices that you will use in chronological order in column 1 of your work sheet. If your data is January 1970 through December 1977, for example, you would have 96 observations listed in chronological order.

2. Calculate a 12-month moving total by adding prices 1 through 12. Record this total by observation or price 6 (June 1970 if the data are January 1970 through December 1977) in column 2.

3. Calculate a 12-month moving total by adding prices 2 through 13 and enter this in column 2 by observation 7. (For ease of computation, keep the 12-month moving total from step 2 in the calculator, add the 13th price and subtract the 1st to get the 12-month moving total for prices 2 through 13.) Continue this process in column 2. There will be 5 blanks at the beginning of this column, 6 at the end.

4. Calculate a 2-month moving total of column 2 and enter this in column 3 starting with the 7th observation. There will be 6 blanks at the beginning and 6 blanks at the end of this column.

5. Divide column 3 by 24 and enter this in column 4 starting beside original observation number 7. This is the centered 12-month moving average. Carry at least 3 places to the right of the decimal.

6. Divide the original prices in column 1 by the moving average in column 4, and enter these individual monthly indices in column 5 starting beside observation number 7. There will be no indices for the first 6 rows and none for the last 6 rows. Carry at least 3 places to the right of the decimal.

7. From column 5, take all the index values for each month and average them. You will always have n-1 indices to average for each month where n = the number of complete years of data.

8. Express the averages from step 7 as percentages. Plot them if preferred to allow a visual picture of the seasonal pattern as represented by your seasonal index.

To illustrate these steps, monthly prices of U.S., SM 1 1/16" cotton 1972–1977 were used. In practice, more years should be used unless there is reason to believe the seasonal pattern has undergone a permanent change in the earlier years. Shown below is the beginning and end of the work sheet to illustrate procedure.

Worksheet

Year, Month		Col. 1 Price (¢/lb.)	Col. 2 12-month Moving Total	Col. 3 2-month Moving Total	Col. 4 Col. 3 ÷ 24	Col. 5 Col. 1 ÷ Col. 4
1972	J	41.45				
	F	41.68				
	M	40.17				
	A	37.56				
	M	36.88				
	J	35.15	438.63			
	J	34.06	439.56	878.19	36.591	.931
	A	32.49	441.38	880.94	36.706	.885
	S	31.28	447.12	888.50	37.021	.855
	O	32.22	455.78	902.90	37.620	.856
	N	36.69	470.65	926.43	38.601	.951
	D	39.00	491.50	962.15	40.090	.973
1973	J	42.38	522.44	1013.95	42.248	1.003
	F	43.50	569.75	1092.19	45.508	.956
	M	45.91	628.66	1198.41	49.934	.919
	A	46.22	685.19	1313.85	54.744	.844
...	...	...	...	...	...	...
1977	J	78.88	989.12	1999.26	83.303	.947
	F	85.00	968.85	1957.97	81.582	1.042
	M	88.05	947.39	1916.24	79.843	1.103
	A	86.12	919.32	1866.71	77.780	1.107
	M	83.06	891.39	1810.71	75.446	1.101
	J	72.50	867.71	1759.10	73.296	.989
	J	66.50				
	A	63.56				
	S	62.10				
	O	61.31				
	N	59.63				
	D	61.00				

Averaging the index values for each month from column 5 gives us the seasonal index.

Month	Index
Jan.	102.0
Feb.	99.9
Mar.	98.8
Apr.	96.8
May	96.8
June	96.9
July	100.5
Aug.	102.3
Sept.	102.9
Oct.	102.8
Nov.	99.5
Dec.	101.0

After the seasonal index is calculated, it should always be checked to see if the average is 1.00 (or 100%). For the index above, the total of the 12 indices shown is 1200.2. The average is 100.017. This is not enough to worry about but the indices can be adjusted to "force" an average of 100 by dividing each index by 1.00017. To illustrate,

$$102.0 \div 1.00017 = 101.98 \text{ for January.}$$

If the average is farther from 100, the adjustment would, of course, be more significant.

part four

Commodity Futures and Hedging

Prices exploded in terms of level and variability in the 1970s. The increased exposure to price risk has brought changes. One of the most evident is the increased interest in commodity futures and hedging.

The trends will continue. Prices will be volatile. Interest in commodity futures will grow. We will be caught with too little reference material of the type needed by the marketing student, decision maker, and analyst.

Materials presented in this section are not found in the currently available marketing texts. But the texts written in the next five to 10 years will pay more attention to trade in commodity futures unless the authors ignore the needs of the times. The need is there today but it has been slow to find its way into the classroom.

Understanding the role of trade in commodity futures is the place to start. Futures trade is a factor in price discovery processes. Perhaps more importantly, futures trade provides a hedging mechanism that allows the

195

decision maker to gain a measure of protection against the risk of cash price fluctuations. To hedge effectively requires an understanding of trade in commodity futures, who trades and why, and the ability to use the technical aids. The objective of Part IV is to promote this type of understanding and this type of ability.

chapter eight

Role of Commodity Futures in the Marketing System

Trade in commodity futures presents both the old and new. Grain futures have been traded for decades in the U.S. Futures contracts in the livestock and meat commodities are a more recent development. Live cattle futures, for example, were initiated in November of 1964 for an April 1965 contract. The live hog, the feeder cattle, and pork belly contracts were introduced still later in the 1960s or early 1970s.

Across the years commodity trading has come under attack from producer groups. During periods of declining cash prices, there is a tendency to blame the futures market. Attempts to precipitate legislation to block trade in commodity futures have met with limited success. Trade in onion futures was banned in 1957.[1]

But the negative attitudes toward trade in commodity futures rest primarily with a segment of producers. Most price analysts, marketing economists and many producers feel trade in commodity futures can be an effective tool in the hands of the well-informed decision maker. Given the diverse attitudes, it is important that we understand the role that trade in commodity futures plays in the marketing system and in the process of price discovery. On this base of understanding we can then turn in later chapters to consider management strategies that employ commodity futures.

Economic Basis for Trade

The economic justification for trade in commodity futures includes the following:

1. Trade in commodity futures, by providing a hedging mechanism, gives the producer, processor, or other marketing system participant an opportunity to reduce exposure to the risk of cash price fluctuations.

2. Trade in commodity futures is a factor in price discovery processes.

Without one or both of these roles there would be little economic support for trade in commodity futures.

A HEDGING MECHANISM

Hedging can be referred to as taking opposite positions in the cash and futures markets.[2] The wheat producer who harvests and stores his wheat is "long" in the cash market—he actually has the physical commodity. To hedge that storage operation, he would sell wheat futures—he would go "short" in futures. The hedge can provide protection against (1) a falling cash market, or (2) a rising cash market that does not increase enough during the marketing year to cover the costs of storage.

The mechanics of a hedge are essentially the same whether the product is a storable product such as grain, cotton, and pork bellies or a "perishable" commodity such as live cattle or live hogs. But there are important differences to consider in hedging the two broad commodity groupings. First, the storable commodity will show a seasonal price pattern with low prices during harvest and a tendency for price to rise during the market year as storage costs accumulate. Unless there are significant changes in demand within the year or significant developments in new-crop prospects, this pattern of rising prices within the crop year tends to be predictable and reliable.

Second, the available supply of the seasonally produced storable commodity such as grain is essentially "fixed" for the year. Once the acreage is seeded and the crop is produced, the quantity flowing through the market within the year will respond to price but the total quantity for the year can show little or no response. Conversely, the supply of live cattle, hogs, pork bellies, broilers, and turkeys can be changed within the year by the decisions of producers. For example, cattle placed on feed during the first half of any calendar year will usually reach market weights before the end of the year.

This second distinction is important. It means the available supply of livestock and poultry might be influenced by the trading levels of commodity futures. We will come back to this later when we look at futures trade and price discovery processes.

Hedging a Storable Commodity. Table 8.1 illustrates the basic parts of a hedge on wheat. The producer stores winter wheat after harvest on June 15. He plans to hold the wheat until March of the following calendar year. With a cash price at harvest of $4.00 and storage costs of $.03 per bushel per month, the price needed in March to make the storage program equally profitable to selling in June—the "breakeven" price—would be about $4.27 (or the $4.00 in June plus $.27 per bushel storage costs until March).

If the producer can sell March wheat futures in a sufficient volume to "cover" his stored crop at a price equal to or above $4.27, he has "locked in" a margin large enough to protect himself against variable cash prices. Note that Table 8.1 illustrates what will occur if (1) the cash price moves up to only $4.00, and (2) if the cash price moves to the $4.50 level. In each case, the net from the hedged storage operation is the margin that was locked in when the futures were sold at $4.35.

The producer of wheat, corn, soybeans, oats, cotton, etc., can also hedge a growing crop. To illustrate, consider the position of the midwestern corn producer who is concerned over the possibility of a bumper crop and low harvest period prices. The hedge is set by selling December corn futures. Any break in cash price will be accompanied by a downward move in the corn futures. The money lost in the cash market is offset by buying back the futures at a price below the price at which they were sold.

The producer of a crop for which futures contracts are traded is always a "short hedger". He has the cash crop and sells futures to protect against falling markets. Futures contracts are traded for wheat, corn, oats, soybeans, soybean meal, soybean oil, cotton, potatoes, sugar, orange juice, and selected other non-livestock commodities.[3]

Processors may be either short hedgers or long hedgers. If falling prices are anticipated by their analysts, the processor can protect against an inventory loss on stored raw materials (wheat, sugar, soybeans, etc.) by selling commodity futures. Conversely, if higher prices are expected, buying futures contracts provides protection against rising prices of raw mate-

Table 8.1
Illustration of a Hedge for a Stored Wheat Crop [a]

Date	Action Taken	Outcome
June 15	Places wheat in storage. Estimates break-even price for storage until March 1. Break-even is harvest-period price plus cost of carrying (storage, interest, insurance, shrink, and spoilage). Harvest price = $4.00 Carrying cost = .27 Break-even = $4.27	
June 15	Sells March futures at $4.35. Lock-in margin = $4.35 − 4.27 = $.08 per bu.	
March 1	Sells cash wheat at $4.50, buys March futures at $4.50.	Net = $4.50 − 4.27 = $.23 from cash Net = $4.35 − 4.50 = −$.15 from futures Net to hedged program = $.08
March 1	Sells cash wheat at $4.00, buys March futures at $4.00.	Net = $4.00 − 4.27 = −$.27 from cash Net = $4.35 − 4.00 = $.35 from futures Net to hedged program = $.08

[a]The experienced student will note we ignore the costs of the futures trade and any need to incorporate a futures-cash basis in this analysis. These elements will be brought in later after the basics are illustrated.

rials. This is a long hedge. For example, Pillsbury might buy sugar futures when the company analysts are expecting higher prices for sugar, an important raw material.

Whether the hedge is to protect against rising or falling cash prices, the hedge works because the cash and futures prices tend to converge—tend to come together—during the month in which the futures contract matures. Figure 8.1 illustrates. Note the tendency for the cash and futures markets to move closer together as the maturity date of the futures contract approaches.[4]

The concept of hedging is made operational by this tendency for cash and futures to converge. The difference between futures quotes and cash prices at any particular time (on any particular day) is called the *basis*. Clearly, the behavior of the basis is important to the hedger. The basis may vary during the trading life of the futures contract but is forced toward zero as the futures contract moves toward the expiration date.

More specifically, the basis approaches the cost of delivering the product under the provisions of the futures contract. No economic forces will guarantee the basis will go to zero. During the delivery period,[5] the futures and cash will be forced to converge on a value of the basis approximating the cost of delivery as follows:

1. If the futures price is above cash, traders will sell futures, buy the lower priced cash product, and deliver under the provisions of the futures contract. This will be profitable so long as the futures price is above cash by more than the costs of completing the trades and delivery processes involved. Such action puts selling pressure on

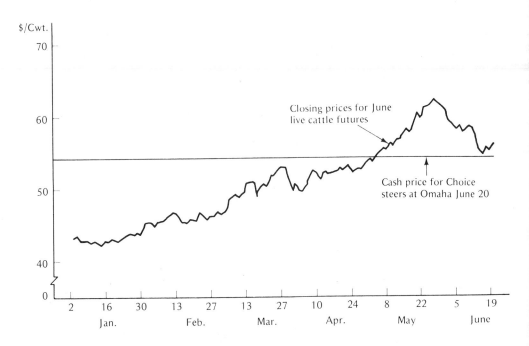

FIGURE 8.1 PLOT OF CLOSING PRICES FOR JUNE 1978 LIVE CATTLE FUTURES, JANUARY–JUNE 1978, AND CLOSING CASH PRICE

the futures and buying pressure on the cash prices, which forces the basis toward an approximation of delivery costs.

2. If the futures price is below cash, traders will buy the futures contract, accept delivery, and sell the product in the higher cash market. Processors who can use the product will buy futures and accept delivery rather than buy the higher priced cash product. This puts buying pressure on the futures, selling pressure on the cash price, and forces convergence.

Hedging a Non-Storable or Flow Commodity.   The mechanics of a hedge on a commodity such as live cattle are similar to those employed in the storable commodities. Since the product is available in a continuous flow rather than as a stock, we will find (in later chapters) the decision on whether and when to hedge is made using somewhat different criteria. But the basic elements of the hedge are the same.

Calculating a break-even price differs since we are dealing with a commodity that changes its form during the period the hedge is being employed. Table 8.2 illustrates. The break-even price that is needed is the price required to cover the costs of producing market-ready fed cattle. This cost is comprised of the cost of the feeder animal when placed on feed and the cost of the gain during the feeding process.

The underlying forces that make the hedge work are also essentially

---

Table 8.2
Illustration of the Short Hedge for a Cattle Feeding Operation

Date	Action Taken	Outcome
January 1	Buys 600-lb. feeder steers at an into-the-lot cost of $60 per cwt. Estimates the costs of 500 lbs. gain at $50 per cwt. Break-even price on a 1100 lb. Choice steer sold with a 4% shrink is $[6(\$60) + 5(\$50)] \div .96(11)$ $= (\$360 + 250) \div 10.56$ cwt. $= \$57.76$ per cwt.	
January 1	Sells June cattle futures at $61 per cwt. to give a lock-in margin of $61 − 57.76 − 1.00 estimate of costs of delivery = $2.24 per cwt.	
June 10	Sells cash cattle at $50 per cwt., buys back futures at $51 per cwt.	Net: $10 per cwt. in futures −7.76 per cwt. in cash = $2.24 overall

the same as for the grains and fibers. During the delivery month, the threat of delivery by those who have sold futures keeps the futures price from closing above cash by more than the costs of delivery. Conversely, futures cannot close below cash because meat packers who have bought futures, a long hedge, would simply hold their long position and accept delivery of the cattle. This takes their buying influence out of the cash cattle market and helps to bring cash prices down. Such holding action prompts higher bids by earlier sellers of futures who are trying to buy and liquidate their position. This bidding action forces futures prices higher until the equality between cash plus delivery costs and futures price is approximated.

PRICE DISCOVERY PROCESSES

Trade in commodity futures becomes a force in price discovery processes. At any point in time, the trading level for a distant futures option represents the consensus of traders' opinions as to what the cash price will be in that future period.[6] For commodities harvested once a year, futures quotes become a factor in production, storage, and sales decisions. For the products produced on a continuous basis, futures become a factor in decisions on production level and decisions on when to sell.

The expected pattern in prices for a storable commodity within the market year shows low prices during the harvest period and a tendency for price to rise during the year based on storage costs. Unless some other economic force enters the picture, the futures quotes for the commodity typically reflect this pattern. For example, the crop and market year for winter wheat is from June 1 through May 31. Prices are generally low during June and July, rise reflecting storage costs through the following February, then begin to decline toward the harvest months for the new crop.

Planting decisions on winter wheat are made from August through October. The level at which the July futures contract for the following calendar year is trading may influence those decisions. Where there are alternative uses for the land and resources, a relatively low quote on the July option during planting season can decrease seeded acreage. Conversely, a relatively high quote can encourage increased acreage and increased production. Therefore, the levels at which wheat futures are trading can become a factor in decisions that determine plantings, and, with an appropriate time lag, influence supply during the following harvest period. The prospective crop is monitored by buyers, sellers, and traders throughout the year and becomes a direct input in their combined efforts to discover wheat prices during the crop year.

The impact of trade in futures is similar for other storable commodities such as oats, barley, grain sorghum, cotton, corn, and soybeans. Crop and market years are different (the crop year for corn is October 1 through September 30, for example) but the process is essentially the same. Planting decisions can be affected by futures quotes. The impact varies across crops with absolute price levels and with the extent to which flexibility in resource use exists.

For most storable commodities, price within the crop and market year is a direct function of the futures quotes. Table 8.3 demonstrates how the bid price by a local elevator in the major winter wheat states of Kansas, Nebraska, Oklahoma, and Texas is determined. The process starts with the most recent closing quote from the nearby Kansas City wheat futures,[7] the exchange on which the winter wheat futures contract is traded. The "Gulf basis" is added to this quote. This basis is a reflection of the difference in value of wheat between Kansas City and the major export point at Houston. Wheat ready for export is worth more than wheat at Kansas City. From the sum of the Kansas City futures and the Gulf basis, the local elevator manager subtracts what we would call a "local basis" to determine his bid price for wheat on any particular day. The local basis is an approximation of the transportation costs from the local point to the Gulf plus an operating margin for the local elevator. It may be 60 cents per bushel in southern Oklahoma, 65 cents per bushel in western Kansas, etc., reflecting differences in rail rates and/or trucking costs to the Gulf. Operating margins usually are fairly competitive and do not vary a great deal across elevators in the same area.

The variable component of the pricing process is the Gulf basis. Exporting firms "bid up" the Gulf basis when wheat is needed to meet orders. The higher bids prompt producers to sell. Wheat comes out of storage and moves to the Gulf. Within a crop year, this basis may vary as much as 20 cents to 30 cents per bushel reflecting the strength of export demand. The behavior of the Gulf basis is watched by the trade as a barometer of the strength of export demand.

Table 8.3
Determination of the Cash Bid Price at the Local Elevator Level in the Hard Red Winter Wheat Belt

	Record the closing price of the nearby Kansas City wheat futures	$3.95
Add	Gulf to Kansas City basis	.50
		$4.45
Subtract	Gulf to local basis	.65
	Local cash bid	$3.80[a]

[a] The $3.80 cash bid is for a given point in time when the $3.95 futures close, the $.50 Gulf to Kansas City basis and the $.65 Gulf to local basis are in effect.

When futures prices change, therefore, the local cash bids tend to move in the same direction and roughly in the same magnitude as the change in futures quotes. On some occasions there is an anticipatory dimension in the market. If the trading levels for soybean futures on the Chicago Board of Trade close lower by 10–15 cents per bushel on Friday, local elevator managers in the soybean areas may "take protection" and lower their posted bids over the weekend. The reason for such moves is clear. The local elevator manager operates on a margin. His cash buying price reflects this margin and allows him to immediately protect his position by either reselling the beans to an exporter or setting a hedge by selling soybean futures. If the manager expects a further decline in soybean futures on Monday, he "takes protection" by lowering his cash bid.

Procedures may vary slightly for the other major storable commodities such as corn and cotton but the direct use of a futures quote in setting price bids is typical. The size of the Gulf (or other) basis and the local basis may vary reflecting local conditions and different transportation costs but the procedure is much the same.[8]

As explained in Chapter 6, a primary function of the pricing mechanism is to ration the exhaustible domestic stock of the commodity so that it will last through the market year until the next harvest. Trade in commodity futures becomes a factor in "discovering" the intermonth price differentials that will accomplish this rationing function.

At any point in time, the quotes on distant futures indicate what margin the producer, elevator manager, processor, or cattle feeder who is considering storing grain can lock in with a hedge. This has impact on his yes-no decision concerning storing and affects how the grain is released from the exhaustible stock of grain available within the year. Trading levels of the futures take into account the need for storage and reflect this in the inter-month price levels. In winter wheat, for example, the first indication of seeded acreage for the crop year is available in December. This gives a base for initial estimates of the size of the new crop and has impact on the demand for storage.

In a year when stocks are light and the early indications are for a relatively small crop, the futures will tend to register a full carrying charge during the market year. Quotes for March and May would tend to reflect total cumulative storage costs (or more) over an earlier month such as September. This motivates those holding cash grain to give strong consideration to carrying more of their product until late in the crop year where it will be needed to supplement the projected short crop.

Conversely, the prospects of a bumper crop tend to reverse the intermonth pattern shown in the futures quotes. Options such as March or May in the second half of the crop year for wheat may carry little or no premium over earlier contracts such as September or December. When the stocks are small and a big crop is anticipated, an inverted carrying charge market may develop with September or December trading above March and May. The futures give no encouragement to hold grain in terms of presenting an opportunity to hedge or "lock in" a profit to storage.

One of the periods of key importance during the crop year is the last three to four months as the new harvest period approaches. The process of price discovery becomes more complex during this period. Developments in weather that influence expectations on the new crop become an important factor in the market. The volume of old-crop grain that is released from storage responds to changes in new-crop expectations. Price is the motivating influence.

Figure 8.2 illustrates what happens if expectations for the new crop deteriorate due to weather, disease, etc. The supply curve for the new crop shifts to the left or decreases, and, for a given demand, the expected harvest period price increases to OP_2. This increase in price shifts the demand for old-crop grain up and to the right to $D'D'$, which pushes price higher on old crop stocks to OP'_2. With some time lag, this higher price for old-crop grain increases the demand for the new crop and the process moves toward an equilibrium situation until a new "shock" is felt. Futures quotes tend to register these developments.

The role played by futures trade in price discovery processes for non-storable commodities produced on a year-round basis is somewhat

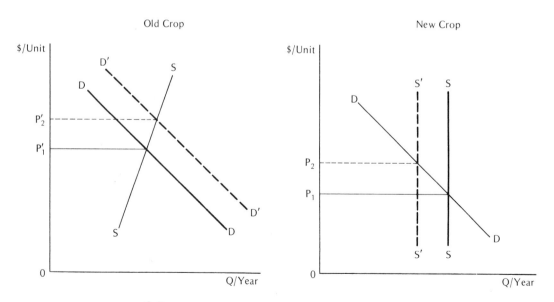

FIGURE 8.2 IMPACT OF A DECREASE IN SUPPLY EXPECTATIONS FOR NEW-CROP GRAIN ON DEMAND FOR OLD-CROP GRAIN

different. Production levels can be and are changed within the year. The number of broilers can be changed within the year by changing the egg set. Pork production during the second half of the calendar year is directly affected by the number of sows farrowed during the first half of the year. The number of cattle being placed in feedlots during any particular month will affect fed cattle slaughter 100 to 150 days later when the cattle move from the feedlot to the packing plant.

To the extent the current price levels of distant futures options influence production decisions, the supply of product in the distant months is influenced. Observation suggests the response is often significant. Periodically, when the prices of distant slaughter cattle futures trade up to relatively high levels, the following set of actions by cattle feeders can be observed:

1. Placements of cattle on feed increase;

2. Price levels of feeder cattle are bid up as cattle feeders bid aggressively for the available supply of feeder cattle; and

3. Feed grain prices may also increase as added buying of grains exerts an influence.

But such reactions can be self-defeating. The increased placements tend to come out of the feedlots as finished cattle later in the year. In this later time period, cattle prices can come under pressure due to the increase in marketings.

Similar patterns of activity can be observed in hogs and in broilers. Most slaughter hogs are six to eight months old when marketed. A larger pig crop from increased farrowings can be ready for market in six to eight months. The level at which live hog futures are trading is not the *only* factor that changes farrowing plans. In many instances other economic forces may be more important. But the futures are a force that is receiving increasing attention.

Using futures prices in this way can lead to problems for the producer if no hedge is employed. For example, the cattle feeder who placed cattle during July and August while prices of the December futures were high may see those favorable price expectations disappear under the weight of increased marketings during November and December. The extent of the price impact will of course vary with how many cattle are placed during July and August. Table 8.4 illustrates the net outcome from hedged and unhedged feeding operations when the response in the form of increased placements is enough to contribute to a "break" in the market in the later time period.[9]

Increasingly, price levels for livestock futures are a factor in price discovery processes in a broader context. The concept of derived demand

Table 8.4
Illustration of the Impact of Increased Placements in Response to High Prices of Live Cattle Futures

Setting:	July and early August of 1974. Average closes for the December live cattle futures increased from $42.70 the week ending July 6 to $49.08 the week ending August 3.
Actions:	A strong surge in placements evolved as the December futures traded higher. Choice 600–700 lb. feeder steer prices increased over $4 per cwt. in the last 3 weeks of July. Corn prices which averaged $3.14 the week ending July 6 (No. 2 yellow, Chicago) averaged $3.74 the week ending July 27 as corn and feeder cattle were bought aggressively by cattle feeders.
Outcomes:	A sharp increase in fed marketings in November and December helped send cattle prices tumbling. The December live cattle futures went off the board at $37.90 and cash cattle were around $37.00. The feeders who hedged the July and early August placements netted from $30 to $50 per head. The feeders who placed at least partially in response to the high futures quotes and did not hedge lost $70 to $100 per head.

was discussed in Chapter 7. Table 7.4 in Chapter 7 illustrated the concept by recording a significant change in the price relationships between slaughter cattle and feeder cattle, a primary input to the feeding complex. As slaughter cattle prices decreased with constant or rising corn prices, the prices paid for feeder cattle moved from a significant premium over slaughter cattle to a $15 per cwt. discount. This occurred as efforts continued to "discover" the prices for feeder cattle which would restore profitability to the cattle feeding operation.

Livestock futures enter the price discovery process when the cattle feeder attempts to guarantee a relationship between his selling price and costs. To illustrate, consider the position of the manager who is concerned about high costs of feeder cattle in the late spring or summer months. Early in the year—perhaps in January or February—before seasonal price strength emerges, he can consider taking the following actions:

1. Sell live slaughter cattle futures for the following February;

2. Buy feeder cattle futures for August; and

3. Buy corn futures for July or September.

Given the prices at which he can buy feeder cattle futures and corn futures, our cattle feeder can estimate the break-even cost of cattle placed in August to finish in the following January or February. Given his estimated break-even, he can then look at the trading level for the February slaughter cattle futures and see whether he can lock in a margin of profit.

In this manner and for given levels of the slaughter cattle futures and corn futures, influence is exerted on the only variable that the cattle feeder can influence—feeder cattle prices. This means trading levels for economically related livestock and grains become an input into price discovery processes for feeder cattle. The rapidity and efficiency with which the process of price discovery moves to restore a balance between product prices and input or raw material prices is extremely important. There is an unavoidable time lag in the adjustments. In Table 8.5, feeder cattle placed in November–February at a price around $50 came out as finished cattle four to six months later in a price range of $35 to $40. With the grain prices that prevailed, this meant substantial losses. The longer such an imbalance persists, the more economic damage to the cattle feeding complex.[10] To the extent that producers watch for a profitable combination of corn, feeder cattle, and live cattle futures and take no action until such appears, trade in futures is very much a part of the price discovery process.

Table 8.5

The Changing Profit Picture on Cattle Placed on Feed During a Selected Period in 1973–74

	Monthly Average Prices		
Year, Month	*Choice 900–1100#* *Steers, Omaha*	*Choice 600–700#* *Steers, Kansas City*	*No. 2 Yellow* *Corn, Omaha*
	$ per cwt.	$ per cwt.	$ per bu.
1973 July	48.05	56.49	2.32
Aug.	53.61	62.40	2.71
Sept.	45.45	55.06	2.37
Oct.	41.79	51.86	2.34
Nov.	39.88	51.02	2.73
Dec.	38.90	47.71	2.49
1974 Jan.	47.68	50.58	2.71
Feb.	46.12	50.80	2.95
March	42.36	44.81	2.76
Apr.	41.18	44.15	2.49
May	40.04	40.14	2.51
June	37.33	35.10	2.68

Source: *Livestock and Meat Situation* and *Feed Situation*, ERS, USDA.

Summary

Trade in commodity futures provides a hedging mechanism and becomes a factor in price discovery processes. By providing the opportunity to hedge, trade in commodity futures puts the marketing system decision maker in a position to do something about the risk of cash price fluctuations. And since futures price quotes for any particular day are highly visible and are widely communicated, we can be sure their role in the price discovery process will not be overlooked.

Actually, the two basic functions are related. For example, futures prices record the impact of new information or new expectations. To the extent these price changes alter producers' production or marketing decisions, the process of price discovery is influenced directly. The level of production, the quantity held in storage, or the quantity released from storage can be affected—and a situation that encourages hedging or that allows the placing of a profitable hedge can emerge.

Whether the two roles are viewed together or independently, the importance of trade in commodity futures in our marketing systems cannot be denied. And the volume of trade will continue to accelerate. But caution is in order. The futures can be an effective tool if the user understands trade in commodity futures, makes objective decisions on whether and when to get involved, and does not misuse futures quotes by treating them as cash price predictions. Futures markets do not eliminate the need for good management.

Footnotes

1. Trade in onion futures was banned by Congressional action on the grounds such trade was accentuating cash price variability. Many analysts did not believe the evidence was conclusive, however. See Roger Gray, "Onions Revisited", *J. of Farm Econ.*, Vol. 45, May 1963.

2. A brief treatment of the basics of trade in commodity futures and the mechanics of hedging is found in Appendix A to this chapter. The student with little or no exposure to futures markets and hedging should read Appendix A before proceeding.

3. A list of the important commodities and the exchanges on which they are traded is provided as part of Appendix A. Also shown are contract sizes, even though these can change over time.

4. "Maturity date" means the last day the contract trades. For example, the August live cattle contract will expire or "go off the board" at 12:00 noon on August 20 or on the last trading day prior to August 20 if the 20th is a holiday or on a weekend. These provisions are spelled out in detail in the futures contract and are working knowledge of most commodity brokers.

5. The "delivery period" is the period established during which sellers of futures contracts who decide to deliver the physical commodity under the provisions of the futures contract can notify the exchange of their intent and proceed with actual physical delivery. Details on when and how to announce intent to deliver, how to deliver, etc., vary with commodities and are spelled out in the futures contract.

6. This does *not* mean the futures quote is a good prediction of cash prices in the later time period. The consensus on any particular day is a function of expectations of the buyers and sellers of the futures. These expectations can and will change over time as the body of available information changes and with the ability of those trading to interpret the available information. What we need to understand here is how trading levels are reflected in the price discovery process.

7. The nearby contract is the closest contract in terms of time. Contracts for hard red winter wheat are traded on the Kansas City exchange for the months of July, September, December, March, and May. The May contract will be used from March 1 until May 1, for example. Starting with May 1, the prices will be based on the July contract. The pricing process moves to the next contract instead of using the nearby into the maturity month and into the delivery period.

8. For many commodities such as corn, soybeans, oats, cotton, and spring wheat the cash bid process is simpler than with hard red winter wheat. Cash quotes reflect a single futures-cash basis below the nearby futures on the Chicago exchange (corn, oats, soybeans, spring wheat, etc.) or the New York exchange (cotton). This basis is typically negative and when exporters need grain or cotton, they simply bid higher in the cash market and the basis decreases in absolute terms.

9. Table 8.4 is constructed based on events that took place in 1974. Other examples can be found but the developments of this period were so apparent it constitutes a good base period for illustration.

10. It should be noted that the lower prices for feeder cattle do nothing to relieve any cost-price pressure on the stocker operator or cow-calf man who produces the feeder cattle.

Questions

1. Briefly describe the concept and purpose of a hedge.

2. Explain the forces that prevent a futures contract from closing on its last trading day at a price greater than the cash price plus the costs of delivery under the provisions of the futures contract.

3. Can the level at which futures contracts are trading influence the supply of a commodity within the year? Explain and illustrate.

4. Outline the way in which futures quotes are used in determining cash bids for grains. How do you think cash bids to producers would be affected if there was no trade in commodity futures?

5. Based on the brief discussion in this chapter, what advice do you have for a decision maker who watches futures quotes and makes his production, storage, and marketing decisions based on those quotes?

Selected References

Gray, Roger, "Onions Revisited", *J. of Farm Econ.*, Vol. 45, May 1963.

Gray, Roger W., "Price Effects of a Lack of Speculation", *Food Research Institute Studies*, Supp. to Vol. 7, 1967.

Hieronymus, Thomas A., *Economics of Futures Trade for Commercial and Personal Profit*. New York, N.Y.: Commodity Research Bureau, 1971.

Taylor, Gregory S. and Raymond M. Leuthold, "The Influence of Futures Trading on Cash Cattle Price Variations", *Food Research Institute Studies*, Vol. 13, 1974.

Working, Holbrook, "Futures Trading and Hedging", *Amer. Econ. Rev.*, Vol. 33, pp. 314–343, 1953.

Appendix 8.A

Basics of Trade in Commodity
Futures and Hedging

Trade in commodity futures can be a tough concept for the beginning
student. To help insure understanding of the basics, this appendix covers
some of the trouble spots. There is no formal structure. The topics are introduced and treated in a simple fashion. Coverage at a more sophisticated
level is reserved for the main body of Chapter 8, and Chapters 9 and 10.

Questions and Answers

1. What is being traded?

    Trade is in terms of commitments to a course of action. Selling a
    futures contract involves incurring a binding obligation to deliver
    the commodity as specified in the futures contract. Buying a futures
    contract brings an obligation to accept delivery of the commodity as
    specified in the futures contract. In practice, few deliveries are
    made. For most commodities, the vast majority of the obligations
    are cancelled or offset by buying back the futures that were sold (or
    selling those that were bought).

2. Who trades commodity futures and why do they trade?

    There are two types of traders: hedgers and speculators. Hedgers
    are seeking protection against the risk of cash price fluctuations.
    Speculators are seeking profits from moves up or down in the trad-
    ing levels of commodity futures.

3. Why are speculators needed?

    Speculators are essential to the providing of an opportunity to
    hedge. They accept the risk the hedger wishes to protect against.
    Speculators also provide the volume and liquidity so important to
    the hedger. The cotton producer who wishes to sell cotton futures
    to establish a hedge needs someone who will "step up" and be
    willing to buy the contracts he wants to sell. The speculator fills this
    role and by contributing to the volume of trade and liquidity of the
    market, helps to guarantee the hedger *will* be able to make the
    trades to establish a hedge.

4. Where and how is trade conducted?

Trade in commodity futures is conducted within the facilities and under the auspices of organized commodity exchanges. Among the more important are the Chicago Board of Trade, the Chicago Mercantile Exchange, the New York Commodity Exchange, the Kansas City Board of Trade, the Minneapolis Commodity Exchange, and the Mid-America Commodity Exchange. Trade is conducted by the "open outcry" auction system. Consider the following:

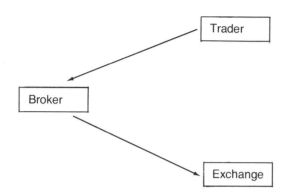

The trader calls his broker and places an order.

The broker sends the order by wire or phone to the floor of the exchange. A floor broker accepts the order, takes the order to the trading floor, and offers to sell or buy consistent with the trader's order.

Buy and sell orders are matched and filled on the floor. The paper work is handled back through the broker who passes the information on to his client (the trader) and maintains an account for his client.

5. What is needed to begin trade?

An account must be opened with a broker who is authorized to trade in commodity futures as a member of the exchange. Certain margin monies must be deposited with the broker before trade can occur. This is "surety" money to protect the broker if the trades lose money. The broker is responsible to the exchange and must therefore protect himself against having to accept losses incurred by clients.

6. Is trade on the exchanges supervised or regulated by any governmental agency?

The exchanges adopt their own rules, and, to a significant extent, police themselves. Since the early 1970s, the Commodity Futures Trading Commission (CFTC) has existed as a federal agency to oversee trade in commodity futures.

7. Are there different types of orders?

    Market order: This is an order that sells or buys at the price that can be attained when the order reaches the floor of the exchange. A market order such as "sell December cotton at the market" will be filled at the first available price when the order clears through a broker and reaches the floor of the exchange.

    Limit order: A specific price is included in the order and the order is filled only if it can be filled at the specific price or better. For example, the order "sell July wheat at $3.50" will be filled only if July wheat can be sold at $3.50 or higher. The order "buy March feeder cattle at $57.50" will be filled only if March feeder cattle can be bought at $57.50 or lower. With this type of order, there is no guarantee the order will be filled. The specific price may not be in the trading range for the particular day. It is possible the limit price will be touched or penetrated by a small amount and the order will not be filled if the market moves quickly.

    Stop order: The stop order includes a specific price and becomes a market order if penetrated. A "sell December live cattle at $58.00 stop" will become a market order if the trading level goes through $58.00 *from above.* An order such as "buy November soybeans at $7.00 stop" will become a market order if the trading level goes through $7.00 *from below.* Stop orders are used to limit losses or to enter the market when a major move in trading levels develops. For example, the "sell December live cattle at $58.00 stop" could be used to limit losses by the speculator who bought at $59.00, or it could be used by the hedger to sell December cattle if the market breaks lower from the $59.00 level.

    Stop close only order: This order is activated only if the closing price for the day penetrates a specified level. The order "buy 1 February pork belly at $82.05 stop close only" will be activated only if the February contract closes above $82.05. If the market closes at $82.20, for example, one February contract of 36,000 lbs. of frozen pork bellies would be bought at or near the close of $82.20.

    Other types of orders exist but these four are the basic ones. Chapters 9 and 10 will demonstrate use of the orders.

8. How is trade reported?

    Trade is reported in most major newspapers, especially morning papers and business papers such as the *Wall Street Journal,* in accordance with the following format:

		Commodity			
Month	Open	High	Low	Close	Change
August	55.10	55.60	54.90	55.45	+.25

If this were for August live hogs, for example, we would know that:

(1) Trade began or "opened" on this particular day at $55.10 per cwt.;
(2) The high trade or trades of the day occurred at $55.60;
(3) The low trade or trades occurred at $54.90;
(4) The last trade or trades occurred at a closing price of $55.45; and
(5) The closing price of $55.45 was $.25 per cwt. above the closing price of the previous day.

The opening price and the closing price will often be quoted as ranges. For examples, if the closing price above had been 55.45–.55, this means there were trades at levels from 55.45 to 55.55 as trade in August live hogs was completed at 12:55 CDT on the Chicago Mercantile Exchange. The exchange releases a "settlement" price, usually the midpoint or near the midpoint of the closing range, but the newspapers seldom pick this up and often use one side of the closing range.

9. What about margin requirements and margin calls?

There are two types of margin requirements: initial margins and maintenance margins. The initial margin is the money the trader must have on deposit with his broker, per contract, before trades can be made. A minimum is set by the exchange but brokerage firms can and often do require something above the exchange minimum. For example, a particular firm might require $1200 per contract for live cattle futures of 40,000 lbs. live weight. The maintenance margin is a threshold level that triggers a margin request or a request for more money to be deposited with the broker. Let's assume the maintenance margin is $800 per live cattle futures contract and illustrate as follows:

Date	Action
Feb. 1	Places cattle on feed, wires $1200 per contract to his broker, and sells August live cattle futures at $58.00 per cwt.

March 1   August futures close at $59.50. This means a debit in the account with the broker of $600--58.00-59.50 = -$1.50 per cwt. and each contract is 400 cwt. A margin call of $600 per contract would be sent to the cattle feeder to bring the account balance back up to $1200 per contract.

If the price continues to rise, more margin requests would be sent. If the price falls well below $58.00, the cattle feeder can ask for and receive all excess over $1200 per contract as profits accumulate.

10. To know how to read the literature and follow the markets, does a person need to know special terms? Yes.

Volume: the number of contracts traded during the day;

Open Interest: the number of outstanding contracts held by buyers and sellers (there must be a buyer for each seller and vice versa);

Bulls: traders who think the market will go higher;

Bullish: feeling the market will go higher;

Bears: traders who think the market will go lower;

Bearish: feeling the market will go lower;

Long: holding a "buy" position in the market;

Short: holding a "sell" position in the market;

Basis: the difference between futures and cash price at any point in time;

Limit move: the maximum change in price on a futures contract from the previous day's closing price (10 cents per bu. in corn, $1.50 per cwt. in live cattle, etc.);

Hedger: trader who takes the opposite position in cash and futures markets, seeking protection against cash price fluctuations and/or profits from his hedging operations;

Speculator: trader who seeks to make profits from moves in commodity futures by buying low and selling high or selling high and buying low;

Locals: traders on the floor of the exchanges who are primarily short-term speculators;

Commercials: traders in commodity futures who either have or represent clients who have interests in the cash product;

Fundamentals: the supply-demand forces at work in the market that influence level and direction of trade;

Fundamentalist: trader who subscribes to the supply-demand forces as being the relevant determinants of trading levels and price directions for commodity futures;
Technical: in contrast to fundamentals, refers to charts, chart positions, chart signals, and other technical means of trying to determine direction in the market;

Technician: trader who subscribes to the technical forces as being the relevant determinants of trading levels and price directions for commodity futures;

Spread: a trade that buys one futures contract and sells another, either for the same or different commodities, in an attempt to profit from changes in the relationship between the two contracts; and

Delivery period: period during the last month a futures contract trades when deliveries of the actual physical product under the provisions of the futures contract are allowed.

11. What are the key components of a hedge?

Break-even price: the cash price that would be required to break even for the operation in question.

Lock-in margin: the difference between the break-even price and the price at which futures are sold minus any adjustments for cost of delivery or other discounts.

12. How does a hedge work?

Date	Action
May 15	Plants soybeans and estimates break-even price at $4.50 per bushel.
	Checks November futures and finds they are trading at $6.50. Adjusts the $6.50 quote by $.30 to reflect the normal difference during early November between November futures and local cash.
May 16	Sells November futures at $6.50 and calculates a *lock-in margin* of ($6.50 − .30) −4.50 = $1.70 per bushel.

Regardless of the absolute level of price, the $1.70 will be realized when the cash product is sold and the futures bought back so long as the futures are $.30 above cash when the operation is completed.

13. Why does a hedge work?

   The hedge works because the futures market and cash market tend to come together as the futures contract approaches the final days of trading. If cash markets have fallen since the hedge was established, losses will develop in the cash operation. But futures will trade down with the cash market, and buying back futures well below the level at which they were sold will provide profits on the futures side of the hedge to offset the losses on the cash side.

14. How can we be sure the futures and cash markets will converge?

   Actions in the marketplace guarantee this. If futures during the delivery period are above cash by more than the cost of delivery, traders on or near the par delivery markets can buy the cash product, sell futures, and deliver—making a profit after paying the delivery costs. This forces convergence by putting buying pressure in the cash market and removing buying pressure from the futures. If futures are well below cash, traders who are long in futures would refrain from selling futures to cancel their position, accept delivery, and sell the physical product in the higher priced cash market.

15. Are risks involved with a hedge?

   The risks that remain are the risks associated with the lack of convergence to the expected level. This can be called *basis risk* and the hedge will not protect against this type of risk. In answering question 12 above, for example, the cash minus futures basis during November has been −30¢. Therefore, we would expect the basis to be near −30¢ in November when the cash beans are sold and the futures bought back. But if the basis is −40¢, we get

   Actual margin = $1.60 vs. lock-in margin of $1.70.

   Or if the basis is −20¢

   Actual margin = $1.80 vs. lock-in margin of $1.70.

16. If I do decide to deliver the commodity, what price do I get?

   The price at which the futures contract was originally sold. The net from delivery will be this price minus the costs of delivery.

17. If I hedge by selling futures at a very high price, doesn't this mean I will have to deliver to realize the high price?

   No. Whether prices have fallen or risen since the hedge was set has nothing to do with the wisdom of delivery. Whether delivery is wise—and it seldom is—depends on how much the net will be from delivery as compared to the net from selling the cash product and buying back the futures. And these nets are a function of the futures-cash relationship—the extent to which convergence has occurred—as trade in the futures contract nears completion.

18.   How do I get started?

Slowly, very slowly. Take the time to study and understand first. Learn to read and interpret charts. Develop an understanding of what is and is not possible in a hedging or speculative program. Trade seriously "on paper" first. Know what you are after, develop or adopt a system you believe will work, and stick with it.

19.   What is the single most important factor in success as a commodity trader?

Trading discipline—having the patience and control to stick with your system and wait for the right opportunity. Many traders master the techniques. The successful ones acquire or develop discipline.

20.   Where are the major commodities traded and what size are the contracts?

Commodity	Exchange	Contract Size
Corn	Chicago Board of Trade (CBT)	5,000 bu.
	Mid-America Exchange (MAE)	1,000 bu.
Soybeans	CBT	5,000 bu.
	MAE	1,000 bu.
Wheat	CBT (winter and spring wheats)	5,000 bu.
	MAE (winter and spring wheats)	1,000 bu.
	Kansas City Board of Trade (KBT, hard red winter)	5,000 bu.
	Minneapolis Board of Trade (MPLS, durum wheats)	5,000 bu.
Cotton	New York Commodity Exchange (NY)	50,000 lbs.
Cattle	Chicago Mercantile Exchange (CME)	40,000 lbs. live weight
	MAE	20,000 lbs. live weight
Feeder Cattle	CME	42,000 lbs. live weight
Hogs	CME	30,000 lbs. live weight
	MAE	15,000 lbs. live weight
Pork Bellies	CME	36,000 lbs. live weight

chapter nine

Trade in Commodity Futures

In Chapter 8, the role of the commodity markets in the marketing system was discussed. Trade in commodity futures provides a hedging mechanism that can be used to transfer price risk and becomes a factor in price discovery processes. Effective use of the commodity futures requires understanding the bases on which trade is conducted and being aware of widely used trading techniques. In this chapter the economic and technical dimensions of trade in commodity futures are explored. Chapter 10 will then develop strategies that the decision maker might employ in hedging programs.

Bases for Commodity Trade

The forces involved in commodity trade are usually identified as fundamental and technical. Both are important. An understanding of the two and how they exert influence in the market is a necessary prerequisite to effective trading.

FUNDAMENTAL FORCES

The fundamental forces are those that deal with the basic economic concepts of supply and demand. Traders who stress the fundamental dimensions of the market watch indicators that have the potential to shift supply, demand, or both. Positions are taken in the futures market based on decision makers' interpretations of the supply-demand picture.

Table 9.1 illustrates the fundamental information that influences the trading level of corn futures. Total supply for the crop year beginning on October 1 is made up of beginning stocks plus production. The demand or "disappearance" components consist of domestic demand for feeding purposes, for seed, food and industrial uses, and exports. For a given set of these supply-demand indicators, futures prices tend to focus in on an equilibrium or market-clearing level. Fluctuations in trading levels are due primarily to varying interpretations of the supply-demand forces, to rumors of new or pending developments that will change supply or demand, and to the influence of other grains or the oilseeds such as soybeans and soybean meal.

Significant changes in the fundamental picture are usually accompanied by significant changes in the trading level of futures for the commodity where the change in fundamentals has evolved. The clearest examples of this are seen in the price reactions to a new USDA estimate of corn production, cotton production, or a *Cattle on Feed* report. In corn, for example, it is not the fact that the estimate is changed from earlier esti-

Table 9.1
Supply-Demand Balance Sheet for Corn for
1977–78 [a]

Item	Million Bushels
Beginning Stocks	884
Production	6,357
Imports	1
Total Supply	7,242
Feed	3,750
Food, seed, industrial	535
Exports	1,750
Total Disappearance	6,035
Ending Stocks	1,207

[a]For the crop year beginning October 1. The table values are estimates from the June 23, 1978 issue of *Agricultural Supply and Demand Estimates*, USDA.

mates that causes the sharp price reaction. Prices react when the change is of a sufficient magnitude to be a surprise to the trade, and exceeds traders' expectations as to what the increase or decrease would be. If the change is within the range of traders' expectations, little or no price reaction will occur. In other words, the market has "discounted" the new estimate and prices have made their adjustment in anticipation of the report. In Figure 9.1, the move in expected supply from S_0S_0 to S_1S_1 could be a reaction to dry weather during the summer months. December corn futures move up and trade around a price of OP_1. But if the September crop production report by the USDA puts corn supply at S_2S_2, the December futures will trade sharply higher. The adjustment by the trade was not enough, further drought damage needs to be "discounted," and higher prices will be the result.

The fundamental forces for a commodity such as live cattle, which are produced year round, are different but the general relationships to futures trade hold. As in the grain complex, it is the piece of information that is a surprise that moves trading levels of the futures. In cattle, it may be a report of the number of cattle on feed that is inconsistent with traders' expectations. In hogs, unexpectedly high farrowings could be the piece of information that precipitates a downward adjustment in trading levels for live hog futures.

The fundamental forces of supply and demand that underlie the market are never known with certainty. The trading level for a commodity futures contract on any particular trading day represents a consensus as to what the price of the product will be at the future date or in the future month. But the traders formulating that consensus may have varying degrees of access to basic supply-demand information. Clearly, their analytical abilities and capacities to interpret the information at their disposal will differ. And the consensus on any day is based on a particular body of information in existence on that day. When the body of information changes, the consensus will also change—and price levels react.

STORABLE COMMODITIES

For the commodities such as wheat, corn, or cotton the components of the fundamental picture are clear. Since production is on a seasonal basis, the domestic supply of the product is largely fixed at the end of the harvest period. The hedgers, who are seeking protection, and the speculators who trade from a fundamental picture will examine:

1. Total supply comprised of beginning stocks plus production or expected production;

2. Expected total disappearance including exports and domestic use;

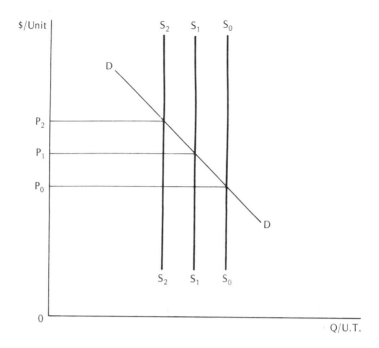

FIGURE 9.1   ILLUSTRATION OF CHANGING EXPECTATIONS OF CORN PRODUC-
TION ON PRICE OF DECEMBER FUTURES

3. Expected ending stocks given the total supply and estimates of total disappearance; and

4. Prospects for the upcoming crop.

These pieces of information must be incorporated into some type of analytical framework to allow formation of price expectations.

For the storable commodities, a great deal of attention has been paid to ending stocks and the relationship between ending stocks and yearly average price. Figure 9.2 illustrates the relationship between ending stocks and yearly average price for wheat. When the ending stocks move very much above 500 million bushels, prices tend to be relatively low and stable. When the ending stocks shrink to levels well below 500 million bushels, prices tend to move sharply higher and exhibit more volatility.[1]

The task of the fundamental analyst is to integrate the various pieces of information and formulate price expectations. Ending stocks are important but during the several months before the end of the crop year (May 30 for wheat, August 31 for soybeans, September 30 for corn) a combination of expected ending stocks and projected new-crop production becomes relevant. Also to be considered are such factors as the following:

1. The normal seasonal price pattern. A seasonal index based on a 12-month moving average as explained in Chapter 7 is useful.

2. Expected developments in exports. Weather in other major producing countries should be monitored. Changes in the health of the economy of major buyers such as Japan and the western European countries influence their ability to buy.

3. Grain stocks on a world-wide basis. Expectations of continued decreases in world stocks provide a strong undertone of support to the market. Prices tend to rise during years when consumption exceeds production and stocks decrease.

The overall package of information may vary among decision makers but any decision maker who trades using the fundamental picture must (1) assemble information, and (2) incorporate that information into an analytical framework for decision purposes.

Consider the position of the soybean producer who is trying to decide whether to hedge a growing bean crop. Chapter 10 will deal with complex

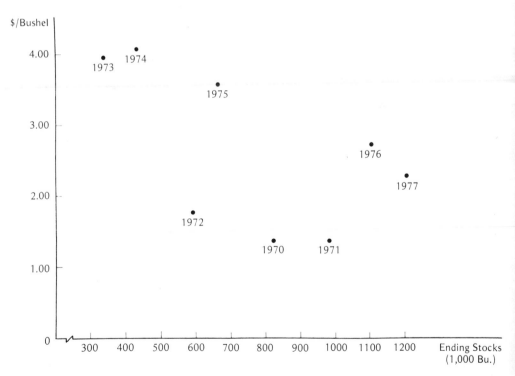

FIGURE 9.2 RELATIONSHIP BETWEEN ENDING STOCKS AND PRICES RECEIVED BY FARMERS FOR WHEAT, U.S., 1970–77

hedging strategies. At this point, we will assume the producer is going to make a yes-no decision on hedging and hold the hedge until the cash beans are sold.

The first need is an estimate of what the price will be at harvest. With soybean plantings primarily in May, this means the needed price expectation must be made months in advance. Among the important pieces of economic information are:

1. Stocks of soybeans, soybean meal, and soybean oil during the spring months.

2. Prospective plantings of soybeans. Estimates of plantings are released by the USDA during the third week of January and April for intentions of January 1 and April 1, respectively.

3. Production in other major producing countries, primarily Brazil. Harvest of Brazilean beans is completed during April and May and this is important information with regard to the total world supply.

After accumulating this and possibly other fundamental information, the producer must decide on a price expectation or forecast to use in deciding whether to hedge his crop. Figure 9.3 illustrates the situation and

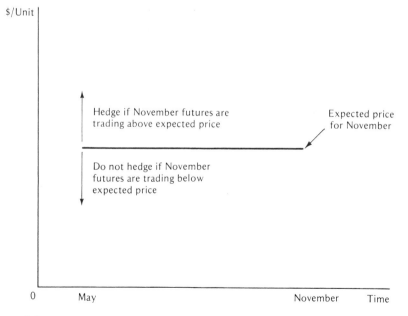

FIGURE 9.3 CONCEPTUAL FRAMEWORK FOR DECIDING WHETHER TO HEDGE SOYBEANS BASED ON EXPECTATIONS DURING PLANTING SEASON

provides a conceptual base that can be used in making the hedge-no hedge decision. If the November soybean futures are trading significantly above the expected cash price, a decision to hedge would appear to be a logical decision. A decision to not hedge would appear logical if the futures are trading below the cash price expectation.[2]

The speculator who trades on the basis of fundamental information conducts a similar analysis but with a different objective in mind. His aim is to determine the direction in which fundamental forces will push price and to take a position that will earn a profit if his analysis proves to be correct.

Figure 9.4 illustrates the type of market the speculator trading on the basis of fundamental information would like to see.[3] During the October-November harvest period, prices were in the $6.00–$6.80 range. Prices moved slightly higher during early January and February and "took off" to higher ground in late February. Through early February, the fundamental analysts were monitoring the following developments:

1. Total supply for the crop year, which began September 1, was down relative to the previous year. Both harvested acreage and per acre yields were down and the beginning stocks were small.

2. Export demand for soybeans, soybean meal, and soybean oil was strong from October through January. Weekly export levels were comparable to year-earlier levels when the total supply of available beans was much larger.

3. The domestic crush of beans was relatively high based on a strong demand for soybean meal and soybean oil.

Projecting the January-February levels of disappearance—exports plus domestic—the fundamental analyst concluded there would be zero ending stocks. Disappearance would apparently have to be controlled or rationed. In an exchange economy, higher prices are the rationing mechanism. Based on this conclusion, the speculator trading on fundamental information might have decided to buy August soybean futures in late February around the $7.50 level. Holding such a position to the $10.00 level would mean a gross profit of $12,500 per contract.[4]

NON-STORABLE COMMODITIES

The important difference in the fundamental price picture for the non-storable commodity is the possibility of changes in domestic supply within the year. Examples include slaughter cattle, hogs, broilers, pork bellies, and turkeys.

As with the storable commodity, the fundamental analyst will be examining the economic forces that affect supply and demand. The proce-

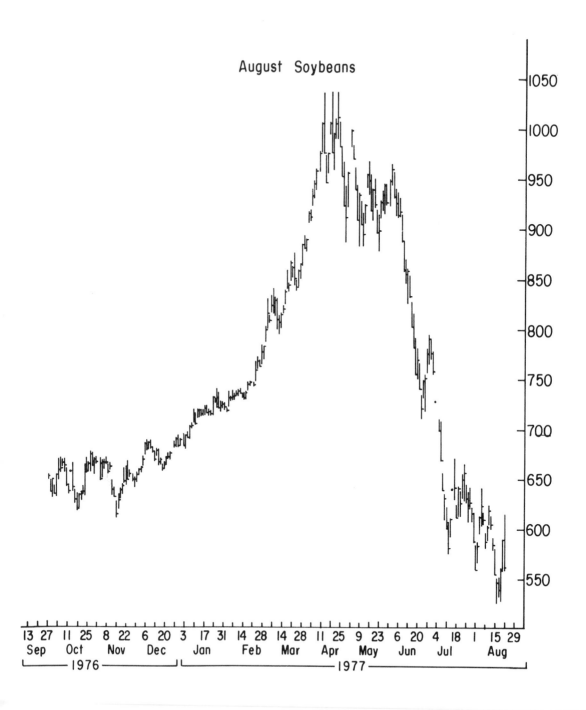

FIGURE 9.4   TRADING PATTERN FOR AUGUST 1977 SOYBEANS

dure is similar. Using slaughter hogs to briefly illustrate, the analyst will be monitoring such information as:

1. The number of hogs and pigs on farms for breeding purposes and the number kept for market by weight groups. This information is available in late March, June, September, and December for conditions as of the first of the respective months from the USDA's *Hogs and Pigs* report. Projecting the number in each weight group to a finished or slaughter weight gives an initial and useful estimate of hog slaughter in any particular month or quarter.

2. Farrowings and farrowing intentions are important pieces of information also available from the USDA's *Hogs and Pigs* report. The number of pigs farrowed in a particular quarter will directly influence the number of slaughter hogs going to market six to eight months later.

3. Seasonal price patterns in hogs are important. Prices are generally strong in February and again in the June–August period. A seasonal index for hogs was shown in Table 7.6.

4. The status of the production and price cycles in hogs is also important. During any particular year, the building or liquidation phases of the cycle can affect supply and have a pronounced impact on price.

Figure 9.5 gives an indication of the impact a significant change in fundamental information can have on trading levels for live hog futures. The *Hogs and Pigs* report released by the USDA on March 21 revealed the number of hogs and pigs on farms was well below the expectations of most traders. Prices traded significantly higher in the days following the report.

Of major importance in fundamental analysis of a non-storable commodity such as hogs is the possibility of changing the available supply within the year. Producers can and do react to changing profit possibilities by changing the supply of product produced and offered for sale. But the fundamental analyst must exercise caution here in formulating expectations for future hog prices. There is typically a significant time lag between the emergence of a favorable sign such as a higher hog-corn ratio and the availability of expanded production on the market. As discussed in Chapter 7, both a biological and behavioral lag are present.[5]

There is a parallel in the cattle industry, especially in the cattle feeding sector. The three key variables in the profit picture for the cattle feeder are (1) corn or other feed grain prices, (2) price of feeder cattle of weights that could be placed on feed, and (3) the expected price for the finished slaughter steer. With the typical feeding period ranging from 100–180 days, up to

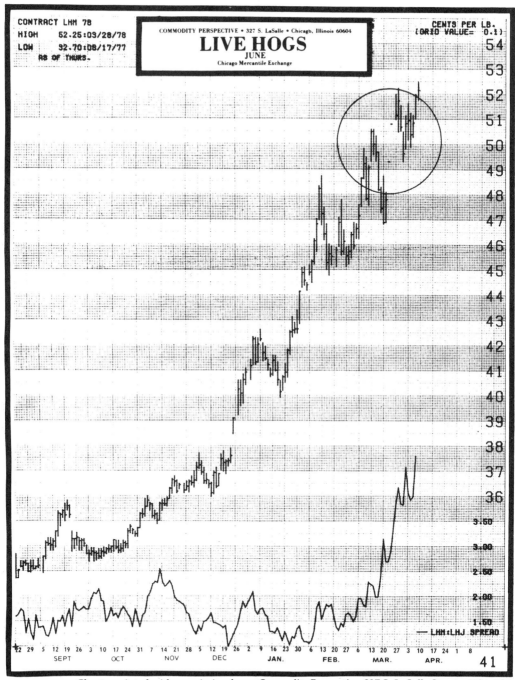

Chart reprinted with permission from: *Commodity Perspective*, 327 S. LaSalle Street, #536, Chicago, Ill. 60604.

FIGURE 9.5 **IMPACT ON LIVE HOG FUTURES OF A** *HOGS AND PIGS* **REPORT WITH NUMBERS BELOW THOSE EXPECTED BY THE TRADE**

six months is required before the cattle finish and are sold. And this gives time for the fundamental supply-demand picture to change.

A direct relationship to the futures market is established by the tendency for cattle feeders to use current or spot quotes in distant live cattle futures as a price expectation for fed cattle. Table 9.2 reviews and supplements coverage in Chapter 8 of the events of 1974. During late July and early August of this particular year, the December live cattle futures traded up to the $50 level. Placements of cattle into feedlots increased as cattle feeders reacted. The weekly average price of feeder steers was "bid up" significantly in late July and August. Placements in the seven major cattle feeding states during July were up 50 percent over June and up seven percent over July of the previous year.

The analyst who monitored these developments was in a position to predict at least the direction of the subsequent move in the December

---

Table 9.2
Developments in Prices, Costs, and the Results of Hedged and Unhedged Feeding Programs During a Selected Period of 1974

Weekly Average Prices

Week Ended	Choice 600–700 lb. Feeder Steers, Okla. City ($/cwt.)	Corn, No. 2 Yellow, Chicago ($/bu.)	December Live Cattle Futures Closes ($/cwt.)
July 6	34.75	3.14	42.70
13	33.95	3.39	43.75
20	32.00	3.56	45.45
27	35.00	3.74	47.92
August 3	36.50	3.69	49.08
10	36.20	3.58	47.85

For cattle placed during week ending August 3:

	Hedged	Unhedged
Break-even cost ($/cwt.)	44.35	44.35
Average Close Dec. Futures	49.08	—
Average Cash, Omaha, Week Ending Dec. 6	37.12	37.12
Average Close Dec. Futures Week Ending Dec. 6	38.62	—
Net After Commissions ($/cwt.)	+3.10	−7.23

futures. As awareness of the increased placements filtered through the trade, expectations for slaughter and beef production in the November-December period were adjusted upward accordingly. The December futures traded down to the mid-$30's and went off the board on the last trading day showing a settlement price of $37.90 per cwt.

Clearly, the capacity to change production levels within the year is an important economic variable when analyzing price patterns and outlook for the non-storable commodity. The trader who trades on the basis of fundamentals must isolate the developments that signal a change in production levels and bring these into his decision model.

TECHNICAL BASES FOR TRADE

The techniques of trade in commodity futures is a broad and complex subject. It is a growing and maturing "art" as new procedures are being developed and tested. In this section, attention will be focused on selected dimensions of technical trading.

If the fundamental picture should be the determinant of *whether* to hedge, the technical picture is clearly the determinant of *when* to hedge. After analyzing the fundamentals to project the direction of price movement, the technical tools can be used to supplement the analysis on direction of price trend and guide the timing of buy-sell actions.

The tools of the technical trader can therefore be conveniently divided into those concerned with day-to-day or even intra-day considerations, and those concerned with market directions over time. A logical approach is to apply the long-run tools to trade in a particular commodity, determine the trend in the market, and then use the short-run tools for a planned program of entry and exit.

LONG-RUN TECHNICAL TOOLS

One of the most widely used approaches to ascertaining the long-run trend in the market involves use of the familiar bar chart. An upward trending market is identified by a "trend line" connecting lows of the daily trading ranges. The trend line is moving higher through successive trading days or weeks. Figure 9.6 provides an illustration. The trend line labeled "AA" slopes upward and continues to signal an upward trending market until the break, which occurs in the encircled area. Two successive closes below the trend line are widely employed as an indication of a change in direction in the market and are a strong sell signal. To integrate this technical dimension with the fundamental approach, we could argue the market has moved as high as the underlying fundamental or supply-demand picture will allow. The market then changes directions, penetrates the technical support provided by the trend line, and proceeds to move lower.

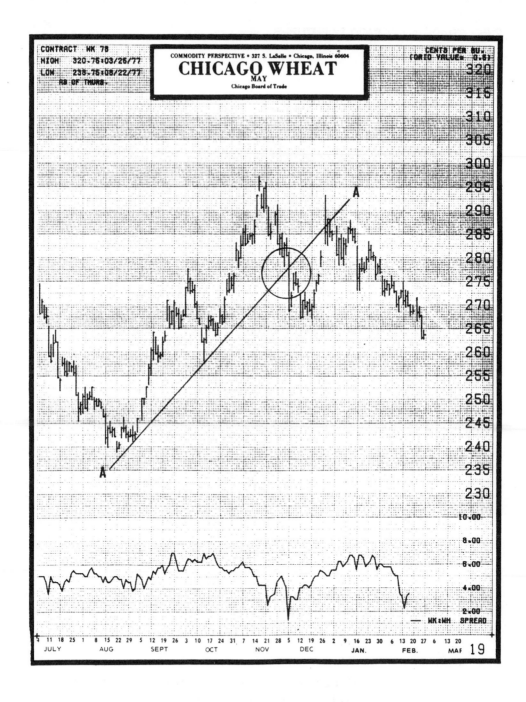

Chart reprinted with permission from: *Commodity Perspective*, 327 S. LaSalle Street, #536, Chicago, Ill. 60604.

FIGURE 9.6 ASCENDING TREND LINE ILLUSTRATING A BREAK WITH A CLOSE BELOW THE TREND LINE

235

A downward trending market is identified by a trend line connecting "tops" or the high end of daily trading ranges. An illustration is shown in Figure 9.7. Interpreting the trend line is similar to that in the upward trending market. Two successive closes *above* the trend line in the encircled area signal a "break out" and a change in the market direction.

An upward or downward trending "trading channel" is an indicator of trend that is closely related to the trend-line approach. Figure 9.8 provides an illustration. An upward trending channel is established as follows:

1. Draw a trend line under the lows to form the bottom of the channel;

2. Examine the trading ranges, especially the short-run price surges, to see whether the tops can be connected with a line roughly parallel to the bottom channel line; and

3. Draw in the top of the channel with a line *parallel* to the bottom and touching the top of the trading range that gives you the widest channel.

The procedure is reversed for a "down channel." Clearly, some experience and judgment are required in determining whether the parallel lines requirement fits the trading ranges on the chart.

Once the channel is established, a "break out" either up or down is possible. An upside break from an upward trending channel as illustrated on Figure 9.8 is a strong bullish sign and indicates added intensity to the upward trend. A break on the downside is analogous to the break when only a trend line is used and indicates a change in market direction.

In using trend lines and channels on a bar chart, a few guidelines should be followed:

1. Trend lines connecting widely separated points on the time continuum have more validity and reliability than trend lines connecting highs or lows only a few days apart. On Figure 9.9, the trend line labeled AA will offer more resistance to a move to lower prices than would the trend line labeled BB. Once the trend line is "honored" by a trading range that moves to it and retracts, the trend line is even stronger. This occurred in the encircled area on Figure 9.9.

2. A trading range that penetrates the trend line should be traded with care. If the close is not below (or above) the trend line, no "break out" has occurred. Figure 9.10 illustrates. In the encircled area, the trading range penetrated the trend line but the market rallied and the close was above the trend line.

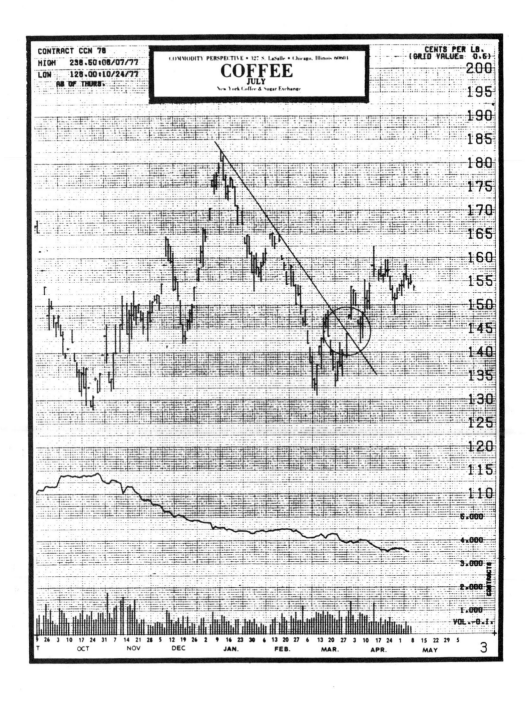

Chart reprinted with permission from: *Commodity Perspective*, 327 S. LaSalle Street, #536, Chicago, Ill. 60604.

FIGURE 9.7 DESCENDING TREND LINE ILLUSTRATING A BREAK WITH A CLOSE ABOVE THE TREND LINE

237

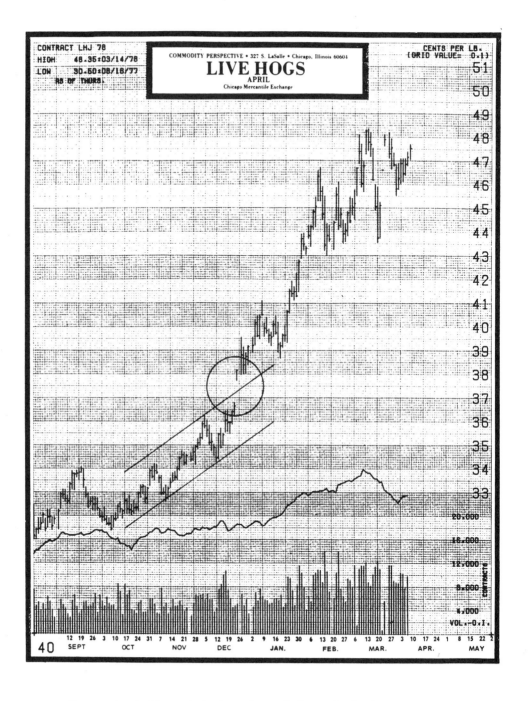

Chart reprinted with permission from: *Commodity Perspective*, 327 S. LaSalle Street, #536, Chicago, Ill. 60604.

FIGURE 9.8   ASCENDING TRADING CHANNEL FEATURING A BREAK OUT TO THE UP SIDE

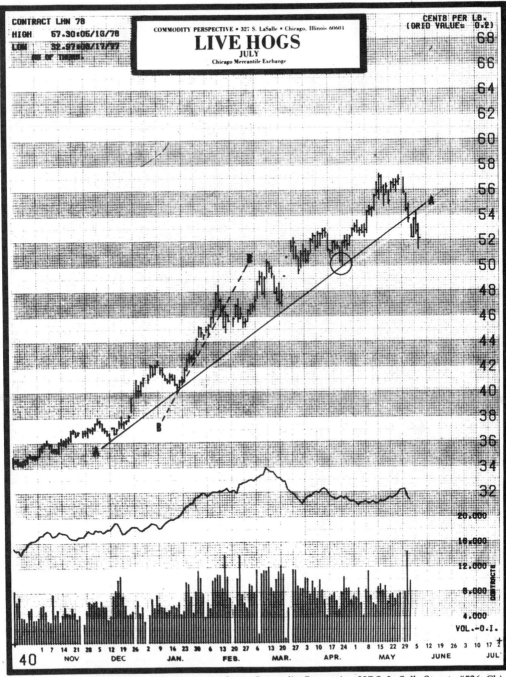

Chart reprinted with permission from: *Commodity Perspective*, 327 S. LaSalle Street, #536, Chicago, Ill. 60604.

FIGURE 9.9   LONG-RUN, SHORT-RUN TREND LINES ILLUSTRATING THE RESISTANCE OFFERED BY THE LONG-RUN TREND

Chart reprinted with permission from: *Commodity Perspective*, 327 S. LaSalle Street, #536, Chicago, Ill. 60604.

FIGURE 9.10   PENETRATION OF THE TREND LINE BUT THE CLOSE FAILS TO CONFIRM A BREAK

3. The potential for a significant follow-through after a break out is greater if the break out occurs on relatively high volume. An illustration can be found on Figure 9.11. The break and close below the trend line occurred on a day when trading volume was high compared to normal. A significant follow-through to the downside then resulted.

4. Open interest can sometimes be used to give an early warning of an impending break. This is especially true when the trend is upward. Continued higher prices require capital to "finance" the move. Having a trader willing to buy is not enough—there must be someone, hedger or speculator, willing to sell at successively higher levels. In other words, new buying *and* new selling are needed to finance a continued bull market and when both are present, open interest climbs. When open interest starts to level off and/or decline, this means the new selling has been exhausted and the selling that is occurring is profit taking or the canceling of long positions. As the trend in open interest switches to horizontal or down, a price break downward may well follow.

In a sideways channel or congestion area, changes in open interest may also be significant. Consider Figure 9.12. The market moved down and formed a congestion area. When open interest began to fall, one possible interpretation is that the large commercial firms had decided the price would not slip lower and were beginning to lift their short hedges. As this perspective spread through the trade, the balance of opinion began to shift and the market was ready to move higher. Producers or commercial firms still interested in lifting hedges will push a move from such a congestion area with a willingness to buy that is supplemented by speculative longs buying the break out.

Other types of trend indicators are, of course, used. Long-run moving averages are favored by some traders. For example, a 10-week moving average of the average weekly close (or the close on Friday or some other particular day) is used to help identify the direction of the market. The trader who uses this tool would use short-run technical indicators to tell him to enter the market on the long side if the 10-week moving average is moving up, on the short side if it is falling.

Various oscillators are used to indicate trend direction. It sometimes appears there are as many approaches as there are traders. Summarizing the area is difficult because what will work in one commodity will often not work in another commodity. Even within a commodity market, there are periods of time or price patterns which evolve which will simply negate the effectiveness of any trend indicator. As a general rule, the trend indicators should be employed as long-run tools with their success measured over time and not based on the first application.

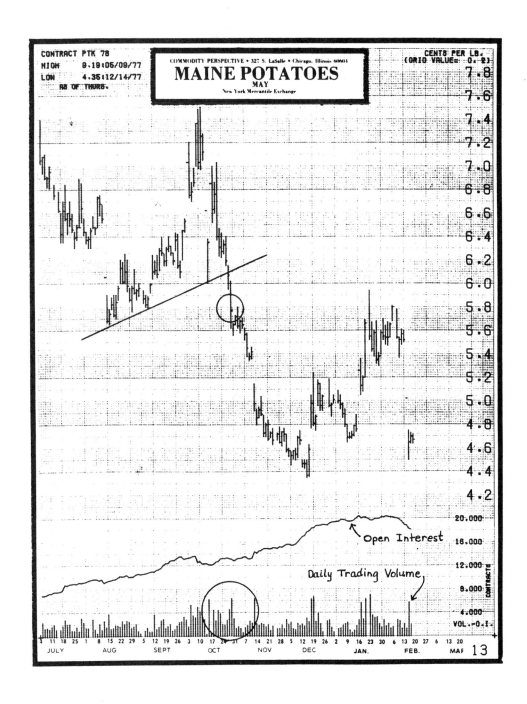

Chart reprinted with permission from: *Commodity Perspective*, 327 S. LaSalle Street, #536, Chicago, Ill. 60604.

FIGURE 9.11   BREAK OUT CONFIRMED BY RELATIVELY HIGH DAILY VOLUME

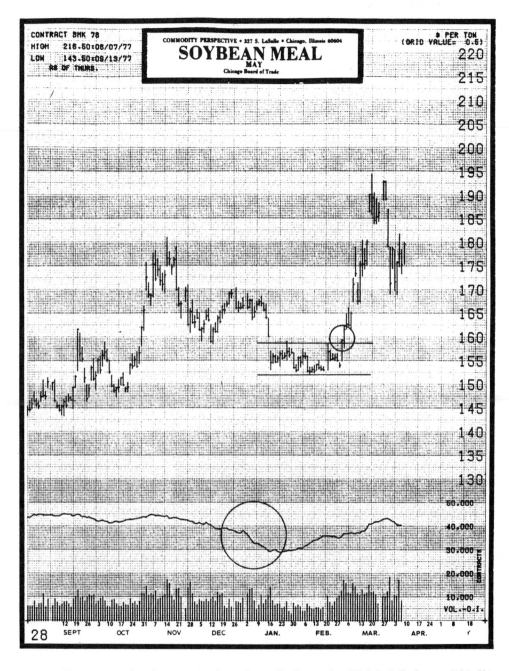

Chart reprinted with permission from: *Commodity Perspective*, 327 S. LaSalle Street, #536, Chicago, Ill. 60604.

FIGURE 9.12 CONGESTION AREA, DECLINING OPEN INTEREST, AND A BREAK OUT TO THE TOP SIDE

243

Moving averages have long been used as both trend indicators and also as a basis for buy and sell decisions in the commodity markets. They have been adopted as technical tools by hedgers who use them to place hedges when the moving averages signal a price move against the hedger. Moving averages are also used by speculators to determine when to buy (sell) when trend indicators are signaling an up (down) market. Some speculative traders ignore the general direction of the market and both buy and sell using the moving average signals.

A sketch of 3- and 10-day moving averages is shown in Figure 9.13.[6] A sell signal is generated at point A when the 3-day crosses the 10-day average from above. A buy signal is generated at point B when the 3-day crosses the 10-day from below.

The theory behind the moving averages is relatively simple. During an up market, the shorter moving average will "lead" (will stay above) the longer moving average. When the market changes directions and turns down, the shorter average turns more quickly and crosses the longer average. This crossing action is used as a sell signal. Buy signals are generated by the shorter average crossing the longer average from below. Figure 9.14 demonstrates with a plot of the 3- and 10-day moving averages below the bar chart for the same time period.

The length of the moving averages is an important determinant of their effectiveness. As a general rule, the shorter sets (such as the 3- and

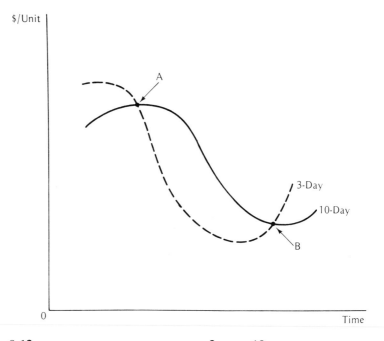

FIGURE 9.13   SELL AND BUY SIGNALS WITH 3- AND 10-DAY MOVING AVERAGES

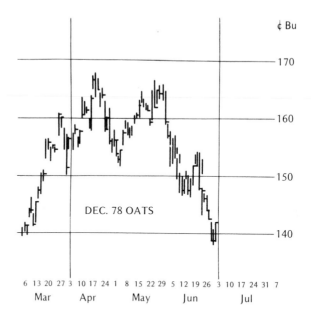

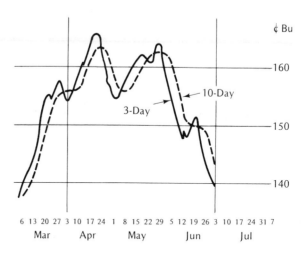

FIGURE 9.14   ILLUSTRATION OF THE RELATIONSHIP BETWEEN THE 3- AND 10-DAY MOVING AVERAGES AND THE BAR CHART

10-day) will generate more frequent sales than a longer set (such as the 5- and 20-day). Even if the base average is the same (say the 10-day) using a 3-day as a lead average will generate more trades than will the 5-day as a lead average. What is needed is a set that meets the following dual and somewhat competitive criteria:

1. The averages need to be responsive to changes in market direction and give signals in time for effective positions to be taken in the market; and

2. The averages need to avoid the "false signals" that occur when the market changes direction in the short run but then resumes the original direction. (In other words, the averages should avoid signaling action each time a small technical correction occurs in the market but the general trend remains intact.)

Table 9.3 illustrates these two points. During the time period shown, the 3- and 10-day combination generated frequent trades but also generated many "false signals". The 5- and 15-day combination generated fewer signals and was better able to correctly stay with the general direction of the market.

Thus, going to a longer set of averages eliminates some of the false signals generated by the shorter sets. But this improvement has a limit. If the set is too long and too slow to generate signals, it is not responsive to changes in market direction and can generate signals that are often actually inversely related to short-run market direction. All moving averages will have trouble in a choppy market that drifts sideways at the same price levels and shows no sustained moves in either direction. Use of a "lead indicator" as a confirmation of the buy or sell decision can help eliminate the problem of false signals and improve the effectiveness of the averages.

Table 9.3

Comparison of 3 and 10 with 5- and 15-Day Moving Averages in a Trading Program for Slaughter Cattle [a]

Averages	No. Trades [b]	Net After Commissions	Per Trade Average
3 and 10	873	$10,010	$11.47
5 and 15	544	$45,356	$83.38

[a]The results from short trades are shown. When the moving averages indicated a bottom and gave a buy signal, the short positions were lifted but no long position was ever taken. The period covered was 1965–1976.
[b]The number of trades needs explanation. The averages were calculated and used to trade *each* contract on the board. Since there are at least 6 contracts being traded at any point in time, up to 6 trades could be initiated on a particular day if the averages gave a signal for all contracts. If only one contract were being traded as part of a hedging program, the number of trades would be around 150 for the 3 and 10 and around 90 for the 5 and 15. Across a 12-year period, this would not be an excessive number of trades.

Source: Wayne D. Purcell, "Effective Hedging of Live Cattle," *Commodities*, Cedar Falls, Iowa: Vol. 6, July 1977.

Table 9.4
Impact of the 4-Day Weighted Moving Average as a Lead Indicator in Long Hedges on Feeder Cattle[a]

Averages Used to Place and Lift Strategies	No. Trades	Per Head Contribution After Commissions
5 and 10	942	$10.71
5, 10 and 4W	738	11.47
5 and 15	707	8.48
5, 15 and 4W	622	9.43

[a]The analysis from which these comparisons are adapted covered the period 1972–76 using a 90-day planning horizon. Each week, the cattle feeder was presumed to look ahead to feeder cattle needs 90 days into the futures and hedge against rising prices for feeder cattle. These are therefore long hedging strategies. Note the use of the 4W lead indicator reduced the number of trades and increased the per head contribution for both sets of averages.

Source: Wayne D. Purcell, "The Long Hedge on Feeder Cattle: A Closer Look," *Commodities*, Cedar Falls, Iowa: Vol. 7, August 1978.

Table 9.4 records the results when a weighted 4-day moving average is used with the 5- and 10-day combination and the 5- and 15-day combination.[7] Using the 5- and 15-day combination to illustrate, the weighted 4-day moving average is used as follows:

> Accept the buy (sell) decision generated when the 5-day crosses the 15-day from below (above) if the 4-day weighted moving average *leads* the 5-day through the 15-day.

This rule means the 4-day weighted must be *below* the 5-day when the 5-day crosses the 15-day from above if the sell signal is to be honored (and *above* the 5-day when the buy signal is generated).

The theory behind the use of a weighted moving average as a lead indicator and a device to confirm the signal is also relatively simple. When a market moves higher and then reverses direction for a short-run setback or technical correction, forces may be set into motion that will ultimately lead to the 5-day crossing the 15-day and signaling a sell. If the market then proceeds to move sharply higher, we have a signal for a "false top" and this can be costly. But the weighted 4-day average is much more responsive to recovery from the technical setback and will turn sharply higher on the basis of higher closes for the most recent trading days. In sum, therefore, the 4-day weighted moving average provides protection against at least part of the false signals that would otherwise be generated. For any particular futures contract and for a given time period, fewer trades will be made and the average profit per trade will usually be greater when the weighted lead indicator is used.

SHORT-RUN TECHNICAL TOOLS

A necessary condition to effective trade in commodity futures is the ability to enter and exit the market at the right time. Whether the trader is a hedger or speculator, timing of trades is extremely important.

Commodity trade, even with the vast array of technical tools at the disposal of the trader, is far from an exact science. The successful traders exhibit what the novice calls a "feel" for the market and a related ability to predict direction of price movement. But most of this ability is not magical—it comes from hard work, careful study of the market, and the informed use of workable technical tools.

The *bar chart* is again the base. In the previous section there was discussion of buying or selling break outs when a trend line is violated. The bar chart deserves more careful study as a basis for short-run guides to action.

Trend-line analysis is the most important direct application of the bar chart. Reading the charts looks simple and easy—but it is neither simple nor easy. Go back and look at the chart shown in Figure 9.6. Ex post, the trend line drawn there is obviously relevant. But there are countless other possibilities. Figure 9.15 reproduces the same chart and shows some of the many "trend lines" that could be drawn in. Watching the chart develop on a day-to-day basis brings some difficult questions on what is and is not a legitimate trend line. The message is becoming clear. The long-run trend lines connecting tops or bottoms widely separated, as we have suggested earlier, are the more valid trend lines. Once these are drawn in, the trader has something he can use to help him enter the market with a more favorable risk-potential tradeoff. Consider the area that is encircled on Figure 9.16. With the major trend line drawn in and established, a buy order just above the trend line (in the encircled area) would have allowed entry into the market with considerable confidence the market would trade higher. A close-only sell stop under the trend line offers protection if the trend line does not hold. As a technical aid to entry and exit from a market, few approaches offer more protection than the major long-run trend line. Repeated observations of trading ranges that go to a major trend line and then retreat make a useful and important point—many traders are looking at the same chart with the same trend line. Orders placed in expectation the trend line will "hold," tend to make it hold, and ensure this technical tool will be operational.

Various formations are used on the bar chart. Most involve attempts to recognize and/or predict "tops" or "bottoms" in the market. With some, there are procedures that allow a projection of how far the market will move once the break out occurs.

One of the most popular chart patterns is the head and shoulders bottom or top. Figure 9.17 illustrates a head and shoulders bottom. As the

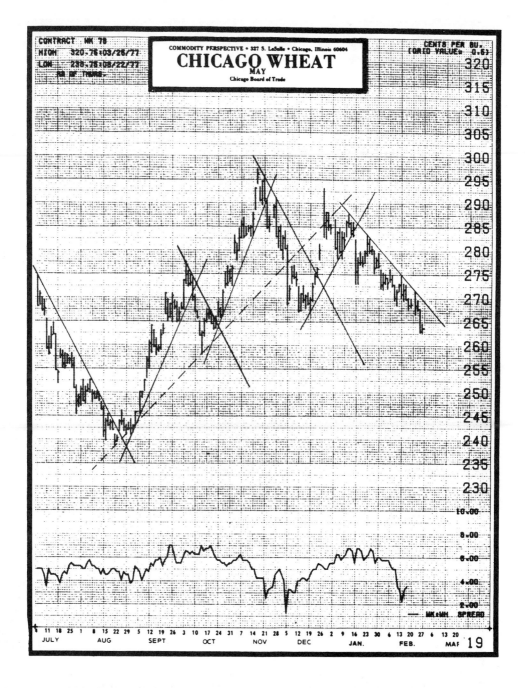

Chart reprinted with permission from: *Commodity Perspective,* 327 S. LaSalle Street, #536, Chicago, Ill. 60604.

FIGURE 9.15   ILLUSTRATION OF THE DIFFICULTIES INVOLVED IN DECIDING WHICH TREND LINES TO USE

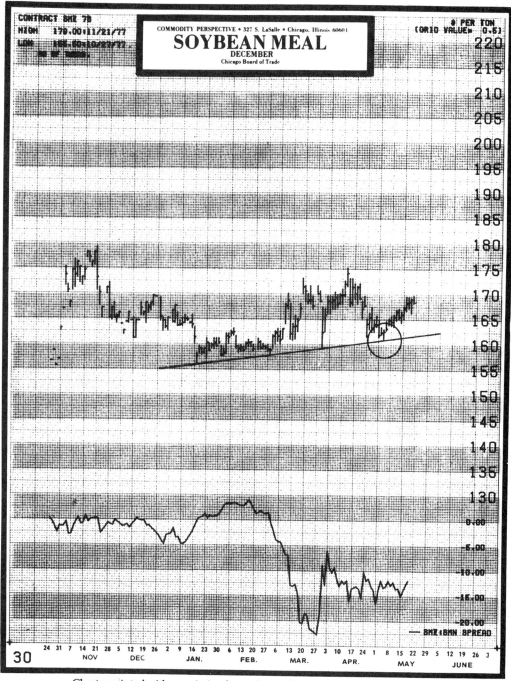

Chart reprinted with permission from: *Commodity Perspective,* 327 S. LaSalle Street, #536, Chicago, Ill. 60604.

FIGURE 9.16   ILLUSTRATION OF USE OF THE MAJOR TREND LINE AS AN OPPORTUNITY TO BUY FUTURES WITH MINIMUM RISK

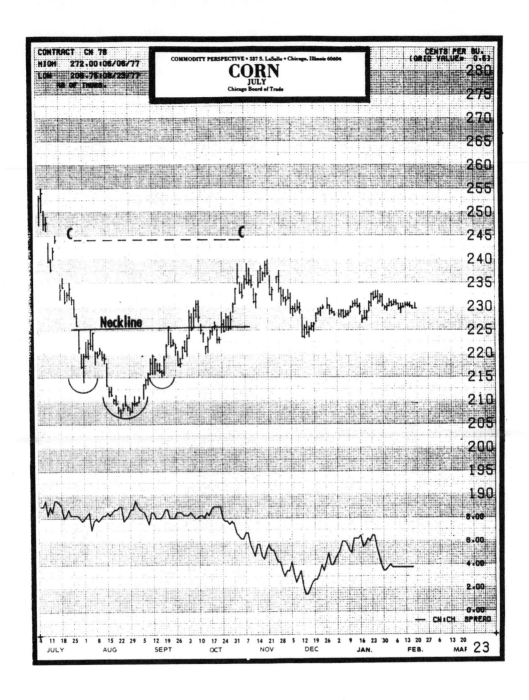

Chart reprinted with permission from: *Commodity Perspective*, 327 S. LaSalle Street, #536, Chicago, Ill. 60604.

FIGURE 9.17 ILLUSTRATION OF A HEAD AND SHOULDERS BOTTOM WITH PRICE PROJECTIONS AFTER A BREAK OUT

left shoulder is being formed, volume tends to increase and then decline as the "neckline" is completed. Price moves slightly lower to form the "head" of the formation and then starts to increase, usually with expanding volume as the head is completed. The right shoulder is formed with falling prices, declining volume during formation of the neckline, and some increase in volume as the shoulder is completed.

A line connecting the highs on each side of the head positions the neckline. A break out develops when price moves through the neckline after the right shoulder is completed. If it is to be a "true" break out, it will occur on a high volume day. Once the break out occurs, the move up will approximate the vertical distance between the bottom of the head and the neckline. On Figure 9.17, this suggests price will rise by an amount X to the level marked by the line CC. Comparable interpretations are valid for the head and shoulders top.

A double or triple bottom or top is often seen on the bar charts. Figure 9.18 illustrates a double top. Prices decline after the move up to level AA. New strength emerges and prices move up to level AA again. When the market falters on this second move up and is unable to push through and close above the earlier highs, the formation of a top becomes more evident. This is especially true if the open interest begins to level off or decline at the higher price levels indicating a decline in the new buying and new selling that is needed to finance still higher prices. If volume is high with the shrinking open interest the picture is even more clear—heavy profit taking is occurring. High volume and increasing open interest as the move down begins tend to confirm the top as new selling begins to develop and drives the price lower. There is no definitive way to project the magnitude of the price movement from such a top or bottom. As a general rule, the price move will be greater the broader the congestion area from which the break comes.

In addition to various types of bottoms and tops, a number of recognizable formations on the bar charts are either congestion areas or consolidation patterns. Both can be a "resting area" in the middle of a major move up or down.

Triangles are an example and are a common formation on bar charts. The so-called ascending triangle typically occurs in a bull market and represents a technical correction or hesitation before a move to still higher prices. Figure 9.19 illustrates this type of triangle. The magnitude of the price move after the break out can be estimated by measuring the distance from the base of the triangle (point A) to the break out (point B) and extending this distance horizontally to point C. Then draw a parallel to the ascending line connecting the lows in the triangle and extend it to the vertical plane over point C, to point D. Price will be expected to reach at least the plane represented by D. For a descending triangle, the procedure is similar but the break out is, of course, projected to a lower price plane.

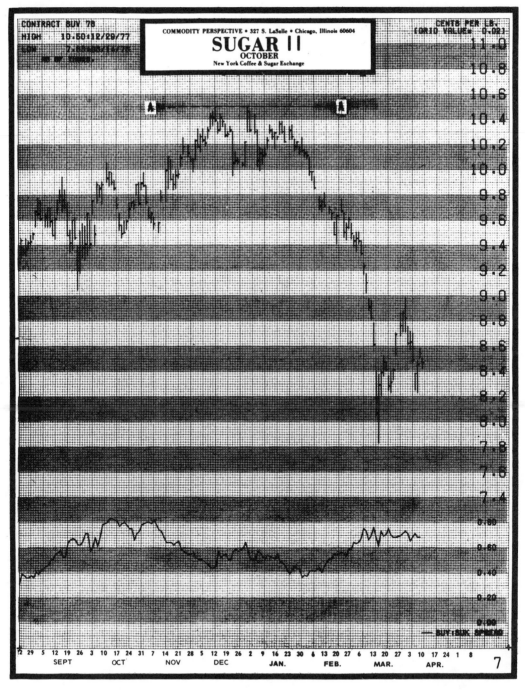

Chart reprinted with permission from: *Commodity Perspective,* 327 S. LaSalle Street, #536, Chicago, Ill. 60604.

FIGURE 9.18   ILLUSTRATION OF A DOUBLE TOP

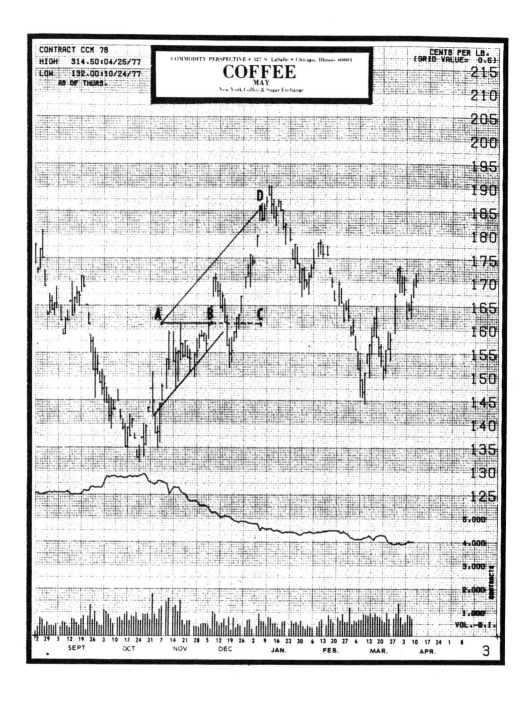

Chart reprinted with permission from: *Commodity Perspective*, 327 S. LaSalle Street, #536, Chicago, Ill. 60604.

FIGURE 9.19   THE ASCENDING TRIANGLE WITH PRICE PROJECTIONS AFTER A BREAK OUT TO THE TOP SIDE

Among the generalizations about analysis and use of price triangles are:

1. The break out is expected to occur in the same direction that price entered the triangle;

2. The price projections are generally considered to be more reliable if they occur between two-thirds and three-fourths of the distance from the base of the triangle to the apex; and

3. Symmetrical triangles (neither ascending nor descending) are valid indicators of probable price direction when a break out occurs but provide no base for a projection of how far price will move.

Rectangles are another frequently observed price formation. They become congestion or consolidation areas and often develop when a triangle fails to hold its shape. Figure 9:20 provides an illustration.

In general, the break out will occur in the same direction in which price was moving when it entered the rectangle. If the break out is up as in the encircled area, the move is expected to reach the price projected by adding the vertical increase or depth of the rectangle to the break-out point—a price PP in Figure 9.20. The longer the rectangle, the greater the tendency for the price move to reach significantly beyond the minimum price projection.

A flag formation is one of the easiest formations to recognize. Flags are consolidation formations and usually constitute a "pause" in a major price move. In Figure 9.21, for example, we see a bear flag formation. The break from higher prices carried to a price level well below the previous congestion area. The mast of the flag is formed by this sharp downward move. The flag formed in the trading days that followed, taking the shape of an ascending channel. When the break out occurs, the minimum price objective is the length of the mast subtracted from the price level at the point of the break out. Procedures are similar for a flag formation in an upward trending or bull market. For both bull and bear flags, a decline in volume is expected during the formation of the flag.

When a flag fails to develop in a major bear or bull move, we often see a pennant develop. Figure 9.22 illustrates a "bull" pennant. The breakout occurs on the top side and the minimum price objective is projected by adding the length of the mast to the break-out point.

Like the flag, the pennant is the result of profit taking by traders. After a strong move up (or down) that forms the mast, profit taking calls at least a temporary halt to the move. Often, this occurs before the move is exhausted so the direction of the break out is usually the same as the direction in which price was moving when it entered the pennant formation.

The *point and figure chart* is another popular type of chart. Some

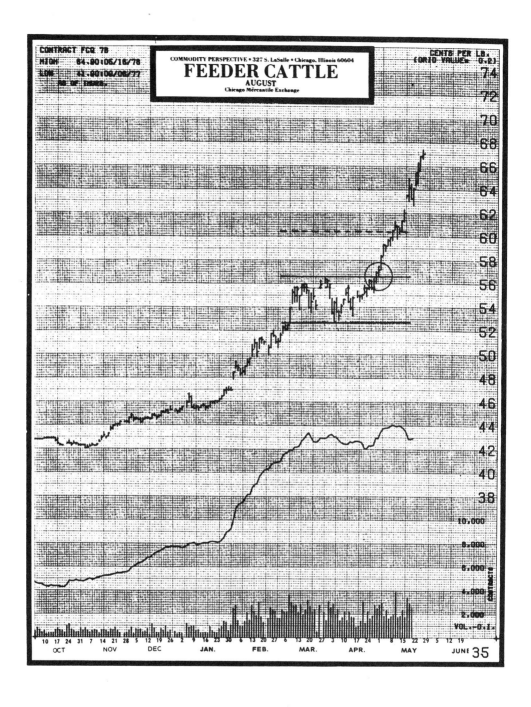

Chart reprinted with permission from: *Commodity Perspective*, 327 S. LaSalle Street, #536, Chicago, Ill. 60604.

FIGURE 9.20   THE RECTANGULAR FORMATION WITH A BREAK TO THE TOP SIDE AND A PROJECTION OF PRICE EXPECTATION

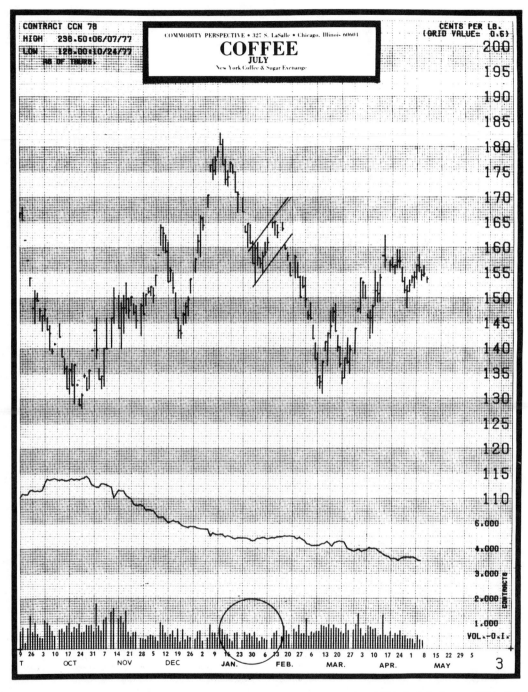

Chart reprinted with permission from: *Commodity Perspective*, 327 S. LaSalle Street, #536, Chicago, Ill. 60604.

FIGURE 9.21 A BEAR FLAG FORMATION CONFIRMED BY DECLINING VOLUME

257

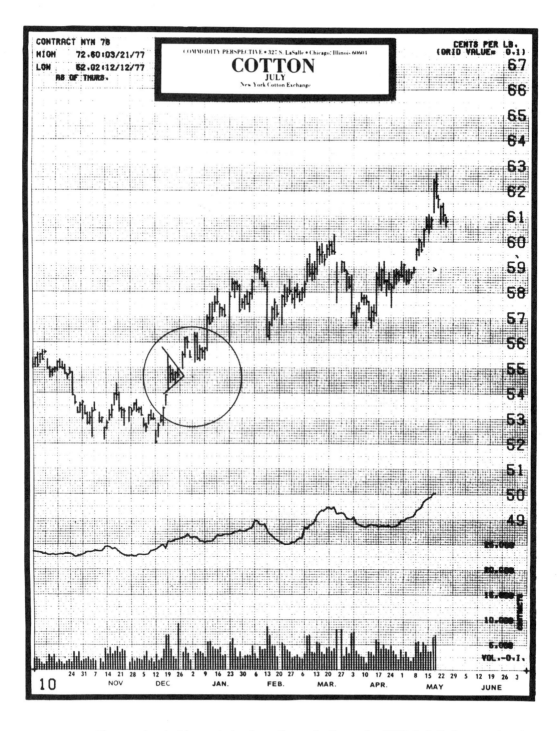

Chart reprinted with permission from: *Commodity Perspective*, 327 S. LaSalle Street, #536, Chicago, Ill. 60604.

FIGURE 9.22   THE PENNANT FORMATION IN A BULL MARKET

analysts prefer it to the bar chart. Others use the bar chart but prefer the point and figure as an aid in deciding when to buy or sell. Perhaps the best approach is to use both types—you can never have too much information if the techniques you employ are valid.

A point and figure chart places less emphasis on the time dimension and concentrates on the trading action and price direction. Coordinate paper is used and decisions must be made on the size (or dollar value) of each cell and what will be required to effect a change in price direction.

Figure 9.23 illustrates with a point and figure chart for live hog futures. Each cell has a value of 20 cents and, in this particular chart, a three-cell reversal requirement is employed. Note there is no time scale on the horizontal axis.

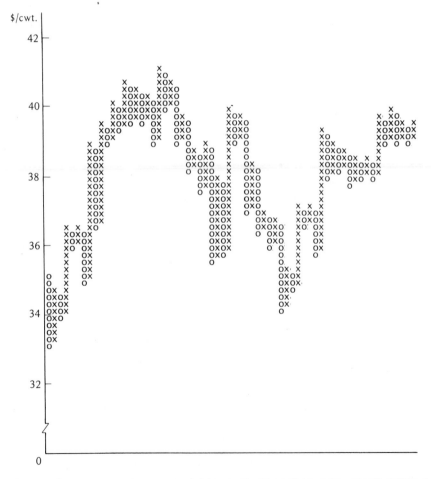

FIGURE 9.23   POINT AND FIGURE CHART FOR OCTOBER LIVE HOGS WITH A 20-CENT CELL SIZE AND A THREE-CELL REVERSAL REQUIREMENT

Charting is begun by observing the high and low of the trading range of the first trading day for the contract.[8] If the trading range spans at least three cells and the close is above the center of the range, enter X's (representing rising prices). If the close is below the center of the range, enter O's (representing falling prices). If the trading range does not span three cells, wait until the next day or the first day three cells *are* filled and start the plot.

Once a beginning direction is established, the daily charting task then drops into an easy routine. Charting rules for each day are:[9]

1. If the price direction is up, look at the high for the day to see if a new cell (or cells) has been filled. Enter X's in all new cells filled by the day's high.

2. If the price direction is up and the high for the next day does not fill one or more new cells, look at the low to see whether the three-box reversal requirement has been met. If you can drop one cell and then plot at least three cells down, there has been a reversal and the price direction has changed. Continue to plot the 0's for lower prices until the daily low fails to fill a new cell and look for a reversal.

3. On any day when no new high (or low) is made and there is no three-day box reversal, plot nothing and wait for the next day.

Both the choice of cell size and reversal requirements influence the movement seen on the chart. There is no single rule that can be applied to these selections. What is needed is a chart that shows significant movements or reversals of direction in price. Choice of a cell size that is too large will suppress movement along both the vertical and horizontal dimensions. A large cell size suggests many days in which no new high (or low) can be plotted and also makes the reversal requirement difficult to meet. Movement along the vertical dimension is restricted when no new plotting is possible and the difficulty in making reversals suppresses movement along the horizontal dimension. On the other hand, small cell sizes and/or "easy" reversal requirements will generate a chart that is volatile in appearance and difficult to use. Though they are somewhat arbitrary and based on experience, the following guidelines can prove useful:

1. If you are plotting nothing on one-third or more of the trading days, your cell size is probably too large.

2. If you plot new cells every trading day and typically fill two or more cells, your cell size is probably too small.

3. For a given choice of cell size, an average of more than one reversal per trading week suggests the reversal requirement is too small. For a given choice of cell size, an average of only one reversal per three or more trading weeks suggests the reversal requirement is too large.

The final test of the cell size and reversal requirement decisions is whether the point and figure chart works. The purpose of the point and figure chart is to enable the reader to identify buy and sell decisions from the chart's patterns of activity. If the cell size and reversal requirements are correct for the particular commodity, certain techniques allow projections of the minimum price move after a break out is identified.

Point and figure charts do an excellent job of recording trading activity in congestion areas. Figure 9.24 shows the point and figure chart used in Figure 9.23 with cell size set at 20¢ and a three-cell reversal requirement. A broad congestion area is built in the area framed by the rectangle. When price moved out of the congestion area on the down side, this was a "sell" signal. If the break out had been up, a "buy" signal would be generated. Point and figure chartists talk of "double tops," "triple bottoms," "spread triple tops," etc., and pay attention to the buy and/or sell signals when price pushes higher past a double top or breaks down through a double or triple bottom. On Figure 9.24, for example, a buy signal is generated at point B when the double top is penetrated. A double bottom and a sell signal are generated at point S.

As with the bar chart, formations such as the triangle can be identified on the point and figure chart. Figure 9.25 records typical formations with related indications of the buy or sell signals.

Trend lines can also be employed on the point and figure chart. Interpretation and use are essentially the same as with the bar chart. Penetration of the trend line provides a signal. With this type of chart, however, there is no indication of whether the closing price confirms the break out. This is one of several reasons why use of both types of charts is advisable.

Price projections following a break out up or down can be made from congestion areas on the point and figure charts. Chartists feel most comfortable with these projections when they are from a congestion area that approximates a symmetrical rectangle in shape.

To illustrate the procedure, consider Figure 9.24. A "break out" occurred when the bottoms around a price level of $38.50 were penetrated and the market traded to lower levels. An estimate of the minimum price objective after the break out can be made as follows:

1. Count the number of columns in the congestion area. Often, this requires judgment since the congestion areas are sometimes ir-

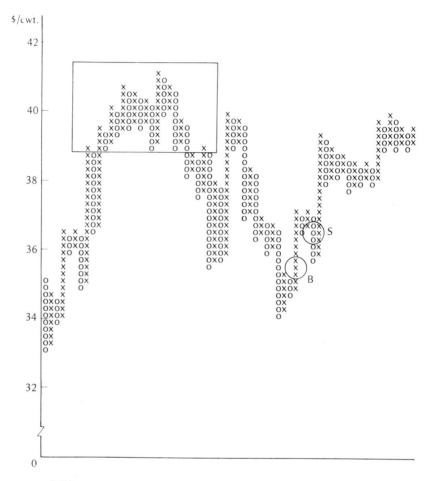

FIGURE 9.24   ILLUSTRATION OF A BREAK FROM A CONGESTION AREA AND SIM-
PLE SELL AND BUY SIGNALS, POINT AND FIGURE CHART FOR LIVE HOGS

regular and lack the symmetry the chartist might like to see. In
Figure 9.24, the congestion area has 16 columns.

2. Multiply the number of columns in the congestion area by the
value of the cell size. We are using a live hog contract with a cell
size of 20 cents to illustrate. Therefore, we multiply 20 cents by 16
to get a product of $3.20.

3. Multiply the product formed in step 2 by the number of cells required for a reversal. Here, we have a three-cell reversal requirement so our final product is 3 × $3.20 = $9.60.

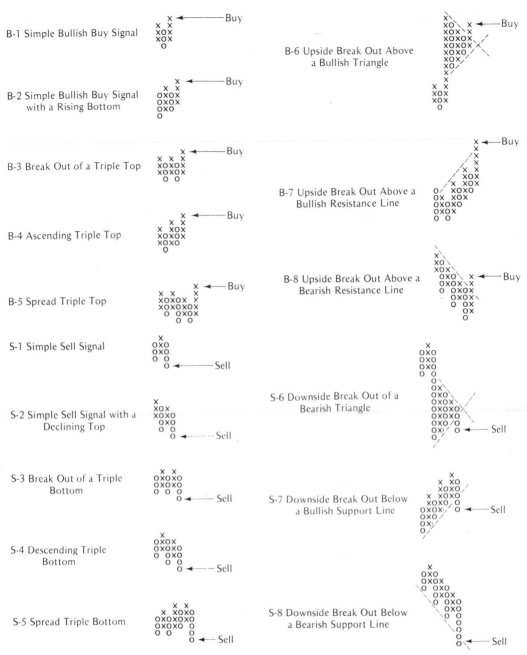

Source: *Using Technical Price Analysis*, Reprint articles from Commodities Magazine, 219 Parkade, Cedar Falls, Iowa.

FIGURE 9.25 ILLUSTRATION OF BASIC BUY AND SELL SIGNALS ON POINT AND FIGURE CHARTS

4. Subtract the $9.60 from the top of the congestion area. In Figure 9.24, the top is at a price level of approximately $41.20. Therefore, our minimum price objective is $41.20 − $9.60 = $31.60. In this instance, the price objective was not attained. The market "held" around $34.00.

Nothing is magical about this procedure. It is important to remember the congestion areas on graphs of commodity trade are, in a very real sense, a tug of war between the bulls and the bears. Varying interpretations of the fundamental supply-demand picture plus technical considerations are brought to the trading arena. It is when some net consensus as to the direction of price movement emerges from this give and take that the break out occurs. The longer the time required to decide on direction, the broader the congestion area and the more definite the feeling about the "correctness" of the break out when it does occur.

A few general guidelines on the use of point and figure charts as a source of buy and sell decisions are as follows:

1. The break out from a congestion area seldom carries directly to the price objective without reversing. Typically, there will be a "set back" to the congestion area or trend line after the initial breakout. Some traders will buy (sell) the break out up (down). Others prefer to wait for the setback and, if it does not come, let the opportunity pass.

2. A break out with no follow through should be traded with extreme care. A top side break out that extends to only two or three cells and then sets back deep into or near the bottom of the congestion area is not likely to be a sound buy signal. The failure of any follow through after a break out from a sizable congestion area suggests the absence of a strong net consensus on which way price should go.

3. It is usually not wise to "chase" the market. If you miss getting into the market on the break out or the subsequent setback, it may be best to wait for a technical correction of the move before entering. Be patient—there is always a tomorrow in the commodity trade. As a rule, any strong move up or down will be followed by a correction of 50–65 percent of that move. There will usually be another chance to enter the market.

The technical tools, charts, and moving averages can provide help in determining when to enter the market, whether the purpose is hedging or speculation. But the effectiveness of the hedging program and the profitability of the speculative trading plan will be significantly influenced by the level at which the trader enters the market. What is needed is a workable compromise between entering at the "right" level and keeping the risk associated with that entry to acceptable or tolerable levels. Knowledge of types of orders and when each should be used will help.

The "market order" is a simple and widely used order. An order to buy or sell a commodity "at the market" will insure the trader of entry into the market.[10] The price will be the price at which the order can be filled when it reaches the floor of the trading exchange. The obvious advantage of this order is that it will insure the trader he will buy or sell. Among the disadvantages is the possibility the price level will move significantly before the order can be filled.

A "limit order" is an order that requires filling at a specific price level or better. For example, an order to sell a particular live cattle futures contract at a limit price of $55 is interpreted as a request to sell live cattle at $55 or higher. A frequently used order, the limit order gives the trader the opportunity to establish a specific price at which he is willing to sell or buy. Whether this proves to be advantageous depends on the ability of the trader to pinpoint, on a particular trading day, a specific price that is likely to be realized.

The limit order can be used to minimize the risk of establishing a position in the market at what later proves to be a relatively poor level. Consider, for example, the position of the corn producer who wishes to hedge 30,000 bushels of corn. Instead of selling six contracts[11] at a specific price, say $2.90, the producer might prefer to sell two at $2.90, two at $3.00 and two at $3.10. In other words, the hedging is done on a "scale up" basis from a specific level by using three limit orders. This reduces the risk of seeing the market move higher after having placed all the orders at a lower price.

The question of "what price?" has not been answered—and it is an interesting question. Once a decision has been made to enter the market, an approach that will often work is to place a limit order at the closing price of the previous trading day. For example, assume the trading range and closing price that generates a "sell" to the trader on a particular day is as follows:

High	$3.20
Low	3.10
Close	3.10

An order to sell at $3.10 or better will be filled the next day in most cases. In general, the trading range for a particular day will contain the closing price from the previous day.

The limit order can also be used to buy or sell in the area of a major trend line that either offers support if price levels are trending downward or resistance if they are trending higher. On Figure 9.26, a limit price at 8.95 cents on March 29 would have offered an opportunity to sell just under a

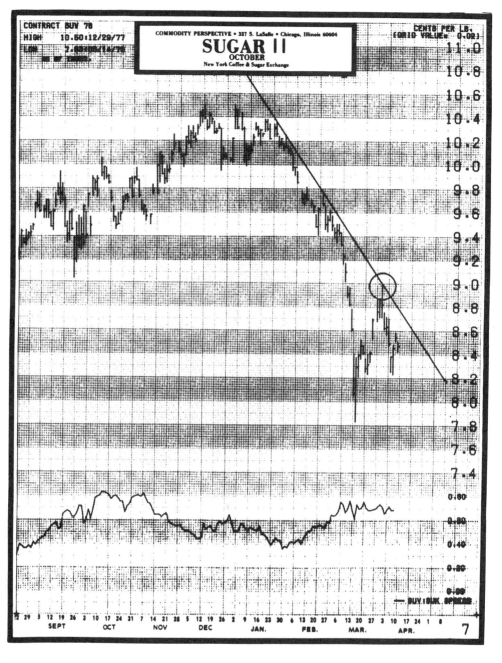

Chart reprinted with permission from: *Commodity Perspective,* 327 S. LaSalle Street, #536, Chicago, Ill. 60604.

FIGURE 9.26   A SELL ORDER AT A LIMIT PRICE UNDER A MAJOR RESISTANCE LINE

major overhead resistance line. The order can be placed early in the day and will be there waiting for the trading range to reach it. If the trend line "holds," the trader has entered the market not only at what appears to be a favorable "level" but he has also minimized the risk during entry.[12]

The "stop" order is frequently used. An order such as "sell 5 December corn at $3.20 stop" will be activated only if the market trades to the $3.20 from higher prices. Obviously, such a "sell stop" order will be placed only at prices below the trading level at the time the order is entered.

There are two primary uses of the "sell stop" or "buy stop" order. By far the most frequent use is as a source of protection for an established position in the market. For example, the trader who has bought corn futures expecting them to trade to higher prices may wish to use sell stop orders to limit his losses in the event his analysis proves incorrect and the corn market drops. If he buys March corn at $3.30, he might choose to place sell stop orders at $3.24½. This would effectively limit his losses to $275 per contract (5,000 × 5½¢ per bu.) if the market trades down instead of up.

Just where protective stops should be placed is a tough question to answer. Among the approaches used are:

1. Money stops. A money stop is used when the trader decides how much money he is willing to risk and places stops to limit the losses to that amount.

2. Chart stops. With this approach, the trader looks at the chart to find a place he might reasonably expect to find "chart support" or "chart resistance." In the discussion of limit orders, an illustration was given of a sell order just below a major trend or resistance line. Many traders will place "buy stop" orders above the trend line in the event the line does not "hold" and the market trades higher. Another approach is to place a "buy stop" just above the tops in a congestion area or a "sell stop" below the lows.[13]

The "stop" order has another application that can be used to advantage, especially by the hedger who is seeking protection against price moves that will threaten the profitability of his cash position. As a congestion area is building, it is often difficult for the trader—whether speculator or hedger—to predict with a high degree of accuracy the direction in which the "break out" will occur. A "sell stop" order under the congestion area will insure the would-be hedger who is long in the cash market he will be short in the futures market if the market breaks downward. The possible dangers here are (1) the move down will be no more than a "running the stops" move with no significant follow-through, and (2) there will be a technical correction or pull back to or into the congestion area after the break out, which could carry to levels above that at which the sell stop order was activated. But the dangers are not that great. Once a break out downward occurs, price will ultimately move significantly lower with a high level of probability.

Once the level at which a stop order is specified is violated, the market becomes a market order. A sell stop at $3.20 on corn might get filled at $3.19 or less in a fast-breaking market. And the situation worsens in the event of a dramatic move in the market. Suppose the sell stop is at $3.20 and the low during a particular day is $3.21 with a close at $3.22. The next morning the market opens "limit down" at $3.12, trades up to $3.14, and closes limit down at $3.12. A standing or "good till cancelled" sell stop order at $3.20 would be filled the next day somewhere from $3.12 to $3.14. This is a hazard with the stop order—but the alternative of no protection is usually considered to be worse.

The "close only stop" completes the list of frequently used orders.[14] With this order, a particular price can be entered—as with the limit order—but the order will be filled only if the *close* is above the price specified in the order for a "buy stop close only" or below the specified price for a "sell stop close only."

The logic and conceptual appeal of this type of order is great. Earlier, cautions were presented about protective stops placed just above or below trend lines, congestion areas, etc. There was concern a buy stop just above a trend line to protect a short position would be activated by a trading range that reaches the stop. If this occurs and the close is back below the trend line, the trader's short position may be wiped out and he then watches from the sidelines as the market trades lower—just as his analysis had indicated. This can be frustrating, demoralizing—and expensive. The "buy stop close only" will take off the trader's short position only if the market *closes* above the price level specified in the order.

Close only stops can also be used as a way to enter the market. A "sell stop close only" order below a trend line or congestion area will put the trader in the market on the short side only if the price closes below the trend line or congestion area—the sign of a legitimate break out. This approach can help eliminate the uncertainty connected with a "sell stop" order that can be activated with no significant follow-through. But there are also hazards. The close only order has the potential to be filled far below the level at which a simple sell order at a particular price would be filled. A close near limit down will set the hedge or the speculative short position but after a substantial part of the price break has been missed. And if the market goes limit down and stays there, the "sell stop close only" order will not be filled—and the trader is not in the market at all.

It is impossible to list specific rules that will always work with orders. A few basics can be gleaned from the literature and through experience:

1. Try to use limit orders to enter the market. Study the charts and enter price levels with a high probability of being filled. If the trading range falls just short of your price and you do not get a "fill," avoid moving your limit price and "chasing" the market. Wait for another opportunity.

2. Use market orders when you are very sure of your analysis in terms of price direction or when a major move is pending in a predictable direction. A market order may well be appropriate when both the fundamental and technical picture suggest a major move in a particular direction or when hedge protection is needed against the possibility of a price move that would wreck the hedger's financial position.

3. Use stops to protect the initial position. This is especially true for the speculator. (If the hedger has set a profitable hedge, he may be willing to let the market move against him and answer any margin calls.) Whether regular or close only stops, it is important to recognize there is no "sure" analysis of commodities trade and that the market can and will trade against you. Many successful traders are right in terms of predicting direction of price movement only 20 to 30 percent of the time but succeed by using stops to limit their losses when they are wrong.

Summary

There are two important approaches to trade in commodity futures. The fundamental approach emphasizes the forces of supply and demand underlying the market. The technical approach pays more attention to the patterns of price movement.

Hedgers and long-term speculative traders usually stress the fundamental approach. The hedger is interested in projecting the direction of price movement in trying to decide whether to hedge. Speculators who follow a strategy of taking a position in the market and holding it for some time are equally interested in the direction of price trends. Trying to isolate the trend and determine the direction in which the market will move requires fundamental analysis.

The trader stressing the fundamentals will need to develop an analytical framework. It need not be highly sophisticated; a balance sheet approach is often used. Alternatives range up to the use of quantitative models such as those discussed in Chapter 7. Regardless of the type of model used, the fundamentalist must develop an ability to analyze the forces of supply and demand and predict the direction of price movement. The ability to predict direction of movement is important to both the hedger and the speculator.

The tools of the technician can be used in both long- and short-run analysis. The bar chart is the base around which other tools are developed. Trend-line analysis gives an indication of the direction of price movement and can be a long-run tool. But when trend lines are penetrated, the analysis becomes a short-run tool that can be invaluable in a planned program of entry and exit.

Many other technical tools are available. Moving beyond simple trend lines, the analysis of formations on the bar charts generates buy and sell signals. Point and figure charts generate buy and sell signals and offer a means of projecting the magnitude of price moves. Moving averages can be used to indicate direction of the market trend and they also generate buy and sell signals.

The successful trading program, whether it is a hedging program or a speculative program, will typically be a mixture of the fundamental and the technical. In the long run, the fundamental forces will prevail. It is supply and demand that ultimately determine price. But the price gyrations before the fundamental forces make themselves clear can be dangerous—and they offer opportunity. A combination of fundamental and technical analysis, knowledge of the mechanics of trading (types of orders, margin requirements, etc.), and the discipline to develop a sound trading program and *stick with it* is the best recipe for trading success.

Footnotes

1. In Chapter 6, the role of price as a rationing mechanism was discussed. When stocks during the crop year are relatively low, higher prices are required to bid the grain from storage and, at the same time, ration the demand side. When stocks continue to shrink, prices move still higher and potential buyers drop out of the market until the demand structure becomes highly inelastic. At these levels, small changes in quantities or in expectations of quantities can and do bring sharp changes in price in the opposite direction.

2. This oversimplifies the situation but the purpose here is to illustrate how fundamental information is brought into the hedging decision. Many other factors become important. The producer's financial position, his overall management ability, the extent to which his is a diversified operation that spreads risk to other crops, etc., will all influence the decision. Too, a "no hedge" decision if the futures are below the cash price expectation can be a very dangerous position if the producer's analysis proves to be faulty and the harvest-period price falls significantly below his expectation on cash price. Chapter 10 will develop strategies that could be used to cope with such situations.

3. Figure 9.4 is a bar chart for August soybean futures. The horizontal axis is divided into 5-day trading weeks. The vertical bar on each trading day shows the trading range from the high price to the low price for the day and the closing or settlement price—the horizontal "dash" on the vertical bar. For example, on May 9 the August contract traded in a price range from $8.85 to $9.40 per bushel and closed or "settled" at $9.355.

4. Buying at $7.50 and selling at $10.00 gives a profit before trading costs of $2.50 per bushel. Each futures contract is for 5,000 bushels giving a gross profit per contract of $12,500.

5. It should be noted, however, that the response to a particular level of the ratio may not be independent of the absolute price levels. A ratio of 20:1 based on $60 hogs and $3 corn may not motivate the increase in production, which would be expected when the 20:1 ratio is comprised of $40 hogs and $2 corn. At $3, the corn crop may be highly profitable as a cash crop and the producer may choose to sell the corn and not feed it. Feeding involves more risk.

6. A 3-day moving average is calculated by adding the closes or settle-

ment prices for the 3 most recent days and dividing this sum by 3. A 10-day moving average is calculated by adding the last 10 settlement prices and dividing the sum by 10. The calculated values are the 3-day and 10-day moving averages respectively for the most recent trading day.

7. The weighted 4-day moving average is calculated as follows:

Day	Closing Price	Weight	Product
t	$60.00	4	$240.00
t-1	59.00	3	177.00
t-2	59.00	2	118.00
t-3	58.50	1	58.50
		10	$593.50

The 4-day weighted moving average for day "t" is $593.50 ÷ 10 ≐ $59.35.

8. Most analysts believe the particular contract should be plotted from the time it is first listed for trade. Some would argue there is so little trading action when the contract is first listed the early months of trade can be ignored with little or no sacrifice. Personally, I feel the entire life of the contract should be plotted to keep the total picture in front of the analyst.

9. Recognizing the difficulty most students have with the plotting procedure, Appendix A to this Chapter explains plotting the point and figure chart in detail.

10. The only exception to this is the infrequent instance when the price has moved either up or down the allowable daily limit from close of the previous day. When this occurs, little or no trading activity occurs. Even in a limit up or limit down situation, however, it is often wise to enter a market order if the trader is sure he wishes to enter the market. For example, when the price is limit up, market orders to buy will be time stamped as they reach the trading floor and filled in that chronological order if sell orders do come in. When the normal daily trading volume averages around 10,000 contracts, several hundred trades will often occur on a day when the price is limit up and no trading range is recorded.

11. Each contract is for 5,000 bushels on the Chicago Board of Trade. Contracts of 1,000 bushels each are traded on the Mid-America Exchange.

12. Remember, trading through such a trend line becomes a "break out"

and a buy signal when a close or two consecutive closes above the trend line materialize. Thus, the risk associated with a sell decision that proves to be incorrect—i.e., the market trades higher—can be substantial so a protective stop is advised.

13. But a caution is needed here. When using charts to place stops, the trader must remember other traders are looking at the same chart patterns. It is not unusual to see a number of stops just above the trend line, just below the lows or at other "apparent" chart positions for stops. When this occurs, floor traders and other professionals may seize the opportunity to push the market toward these stops and "run the stops"—and take advantage of the intra-day price moves this can bring. The astute trader, aware of this, will often avoid the chart positions where stops are likely to cluster by either placing the stops closer to his entry position or, alternatively, leaving enough room so an attempt to "run the stops" will not reach his order.

14. Not all exchanges will accept "close only stops." Check with your broker or otherwise make sure such an order will be accepted and properly filled before attempting to use it.

Questions

1. If the forces of supply and demand do in fact determine price, why would the fundamentalist approach not be the only approach needed in analysis of commodity futures prices?

2. Assume you have opened an account with a broker, have money on deposit and are ready to begin trading commodity futures as a speculator. Describe the trading plan you would follow.

3. If you were going to trade as a hedger instead of a speculator, would your trading plan be different from the one outlined in your answer to question 2? Why or why not?

4. Trade in commodity futures is reported in terms of opening, high, low, and closing prices. Which *one* of these do you feel is the most important in terms of the information it provides? Why?

5. Compare and contrast the bar chart and the point and figure chart in terms of strengths, weaknesses, and ease of use.

Selected References

Arthur, Henry B., "The Nature of Commodity Futures as an Economic and Business Instrument," *Food Research Institute Studies*, Vol. 9, 1972.

Belveal, Lee Dee, *Commodity Speculation: With Profits in Mind.* Wilmette, Ill.: Commodities Press, 1968.

Cohen, A. W., *Three-Point Reversal Method of Point and Figure Stock Market Trading.* Larchmont, N.Y.: Chartcraft, Inc., 1972.

Edwards, Robert D. and John Magee, *Technical Analysis of Stock Trends.* Springfield, Mass.: John Magee, 1966.

Teweles, Richard J., Charles V. Harlow and Herbert L. Stone, *The Commodity Futures Game.* New York, N.Y.: McGraw-Hill, 1974.

Appendix 9.A

Plotting Procedure for
Point and Figure Charts

Plotting point and figure charts is tricky until you have mastered the procedure. Let's continue to use a 20 cent cell size and a three-box reversal requirement to illustrate and plot a live hog futures. A February live hog contract is usually started just after the old contract expires on February 20. Starting on February 21, the plotting procedure is explained in detail below.

Suppose the trading action for the first five days is:

Date	High	Low	Close
2-21	$51.00	$50.00	$50.75
2-22	51.25	50.50	50.95
2-23	51.30	50.70	50.80
2-24	50.75	49.50	49.95
2-25	50.50	49.10	49.40

To begin the chart, the plot for February 21 would look as follows since the range spanned more than three boxes and the close was above the center of the range:

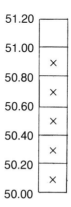

On February 22, a new higher cell was filled by the high so we plot as follows:

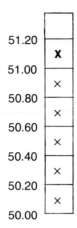

Note one new cell, the $51.00–51.20 cell, was filled so it is plotted with an X.

On February 23, the high of $51.30 does not fill a new higher cell. We look at the low of $50.70 and find we could not drop the $51.00–51.20 cell and then plot three cells down. There has been no new high, no three-cell reversal, so we plot nothing.

On February 24, the situation changes. The high is too low to fill a new cell on the up side (it would take a high of at least $51.40) but this time the three-cell reversal requirement has been met. The plotting action on February 24 is:

The low of $49.50 allows more than the necessary three cells to be plotted after dropping the "reversal cell" of $51.00–51.20. Cells coming back down have been filled to the $49.60 level. (The low would have to be at $49.40 or less, not $49.50, for the $49.40–$49.60 cell to be plotted.)

On February 25, we look only at the low and find it will allow plotting new lower cells. Plotting action is shown below:

51.20		
	×	
51.00		
	×	0
50.80		
	×	0
50.60		
	×	0
50.40		
	×	0
50.20		
	×	0
50.00		
		0
49.80		
		0
49.60		
		0
49.40		
		0
49.20		
49.00		

This procedure is continued throughout the life of the contract. Some chartists enter the month in the cell for the first trading day of a particular month to keep some record of time on the chart. Others prefer to totally suppress the time dimension and adopt the position that trading patterns and direction of price movement are all that matter.

To illustrate the importance of cell size and reversal requirements, we can plot a more complete chart using two different sets of requirements. Adding to the time period illustrated above, we might get this data set:

Date	High	Low	Close
2-21	51.00	50.00	50.75
22	51.25	50.50	50.95

Date	High	Low	Close
23	51.30	50.70	50.80
24	50.75	49.50	49.95
25	50.50	49.10	49.40
28	49.60	49.15	49.30
3- 1	49.65	49.05	49.20
2	49.40	48.80	48.90
3	49.00	48.70	48.75
4	49.10	48.70	49.05
3- 7	49.80	48.70	49.50
8	49.90	49.30	49.60
9	49.95	49.20	49.30
10	50.25	49.15	49.85
11	50.35	49.50	50.15
3-14	50.30	49.80	49.95
15	50.40	49.90	50.30
16	50.50	50.00	50.40
17	50.55	49.80	50.20

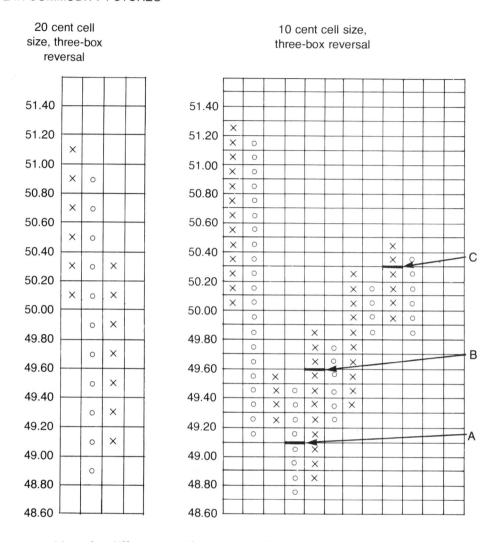

20 cent cell size, three-box reversal

10 cent cell size, three-box reversal

Note the difference in the amount of activity on the charts. The chart with the 20 cent cell size reversed only twice. Plotting the same data, the chart with the 10 cent cell size and a three-box reversal requirement reversed a total of nine times. Comparing the two we would find:

1. Buy and sell signals would come much more often with the 10 cent cell size. Looking only at double tops and double bottoms, there are no signals on this part of the chart with the 20 cent cell size. There is one sell signal (point A) and two buy signals (points B and C) on the chart with the 10 cent cell size.

2. The 20 cent cell size would be preferred for hedging programs. The rapid turnover with the 10 cent cell size is not as consistent with the needs of the hedger who has many other demands on his time.

chapter ten

Hedging Strategies and Techniques

Providing a mechanism to allow hedging is the primary justification for trade in commodity futures. The body of knowledge concerning hedging is continually changing and growing. Certain techniques and approaches will continue to be relevant and of basic importance, however. In this chapter, fundamental analysis and the technical tools associated with chart analysis will be integrated into selected hedging strategies. Most emphasis will be placed on the needs of the producer as a potential short hedger.

The Strategies

No one hedging strategy is best for all potential or actual hedgers. Before a strategy is developed it is imperative that the hedger fully understand his objectives. What does he expect from the program? In general, hedging programs are developed to provide protection against the risk of cash price fluctuations, but how much protection is desired? A basic function of a

281

manager is to accept risk, given the financial ability of the firm to carry risk and the managerial capacity to handle risk. Therefore, we conclude the choice of hedging strategies will depend upon:

1. The financial position of the individual;

2. The managerial capacity or ability to manage risk; and

3. The personal orientation of the manager toward accepting risk.

THE HEDGE AND HOLD STRATEGY

A simple approach to hedging is to place the hedge and hold the position until the cash position is liquidated. The wheat producer who stores winter wheat in June, sells December wheat futures, and lifts the hedge by buying back those futures contracts when he sells his cash wheat in December is using a "hedge and hold" strategy. Similarly, the cattle feeder who sells June live cattle futures to hedge a feeding program begun in January and holds the futures position until the cattle are sold is following a hedge and hold strategy.

Though a simplistic strategy, nothing is wrong with this approach. It is especially appealing to the beginning trader and/or to the trader whose financial position or personal orientation cannot tolerate much risk. And when profitable hedges are set, this brings a much needed businesslike orientation to the situation. Consider the position of a wheat producer who faces the following set of information during the third week in June as he harvests his hard red winter wheat:

1. Local cash price = $3.00 per bu.;

2. December wheat futures on the K.C. exchange are trading at $3.50;

3. The variable costs associated with storage are 2 cents per bu. per month (12 cents for the June–December storage period); and

4. The "basis" for the producer's local market during December is normally −20 cents per bu.[1]

Deducting the 20 cent basis and the 12 cent carrying charges leaves $3.18, a net that can be compared to the cash bid of $3.00. Since all costs of production and harvesting are fixed at this point, the hedged storage program looks better than the cash sale regardless of the cumulative costs in the wheat. The only things that can go wrong once the hedge is set are relatively insignificant to the profitability of the hedge and include the following:

1. The basis in December can be different from the normal −20 cents per bushel. If the basis is larger, the producer is hurt—he is buying back futures which are more than 20 cents over his cash selling price. But if the basis is smaller, the producer is helped—he is buying back futures that are cheap relative to his cash price.

2. The December futures contract can trade above the $3.50 level, which brings margin calls. Seldom, however, will interest on margin call money be enough to really hurt the profitability of the hedge. And there is always the possibility the market will trade down from the $3.50 level, creating a surplus in the hedger's account that is his on request.[2]

3. Unexpected losses such as damage of the wheat during storage, wind damage, water damage, etc., can occur. Good management can keep these risk factors to acceptable levels.

Note the hedger has "locked up" a profit margin on his storage program. He can then turn his managerial ability to other areas of his operation and may accept market risk in some other area where the odds are more favorable.

THE HEDGE AND HOLD STRATEGY: CONTROLLED PLACEMENT OF THE HEDGE

A simple extension of the previous strategy is to exercise managerial control over when the hedge is placed and then hold the hedge until the cash position is liquidated. Chart analysis, moving averages, or other technical tools can be used to help the manager decide just when to place the hedge.

The intuitive appeal to this approach is apparent. The manager may know he intends to hedge his cash position but sees no reason to place the hedge immediately if the futures market appears headed for higher ground. Here, he will need to look at the charts, at moving averages, or other indicators of long-term trend. If the futures are trending upward, the message is simple—wait until the market turns down before setting the hedge. But this involves the ability to "call" direction in the futures. Several approaches are available.

Trend Lines, Chart Patterns.   Trend lines and trading channels can be used to determine the general direction in which the market is moving. Figure 10.1 shows a chart with an upward trending pattern as noted by the trend line marked AA. Following the market up with a "sell stop close only" order $.50–1.00 under the trend line is one logical approach. This precludes

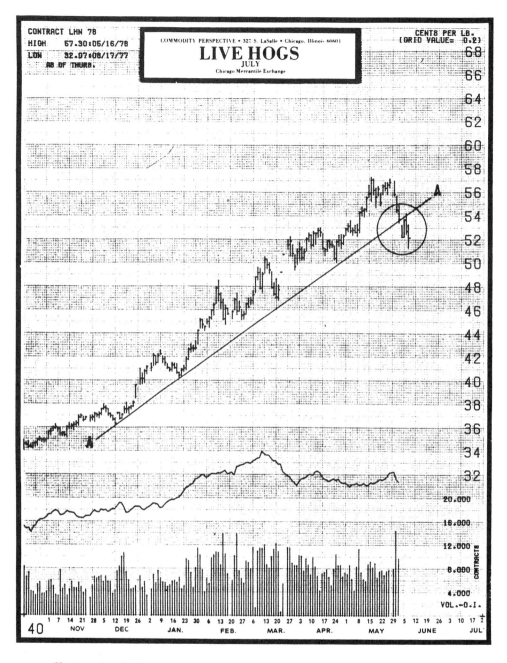

Chart reprinted with permission from: *Commodity Perspective,* 327 S. LaSalle Street, #536, Chicago, Ill. 60604.

FIGURE 10.1   USING THE MAJOR TREND LINE AND CLOSE ONLY SELL STOP ORDERS TO PLACE SHORT HEDGE

the necessity of arbitrarily calling a "top" to the market, lets it trade higher, but insures protection if a break out down occurs. This approach will never put the hedger in the market at the very top of the trading ranges but will be effective. In Figure 10.1, the hedge would have been placed on June 2 when the contract closed at $52.25.

A similar approach could, of course, be used to set the hedge on cattle, corn, or some other commodity. As a general rule, place the sell stop below the trend line by 20 to 30 percent of the daily allowable trading limit. If it closes this much below the trend line, it will usually be a legitimate break through the trend line and a change in market direction.

Much the same trading approach can be used on the point and figure charts. Close only sell stops under a trend line or below an upward trending channel will let the market run its course and turn before the short positions are established.

Moving Averages.   Since the moving averages are designed to indicate tops and bottoms in the markets, a set of the averages can be used to determine when the hedge should be set. In general, the rules are as follows:

1. If the moving averages are indicating a downward trending market, place the hedge immediately. To illustrate, assume a hog producer puts feeder pigs on his feeding floor and considers a hedge. He checks the 10-day and 5-day moving averages (or some other set) and finds the 5-day has moved through the 10-day from above and is below the 10-day. The hedge is placed immediately by selling live hog futures.

2. If the moving averages are indicating an upward trending market, wait until a top is signaled before placing the hedge. Continuing the illustration above, this would mean the live hog futures are not sold and the hedge is not set until the 5-day moving average crosses the 10-day from above and signals a top.

Table 10.1 compares the two strategies discussed to this point for selected commodities. In general, use of the moving averages to set the initial hedge gives slight improvement. Both approaches usually yield a mean return below an approach that uses no hedging at all. This does not mean, however, that these simplistic approaches should be discarded. When used with an aggressive effort to project the cash price and hedge when the adjusted futures are above the cash price projection, the hedge and hold approach can have real merit. And the lower mean return does not tell the entire story. With the hedge, the stream of returns to the operation is much more stable. This means the producer might survive a

Table 10.1
Comparison of the Hedge-and-Hold with the Controlled Placement Hedge-and-Hold, Selected Commodities

Program	Slaughter Cattle [a]		Feeder Cattle [b]		Corn [c]	
	Mean	Std. Dev.	Mean	Std. Dev.	Mean	Std. Dev.
	($ per head)		($ per head)		($ per head)	
No Hedging	−19.65	77.54	31.65	53.21	160.33	39.07
Hedge and Hold	−28.88	56.40	30.57	20.66	150.60	49.88
Hedge and Hold: Controlled Placement (5- and 10-day moving averages)	−23.51	57.00	31.82	22.73	150.39	49.99

[a] Based on analysis of 186 feeding periods of 140 days each in the 1972–75 period. Note the reduction in risk (the smaller standard deviations) *and* the reduction in mean profits that usually comes with the hedge-and-hold strategies. These are *short* hedges only.
[b] Based on analysis of 84 production periods for feeder cattle under alternative production programs during 1972–76. These are *short* hedges only.
[c] These results are in terms of the per head costs of feeding cattle over 238 feeding periods 1972–76. The "no hedge" alternative bought all the corn needed at the beginning of the feeding period at the prevailing price. Both hedging strategies reduced the costs reflecting the upward trending markets of the period. The higher standard deviations reflect the volatility of corn futures during the period. These are *long* hedges only.

Source: Wayne D. Purcell and Thomas Richardson, *Quantitative Models to Predict Quarterly Average Cash Corn Prices and Related Hedging Strategies*, Okla. Ag. Exp. Sta. Bul. B-731, Stillwater, Dec. 1977; Robert A. Brown and Wayne D. Purcell, *Price Production Models and Related Hedging Programs for Feeder Cattle*, Okla. Agr. Exp. Sta. Bul. B-734, Stillwater, Jan. 1978; Wayne D. Purcell, "More Effective Approaches to Hedging?" *Proceedings: 1976 Oklahoma Cattle Feeders Seminar*, Stillwater, Feb. 1976.

price break, which would have wrecked him financially with no hedge protection.

THE PLACE AND LIFT OR SELECTIVE STRATEGY

Any approach that places and lifts hedges based on an analysis of price or some indicator of the direction of market movement has a two-fold objective—to attain protection against the risk of downward breaking prices and to allow the benefits of a rising cash market. Unlike most hedge and hold strategies, this approach can and often will both decrease the variability in the stream of net profits (meaning the risk is decreased) and increase the mean profit or net return per unit. How effective the approach will be rests squarely on the criteria employed in placing and lifting the hedges.

Chart Techniques. Trend lines, analysis of congestion areas, chart formations, etc., can all be brought to bear on the problem. The challenge is simple:

> Have the hedge on in significant downward moving markets and have the hedge off during significant upward moving markets.

How to do it is not quite so simple.

The expert chart analyst will use the charts just as he would if he were a speculator trading the long-range picture based on fundamentals. Sell orders would go in when the analyst sees something on the chart that signals a sell—a breakthrough of a support line, trading up against a resistance line, development of a head and shoulders top, a double top, etc. Stops could be used to protect the short position but since hedging is the objective, they could be set higher than the close stops the speculator might set. When a bottom and a related buy signal develop, the hedges are lifted. If the market then trades higher, the hedger using this strategy stands aside and lets the market trade up—and benefits from the rising cash market. The long position in cash might be liquidated before the charts indicate a top and the hedge is replaced. If a new top is indicated before the cash product is sold, the hedge is put on again and then lifted when the cash product is sold.

Figure 10.2 illustrates this procedure using trend lines. Hedges are set in the areas marked with "S" and lifted in the areas marked with "B." Note the hedge was set and lifted several times during just part of the trading life of this May wheat contract.

Using the closing price for the day after the chart signals are generated to calculate profits and losses, this procedure would have yielded a profit after commissions of 14.3 cents per bushel. The profitability of the total operation would, of course, depend on the cash side as well but the "shorts only" approach would have made a significant contribution. Looking closely at the chart suggests a "hedge and hold" strategy might have helped if the hedge period was started when the futures prices were trading at high levels.

But as noted in Chapter 9, this type of chart analysis is deceiving in its apparent simplicity. The trend lines shown in Figure 10.2 were drawn in after the entire chart had been plotted and are, after the fact, fairly obvious. But as the chart patterns develop, the task of getting the correct trend lines established is a tough one. Cover part of the chart with a sheet of paper and slowly move it to the right. The patterns are not that clear and the trend lines are not obvious until after the fact. In drawing in the trend lines in Figure 10.2, two simple and somewhat arbitrary criteria were employed:

1. No two bottoms or tops were connected unless they were separated by at least 10 trading days. As noted in Chapter 9, the trend lines that are separated by more time tend to be the more valid trend lines.

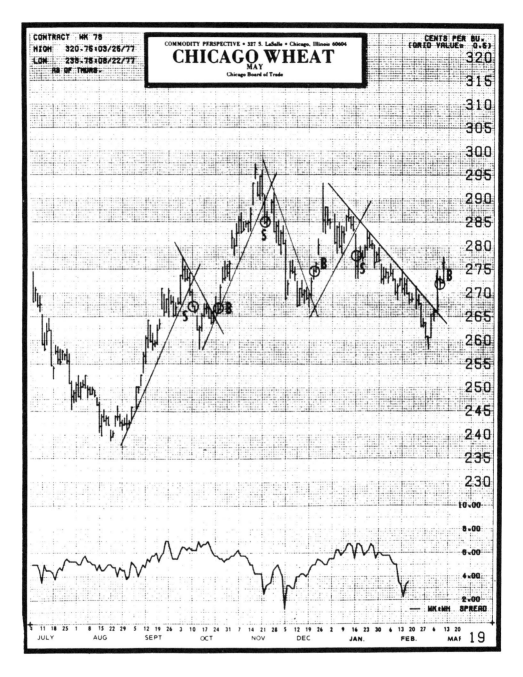

Chart reprinted with permission from: *Commodity Perspective*, 327 S. LaSalle Street, #536, Chicago, Ill. 60604.

FIGURE 10.2   TREND LINES AS AIDS IN DETERMINING WHEN TO PLACE AND
LIFT HEDGES

2. Extremely "steep" trend lines were not used even if the requirement in No. 1 above was met. No trend line was drawn that had a slope of more than 2:1 (rise to run) on the chart.[3] Observation suggests such lines would be short-run only and are created by technical adjustments in the market. This criterion eliminates the frequent in-and-out trades.

Moving Averages.   The difficulty and frustration of reading the charts can be avoided by using an objective approach such as the moving averages. If the correct combination for any particular commodity can be isolated, the moving averages are very effective.

Drawing on the discussion in Chapter 9, a few observations on use of moving averages in hedging programs can help establish a perspective:

1. Moving averages work best in markets with relatively large, sustained moves in price. It is very difficult to find a set of moving averages that can effectively handle hedges in a market characterized by choppy, sideways trade.

2. Any set of moving averages is vulnerable to the technical correction. In Figure 10.3, the market started a major downward trend from the $1.83 price level. Then came a technical correction in a price range of $1.53 to $1.655. Most sets of moving averages would signal a bottom here and cause the hedge to be lifted but there is little or no follow-through on the up side. Such trades can and usually do lose money in that the level at which the "false bottom" is corrected and the contracts are sold again can be below the price level at which the hedge was prematurely lifted.

3. Over the long run, the use of moving averages in a hedging program will typically contribute to the overall profitability of the operation. But periods of short-run new losses are always possible.

4. The primary appeal of the moving averages comes from the fact the hedger who follows the dictates of a properly selected set of averages will never bear the full burden of a bad break in prices. The averages will dictate a sell decision, signal a hedge, and protect against most of the "down" in a sharply breaking market. On the other side of the coin, the hedger using moving averages to place and lift hedges will never be caught so that an established hedge will eliminate all the benefits of a rising cash market.

5. Analysis has shown the financial position of the firm is protected by hedge programs based on moving averages. The "worst loss" for a particular set of cattle, a set of hogs, or a grain operation is

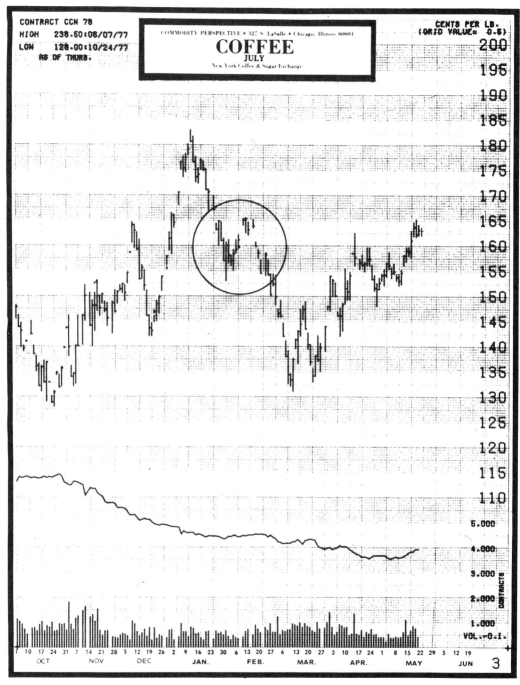

Chart reprinted with permission from: *Commodity Perspective*, 327 S. LaSalle Street, #536, Chicago, Ill. 60604.

FIGURE 10.3 ILLUSTRATION OF THE TECHNICAL CORRECTION IN A DOWN TREND, WHICH CAUSES PROBLEMS FOR THE MOVING AVERAGES

Table 10.2

Comparison of Alternative Hedging Programs on 216 Simulated Sets of Cattle Across January 1972–January 1976

Strategy	*Average Profits in $ per Head*
Feeding Only	−18.54
Feeding, Hedge all Cattle When Placed and Hold Hedges Until Cattle Are Sold	−25.75
Feeding, Controlled Placement of Hedge Using 5- and 10-Day Moving Averages and Hold Hedges Until Cattle Are Sold	−20.74
Feeding, Place and Lift Hedges Using Sell and Buy Signals From 5- and 10-Day Moving Averages	9.78

Source: Wayne D. Purcell, "Managing Total Market Risk in Feeding Operations: Empirical Applications" *Proceedings: 1977 Oklahoma Cattle Feeders Seminar*, Stillwater, Feb. 1977.

less with a selective hedging program using moving averages than with either "no hedge" or "hedge and hold" strategies.[4]

Tables 10.2 and 10.3 provide the results of analysis designed to test the effectiveness of short hedging strategies using moving averages. Table 10.4 examines the long hedge for the cattle feeder who might be concerned with rising costs of corn or rising costs of feeder cattle he will have to buy to replace the cattle on feed.

Table 10.3

Contribution to the Net Profits of a Cattle Feeding Program of Selected Moving Averages Across the Period 1965–76

Hedging Program	*Net Contribution After Commissions in $ per Head* [a]
No Hedging	0
3- and 10-day moving averages	.30
5- and 10-day moving averages	.70
5- and 15-day moving averages	2.19
5-, 15-day and 4-day weighted moving averages	3.02

[a]Examination of the results indicates little or no contribution during the relatively stable and quiet markets of 1965–72. The contribution per head would increase tremendously if the analysis were restricted to the volatile markets of 1972–76.
Source: Wayne D. Purcell, "Effective Hedging of Live Cattle" *Commodities*, Cedar Falls, Iowa. Vol. 6, July 1977.

Table 10.4
Contribution to the Net Profit of a Cattle Feeding Program for Selected Hedging Programs, Long Hedge on Feeder Cattle and Corn

Hedging Program	Contribution After Commissions in $ per Head	
	Feeder Cattle [a]	Corn [b]
No Hedging	0	0
Hedge at Beginning of the Period and Hold	.10	8.50
Place and Lift Hedges Using 3- and 10-Day Moving Averages	19.79	not available
Place and Lift Hedges Using 5- and 10-Day Moving Averages	20.09	9.38
Place and Lift Hedges Using 5-, 10- and 4-Day Weighted Moving Averages	20.12	not available
Place and Lift Hedges Using 5-, 15- and 4-Day Weighted Moving Averages	17.80	not available

[a] This analysis was based on 180-day planning periods for feeder cattle. Each week during 1972–77, the situation was analyzed in terms of cattle needs 180 days in the future. A new "planning period" was started each week.

[b] The analysis for corn was over the period 1972–76. Each week, a feeding period was started and the corn needs for the period were hedged according to the directions of the particular strategy.

Source: Wayne D. Purcell, "The Long Hedge on Feeder Cattle" *Proceedings: 1978 Cattle Feeders' Seminar*, Stillwater, Feb. 1978.

Table 10.5
Suggestions on Moving Averages To Be Used in Selective Hedging Programs for Selected Commodities

Commodity	Suggested Averages
Live Cattle	5, 15 and 4W
Feeder Cattle	5, 10 and 4W
Wheat	5, 10 and 4W

Commodity	Suggested Averages (tentative)
Corn	5 and 10 *or* 5, 10 and 4W
Hogs	5, 10 and 4W
Soybeans	5, 10 and 4W
Cotton	5, 10 and 4W

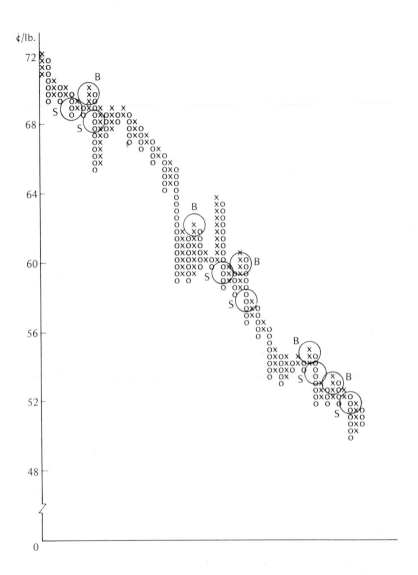

FIGURE 10.4   ILLUSTRATION OF SELL AND BUY SIGNALS USING A DECEMBER COTTON CONTRACT WITH A 40-CENT CELL SIZE AND A 2-CELL REVERSAL REQUIREMENT[a]

[a] The plot is over the period of March–November of 1977 for the December 1977 cotton futures contract. Break outs from double bottoms and double tops were used to place and lift the hedge. The cumulative profits before commissions from the trades shown were approximately 10¢ per lb.

Table 10.5 offers guidelines on which set of moving averages works best with specific commodities. As we move toward the 1980s, we still have a lot to learn about this area. In the upper part of the table are averages for live cattle, feeder cattle, and wheat. Extensive analysis backs these choices. For corn, soybeans, cotton, and hogs the averages shown are more tentative. More work is needed on these and other commodities to determine which particular average is best.

Point and Figure.   Point and figure charts can be employed for a selective hedging program by using sell and buy signals. In Figure 10.4, for example, hedges would be set when the sell signal was generated in the areas marked with S. The hedge would be lifted in the areas marked with B where buy signals are generated. Examination of the chart reveals a pattern familiar to the hedger who uses such technical indicators in a selective hedging program:

1. After some sell signals, the hedge is set but there is little or no follow-through. A buy signal comes a few days later and the hedge is lifted—sometimes at a loss.

2. When a major top to the market develops, sell signals are generated and precede a major move down in price. The point and figure approach will have the hedge set in time to give protection against these major price breaks. Conversely, the buy signals will

---

Table 10.6
Suggested Box Size and Reversal Requirements for Point and Figure Charting of Selected Commodities

Commodity	Box Size	Reversal Requirement
	(¢ per cwt., lb. or bu.)	(no. boxes)
Live Cattle	20¢/cwt.	3
	25¢/cwt.	2
Feeder Cattle	20¢/cwt.	3
	25¢/cwt.	2
Live Hogs	20¢/cwt.	3
Cotton	40¢/lb.	2
Wheat	4¢/bu.	2
Corn	2¢/bu.	3
Soybeans	4¢/bu.	3
	5¢/bu.	2

take the hedge off and allow the hedger to get the benefit of most of the sustained price recoveries.

This particular chart is a point and figure chart for a December cotton contract with a 40 cent box or cell size and a two-box reversal requirement. How effective the approach will be is largely determined by the related choices on box size and reversal requirements. We discussed these issues in Chapter 9 and noted the choice of box size and reversal requirements involves judgment, experience, and consideration of the market involved. Table 10.6 lists recommended box size and reversal requirements for several key commodities. What works best will change over time as the behavior of the futures markets changes but the user should try to select combinations that are responsive to changes in market direction but not likely to generate an excessive number of false signals.

The Hold-Sell and Related Hedging Decision

As noted on several occasions, many factors enter into the decision on whether to hedge. The cash price outlook, the financial position of the manager, the attitude of the manager toward risk, etc., all become involved. These considerations carry the implicit assumption the manager is long in the cash product.

For storable commodities, there is typically a direct tie between futures prices and cash prices. The grains are a primary example and will be used here to illustrate.

In Chapter 8, we discussed the relationship between futures and cash prices for grains. At a local market in the hard red winter wheat belt that runs from Texas northward into the Dakotas, the cash bid on any particular day is determined as follows:

Nearby Kansas City futures close	$3.70
Add Gulf-Kansas City basis	.30
Subtract Gulf-local basis	.60
Local cash bid	$3.40

The local cash bid is thus 30 cents under the Kansas City futures. The two components of the bid are important. The 60 cents is essentially a reflection of the costs of moving the wheat from the local point to the Gulf. It trends higher over time, reflecting increasing transportation costs but is essentially constant within a crop year. As we have seen in earlier discussions, it is the Gulf-Kansas City basis that is potentially variable and that can become an important barometer of the price-making forces in the market.

Local prices are built from a demand that is primarily a derived demand based on export prices at the Gulf (Houston, Galveston for hard red winter wheat). By changing their bid at the Gulf relative to the Kansas City futures—by changing the Gulf-Kansas City basis—exporters can register the short-run intensity of their demand for wheat. For example, increasing the Gulf-Kansas City basis by 5 cents per bu. would tend to increase the local bid by that amount. Bidding up the basis, especially when it is bid above its "normal" level for a particular season of the year, is the exporters' way of saying "we want wheat."

The behavior and level of the basis thus becomes an important piece of information to the producer in making his hold-sell decision. In general, when the Gulf-Kansas City basis is unusually high at harvest time, this is interpreted as a signal to sell cash wheat. Conversely, when the basis is unusually small this should be taken as a signal to store cash wheat rather than selling. And this situation also tends to suggest a hedge since widening of the basis means an improving cash price relative to futures—the ideal set of circumstances for the hedger.

Figure 10.5 shows a sketch of a "normal" seasonal pattern for the Gulf-Kansas City basis. Note the basis tends to increase significantly within the crop year after the harvest period. A few general guidelines as to how this information can be used are as follows:[5]

1. Sell cash wheat at harvest if the sell-hold decision is the only alternative being considered and the basis is significantly *above* its normal harvest-period level.

2. Sell cash wheat at harvest and buy futures if a decision to be long in wheat has been made and the basis is significantly *above* its normal harvest-period level.

3. Store cash wheat if a sell-hold decision is the only alternative being considered and the basis at harvest is significantly *below* its normal level.

4. Store cash wheat and hedge if the hedge-no hedge alternative is being considered and the basis is significantly *below* its normal harvest-period level.

Table 10.7 gives illustrations of the potential in working with the basis. In years of heavy supplies and relatively stable prices, the potential move in the basis may be more than the potential tied to movements in absolute price levels. The potential is there because of the decisions and actions of producers. Large total supplies, made up of large ending stocks or bumper crops or some combination of the two, typically bring sharply depressed cash prices at harvest. Producers tend to look at the low cash

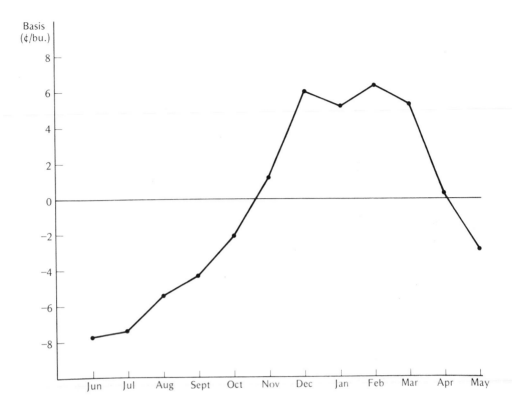

FIGURE 10.5   A NORMAL SEASONAL PATTERN FOR THE GULF-KANSAS CITY BASIS FOR HARD RED WINTER WHEAT[a]

[a]This pattern is based on a 12-month centered moving average of the monthly differences between the Gulf cash quote and the Kansas City *March* futures (Gulf-Kansas City March).

bids and hold in hopes of better prices. Thus, in spite of large supplies and low prices, the stocks can be in "tight hands" and not really available to the buying elevators and exporters. When exporters have orders to fill, they may be forced to bid up the basis to stimulate movement of wheat or other grain from storage into market channels.

Similar opportunities emerge in the other grains. Figure 10.6 shows a sketch of the normal central Iowa basis for cash corn against the nearby Chicago futures contract and a hypothetical pattern for one particular year. During some harvest periods, the opportunity to take advantage of an expected change in the basis emerges. At point A, for example, the relatively small basis suggests cash prices are unusually high during harvest

Table 10.7
Net Results of Selected Strategies During Years When the Basis Is Unusually Favorable at Harvest [a]

Strategies

Date	Sell at Harvest	Store	Store and Hedge	Sell Corn and Buy Futures
Nov. (year t)	Sells cash corn @ $3.00	Stores corn and estimates cost of carrying to September @ 25¢ per bu.	Stores corn and sells September futures @ $3.30 with basis at −30¢ during November	Sells cash corn @ $3.00 and buys September futures @ $3.30 expecting the basis to move out (become more negative) from the −30¢
Sept. (year t+1): Price increase	—	Sells corn @ $3.50 Net: 25¢ above selling at harvest	Sells corn @ $3.50 and buys back September futures @ $3.90 with basis @ −40¢ Net: −35¢ plus costs of the hedge compared to selling at harvest	Sells September futures @ $3.90 with basis @ −40¢ Net: 60¢ minus the costs of futures trade above selling at harvest
Sept. (year t+1): Price decrease	—	Sells corn @ $2.50 Net: −75¢ compared to selling @ harvest	Sells corn @ $2.50 and buys back September futures @ $2.90 with basis @ −40¢. Net: −35¢ plus costs of futures trade compared to selling @ harvest.	Sells September futures @ $2.90 with basis @ −40¢ Net: −40¢ plus costs of futures trade compared to selling @ harvest

[a] When the basis is unusually narrow at harvest, the market is saying "sell cash corn." The producer who believes, based on his analysis, prices will rise during the year should still sell his cash corn. He can buy futures if he insists on being "long corn" and speculate in the futures instead of speculating in cash corn. The probability of the basis that is unusually favorable (small negative value) at harvest deteriorating during the market year is high. If this happens, the producer could be better off being long in futures since futures go up relative to cash.

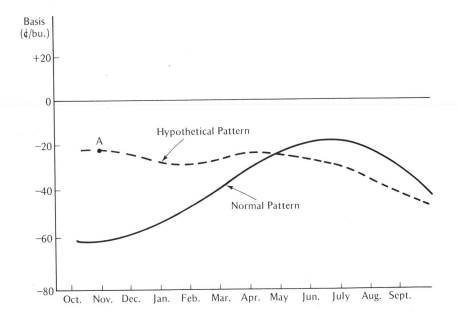

FIGURE 10.6   **THE FUTURES-CASH BASIS FOR CORN IN CENTRAL IOWA**

relative to the futures market. Under these circumstances, selling cash corn at harvest appears advisable. If, given an analysis of the situation, the producer feels storage would have been profitable in this particular year, he could buy futures and speculate in futures instead of in cash corn.

For the non-storable commodity, such as cattle or hogs, the options open to the decision maker are a bit different. Since the product is marketable only when it reaches certain weights and/or grades, the hold-sell decision is not the key decision. But knowledge of the basis and its normal pattern of behavior can also be important.

In any local market, the basis for cattle may vary seasonally within the year. In Figure 10.7, the average futures-cash basis over a period of three years is plotted for the cattle feeder in the Texas Panhandle. During the late spring months and again in the December–January period, cash prices in the Texas Panhandle increase relative to the nearby futures contract. This can make a hedge very effective since the feeder sells in a high cash market relative to the futures.

There are other opportunities. Close examination reveals significant seasonal changes in the basis for slaughter heifers. Good grade steers show a seasonal change in their relationship to Choice steers and the relationship varies from one market to the next. Slaughter hogs that are heavier than the allowable delivery weights tend to show a smaller discount (negative

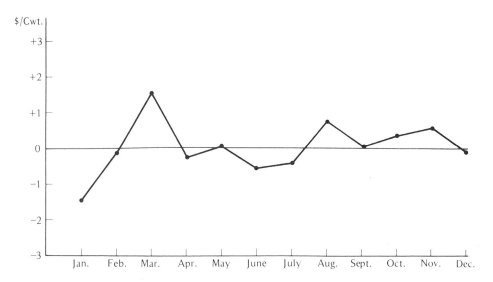

FIGURE 10.7   AVERAGE FUTURES-CASH BASIS, BY MONTHS, 1975–77 FOR THE
TEXAS PANHANDLE CASH MARKET[a]

[a]Calculated by subtracting the weekly average cash price, Texas Panhandle, from the average closes of the nearby futures during the second full trading week of each month. These differences were then averaged for each month across the three years 1975–77.

basis) in February and again in the summer months. Knowledge of the normal basis pattern and how to take advantage of unusual developments requires that the manager know the situation for his market, understand the particulars of the hold-sell and hedge decisions as they relate to basis behavior, and be prepared to act when an opportunity presents itself.

Summary

Numerous approaches are available in developing a hedging program. Which program is best will be a function of what the decision maker is trying to accomplish, his financial position and ability to carry price risk, and his ability to manage risk. Since these factors vary widely, no one best hedging strategy works for all.

Most hedging programs will accomplish a reduction in risk as reflected in lower variances or other measures of variability in the income stream. But the reduction in risk often comes at the expense of a significant decrease in the average profit level. This has prompted interest in hedging strategies that show an ability to reduce risk with little or no decrease in average profits.

Alternatives range from the simple place-and-hold strategies to more complex programs that place and lift hedges using the results of fundamental analysis or a technical indicator of change in market direction. The objective of the place-and-lift or selective approaches to hedging is simple—to have the hedge in place when the market is going against you and to have the hedge off to allow the benefits of the cash market when moves in the cash market are in your favor. If it can be done, this is the best of all worlds.

Much work remains to be done but some of the selective strategies using chart signals or such technical tools as the moving averages show an ability to decrease the risk and increase profits. The moving average strategies in particular have appeared because they offer:

1. Simplicity of calculation and interpretation;

2. An objective approach that removes the decision maker from the game of emotion and guessing; and

3. An empirically verified ability to increase profitability of the overall operation when a set of averages that "fits" the price moves for a particular commodity has been selected.

In this text, we have discussed on numerous occasions the importance of price. The increasing volatility of most commodity markets is apparent. Most marketing texts currently in use spend very little time on trade in commodity futures and hedging strategies. This must change. By 1985, a majority of producers will join the majority of processors, handlers, exporters, etc., who are actively using commodity futures. Understanding hedging is important today and will be critically important in the future.

Footnotes

1. This concept of basis keeps coming up. Here, we are suggesting the futures tend to average around 20 cents above local cash during December. The importance of the producer knowing the normal level and behavior of this basis cannot be overemphasized.

2. There remains a strong fear of the notorious margin call. Producers who should know better see the money as being "lost." But the only real cost is interest on the added margin money. As we have seen in earlier discussions, the lock-in margin will be realized and interest costs on extra margin are seldom enough to seriously threaten the profits of the hedge.

3. Unfortunately, this criterion cannot be used as a general guideline because the scale selected for the vertical axis will influence the slope of the trend lines. Whatever the scale, the point holds—the unusually "steep" trend lines are usually strictly short run and are not necessarily indicative of the trend in the market.

4. Detailed examination of the results of analyses indicates the moving averages accomplish the increase in mean returns over time by decreasing the magnitude of losses. This is especially true of the large losses. While the unhedged or the hedge and hold alternatives will occasionally be hit by huge losses, the moving average programs are effective in reducing the severity of the large losses.

5. In evaluating these possible courses of action it is important to keep in mind that the decision to hold grain (to be long in the market) is made on the basis of an analysis of the outlook in the market. If the decision to be long has been made, then consideration of the level and behavior of the basis can help determine whether being long in the cash market or in the futures market is likely to be the most profitable.

Questions

1. What is "selective hedging"?

2. Outline the trading plan you would recommend to the novice hedger who is just getting started.

3. Discuss and illustrate the notion of a "false signal" when moving averages are used to buy and sell futures.

4. Some agricultural producers are prone to dismiss the idea of hedging because they see this as "gambling on the futures market." How would you respond to such a statement?

5. Describe the hedging plan you would recommend for
   (a) the young cotton farmer in Mississippi who is just getting started and who has a very weak financial picture, and
   (b) the large corn farmer in Iowa who has no long-term debt and has a sound financial picture.

Selected References

Brown, Robert A., and Wayne D. Purcell, *Price Prediction Models and Related Hedging Programs for Feeder Cattle.* Stillwater: Okla. Agr. Exp. Sta. Bul. B-734, January 1978.

Franzmann, John R., *Technical Analysis of Futures Markets: A Tool For The Hedger, Part I.''* Stillwater: Okla. Current Farm Econ., Vol. 48, Dec. 1975.

Heifner, Richard G., "Optimal Hedging Levels and Hedging Effectiveness in Cattle Feeding", *Agr. Econ. Res.* Vol. 24, 1972.

McCoy, John H. and Robert V. Price, *Cattle Hedging Strategies.* Manhattan: Kansas Agr. Exp. Sta. Bul. No. 591, August 1975.

Purcell, Wayne D. and Thomas Richardson, *Quantitative Models to Predict Quarterly Average Cash Prices and Related Hedging Strategies,* Stillwater: Okla. Agr. Exp. Sta. Bul. B-731, December 1977.

part five

Decision Models, Techniques, Market Strategies

Understanding the operating environment, prices, and the commodity markets starts to bear fruit when these various parts are integrated into decision models and marketing strategies. In the area of uncertainty, the need for help is acute. The Bayesian approach provides a logical and effective framework. For problem situations where subjective probabilities are all that is available, Bayesian decision theory and the related analytical approaches can help.

Any marketing program has to start with an understanding of the consumer. Particular strategies for advertising, pricing, new product development, or entry into new markets will miss their mark unless they are based on a sound awareness of the consumer and consumer behavior. With a sound foundation, any type of decision situation can be handled. This does not mean the decision will always be right. What it means is that the probability of being right is higher if there *is* a marketing strategy, there *is* some type of decision model, and there *is* an awareness that tough problems, even under conditions of uncertainty, have to be faced.

In Part V, we deal with the necessity of spending time and effort on marketing strategies and in making marketing decisions. Models, analytical techniques, and strategies are explained and illustrated to help the student take another step toward becoming a more effective market analyst and decision maker.

chapter eleven

Decision Processes and Criteria

Marketing decisions are important because of their implications to the economic well-being of the firm. Marketing decisions are difficult because they involve deciding whether to act, when to act, and which way price will move. These and other dimensions of the decision process must be handled with less than perfect information. In this chapter, we look at the setting within which marketing decisions are made and describe some of the tools that can be used to facilitate more effective decisions.

Criteria

Decisions must be made with some criterion or criteria in mind. Goals must be established. Is profit maximization a primary goal? Or are growth and expansion more important? Will substantial levels of risk be accepted to allow consideration of alternatives that offer more profit potential? Is stability of the income flow more important than the level of income? What about the financial position of the firm—and its ability to carry risk?

Goals are long-run guides to action. Once the goal or goals of the firm are set, strategies and related decision models can be established. Models are important because of the complexity of the environment within which the marketing decision must be made and the many variables that must be considered.

STATES OF KNOWLEDGE

In considering decision situations, three states of knowledge can be identified. The distinction among the three is on the basis of the level of knowledge concerning the operating environment within which the decision must be made. The concept of an operating environment can be illustrated by the use of a payoff table such as that shown in Table 11.1. Across the top are alternative "states of nature." These are descriptions of the environment within which a course of action can be taken. They may be different price levels, the ways in which consumers might react to a new product or service, levels of rainfall, etc. Down the side are alternative strategies. In the body of the table are the outcomes for each strategy if a particular state of nature evolves. For example, O_{12} will be the outcome if strategy S_1 is chosen and state of nature N_2 evolves.

Each possible outcome is a net return figure or an estimate of returns to fixed resources. Thus, each outcome represents the equivalent of a budget for a specific course of action or strategy and state of nature. For example, S_1 might be a strategy that calls for shifting acreage from corn to soybeans, and N_2 could be the soybean price if national soybean acreage increases by two to four percent. The outcome O_{12} would require an estimate of soybean prices if other farmers shift and acreage increases two to four percent.

If the decision maker knows which state of nature will occur, this is a

Table 11.1
The Important Parts of a Payoff Table

Strategies	States of Nature			
	N_1	N_2	—	N_n
S_1	O_{11}	O_{12}	—	
S_2	O_{21}	—		
|				|
|				|
S_m				O_{mn}

certainty situation.[1] Important real-world decisions under conditions of certainty include those situations with such a large number of alternative courses of action that the situation is complex. Examples include the least-cost distribution of a product from 10 production sites to 20 distribution centers when the production costs, transportation rates, and quantities are known. Least-cost rations in livestock production or ingredient mixes for processed meats provide other situations when the technical coefficients, prices, etc., are known but the question of which is the least-cost mix is complex and difficult. When the decision maker has or can calculate objective probabilities[2] for the alternative states of nature, then we have a *risk* situation. Table 11.2 illustrates in the form of a payoff table. Across the top are four states of nature that reflect levels of rainfall. The strategies listed down the side are alternative crop combinations. In the body of the table are "payoffs" for the 12 strategy and state of nature combinations. For example, if crop B is planted and the rainfall accumulation is in the 35 to 39 range, then the payoff per acre will be $40.

Each state of nature has a probability of occurrence. In risk situations, the probabilities meet the following conditions:

1. The probabilities are objective in that they are based on a data history that allows frequency counts in calculating the probabilities.

2. The probabilities for the states of nature must sum to 1.0. This means the states of nature listed cover all possibilities with a significant probability of occurrence.

3. The probabilities are associated with states of nature that are mutually exclusive. That is, no two or more states of nature can occur at the same time.

Given completion of the various elements of the payoff table, the questions of which strategy is best and how it should be selected emerge. Which is best goes back to the long-range goals of the firm. If the goal is to maximize returns to the firm over time, the decision criterion to be employed is:

Select the strategy with the highest expected value.

The expected value[3] of a particular strategy involves weighting the payoff for each state of nature by the probability of occurrence for that particular state of nature. In effect, then, the expected value of any particular strategy is the weighted average of that strategy with the probabilities attached to the states of nature being used as weights.[4] Selecting the strategy with the highest expected value will, over time, maximize the net returns to the operation.

Table 11.2
A Payoff Table Illustrating the Risk Situation

States of Nature (Annual Rainfall) [a]

Strategies (Crop Combinations)	N_1: 25–29 ($\frac{2}{10}$)	N_2: 30–34 ($\frac{3}{10}$)	N_3: 35–39 ($\frac{3}{10}$)	N_4: 40–44
S_1: All Crop A	30	33	36	40
S_2: 50% A-50% B	25	31.5	38	45
S_3: All Crop B	20	30	40	50

[a] The fractions shown in ( )s by each state of nature are the probabilities of occurrence.

Many examples of risk situations face the decision maker in our production-marketing systems. When rainfall, temperature, or other dimensions of nature are involved, a risk situation exists. Crop production, gain by livestock, death loss, crop failure, and many growth processes operate in an environment of risk. Often, price or the outlook for price moves of particular magnitude is treated as a risk situation. Some decision makers are willing to base expected price increases or decreases on the historical pattern—how many years of the past 20 price increased over 20 percent, how many years the increase was in the 15 to 20 percent range, etc. When the states of nature are defined so that objective probabilities are associated with those states of nature, we are dealing with a risk situation.

Where marketing decisions are concerned, the state of knowledge that is both most prevalent and the most difficult is the *uncertainty* situation. Here, there are no objective probabilities associated with the states of nature. And, unlike the risk situation, there is no universally accepted decision rule or criterion. Over time, two different approaches have been tried in an attempt to cope with the difficult decisions that have to be made in a world of uncertainty. The "game theoretic" criteria have been around for a long time. They are criteria developed primarily by different analysts in their attempts to develop a workable approach to the uncertainty situation. Since the 1940s, the Bayesian approach, an approach based on Bayesian statistics, has received widespread attention and has essentially displaced the game theoretic approaches.

Uncertainty: Game Theoretic Approaches[5]

Among the game theoretic approaches are the MAXIMIN, the MAXIMAX, and the Savage Regret criterion. Table 11.3 illustrates the MAXIMIN criterion.

The MAXIMIN is a conservative and pessimistic approach. It focuses on the minimum payoff under each strategy and selects the strategy that

Table 11.3
Payoff Table To Illustrate the MAXIMIN Approach
to Decisions Under Conditions of Uncertainty

	States of Nature		
Strategies	N_1	N_2	N_3
S_1	120	65	150
S_2	80	70	80
S_3	200	60	240

offers the largest of the minimum payoffs. The approach carries an implicit assumption that nature will do her worst and treats nature as a conscious adversary. Using this criterion to evaluate Table 11.3 dictates a selection of strategy 2. Note the solution borders on the ridiculous since the potential of strategy 2 would appear to be well below that of the other strategies.

The MAXIMAX criterion focuses attention on the largest payoff for each strategy, and then selects the strategy with the largest payoff. It is therefore an optimistic "go for broke" criterion. Applying this criterion to Table 11.4 dictates selection of strategy 1.

The MAXIMIN and MAXIMAX criteria have several characteristics in common:

1. They fail to use, and therefore "waste," part of the information contained in the payoff table since they focus attention on the extreme values;

2. They are capable of generating ridiculous decisions because they do focus on the extremes and pay no attention to the outcomes of other strategy and state of nature combinations; and

Table 11.4
Payoff Table To Illustrate the MAXIMAX
Approach to Decisions Under Conditions
of Uncertainty

	States of Nature		
Strategies	N_1	N_2	N_3
S_1	−50	0	105
S_2	80	90	100
S_3	90	95	90

3. They both ignore any judgment, expertise, or knowledge the decision maker could bring to the problem. The decision maker has no role to play in the process once the decision to use the particular criterion has been made.

The Savage Regret approach generates a regret matrix from the original payoff matrix. The criterion then becomes one of minimizing the regret or "pain" from the various payoffs. An optimism-pessimism index is employed in the calculations; all components of the payoff table are considered; and the decision maker is brought into the process in establishing the index level. But the approach has apparent weaknesses. The decision on the index level is arbitrary and void of any analytical rigor. The approach provides no opportunity for a self-correcting process before the final decision is made.

Uncertainty: Bayesian Approach[6]

The Bayesian approach to decisions under conditions of uncertainty differs significantly from the game theoretic approaches. Bayesian or subjective probabilities for the states of nature are used. The knowledge, experience, and judgment of the decision maker are used in establishing the probabilities. An analytically rigorous procedure for bringing in new information and revising the initial probabilities that are assigned is available. In capsule form, the steps in the Bayesian approach are:

1. The payoff table is set up. Alternative states of nature are defined and strategies are formulated.

2. Based on the experience, knowledge, and judgment of the decision maker, probabilities are assigned to the states of nature. These are *prior* probabilities.

3. If the decision maker is ready to make a decision after the prior probabilities are assigned, he calculates the expected value of each strategy and selects the strategy with the highest expected value.

4. If he or she feels more information is needed before making a decision, the decision maker enters an information search period that is part of the posterior analysis. This phase can range from an informal information gathering approach (such as telephoning several "experts") to a scientific and possibly elaborate market survey (such as a sampling of consumer preferences or opinions). Theoretically, the search process is started and continued as long as the marginal value of new information exceeds its marginal cost.

5. The new information is combined with the existing information base, the prior probabilities are revised, and posterior probabilities are developed. A liberal interpretation of what constitutes Bayesian analysis would allow the two bodies of information to be integrated by the decision maker, and the prior probabilities to be revised on the basis of judgment. A more rigorous approach involves using conditional probabilities and a mathematical formulation, which generates quantitative estimates of the posterior probabilities.

Once the probabilities are assigned to the states of nature, the procedure followed in evaluating the payoff table is the same as that in the risk situation. The expected values are calculated for the strategies, and the strategy that has the maximum expected value is selected. The procedures involved in calculating the posterior probabilities require more explanation, however.

To illustrate, assume we have a wheat producer who is trying to decide whether to store his wheat from the harvest period (June) until the following March. He estimates his cost of on-farm storage over this time period at 20 cents per bu. He formulates three alternative states of nature and defines them as:

N_1 = price will rise 10–19¢ per bushel during the storage period;

N_2 = price will rise 20–29¢ per bushel; and

N_3 = price will rise 30–39¢ per bushel.

His alternative strategies are simple and are defined as:

S_1 = sell wheat during the harvest period, and

S_2 = hold wheat until March and sell.

Using 15¢, 25¢, and 35¢ tor states of nature N_1, N_2, and N_3 respectively, the producer adds 5¢ to his storage costs to discount the added risk. He then calculates the payoffs shown in Table 11.5.[7] Drawing on his store of knowledge and past experience in the wheat market, the producer assigns prior probabilities as follows:

$$P(N_1) = .40$$
$$P(N_2) = .40$$
$$P(N_3) = .20$$

If a decision is made at this point, the decision will be to sell during harvest. Strategy S_1 has an expected value of 0 compared to −2 cents for strategy S_2. But our producer begins to feel uncomfortable about the situa-

Table 11.5
Payoff Table for a Hold-Sell Decision on Wheat

	States of Nature		
Strategies	N_1 (.4)	N_2 (.4)	N_3 (.2)
S_1	0	0	0
S_2	−10	0	+10

tion. He knows that in recent years strong export demand has shown the potential to push wheat prices up during the market year. If export demand is strong this year, a price rise of 30–40 cents is certainly possible. He decides to delay the decision and accumulate more information. He will telephone the Grain Marketing Extension Specialist at 10 land grant universities throughout the wheat producing region to get their expectations on export demand. Before making the calls, he decides on the following possible results and relates them to his states of nature:

Z_1 = Less than 4 of the 10 expect unusual strength in export demand, suggesting N_1 will be the state of nature;

Z_2 = From 4 to 6 of the 10 expect unusual strength in export demand, suggesting N_2 will be the state of nature; and

Z_3 = More than 6 of the 10 expect unusual strength in export demand, suggesting N_3 will be the state of nature.

Before making the calls, our decision maker has to deal with the issue of reliability of his simple and less than scientific poll. Thinking back over the recent years and the track records of the extension specialists, he concludes his survey will have a 70 percent reliability factor—i.e., will be right 70 percent of the time. In terms of probabilities, this converts to the following:

$$P(Z_1|N_1) = .7$$
$$P(Z_2|N_2) = .7$$
$$P(Z_3|N_3) = .7$$

The expression ($P(Z_1|N_1) = .7$ is a conditional probability and is read "the probability of observing Z_1 given that N_1 is the true state of nature is .7." The other expressions are interpreted accordingly.

A decision must also be made about the "error component." What, for example, is the probability of observing Z_1 given that N_2 is the true state of nature? What is the probability of observing Z_3 given N_1 is the true state of nature? Logic and rationale must be exercised here. Examine the following sets of conditional probabilities:

$P(Z_1|N_1) = .70$ $P(Z_2|N_1) = .15$ $P(Z_3|N_1) = .10$
$P(Z_1|N_2) = .20$ $P(Z_2|N_2) = .70$ $P(Z_3|N_2) = .20$
$P(Z_1|N_3) = .10$ $P(Z_2|N_3) = .15$ $P(Z_3|N_3) = .70$

Note the differences—and think about this before proceeding. It appears logical $P(Z_1|N_2)$ should be greater than $P(Z_1|N_3)$. The result Z_1 suggests no unusual strength in demand. Given this, we would expect a 20–29 cent rise to be more probable than a 30–39 cent rise. The reasoning is reversed when thinking of the conditional probabilities associated with Z_3. N_2 would be more nearly consistent with Z_3 as a survey result than would N_1. If Z_2 is the observed result, there is little basis for arguing either N_1 or N_3 is more probable. The probability of the survey being wrong is split between N_1 and N_3.[8]

With this as background we can proceed with the calculations for the posterior probabilities. Note both the prior probabilities and the survey results are involved in the calculations. Assuming our producer observes Z_3 as a result of his survey, the posterior probabilities are calculated as follows:

$$P(N_1|Z_3) = \frac{P(N_1) \cdot P(Z_3|N_1)}{\sum\limits_{j=1}^{3} P(Z_3|N_j) \cdot P(N_j)}$$

$$= \frac{.4(.1)}{(.1)(.4) + (.2)(.4) + (.7)(.2)}$$

$$= \frac{.04}{.26} = .15$$

$$P(N_2|Z_3) = \frac{P(N_2) \cdot P(Z_3|N_2)}{\sum\limits_{j=1}^{3} P(Z_3|N_j) \cdot P(N_j)}$$

$$= \frac{.4(.2)}{.26} = \frac{.08}{.26} = .31$$

$$P(N_3|Z_3) = \frac{P(N_3) \cdot P(Z_3|N_3)}{\sum\limits_{j=1}^{3} P(Z_3|N_j) \cdot P(N_j)}$$

$$= \frac{.2(.7)}{.26} = \frac{.14}{.26} = .54$$

Focusing on $P(N_1|Z_3)$, let's examine what goes into the calculation. In the numerator, $P(N_1)$ is the prior probability. This original assignment was based on the producer's store of knowledge, experience, and judgment and is kept in the calculation for that reason. The $P(Z_3|N_1)$ is the probability of observing Z_3 as a survey result when N_1 is the true state of nature. Said another way, this is the probability the survey will incorrectly signal N_3 as the state of nature (since Z_3 suggests N_3) when N_1 is the true state of nature. In the denominator, we have the joint probability of observing survey result Z_3 and the prior probabilities across all states of nature. This probability, once calculated, stays the same for $P(N_2|Z_3)$ and $P(N_3|Z_3)$.

When the calculations are completed, the revised or posterior probabilities are:

$$P(N_1) = .15$$
$$P(N_2) = .31$$
$$P(N_3) = .54$$

Compared to the prior probabilities, $P(N_3)$ has increased significantly. This is logical since the added information suggested the strong export demand needed to push price higher might be there this particular year. Evaluating the payoff table using these revised probabilities yields:

$$E(S_1) = 0$$
$$E(S_2) = .15\,(-10) + .31\,(0) + .54\,(10)$$
$$= 3.9$$

Strategy S_2 would now be the choice. The expected value calls for a 3.9 cents per bu. increase after covering storage costs and the 5 cents "discount factor" to allow for the uncertainty of holding grain in volatile markets.

Other illustrations of the Bayesian approach are included in Appendix 11A. The Bayesian approach is a logical approach to decisions under uncertain conditions. If the posterior probabilities are not calculated mathematically, the approach still makes sense. The available knowledge of the decision maker is brought to the problem. Strategies are developed given various states of nature to which the strategies might reasonably be exposed. Based on knowledge and judgment, probabilities are assigned to the states of nature. If the decision maker is ready to take action, he evaluates the payoff table using these assigned probabilities and selects the strategy with the highest expected value. If he is not comfortable with his available knowledge, he delays action until he can gather additional information. This additional information is then used in combination with his original expectations on the states of nature to generate new and revised probabilities. Whether the process is entirely qualitative with no mathematical calculations at all, or whether a mathematical approach is taken, the process is logical and an orderly way of attacking the decision situation.

What can be more logical than formulating strategies, thinking about the alternatives the operating environment can bring, deciding which one is likely to crop up, and then proceeding to make a decision?

APPLICATION: SEASONAL PRICE PATTERNS

The concept of Bayesian statistics and bringing the decision maker into the middle of the process and taking advantage of his store of knowledge have broad application as a decision model. The approach is especially useful when there is a need to cope with the unexpected development in the marketplace.

Consider the problem facing the decision maker who uses the seasonal index but realizes developments within a particular year threaten to distort the normal seasonal pattern. What is needed is some logical and consistent way of incorporating the impact of the forces at work in the market into his model.

Visualize the position of the soybean producer harvesting in November who is trying to decide whether to store his beans and, if he stores, whether to hedge his position. He has accumulated the following information.

1. The seasonal index values for November and June are 96 and 104 respectively;

2. Costs of storing from November to June on the farm are estimated at 25 cents per bu; and

3. The harvest period price has fluctuated but remains in the $6.00 per bu. area.

If the normal seasonal pattern emerges, our producer is looking at a handsome profit to his storage operation. Using the seasonal index as a simple projection model, the expected price for June could be calculated as follows:

$$\frac{\text{November Index}}{\text{November Price}} = \frac{\text{June Index}}{X}$$

$$\frac{96}{\$6.00} = \frac{104}{X}$$

$$X = \$6.50$$

With storage costs estimated at 25 cents, a price move up of 50 cents during the year would give a profit to the storage operation of 25 cents per bu.

But more examination suggests this may not be a "normal" year in terms of the seasonal pattern. Other forces are at work in the market. A bit of digging reveals the following information:

1. The spot or current quotes (during November) for the July soybean futures are fluctuating around $6.30;

2. Available information suggests Brazil, with harvest in the April–May period, will show a significant increase in production;

3. Harvest-period prices for corn are being pressured down toward the $2.40–2.50 per bu. range and many analysts are expecting corn prices to go lower;

4. The soybean harvest is expected to produce a crop in excess of projected total disappearance for the crop year, which means a year-to-year increase in ending stocks;

5. Cotton prices have faltered and are at or below most estimates of the cost of producing cotton; and

6. Exports of beans, oil and meal are strong with weekly totals running above year-earlier levels. Domestic disappearance is also above year-earlier levels.

Let's now examine each of these pieces of information and see how our producer could use them.

The $6.30 trading level for the July soybeans represents a consensus of the traders of July futures as to what prices will be in July. Our producer looks at this $6.30 level, subtracts his normal June basis of 20 cents, and decides the trade expects a cash price in June of $6.10. Caution is needed here. Futures quotes are not accurate predictors of cash price and *should not be used as such*. But the intra-year pattern in trading levels of futures *is* indicative of the thinking of the traders. In this instance, the trade is saying the normal seasonal increment between November and June may not be there in this particular year. This message is worth noting.

Among the reasons the trade is registering a negative outlook is the situation in Brazil. Since the mid-1970s, Brazil has increased soybean production and become an increasingly important factor in the world trade of soybeans.[9] A high percentage of Brazil's production will enter the world market in the form of beans or after processing into meal and oil. This increased supply will influence the June market and could push prices down.

Corn prices are important. Historically, corn belt producers have shifted acreage from corn to beans when the beans-to-corn price ratio is 2.5:1 or greater as the planting decisions are made.[10] Some producers will already have seed and herbicide commitments but there still remains room for significant shifts in plantings. The possibility of acreage shifts to beans and away from corn makes for uncertainty concerning bean prices in the late spring and summer months. Our producer realizes this is one of the reasons the July futures are down relative to November. But he is concerned the shifts will be large and put even more downward pressure on prices during the summer months as the harvest period approaches.

The important relationship between ending stocks and price is widely recognized—and our producer is aware of that relationship. When ending stocks are expected to increase, price tends to move lower. The discussion and illustrations of Chapters 7 and 9 stressed the importance of ending stocks. Such stocks are a very accessible form of supply, are available without the uncertainties surrounding a growing crop, and are one of the single most important variables in determining price. When a significant increase in ending stocks is anticipated, expect to see the higher levels of stocks become a restraining influence on any seasonal increases in prices—especially in the second half of the crop year.

Cotton prices are important. In the delta areas of Mississippi, Louisiana, Arkansas, and in parts of Texas and other cotton-producing states in the Southeast, it is cotton instead of corn that competes with soybeans for the planted acreage. Falling prices of cotton tend to move acreage out of cotton into soybeans when bean prices suggest more profit per acre. This adds to the acreage that might be shifted to beans and accentuates the concern over soybean prices.

Strong export sales are on the positive side of the ledger. It is to the export arena that one must look for developments that could significantly increase total disappearance or use and prevent the buildup of stocks. Domestic disappearance or the domestic crush can and does vary from year to year but does not offer the potential for change that is found in exports. But with the potential in exports comes variability and uncertainty. The strength in export buying can disappear as quickly as it surfaces. And the situation is especially dangerous when a large Brazilian crop appears possible.

The producer has seen these various forces at work in the soybean market. But each year is different and just what will happen in this particular year is uncertain. In attempting to pull the various economic forces together, the producer establishes the set of probabilities shown in Table 11.6. He sees some possibility the price pattern that evolves could be consistent with a June index value as high as 104. But the probabilities he attaches to lower values of the index indicate he expects a lower price or is interested in discounting for the uncertainty of the situation.

The expected value of the June index for this particular year, based on the probabilities shown in Table 11.6, is 100. Using an index value of 100 gives an "expected" price for June of $6.25. Other prices are possible but the expected price—the price consistent with the expected value of the

Table 11.6
Subjective Probabilities for a Seasonal Index
Value: Allowing for Uncertainty

Index Value	Subjective Probability
104	.1
102	.2
100	.4
98	.2
96	.1

index of 100—is $6.25. With this, our producer is in a dilemma. If the $6.25 cash price prevails in June, the price increase during the November to June period will be 25 cents—just equal his estimated storage costs. Should he sell or store? And if he decides to store, should he hedge with the July futures trading at $6.30?

The decision on whether to store is a toss-up. If the 25 cent figure includes interest charges, a fair return on the investment, etc., storing makes sense if the 25 cents can be covered with some assurance. But herein lies the problem. At current trading levels of the July soybean futures contract, only 10 cents per bu. could be "locked in."[11] The decision process should proceed as follows:

1. If the basis at harvest is unusually favorable to the producer, sell the cash beans at harvest and take no position in the futures.[12] Given the information available, this does not appear to be a year in which the probability of profiting from being long in beans, whether cash or futures, is very high.

2. If the basis is unfavorable, meaning cash is below futures by an unusually large magnitude, hold the cash beans and look to the futures market to protect the cash position. Among the approaches that can be taken are:

   a. Place the hedge if the July futures contract trades up to a level that allows "locking in" at least 25 cents;

   b. If the futures market is trending upward, use moving averages or some other technical indicator to help identify a top in the market for July soybean futures and place the hedge when the market tops; or

   c. Use an appropriate set of moving averages or other technical indicator to place and lift the hedge depending on the movements in the market.

Holding the beans in a year in which significant price appreciation is unlikely will be risky. And waiting for the opportunity to lock in a particular amount, while it looks like a conservative approach, is especially risky. The opportunity may never come. Using a set of moving averages as demonstrated in Chapter 10 has logic and potential on its side. If the market turns down and heads into a bad price break, the averages will signal a hedge and protect the position. But if the market does surge higher, the averages will lift the hedge and allow the benefit of any increase in cash price. And this or some similar approach that places and lifts the hedge based on changes in market direction offers the potential of contributing profits from the futures side of the hedged operation. It is important to remember, however, that the technical system must fit the soybean market and the producer must have the discipline to stick with his system.

APPLICATION: REPLACEMENT DECISIONS

Another type of decision that lends itself to the application of Bayesian type probabilities is the replacement decision. Anything that is done year round and on a batch basis requires making a replacement decision if the objective is to maximize returns to the operation over time. Cattle feeding, hog feeding, broilers, turkeys—production of all these is often year round and on a batch basis. A point needs emphasizing here before we proceed. Maximizing profits to *each* batch is *not* consistent with maximizing profits over time.[13]

Let's use a cattle feeding operation to illustrate. Figure 11.1 demonstrates the shape of the total net revenue curves (TNR) and related average (ANR) and marginal net revenue (MNR). Note these are *net revenue* curves—profit curves. The logic behind the shape of the TNR curve goes back to the nature of the production function for cattle. Recall that total physical product (TPP) increases at a decreasing rate throughout Stage II, the rational stage of production. Given this physical relationship, costs tend to increase at an increasing rate. Since the cattle will not be sold until they grade Choice, there is only one price—the Choice price—used in calculating total revenue. The TNR function is therefore a smooth curve with its concave curvature coming from the curvature of the TPP curve. The ANR curve is simply the TNR curve divided by the number of days on feed, and the MNR curve is the change in TNR for an additional feeding day. There will be a set of these curves for each set of cattle on feed. And for any replacement set of cattle that could be bought and put on feed, there is an *expected* set of revenue curves based on estimates of cost of the cattle, cost of gain, and selling price for the finished steers. Given these two sets of curves, the decision criterion that will maximize profit to the feeding program over time can be stated as follows:

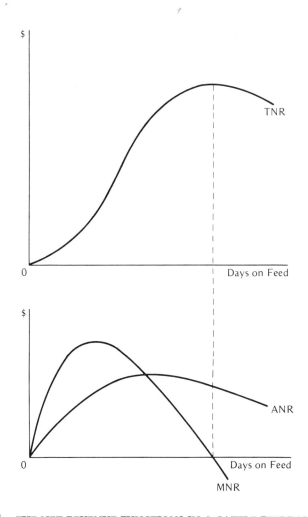

FIGURE 11.1   THE NET REVENUE FUNCTIONS IN A CATTLE FEEDING OPERATION

Replace the current set of cattle when the MNR of the current set equals the maximum expected value of the ANR of the replacement set.

The logic of the approach is sound. For the continuous feeding operation, there is an opportunity cost of feeding the current set. That opportunity cost is the profits the replacement set of cattle would be making if those cattle were on feed. There is a point at which continued feeding of the current set, even though profits per head are still increasing, will contribute less to the total profit stream over time than will the replacement set of cattle.[14]

Figure 11.2 illustrates and also provides a framework within which the impact of changes in key economic variables can be analyzed. The net revenue curves for both the current and replacement cattle are drawn for a fixed set of the economic variables that would shift the curves. For the current cattle, the price of finished cattle is about the only economic force that is still variable as the cattle approach market-ready weights. The buying price of the cattle four to six months earlier, the cost of the feed that has gone into the cattle, the impact of death loss, etc., are now largely fixed. But the net revenue curves will shift with changes in the expected selling price of finished cattle. Higher cash prices will shift the curves up, lower cash prices will shift the curves down. If nothing changes in terms of expectations for the replacement cattle, anticipation of higher selling prices in the short run will delay the optimal time of replacement. Figure 11.3 illustrates. For higher selling prices, we see a shift from MNR to MNR' and the optimal replacement point is delayed from R to R'.

Many factors can still affect expectations on the replacement set of cattle. The buying price of the cattle, costs of feed, expectations on the selling price of the cattle four to six months later—all these things can and do change from week to week or even day to day. If the net revenue functions for the current cattle are stable, anything that decreases the expectations for the replacement set will delay the replacement point. Conversely, anything that increases expectations for the replacement set will speed up the replacement point. If revenue functions for both sets of cattle are changing, it is a matter of which change has the most impact.[15]

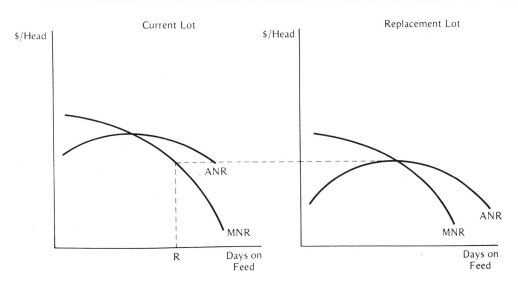

R = Optimum Replacement Date

FIGURE 11.2   ANALYTICAL FRAMEWORK TO DETERMINE THE OPTIMUM RE-
PLACEMENT DATE

It is with the expectations on the replacement cattle that the probabilistic dimension is needed. Some of the variables affecting the projected profitability of the replacement cattle can be "tied down." Feed grains can be bought in advance or hedged using corn futures. Finish dates can be projected and hedges set on the finished slaughter cattle. But uncertainty remains. Basis changes in corn and in the slaughter cattle can influence the outcome of the hedges. Gains can be less than anticipated, which increases costs. Whatever the uncertainty, it can be brought into the decision process by assigning probabilities to a set of net revenue functions for the replacement cattle.

Figure 11.4 illustrates. A total of five ANR functions are shown. Subjective probabilities can be attached to each. Uncertainty can be reflected in the probability assignments. If the manager would like to discount the expectations on the replacement cattle because a four to six months planning horizon is involved, this can be done through the probability levels assigned to each ANR function. Using the maximum value from each ANR function, the expected value becomes a logical measure to use in the decision criterion. In practical terms, the criterion becomes the following:

$$\text{Replace when } MNR_{CL} = E \, (Max \, ANR_{RL})$$

where:

MNR_{CL} = marginal net revenue of the current lot, and
ANR_{RL} = average net revenue of the replacement lot.

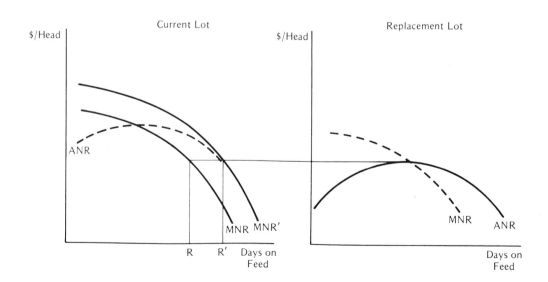

FIGURE 11.3   IMPACT OF A HIGHER PRICE FOR THE CURRENT LOT OF CATTLE ON THE OPTIMUM REPLACEMENT DATE

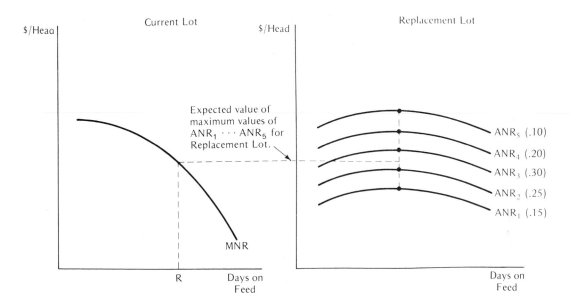

FIGURE 11.4   A BAYESIAN APPROACH TO THE UNCERTAINTY IN THE AVERAGE NET REVENUE PICTURE FOR THE REPLACEMENT LOT

Programming Alternatives

In the age of the computer, many marketing decisions can be effectively handled with the computer. The programming alternatives range from simplistic routines such as linear programming to highly sophisticated simulation procedures. In the section we explore selected alternatives briefly. The purpose is to develop awareness of programming alternatives and how they can be used, not to deal with the mechanics of programming.

LINEAR PROGRAMMING

Computerized linear programming routines allow maximization (or minimization) subject to a specified set of restraints. Generally, the computerized routine is used when the situation is too complex for simple exposition. For example, a processing firm producing 10 different products using 20 different raw materials is interested in the product combination that will maximize profits. Each of the 10 product alternatives has a specific cost and profit potential.

Looking at the two-product case helps to clarify what linear programming is all about. To illustrate, assume we have a meat processing firm that can produce two products. Call them A and B, and the following situation holds:

1. A and B both require two raw materials, R_1 and R_2. Up to 200 lbs. of R_1 and up to 300 lbs. of R_2 are available per day from the processor's slaughter operation.

2. Each pound of A requires .25 lbs. of R_1 and .5 lbs. of R_2. Each pound of B requires .2 lbs. of R_1 and .25 lbs. of R_2.

3. Product A shows a profit of $1.00 per lb. and product B shows a profit of $.70 per lb.

The problem is to determine how many lbs. of A and B should be produced to maximize profits.

$$\text{Let: } X_1 = \text{units of A to be produced}$$
$$X_2 = \text{units of B to be produced}$$
$$\pi = \text{profit}$$
$$\text{Maximize: } \pi = 1.00\,X_1 + .70\,X_2$$
$$\text{Subject to: } .25\,X_1 + .2X_2 \leq 200$$
$$.5X_1 + .25X_2 \leq 300$$
$$X_1, X_2 \geq 0$$

What we see here is a profit equation that we wish to maximize subject to two constraint equations and the obvious requirement that the quantities of both A and B produced be zero or greater. In more direct terms, the constraint equations are saying production of A and B in quantities X_1 and X_2 cannot use more than 200 lbs. of R_1 or more than 300 lbs. of R_2. These constraints are shown graphically in Figure 11.5. The shaded area is the "feasible area," of production—i.e., the dark shaded line becomes a production possibilities curve or boundary. All areas on and below the production possibilities curve are combinations of A and B that could be produced. The most profitable combination of A and B, with per-unit profits of $1.00 and $.70 respectively, is the combination at the point marked "C." This is true so long as the slope of the profit function is such that the highest possible profit line touches the production boundary at point C.[16]

When more than two products and two inputs are involved, the use of graphical procedures becomes impractical. But the processes are the same. To illustrate, let's trace the approach taken by a firm that slaughters live cattle and then breaks the dressed carcasses into primal, sub-primal, or retail cuts. Relevant information is as follows:

1. The plant has an operating capacity of 100 carcasses per hour. Each possible "cut"—from primals to retail cuts—requires time on the breaking line and varying amounts of time going through the saws and cutting procedures. Costs of generating each type of "cut" have been estimated by calculating the machine time, man-hours

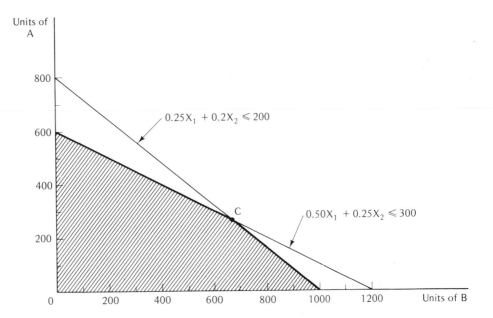

11.5   ILLUSTRATION OF THE LINEAR PROGRAMMING SOLUTION IN A
SIMPLE TWO-PRODUCT WORLD

required, and allocating a share of overhead to the finished product.

2. Profits for the various "cuts" vary with changes in market price
   relationships between primals, sub-primals, and retail cuts.

3. The technical coefficients with regard to the yield of various cuts
   vary with the type of carcass. For example, a Choice yield grade 2
   carcass will not yield the same mix or combination of trimmed cuts
   of finished product which the Choice yield grade 4 will yield.
   These differences have been estimated for the various yield
   grades.

More detail could be added but this should serve to illustrate. The firm
manager is interested in maximizing profits to his investment given the
particular type of cattle and dressed carcasses he has available. The critical
question can be stated as follows:

> For a given set of prices in the market place, what combination of
> products will maximize profits?

The best approach to this problem is to first do a good job of estimating
costs for each of the various finished products. Then make sure all techni-

cal coefficients are accurate and are revised as new technology is available or as new regulations are issued on the use of preservatives, etc., which will influence the cost of production. Next, work with a computer analyst to get a program set up that will allow analysis of profit maximizing routines. Buy a computer with the capacity to handle the problem or rent time on a computer system from a university or private concern. Each time there is a significant change in the price relationships among the various finished products that can be produced, change the prices in the program and rerun to see what, if any, changes should be considered in the product mix being generated.

There are many other market-related decisions where linear programming is a valuable management tool. It is equally relevant for problems where cost minimization, not profit maximization, is the primary need. In processed meats, for example, programs can be set up to generate the least-cost ingredient mix for a particular processed meat subject to available raw materials and any desired or legal restraints on water content, protein level, cereal level, etc. Transportation is another area where cost minimization procedures are important. Imagine trying to decide the least-cost way to serve 20 customers in 20 different cities from as few as five distribution points. With accurate data on cost of shipping, quantity at the supply points, and need at the demand points, a computer can give you the answer in seconds.

SIMULATION

There are many additional programming alternatives—non-linear programming, quadratic programming, integer programming—the list could go on. Most are beyond the scope of this book. But the concept of simulation deserves attention. The term is so broadly used that brief consideration of exactly what is meant by simulation is worthwhile. We will also take a look at how simulation techniques can be used in analyzing the comparative effectiveness of alternative marketing structures.

In its broadest sense, simulation refers to virtually any attempt to "simulate" or approximate the real world via models. To a skilled market systems analyst, however, the term simulation will often mean something else. He will use the term to describe efforts to model the dynamics or the time-related interactive or behavioral dimension of real world processes.

The question of what is and is not simulation is less important than knowing what can be done. In general, the advent of simulation and simulation techniques in the social sciences has been correlated with the advancements in theory and practice in the engineering fields. Many of the techniques being used in simulation studies are adopted from fields such as electrical engineering. But it is not just the techniques that are needed. In the marketing field, interest in simulation came when we finally saw more interest in the total marketing system.

In a study of the Oklahoma beef marketing system, Nelson attempted to conceptualize and simulate the processes from the cow-calf level through the breaking of the dressed beef carcass.[17] In very brief terms, the following steps were completed:

1. Growth curves were estimated for each of 13 breed-types of cattle.

2. A mathematical program was developed to simulate inputs, output (quality grade: yield grade, etc.) for each of the 13 breed-types at varying percentages of the mature weight of the cattle.

3. The information from the previous steps was incorporated into a linear programming model. The model analyzed the economic processes from production to breaking (fabricating) given different ways of organizing the industry and different information structures in terms of accuracy and sophistication of the information used.

4. Output from the linear programming model was generated when maximizing profits to each of the subsystems and to the "team" (or totally integrated system). The output included type of cattle, weights, grades, costs of producing lean retail cuts, profits per head at the various stages from cow-calf through the breaking or fabricating stage, and return on system investment for the vertically integrated or "team" approach to industry organization. Comparisons of costs and other measures of efficiency were made across organizational structures and across the type of information structure used.

The research effort was obviously complex and will not be presented in more detail here. Interesting results included the following:

1. The cost of producing lean meat was not significantly affected by the accuracy and level of sophistication in the information used. When quality grade and yield grade were estimated for live cattle as part of the exchange process versus trading using carcass grades, the cost of producing lean meat was not significantly higher.

2. Using the more sophisticated approaches to exchange involving actual yield grade and actual quality grade versus estimates tended to transfer income from the processing subsector back toward the producing subsector.

3. The vertically integrated or "team approach" produced lean meat at a cost significantly below those realized when separate ownership of the various functions was allowed and coordination was left up to the price system.

4. Restricting the rest of the system to the particular type of cattle that maximized profits to just the cow-calf operator resulted in significantly higher costs of producing lean beef.

The simulation area offers exciting potential but does require sophisticated analytical skills. For purposes of this book, students need at least a limited understanding of what the concept is and some idea of where and how it can be applied.

Summary

Most marketing decisions are made under conditions of risk or uncertainty. Sound analytical processes and decision models are needed if the marketing program is to be successful.

Decisions under risk conditions benefit from the capacity to generate objective probabilities for the various states of nature to which the alternative strategies might be exposed. A carefully constructed payoff table can be evaluated by calculating the expected value of each strategy. Choosing the strategy with the largest expected value will maximize returns to the operation over time.

Under conditions of uncertainty, the situation is more complex. There are no objective probabilities and no single and universally accepted decision criterion. The game theoretic approaches have not proven to be highly effective. Most attention is now being focused on Bayesian analysis.

The Bayesian approach is a logical approach to making decisions under uncertain conditions. The knowledge and experience of the decision maker are used in constructing the payoff table and assigning prior probabilities to the states of nature. If more information is needed before a decision is made, the procedure allows for the accumulation of new information and its incorporation into the decision process in an analytically rigorous fashion. The prior probabilities are employed along with the new information and revised or posterior probabilities are then calculated. The payoff table is evaluated and the strategy with the highest expected value is selected.

The general Bayesian approach can be used as a model whenever uncertainty exists. A seasonal index can be modified to reflect the existence of unusual forces in the marketplace by using Bayesian probabilities. Whether the problem is simple or complex and requires sophisticated simulation or modeling procedures, the Bayesian approach appears to be a logical and functional approach in the uncertain and volatile markets with which the decision maker must deal.

Footnotes

1. Knowing which state of nature will occur is equivalent to that particular state of nature having a probability of occurrence of 1.0.

2. Objective probabilities are defined as probabilities based on frequency counts. For example, the probability of a particular area receiving from 30–34 inches of rainfall is 3/10 if the last 100 years of data were to show the following:

Cumulative Rainfall	Times Observed (frequency)
25–29"	20
30–34"	30
35–39"	30
40–44"	20

3. Technically, expected value is defined as

$$E(X) = \sum_{i=1}^{n} (X_i) \, P(X_i)$$

where:

$E(X)$ = the expected value of the event X,
X_i = the ith value of X, and
$P(X_i)$ = the probability of occurrence of the ith value of X.

4. To illustrate, the expected values of the 3 strategies in Table 11.2 are:

$E(S_1) = 30(2/10) + 33(3/10) + 36(3/10) + 40(2/10) = 34.70$
$E(S_2) = 25(2/10) + 31.5(3/10) + 38(3/10) + 45(2/10) = 34.85$
$E(S_3) = 20(2/10) + 30(3/10) + 40(3/10) + 50(2/10) = 35.00$

Following the criterion, we would pick S_3 and plant all crop B.

5. For more complete coverage of these approaches, refer to the reference by King at the end of the chapter. The coverage here will be restricted to that needed to illustrate selected approaches and their apparent shortcomings.

6. Appendix A to this chapter discusses the steps in the Bayesian approach in more detail. The beginning student or the student who begins to experience problems in dealing with the concept of a Bayesian or "subjective" probability should read the appendix first. The discussion there and the examples shown should help.

7. Note the payoff to selling at harvest, S_1, is zero for all states of nature. The price increment during the year will clearly not affect this strategy. The payoffs for S_2 are shown as returns to the storage operation. There is no reason to bring the costs up through the harvest into the calculated payoffs since they are fixed, are the same for the two strategies, and would not affect the outcome.

8. If the 70 percent reliability factor is not good enough, the decision maker has an option. He can seek still more information, call even more analysts, and try to increase the reliability of his poll. The conditional probabilities $(P(Z_1|N_1)$, $P(Z_2|N_2)$ and $P(Z_3|N_3))$ might then be raised to .8. It is always possible to cut down on the probability of error but more observations always cost money.

9. In the first half of the 1970s, a policy decision was made by Brazil to expand soybean production. Production increased rapidly and by 1977 and 1978, was at or above 10 million metric tons. By this time, processing capacity in Brazil has been expanded to the 13 million ton level. Consequently, some of the exporting activity from Brazil is and will be in the form of meal and oil but these movements have an impact on the world price for beans.

10. Weather is also an important factor. If rains keep the midwestern farmer out of the field until late May or early June, he is more likely to seed his acreage to soybeans than to corn. Soybeans have a shorter growing season requirement and handle drought problems better. History shows late-seeded corn crops can be heavily damaged by mid-summer drought. It has been years in which the price ratio was above 2.5:1 and the plantings were late that we have seen a significant move to soybeans. Such a move should worry the astute producer who knows excessive supplies can result.

11. To review, the lock-in margin is the futures less the local basis less costs. Here, the producer could sell July futures at $6.30 and with a 20 cent basis, "guarantee" a price equivalent of $6.10. But this is only 10 cents a bushel over selling at harvest and the storage costs are estimated at 25 cents.

12. This point was discussed in Chapter 10. It bears repeating: the producer must know the range for the basis in his market to know when he is seeing an unusually wide or narrow basis.

13. The logic of this statement will be confirmed as the discussion unfolds. For the mathematical student looking for mathematical proof or the student interested in pursuing this area, a good place to start is the article by Faris listed in the references at the end of the chapter. The article by Nelson and Purcell constitutes extension and refinement of the concept.

14. This explains why cattle fed in the corn belt, where feeding is often once a year, are fed to heavier weights than the cattle in the Southwest. For the once-a-year feeder, there is no opportunity cost in form of an alternative set of cattle and he should feed to the point MNR goes to zero.

15. A bit of practice is recommended here. Draw a set of curves like those in Figure 11.2. Assume a change or changes in the important economic variables—current price of slaughter cattle, price of feeder cattle, price of corn, rate of gain, projected price of slaughter cattle, quotes for distant futures if the cattle are to be hedged—and make sure the resulting change in the replacement point is logical.

16. This is the product-product case covered in most beginning economic theory texts. The general case is as follows:

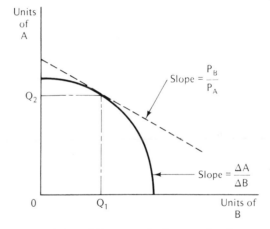

The combination of A and B to maximize profits for any given combination of prices can be found by moving an iso-income curve up and to the right with slope P_B/P_A. At the highest point of tangency, the rate at which A can be substituted for B in the production process $\Delta A/\Delta B$ is equal the rate at which they substitute in the market place P_B/P_A. Above, the optimal combination is OQ_1 of B and OQ_2 of A. In Figure 11.4, the combination at point C will be the correct combination until the price ratios change enough to allow an iso-income line that hits the production possibilities curve on one of the axes to represent a higher level of income than when it goes through point C. Either A or B, but not both, would be produced under such prices.

17. The work was conducted by Nelson and Purcell at Oklahoma State University. The dissertation by Nelson is referenced at the end of the chapter.

Questions

1. What is the difference between risk and uncertainty?

2. Critique the Bayesian approach to decisions under uncertainty with special attention to its strengths and weaknesses.

3. Describe a simple problem and construct the payoff table that would be needed to analyze the problem and decide on a relevant course of action.

4. The terminology "discounting for uncertainty" appears often in economics and in marketing decisions. How can Bayesian analysis be used to discount for uncertainty? Explain and illustrate.

5. The once-a-year cattle feeder will typically feed a pen of cattle longer than the year-round feeder would feed the same cattle. Are there circumstances in which both would feed to the same point? Explain and illustrate.

Selected References

Bierman, Harold, Charles P. Bonini and Warren H. Hausman, *Quantitative Analysis for Business Decisions*. Homewood, Illinois: Richard D. Irwin, 1969.

Faris, J. E., "Analytical Techniques Used in Determining the Optimum Replacement Pattern," *J. of Farm Econ.*, Vol. 42, November 1960.

Green, Paul E., "Uncertainty, Information and Marketing Decisions," *Theory in Marketing*, Reavis Cox and Wroe Alderson, eds. Chicago, Ill.: Richard D. Irwin, 1950.

King, William R., *Quantitative Analysis for Marketing Management*. New York, N.Y.: McGraw-Hill, 1967.

Kohls, Richard L., "Decision Making in Integrated Production and Marketing Systems," *J. of Farm Econ.*, Vol. 40, December 1958.

Leuthold, Raymond M., "On Combining Information Theory and Bayesian Analysis," *Canadian J. of Agri. Econ.*, Vol. 19, November 1971.

Nelson, Kenneth E., *A System Analysis of Information and Communication in Beef Marketing*, Unpublished PhD Dissertation, Oklahoma State University, Stillwater, May 1976.

Nelson, Kenneth E. and Wayne D. Purcell, "A Quantitative Approach to the Feedlot Replacement Decision," *Southern J. of Agr. Econ.*, Vol. 4, July 1972.

Appendix 11.A

Basics of Bayesian Analysis

Probabilities are important to Bayesian analysis. We will start with a brief look at probability and then go through the various steps in the Bayesian approach. After those basics are covered, we can then look at illustrations of how Bayesian analysis is used.

Probability

In the chapter, objective probabilities are mentioned. This is the distinguishing feature of the risk situation. There are objective probabilities attached to the states of nature. For purposes of this text, we can treat objective probabilities as equivalent to those probabilities based on frequency counts. We therefore define the probability of an event X_k in a family of possible events X_i where $i = 1 \ldots n$ as

$$P(X_k) = \frac{fX_k}{\sum\limits_{i=1}^{n} fX_i} = \frac{\text{frequency of } X_k}{\text{frequency of all values of X}}$$

The probability of the particular value of X, or X_k, is thus defined as the number of times X_k is observed divided by the total number of observations on the family of events X_i.

To illustrate, assume we are interested in knowing the probability of getting 30–34 inches of rainfall in our area during the coming year. Checking data for the past 50 years, the rainfall amounts and their associated frequencies are:

Rainfall During Year (inches)	No. Times Observed (frequency)
15–19	0
20–24	4
25–29	16
30–34	20
35–39	6
40–44	3
45–49	1

The probability of receiving 30–34 inches of rainfall is

$$P(30\text{–}34'') = \frac{f\,(30\text{–}34'')}{\displaystyle\sum_{i=1}^{n} f(R_i)} = \frac{20}{50} = .4$$

where R_i = the rainfall interval,
n = 50.

This probability could be important in deciding whether to invest in irrigation equipment, whether to plant a crop that needs at least 25 inches of rainfall, etc.

If price is the area of concern, frequency counts can often be used. Assume the decision situation involves trying to decide whether to sign a cash contract for a growing cotton crop with the local gin for December 1 delivery. The gin manager has offered a price which is 10 percent below the current (July 1) cash price. Data for the past 25 years show the following picture:

Price decline July 1–December 1

(in percent)	No. Times Observed
D_1: + 5 to + 1	3
D_2: 0 to − 4	8
D_3: − 5 to − 9	9
D_4: −10 to −14	4
D_5: −15 to −19	1

The probability of a price decline of 10 percent or more is

$$P(D_4 + D_5) = \frac{f(D_4) + f(D_5)}{\displaystyle\sum_{i=1}^{n} f(D_i)} = \frac{5}{25} = .2$$

where: D_i = the range of decreases shown by the data,
n = 25.

These data suggest the probability of a price decline of 10 percent or more is only .2. Such information will help in deciding whether to sign the cash contract.

In a risk situation, it is this type of probability that is available for the various states of nature. If a sell-store decision needs to be made, the decision maker might be interested in the magnitude and frequency of price increases from harvest to the end of the intended storage period. Assume the past 25 years show the following:

Price Increase	Frequency
(¢/bu.)	
− 9 to − 5	1
− 4 to 0	3
1 to 5	6
6 to 10	5
11 to 15	7
16 to 20	2
21 to 25	1

These frequency counts can be converted to probabilities and used in a payoff table:

States of Nature in Form of Price Increases (Probabilities)

Strategies	$N_1\left(\frac{1}{25}\right)$ −9 to −5	$N_2\left(\frac{3}{25}\right)$ −4 to 0	$N_3\left(\frac{6}{25}\right)$ 1 to 5	$N_4\left(\frac{5}{25}\right)$ 6 to 10	$N_5\left(\frac{7}{25}\right)$ 11 to 15	$N_6\left(\frac{2}{25}\right)$ 16 to 20	$N_7\left(\frac{1}{25}\right)$ 21 to 25
S_1: Sell at harvest	0	0	0	0	0	0	0
S_2: Store	−17	−12	−7	−2	+3	+8	+13

Following the criterion of choosing the strategy with the maximum expected value, we get

$E(S_1) = 0$

$E(S_2) = 1/25\,(-17) + 3/25\,(-12) + 6/25\,(-7) + 5/25\,(-2) + 7/25\,(3) + 2/25\,(8) + 1/25\,(13) = -2.9$

We would sell at harvest since the expected value of the "store" strategy is negative.

The entries in the payoff table show the net returns to storage. For strategy S_1, no storage is involved so the net returns to all states of nature are zero. In other words, the change in price during the storage period cannot, in any way, influence what happens if the grain is sold at harvest. Payoffs under strategy S_2 reflect a 10 cent per bu. variable cost of storage in on-farm storage bins. Using the midpoint of the price range and the 10 cent cost, the net return can be calculated. For example, the payoff for combination S_2N_3 is −7 cents because of an expected price increase of 3 cents and a cost of 10 cents.

Bayesian or subjective probabilities are different. There are no frequency counts. The probabilities are assigned or calculated based on the knowledge and judgment of the decision maker. To illustrate why it is a

Bayesian-type probability or no probability at all, consider the position of the marketing manager of an agri-business firm who is planning to introduce a new product. He has no place to turn for probabilities of success or failure based on frequency counts because this particular product-market mix has never been tried before. The skeptic might argue we could use frequency counts based on all new products but that approach is not acceptable. Each situation and each new product is different. What happens to all or similar products is relevant information but it will be used by the marketing manager to assign probabilities of a subjective nature.

Most prices and price movements also fall into the realm of uncertainty. Counting the frequency of various price increments as we did in the earlier illustration is not strictly correct. The setting for each of those years was a bit different, the forces of inflation move price higher over a 25-year period, and we are guilty to a degree of adding apples and oranges when we try to put the price moves into categories. This type of problem would best be handled as an uncertainty situation.

As part of the Bayesian approach we will deal with conditional probabilities. It is useful to think of all Bayesian probabilities as conditional probabilities. Technically, we write the conditional probability of some event X given the existence of some other event Y as $P(X|Y)$. If X is the event of being over 6 ft. tall, we would expect the probability of X to be different depending upon whether we are dealing with a male or female. In other words, $P(X)$ is *conditioned by* the value which Y takes.

Therefore, when a decision maker assigns a subjective or Bayesian-type probability to a particular event, it is a conditional probability based on the body of knowledge at his disposal. If that body of knowledge changes, the probability assigned will also tend to change.

Bayesian Analysis

In simple terms, the Bayesian approach

1. Brings the decision maker's knowledge into the situation and requires an assignment of *prior* probabilities to the states of nature,

2. Allows for a decision at this point or the postponement of the decision until more information can be gathered, and

3. Provides a rigorous procedure for bringing in the new information, integrating it with the information at the disposal of the decision maker, and calculating revised or *posterior* probabilities.

To clarify what is involved, let's go through the procedure step by step.

STEP 1: BUILD THE PAYOFF TABLE

The important components are the strategies, the states of nature, and the payoff entries in the body of the table. The strategies are usually fairly easy. If the decision is to hold or sell, the strategies will simply be

S_1: sell now, and S_2: hold and sell later.

The "hold" alternative could, of course, be divided into several time periods or several ending dates could be used. This would create several "hold" strategies instead of just one. When the strategies being considered involve trying to match what is planted with the outlook in the market, there may be several crop combinations. The producer in the Mississippi Delta might want to look at the following acreage combinations:

S_1: 75% cotton, 25% soybeans,

S_2: 50% cotton, 50% soybeans,

S_3: 25% cotton, 75% soybeans, and

S_4: 0% cotton, 100% soybeans.

The states of nature are tougher—there is no short cut to some hard thinking here. What are the dimensions of the operating environment that will have the most significant impact on the outcome of strategies? Without going to more complex modeling procedures, the payoff table can handle only one dimension in the states of nature. For the marketing and market-related decision, price or expectations on price behavior is often the key unknown. This means incorporating the impact of other economic forces into price levels or price patterns.

To illustrate, the Mississippi farmer will be concerned about harvest-period prices for cotton and soybeans in making his decision. But he knows the reaction of other producers who have the option of planting beans or cotton will be important in determining those price relationships. This means he must attempt to incorporate expectations of those reactions into the price levels he assigns. The end result might look like those below. He holds the beans at $5.50 since changes in the cotton producing areas will not affect bean prices as much. Beans are also planted in the corn belt and other areas.

N_1: $55.00 cotton, $5.50 beans

N_2: 57.50 cotton, 5.50 beans

N_3: 60.00 cotton, 5.50 beans

N_4: 62.50 cotton, 5.50 beans

N_5: 65.00 cotton, 5.50 beans

The payoff entries in the body of the table are not that difficult *if* the decision maker has good records and knows his operation. Continuing the cotton-soybean illustration, the producer will need good estimates of yields and costs assuming essentially normal weather. Given these data, the net returns per acre for a particular strategy-state of nature combination can be calculated. Assume, for example, the expected yields are 1 bale of cotton and 30 bushels of soybeans per acre. Per acre costs to generate these yields are $40 for cotton and $145 for soybeans. The table value for combination S_2N_2 will be:

$57.50 − 40 = $17.50/acre if planted to cotton, and
$165 − 145 = $20/acre if planted to beans.
$$\frac{17.50 + 20}{2} = \$18.75 \text{ per acre for the 50\% cotton and 50\% soybean combi-}$$
nation at prices of $57.50 and $5.50 respectively.

STEP 2: ASSIGN THE PRIOR PROBABILITIES

The need is simple—probabilities for a set of prices for cotton. The underlying assumption is that when acreage of one crop goes up, the other will go down. The prices of cotton are expected to react accordingly.

Brought to the situation will be the producer's past experience and what he has learned working with university personnel, reading outlook material and talking with representatives of the advisory service to which he subscribes. The probabilities must be assigned. The task is nebulous, intangible, and tough but it must be done. The alternative is to drift into some combination of cotton and beans and never really address the problem. Let's establish a set with which to work:

$$P(N_1) = .1$$
$$P(N_2) = .1$$
$$P(N_3) = .4$$
$$P(N_4) = .3$$
$$P(N_5) = .1$$

Table 11.A1 shows the complete payoff table.

Table 11.A1
Payoff Table for a Decision on Cotton and Soybean Acreage

States of Nature

Strategies	N_1 $55.00(.1)$	N_2 $57.50(.1)$	N_3 $60.00(.4)$	N_4 $62.50(3)$	N_5 $65.00(.1)$
S_1: 75% cotton	16.25	18.125	20.00	21.875	23.75
S_2: 50% cotton	17.50	18.75	20.00	21.25	22.50
S_3: 25% cotton	18.75	19.375	20.00	20.625	21.25
S_4: 0% cotton	20.00	20.00	20.00	20.00	20.00

$$E(S_1) = 16.25\,(.1) + 18.125\,(.1) + 20(.4) + 21.875\,(.3) + 23.75\,(.1) = 20.375$$
$$E(S_2) = 20.25$$
$$E(S_3) = 20.125$$
$$E(S_4) = 20.00$$

The prior analysis would indicate expected profits would be maximized by planting 75% of the acreage to cotton and 25% of the acreage to soybeans.

STEP 3: SELECT A STRATEGY OR DELAY THE DECISION AND CONDUCT A POSTERIOR ANALYSIS

If the producer is not willing to go with the results of the prior analysis, he moves into the posterior analysis. More information is needed on what other producers are likely to do. He visits with his local county extension specialist and decides on a course of action. A postcard survey will be sent to the extension director in all the major cotton producing counties in Mississippi, Louisiana, and Arkansas. A set of possible results are set up and related to the states of nature as follows:

Assigned Number	Average Estimate of Change in Cotton Acreage	Appropriate State of Nature
Z_1	+5% or more	N_1, $55.00 cotton
Z_2	+2 to +4	N_2, $57.50 cotton
Z_3	−1 to +1	N_3, $60.00 cotton
Z_4	−4 to −2	N_4, $62.50 cotton
Z_5	−7 to −5	N_5, $65.00 cotton

The decision is made to attach an 80% reliability factor to the survey. That is,

$$P(Z_1|N_1) = .80$$
$$P(Z_2|N_2) = .80$$
$$P(Z_3|N_3) = .80$$
$$P(Z_4|N_4) = .80$$
$$P(Z_5|N_5) = .80$$

After much deliberation, the decision is made to treat the errors as if they were random. Said another way, the producer decides $P(Z_2|N_1) = P(Z_3|N_1)$ $= \ldots = P(Z_5|N_1)$. Therefore, $P(Z_2|N_1) = .05$ since $P(Z_1|N_1)$ is set at .80 and Z_2, Z_3, Z_4 or Z_5 *could* be observed given that N_1 is the true state of nature.

Let's assume Z_2 is the survey result which is observed. To work with, we have

$$P(Z_2|N_1) = .05$$
$$P(Z_2|N_2) = .80$$
$$P(Z_2|N_3) = .05$$
$$P(Z_2|N_4) = .05$$
$$P(Z_2|N_5) = .05$$

Combining these conditional probabilities with the prior probabilities, we can calculate the posterior probabilities as

$$P(N_1|Z_2) = \frac{P(Z_2|N_1)\,P(N_1)}{\displaystyle\sum_{i=1}^{5} P(Z_2|N_i)\cdot P(N_i)}$$

$$= \frac{(.05)\,(.1)}{(.05)\,(.1) + (.80)\,(.1) + (.05)\,(.4) + (.05)\,(.3) + (.05)\,(.1)}$$

$$= \frac{.005}{.125} = .04$$

$$P(N_2|Z_2) = \frac{(.80)\,(.1)}{.125} = .64$$

$$N(N_3|Z_2) = \frac{(.05)\,(.4)}{.125} = .16$$

$$P(N_4|Z_2) = \frac{(.05)\,(.3)}{.125} = .12$$

$$P(N_5|Z_2) = \frac{(.05)\,(.1)}{.125} = .04$$

Recalculating the expected values, we get

$$E(S_1) = 16.25\,(.04) + 18.125\,(.64) + 20\,(.16) + 21.875\,(.12) +$$
$$(23.75).04$$
$$= 19.025$$
$$E(S_2) = 19.35$$
$$E(S_3) = 19.675$$
$$E(S_4) = 20.00$$

Strategy S_4 has the highest expected value and suggests forgetting cotton and going to soybeans. Note, however, none of the strategies has sharply different expected values. This occurs because of the comparability in profits per acre at these bean and cotton prices.

OTHER ILLUSTRATIONS

Bayesian analysis is appropriate to:

1. Help decide whether a new tractor design would be accepted. The states of nature could be different levels of acceptance. A sample of farmers could be used in conducting the posterior analysis.

2. Shed light on the possible responses of competitors to a price cut. Alternative reactions would constitute the states of nature. Strategies could involve price cuts of varying magnitudes. The price cuts could be tried in test markets if a posterior analysis is needed.

3. Making hold-sell decisions on stocker calves on grass. Price moves during the rest of the planning period would constitute states of nature. Strategies would include different selling dates. Self study and/or a poll of outlook specialists could be used in the posterior analysis.

The list could go on but the point is made. Bayesian analysis is broadly applicable. It is a logical and workable approach to decisions under uncertainty and can be applied with varying levels of quantitative rigor. Continued study of the conceptual framework and the procedures will prove worthwhile.

chapter twelve

Market Systems Analysis

Analysis of market systems can be discussed at levels ranging from simple descriptive statements to highly sophisticated quantitative relationships. There is much yet to be done in terms of developing analytical techniques but such development will not be attempted here. The purpose of this chapter is to supplement the treatment in earlier chapters and describe some approaches that encourage the market analyst and decision maker to use a systems orientation in their work.

The Conceptual Framework

Chapter 2 introduced and described the concept of a market system, and focused attention on the interactions between the stages. The system is challenged to achieve high levels of efficiency and to coordinate what is produced with the consumer demands. But as we have seen, the level of producer-consumer coordination actually achieved will depend on the extent to which activities are coordinated along the interface between technically related stages.

Moving our focus of attention to the interface between any two related stages, what attitudes or economic forces could block coordination of activity? Continuing at the conceptual or theoretical level, we can list:

1. Conflicting goals on the part of decision makers active at the two stages;

2. Lack of knowledge of raw material needs and lack of understanding of production techniques and operational procedures at other levels in the system;

3. Failure to recognize or understand problems facing other stages in the system; and

4. An attitude "Nothing can be gained by coordinating activity or working together" (the zero-sum game paradox).

Any one or any combination of these can lead to a perspective that does not incorporate the concept of a system. Operating from such a limited perspective or orientation can lead to actions that do not help and may even block coordination between the stages.

Very little work has been done to confirm or refute the existence of such barriers to coordination. Part of the reason is lack of a general methodology available for analyzing the system. Most analysts tend to shy away from "systems analysis" because it is perceived as being complex and difficult. But it need not be all that complicated.

One approach is that which was used to look at the beef marketing system.[1] Since surveys are often used to gather information, the question revolved around how surveys could be used to test hypotheses concerning the existence of barriers to coordinated activity. We came up with the idea of "mirror image" questions. A set of questions was developed to guide personal interviews with decision makers at one level of the system. The mirror-image question was developed and directed to decision makers at the related level. The results were analyzed for indication of selected barriers such as goal conflicts and various types of operational inconsistencies.

For example, in an analysis of the feeder-packer subsystem, a sample of cattle feeders was shown several types of information that could be made available to the buying packer. The information ranged from simply presenting the cattle for visual inspection to providing detailed information on weights of the cattle when placed on feed, how long they have been on feed, performance of past cattle with the same or similar genetic background, etc. The feeders were asked which type of information should be presented to the packer-buyer. Although there was a distribution to the responses, a majority of the feeders questioned selected options that minimized the information provided.

The same sets of information were presented to a sample of packers. They were asked which type of information they felt should be made available by the feeders. The packers tended to select the alternatives that provided more information. In responding to a related question, most of the packers indicated they typically discount the price bids on the cattle for which little or no information is available.

In examining the interface between the cow-calf operator and cattle feeders, the issue of what type of feeder cattle should be produced was explored. A set of pictures was shown to a sample of cow-calf operators. They were asked to indicate their feelings about which type of animal they felt they should produce. The same set of pictures was shown to a sample of cattle feeders. The cattle feeders were asked which type of animal they believed would be the best to buy and place on feed. Weights and quality grades were the same for all animals and this was pointed out to the respondents during the interviews. The cattle were selected to demonstrate differences in frame size, in the amount of finish or fat they were carrying, and the implicit potential they presented as money makers in the feedlot and on the breaking table.

The responses of the cow-calf operators clustered around the animal carrying a high degree of finish relative to overall height, length, and frame size. Responses of the cattle feeders clustered around the animal on the other end of the continuum, the steer showing good frame size and carrying very little finish. In related questions, written to supplement the responses to the pictures, a majority of the cow-calf operators said they felt they were producing a type of calf consistent with the needs of the cattle feeders. A majority of the cattle feeders felt just the opposite and indicated they could not get the type of cattle they wanted in terms of frame size and finish.

Other results could be considered but the discussion to this point should serve to illustrate that the mirror-image approach to questioning has potential as an analytical tool. At the time the surveys were conducted, it appears there definitely were barriers to coordinated action in the beef marketing system.

Why the barriers are there and why they have persisted over time deserves more discussion. First, we should recognize the difficulty the individual decision maker will have in "stepping back" and looking beyond his day-to-day activities at what is happening in the system. If the individual sees his operation as being independent and does not see it as an integral part of a total system, he is not likely to recognize the importance of coordination. And if his operating perspective sees no "system" of which he is a part, he is not likely to care whether his activities are coordinated with the needs and activities of others in the system.

A second reason for the barriers points to the pricing mechanism and suggests it has not been able to assign the proper set of recognizable premiums and discounts. If a particular type of steer is worth more to the cattle feeder, we would expect to see the cow-calf operator shift his breeding and production practices to produce that steer if he is paid for doing so. But this requires a price premium that the cow-calf operator can recognize. If no price signal is present or if any signal that is there is not recognized, no change will be forthcoming. Price variability sometimes conceals or distorts the signal. And we must remember the cattle feeder will not pay a premium for a particular type of calf unless he has to—which means either competition among cattle feeders, widespread knowledge of value differentials by producers who insist on bringing this knowledge into price negotiations, or both.[2]

A third reason revolves around lack of knowledge of needs and lack of understanding of problems at other stages in the system. Processors of all types of food and fiber products are plagued with a variable flow of raw material into their facilities. With a relatively high proportion of their costs fixed, the processor can't simply close his doors. He must operate. But few producers fully understand the problem and still fewer recognize any possibility of mutual benefit via coordination.

This problem has been discussed in earlier chapters. For a given plant, we have noted the capacity to keep output levels between quantities such as OQ_1 and OQ_2 in Figure 12.1 is important to the processor. If a variable flow of raw material pulls the output level below OQ_1, per unit cost as measured by ATC increases significantly. Conversely, pushing the

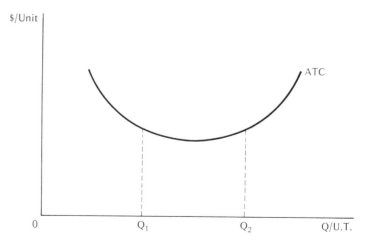

FIGURE 12.1   THE NORMAL RELATIONSHIP BETWEEN COST AND OUTPUT PER UNIT OF TIME

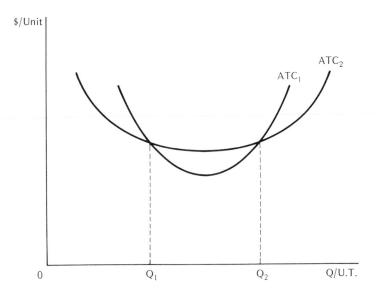

FIGURE 12.2 SPECIALIZED AND GENERALIZED ATC CURVES AND THEIR RELA-
TIONSHIP TO QUANTITY PER UNIT OF TIME

plant beyond its efficient operating level to a level above OQ_2 will increase
costs—but the processor may feel he has to do this to protect his arrangements with raw material suppliers. Over time, average operating costs for a
given plant would be significantly reduced if the processor could rely upon
a stable flow of raw materials—and coordination could give him this.
Coordination could thus mean a net saving to the processor and the possibility of a share of the saving to the cooperating producer. Coordination of
activity *is not necessarily a zero-sum game.*

In the long run, the possibilities extend to more efficient plant design.
If the processor knows he can control the flow of raw materials to keep
weekly output between OQ_1 and OQ_2 in Figure 12.2, he can build a plant
with a cost structure more like ATC_1 instead of ATC_2. The cost curve ATC_1
suggests a highly specialized plant designed to operate efficiently at or near
a stable level of output per day, week, or other unit of time. When the
processor knows he will face a highly variable flow of raw materials, he
builds a flexible plant that can handle variations in output and operates
with a cost structure such as ATC_2. Clearly, the per unit costs over time
could be lower in a plant that operates on a cost structure like ATC_1. There
are, therefore, net benefits to coordination in the long run. A processor
could pass part of the cost savings for the more efficient plant back to producers who work with him in stabilizing flows and everyone would be
helped.[3]

Measures of System Efficiency

Two types of efficiency are important in a marketing system: technical efficiency and pricing efficiency. Both have been mentioned at other points in this book, and both are important.

Technical efficiency refers to the efficiency with which processing, storing, transporting, and other functions within the marketing system are performed. For a given function at a particular point in time, technical efficiency is increased by cutting the cost of performing the function assuming constraints on quality, timeliness of delivery, etc., are met. If we define technical efficiency as $ output/$ input, then an increase in technical efficiency can be mutually beneficial to participants in the market system and to society in general. For example, if a given $ output can be provided at lower cost, this can mean a higher net return to system participants. Competition among system participants tends to insure that at least part of the reduced costs will be passed on to consumers. This can mean either lower prices or, during periods of inflation, smaller price increases than might otherwise be the case.

One measure of system effectiveness is, therefore, the degree of technological progressiveness that prevails. It is usually new technology that allows increases in technical efficiency. If all other factors are equal, the marketing system with the more progressive attitude toward development and adoption of new technology would be judged the more effective system.[4]

A second measure of system effectiveness is the level of pricing efficiency realized. The extent to which needed adjustments in production procedures and related reallocation of resources are completed with a minimum time lag depends upon the level of pricing efficiency achieved.

As a general rule, we can expect the realized level of pricing efficiency to be lower in those marketing systems with major modifications in the product between the producer and the consumer. Changes in product form make the message transfer through each buyer-seller junction more difficult. In the fresh fruits, fresh vegetables, and in fluid milk, for example, there is little processing of the product before it reaches the final consumer. If consumers as a group develop a preference for pink grapefruit, there is little reason to expect this message will not get to producers in the form of a price differential for pink grapefruit. If weight-conscious consumers shift to low-fat milk, the message gets to producers and we see a shift toward the high-producing Holsteins with their lower yield of butterfat. But move to consumer preference for leaner pork and the problem is more complex. Pork takes several distinct forms as it moves through the system. The live hog moves off the farm and is typically sold and priced on a live basis. After slaughter, primal cuts (hams, loins, picnics, bellies) are sold by the packer either directly to a retail chain or to an independent breaker-distributor. Another price is negotiated, this time on the basis of primal cuts. If there is an independent distributor involved, still another price must be negotiated with the retailer. The final pricing act takes place at the retail counter when the consumer buys or turns down the particular price-quality combination being offered.

The product flow from producer to consumer is thus along a complex path. But the message in the form of a price signal has to flow from consumer to producer in the opposite direction along this same complex path. At each pricing point, the message must be passed through so that the correct interpretation is continued. And this is difficult to do. A basic reminder from communication theory is that meaning is not inherent in the symbols, meaning is inherent to the interpretation of the user. A particular grade-price combination or quality-price combination may mean different things to different buyers and sellers.

From this discussion we can hypothesize that in any particular system, pricing efficiency would be increased by changes in the system to require fewer pricing points. This is one of the several motivations for vertical integration. Bringing two or more related stages under the ownership of one management center allows coordination by directive instead of by price.[5]

Another change that has the potential to increase pricing efficiency is the move toward decentralized marketing. For years, the percentage of livestock, grain, and fiber products that passes through the large central or terminal markets has been declining. Direct movement from producer to processor has increased, especially in the livestock markets.

When producers deal directly and on a personal basis with processors or buying agents of the processors, there appears to be an increase in the level of understanding about needs, problems, and the possible benefits of coordination.[6] If this is the case, the probability of extending comparable interpretation to a particular price-quality combination might be higher. But we have to be careful not to over generalize here. Any possible benefits from direct interaction are offset if both parties to the transaction, especially the producer who is in the market only periodically as a seller, are not well informed. This puts the burden on the USDA's market news activities and the private reporting agencies to do a good job of reporting direct trade and all the conditions of exchange that have significant price implications.

In general, we can expect to see at least some pressure for change in the way the market systems are organized when the level of pricing efficiency is not as high as progressive system participants would like to see. But moves toward vertical integration or other changes in organizational structure are not necessarily signs of a progressive marketing system. We could argue that it is just the opposite. Vertical integration might not occur if the system does a good job of promoting changes in grades when needed, has an enlightened attitude toward the need for planning information and market news, understands the cost and efficiency implications of failure to achieve higher levels of vertical coordination, and organizes itself to do something about the problems and deficiencies.

Since there is no one management center for the entire system, it will be up to trade groups and other organizations at the various stages to help effect needed changes. If the current grade standards are not right, then the organized groups in the system might consider supporting research to investigate the area and offer suggestions. The USDA's reports are criticized in terms of accuracy and are charged with exerting a negative influence in the marketplace. If system participants really believe this, then perhaps they should start their own information service or work with the USDA and state agencies to improve what is being offered. These and related types of activities are more nearly indicative of a progressive system. But we are far from this orientation in most of our marketing systems where narrow perspectives, habitual procedure, and institutionalized ways of doing things block change and adjustment.

A third measure of system effectiveness is the degree of stability and order achieved in pricing patterns, production, and growth over time. Both the individual system participant and society in general are hurt by highly variable production and price patterns.

How successful a production-marketing system will be at achieving orderly growth will depend on the degree of exposure to outside shocks such as the world market, on the competitive structure of its production segment, and on the orientation of the system's internal group activities. Trade groups must see the system as a system if they are to enhance the possibilities of achieving stability.

Outside shocks can stimulate developments within the system, which increase variability. An example is what happened in the U.S. production-marketing system for wheat after the USSR entered the market and bought heavily in 1972 and again in 1975. We discussed this in other contexts in earlier chapters. In both years, production in the USSR was pushed below expectations by weather problems. Purchases in the world market by the USSR to offset her shortfall in production pushed wheat prices higher. At this point, the competitive structure of the wheat industry at the producer level took over. Individual producers bought land, equipment, and expanded their operations with $5 wheat in their decision and expectation models. New firms entered the industry and began to produce. Three consecutive crops over 2.0 billion bushels swelled stocks and prices in the production areas fell below $2.00 in the summer of 1977. This brought cries for help and the government was back in the market in 1978 with reserve programs and set aside options to reduce planted acreage and constrain production. Such instability makes effective planning difficult and is bad for producer and consumer alike. The wheat system has shown little ability to regulate itself via internal action and organization.

Price cycles in livestock are both predictable and reliable. In discussing cyclical price patterns in Chapters 6 and 7, we noted that the hog cycle runs 3½ to 4 years and the cattle cycle runs 11 to 12 years in length.

For those who argued in the 1960s the cattle cycle was a thing of the past, the decade of the 1970s brought proof to the contrary. After total inventory numbers reached a historic high at 131.8 million head in 1975, a four-year liquidation that ran through 1978 reduced the inventory by over 15 percent. Prices that had reached historic highs in 1972 and early 1973 tumbled to levels which, with inflation removed, were the lowest in real terms the industry had ever seen. Losses were tremendous, some operations went out of business, and many were refinanced as the industry suffered through a most difficult period.

Out of the problems of the 1970s comes renewed interest in trying to do something to prevent a recurrence of the cycle in the 1980s or, at a minimum, reduce its impact. What would be required is not that difficult. But whether the beef system has or can develop the level of understanding and internal discipline required to deal effectively with the cycle is doubtful.

More complete discussion of the beef cycle, its causes, and its properties was offered in Chapter 7. Here, we need to recognize the basic problem is one of excess—growth rates and cumulative expansion in the cow herd reach levels that produce more slaughter cattle than can be absorbed by the market without a severe reduction in price.[7] The answer would be orderly and stable growth rates consistent with the long-term upward trend in demand. But each producer will still tend to push his production capacity to the limit if his expectations call for higher prices. And since most producers have difficulty seeing beyond the very short run, they are likely to follow the same behavioral pattern again in the 1980s. What is needed is a joint effort by the USDA, land grant universities, trade groups in the beef marketing system, and commercial advisory services to (1) educate producers about the cycle, (2) do a good job of intermediate to long-term outlook and keep this in front of producers, and (3) highlight the warning signs when they begin to appear and stress the negative implciations of excessive growth in the herd.

Whether the beef system can do this remains to be seen. If it can, it will indeed be an impressive performance. The long liquidation that ran through 1978 reduced the cow herd so much that sharply higher prices emerged as the liquidation phase was completed and beef tonnage decreased. To the consumer, this means five to six years of reduced supplies and higher prices during the building phase of the cycle. This comes on the heels of three to four years of abundant supplies and low prices during the liquidation phase. Such variability is bad for everyone in the system.

MARKETING MARGINS

A commonly used measure of system performance is the marketing margin or price spread. But the concept is also frequently misused. Margins or spreads can be useful descriptive statistics if used to show how the consumer's food dollar is divided among participants at different levels of the marketing system. The measures can also provide some input to an analytical framework. If margins continue to trend in one direction over time, this can prompt analysis to determine why the change is occurring and whether it is due to poor performance by some part of the systems. In other words, trying to establish a relationship between changes in the margin and measures of systems performance is sound analysis. But to draw conclusions about inefficiency, excessive profit levels, profiteering or exploitation just because the margin is increasing over time is not analytically sound.

In most instances, the marketing margin or price spread is presented and discussed without indication of the quantity moving through the market. Conceptually, there are three types of marketing margins when quantity is considered:

1. Constant marketing margin,

2. Increasing marketing margin, and

3. Decreasing marketing margin.

When quantity is brought into the discussion, we see that marketing margins reflect the concept of derived demand.

A constant marketing margin is shown in Figure 12.3. Note the spread between the retail and farm level is constant in terms of absolute dollars. For an increasing margin, the absolute dollar difference goes up with larger quantities. The decreasing margin would show a smaller dollar difference as quantity increases. If the margins are in percentage terms, the general relationships are the same, but the farm level demand would not be linear for increasing and decreasing margins.

For most commodities, the increasing margin is the most probable. Retail and even some wholesale prices are sticky and do not fluctuate a great deal in the short run. But the flow of product from the farm level is subject to short-run fluctuations of significant magnitude. With aggregate demand at the farm level highly inelastic, increased product movement can push price sharply lower—and the margin or spread increases with the increase in quantity.

Table 12.1 presents price spread indices for selected commodity groups. The index for meat products indicates the spread has increased 94 percent since the 1967 base year.

To understand how the spread data should and should not be used,

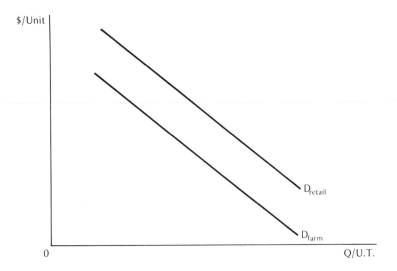

FIGURE 12.3 DEMAND AT RETAIL AND FARM LEVELS WITH A CONSTANT MAR-
KETING MARGIN

we must first understand how the data are generated. Beef is the product
of most interest so we will use it to illustrate. The steps in calculating the
farm-retail spread for beef as a specific product are:

1. Record the price of Choice beef at retail. This price is actually a
   weighted average price of retail cuts from a Choice beef carcass;

2. Calculate the gross value of a Choice steer at the farm level. This is
   done by using an appropriate live cattle price series and multiplying by 2.28, which is the number of lbs. of live steer required for
   one pound at retail;

3. Estimate the value of edible and inedible by-products;

4. Subtract the value of the by-products (step 3) from the gross farm
   value (step 2) to get net farm value; and

5. Subtract the net farm value from the retail price to get the farm-
   retail spread.

The farm-retail price spread for beef is thus a calculated figure using
constant factors to convert values at all levels to pounds of retail equivalent. It is not and was never intended to be a measure of profits or efficiency of the beef marketing system. Observations on what the spread is
and how it should be used include:

Table 12.1
Indexes of Farm-Retail Price Spread for Selected Food Commodities
1967–76

Indexes (1967 = 100)

Year	Meat Products	Dairy Products	Bakery and Cereal Products	Fruits and Vegetables
		(Percent)		
1967	100	100	100	100
1968	102	102	102	105
1969	107	103	105	107
1970	123	109	110	113
1971	122	113	115	118
1972	127	114	113	122
1973	138	119	117	134
1974	168	144	147	155
1975	169	146	177	163
1976	194	154	179	170

Source: *Food, Consumption, Prices, Expenditures,* Economics, Statistics, and Cooperatives Service, USDA, March 1978.

1. The spread is a reflection of values at different levels of the marketing system. Since it includes no measure of quantity, there is no basis without further analysis to determine whether a change in the spread is due to a change in quantity or to some other factor.

2. Spreads are often for only one grade or quality. For example, the price spread for beef is based solely on Choice beef even though other grades are sold. Analysis of spreads and spread behavior should be applied to other grades with caution.

3. At best, price spreads are an estimate of the normal or average spread for the entire industry. They do not, therefore, represent the spread for any sector of the industry or for any particular firm.

4. Price spreads are not estimates of operating margins for industry firms. When spreads increase in the short run, this can mean higher costs, increased profits, or some combination of the two. Over time, the increase in margins can also come from increases in the services being provided by the middleman.

5. Analysis based on price spreads should be restricted to study of the changes in price spreads over time and how these changes compare or relate to changes in other variables or measures of

performance. For example, a price spread that has increased but at a rate below the rate of increase in energy, packaging, transportation, refrigeration, and other costs can mean lower profit margins or increased efficiency by the subsector of the system involved.

Price spreads and marketing margins will continue to receive a great deal of public attention and they will continue to be misused as measures of profits. With strong consumer preferences for services and prepared products, the portion of the consumer's dollar going to the "marketing bill" will continue to increase. Price spreads between the producer and other levels in the system will also increase. The only legitimate concern we have is whether the services being demanded by consumers are being provided as efficiently as possible given current technology. If they are, there is little reason to complain even if increasing costs and/or more demands on the middleman do push the price spreads higher.

Analytical Tools

When we talk about analyzing the effectiveness of a marketing system, we are talking about comparing the effectiveness of a particular system to something. Without attempting to present a complete or exhaustive list, possible comparisons include:

1. Compare the relative effectiveness of a system across alternative ways of coordinating given an organizational structure. For example, we might change the level and type of information available to decision makers and compare the effectiveness of the alternative systems with organizational structure held constant.

2. Compare the relative effectiveness of different ways of organizing the system. For example, a vertically integrated system might be compared to an open market exchange system. We would be comparing the levels of efficiency achieved when coordination is by management directive (vertical integration) versus direction from price and price signals (open market exchange system).

Various approaches to generating the comparisons are possible.

BUDGETING

Budgets can be developed to estimate costs and returns for alternative marketing outlets which require different types and levels of information.

For the livestock producer, this might mean comparing direct sales to sales through organized markets. Or within direct sales, it might mean comparing sales on a live basis to sales on a carcass basis. If the budgets are well done, they should provide direction to the producer as he faces his marketing decision. Perhaps more importantly in the long run, working through the budgets might help the seller in his attempts to understand the terms of trade and focus in on the true price. If the budgets get the seller to this level of understanding, he might also be in a better position to see and accurately interpret price signals.

When comparing alternative organizational structures, budgets can also be used. For example, a carefully constructed budget of costs and returns for an exchange system can be compared to the budgeted costs and returns for a vertically integrated system. Published results from such analyses give the decision maker something to work with in making long-run decisions on coordination with others in the system, or in trying to decide whether to get involved in moves toward vertical integration.

Table 12.2 provides an indication of the type of comparisons budgeting can provide. The results shown are typical of what we usually see in the livestock industry. Costs can usually be reduced by eliminating one or more transfers before the animal reaches the final point of slaughter.

LINEAR PROGRAMMING

Linear programming can be used to compare systems that differ in terms of the information base on which decisions are made, in terms of how the system is organized, or both. In conceptual terms, we see the problem as one of selecting the correct alternative from many alternatives subject to a set of constraints imposed on the entire system. Each of the alternatives, however, requires the equivalent of a budgeting process to establish costs, production coefficients, prices, resources used, etc.

Table 12.3 illustrates the required general format. Across the top are activities A--A_n. This could refer to alternative ways the economic functions could be combined. Down the left side are the various restrictions or constraints. These could range from legal constraints on price to volume constraints that prevent a level of activity that exceeds the operating capacity of the industry involved. Each cell in the table lists the coefficient that shows how the activity in that column draws on the supply of resources specified in that row. Across the bottom is a row that shows the net returns for each of the activities.

What we have, therefore, is a complex problem that requires picking the one activity or a combination of activities that would maximize returns or profits to the system as a whole. Alternatively, we might be interested in minimizing the cost of producing the product and making it available to the

Table 12.2
Budgeted Costs of Open Market and Integrated Systems for Choice Steers from Weaning to Slaughter

Type of Expense	Open Market System	Integrated System	Difference in Costs
	($/head)		
Auction market fees	5.18	0	5.18
Feed for regaining shrinkage	4.83	2.90	1.93
Medication	4.34	2.49	1.85
Order buyer's fees	1.75	0	1.75
Interest	16.10	14.44	1.66
Pasture expense	15.91	14.41	1.50
Death loss	4.43	3.61	.82
Trucking	5.40	4.75	.65
Variable labor	10.84	10.29	.55
Loss to chronic sickness	.76	.57	.19
Subtotal			16.08
Feed for maintenance growth	82.86	87.28	−4.42
Business trips	0	1.00	−1.00
Fixed costs	3.47	3.97	− .50
Subtotal			−5.92
Total advantage to integrated system			$10.16

Source: Donald E. Farris and Raymond A. Dietrich, "Economics of Alternative Beef Production Systems and Locations," *Forage-Fed Beef: Production and Marketing Alternatives in the South,* Southern Coop. Series Bul. 220, June 1977.

consumer. As noted in Chapter 11, linear programming is a mathematical procedure that is well suited to the problems of maximization or minimization.

Continuing to use the livestock sector to illustrate, let's continue the brief discussion of this topic in Chapter 11 and assume we are interested in finding the combination of breed-type of cattle and set of information to be used in buying and selling that would minimize the cost of producing lean beef. In simple terms, we have a problem which might be illustrated as follows:

1. A total of 13 breeds or cross-breeds as types of cattle with which to work;

2. A total of five alternative sets of information that range from buying and selling using rough live estimates of value-related attrib-

Table 12.3
The General Format of a Linear Programming Problem Involving a Number of Activities

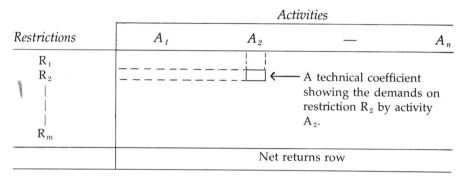

	Activities			
Restrictions	A_1	A_2	—	A_n

A technical coefficient showing the demands on restriction R_2 by activity A_2.

utes such as quality grade and yield grade to buying and selling based on actual carcass grades;

3. A given organizational structure with separate ownership at each stage and price as the coordinating mechanism; and

4. Constraints that take the form of a given number of animals based on some selected herd size, a given or projected feedlot capacity, a given or projected processing capacity, plus other constraints that "pin down" what the system will have in terms of a resource base with which to work in producing a specified amount of beef per capita.

A computerized linear programming routine could be used to analyze this problem. But a few cautions are in order. The results will be no better and no more realistic than the data that go into setting up the matrix that will be analyzed. Let's review some of the required data:

1. The cost of maintaining the cow herd must be estimated for each of the 13 types and incorporated into the final cost estimates of producing lean beef. A large breed requires more resources per cow unit. Some breeds have more calving problems, will wean a smaller calf crop, etc. These differences must be considered and reflected in the cost estimates.

2. A growth curve or production function must be estimated for each of the 13 types. Even if management practices for the cow herd and the ration while in the feedlot are held constant for simplicity, the

growth curve for the different breeds will differ. In general, the larger breeds will have a higher daily feed intake and will have a higher average daily gain.

3. Any differences in the carcass characteristics of the 13 types when they reach slaughter weights must be considered. If slaughtered at the same percentage of their mature weight, the different breeds would not vary greatly in the percentage of the cattle that would grade Choice. But yield grades can differ. And the costs of slaughtering the larger cattle and processing the larger carcasses should be lower on a per pound basis since slaughtering and processing costs tend to be constant on a per head basis.

4. For each of the 13 types, the five different information bases must be developed into cost and price implications.

Overall, a great deal of information is required in preparing to conduct a linear programming analysis. Where estimates go into the data set, results must be interpreted with those estimates in mind.

There are many other applications of linear programming. In the hands of a capable analyst, this tool can generate useful comparisons to guide investment decisions and provide a base of knowledge for policy decisions. Linear programming has been used to compare alternative ways of organizing the transportation system in the U.S. Various marketing systems for the dairy industry have been analyzed and compared using linear programming. When the purpose is to compare alternative systems and the objective is to find the system that either maximizes (as with profits or return on investment), or minimizes (as with costs of doing a job), linear programming is an appropriate tool.

SIMULATION

The concept of simulation was introduced in Chapter 11. As an analytical tool, simulation is generally complex and beyond the scope of this book. But as a concept, discussion of simulation can be kept at a simple level. A relatively new tool, simulation will come into widespread use in analyzing marketing systems. It allows analysis of behavioral and interactive dimensions which are the essence of a marketing system.

In our food and fiber marketing systems, the behavioral dimension is becoming increasingly important. Firms operating at the levels above the production stage have always been aware of this dimension. How the user or the competing producer will react has always been of concern to the fertilizer company as it contemplates introducing nitrogen in a new product form. The reaction or probable reaction by competing firms to a decrease in price may be the most critical dimension of the pricing policy for a large meat packer. But the behavioral dimension is rapidly becoming important at the producer level.

The wisdom of a decision to store wheat in a particular year pivots on what other producers decide to do. Planting decisions become of major importance because of the behavioral dimensions of the system. We noted earlier that planting more soybeans in a year after bean prices were up relative to corn prices can be disastrous if most other producers do the same thing. Trade in commodity futures has come under attack from disgruntled producers who expanded production of a crop, placed more cattle on feed, or farrowed more sows because of high quotes on distant futures—and then saw the price fall because many other producers did the same thing. As information becomes more widespread and as producers who never paid attention before look for help in volatile markets, the system becomes more vulnerable to the behavioral reaction.

Recognizing this behavioral dimension and incorporating it into analyses is becoming increasingly important. It is consistent with the need to focus more attention on the actions and reactions along the interfaces of a marketing system. As the state of knowledge is advanced, simulation techniques are increasingly capable of handling the system's dynamics.

For a simple illustration let's continue to use the livestock sector. In earlier sections, we discussed the idea of different information structures that could be used in trading fed cattle. Let's assume the purpose is to analyze the impact of errors in estimating grades for live cattle on the pricing efficiency of the beef marketing system. Before proceeding to describe the type of analysis, let's first review a few propositions regarding pricing efficiency:

1. The level of pricing efficiency achieved will vary directly with the extent to which the system can pass a price signal back to the producer and relate that signal to a product attribute the producer can recognize and identify;

2. Pricing efficiency will be at its maximum when price levels at the producer level are consistent with the true value of the product as determined higher in the system where true value can be measured; and

3. Pricing errors, defined as differences between the actual price and the true price, inject noise into price as a communication mechanism and reduce the level of pricing efficiency relative to the level that could be realized.

The first thing needed would be a probability distribution of errors made in estimating quality and yield grades for live cattle. This could be developed by having buyers, sellers, or "experts" grade live cattle and follow the cattle through the system until actual carcass grades could be observed. If we make the assumption the probability of positive and negative "misses" is the same, a frequency distribution of errors would look like the distribution in Figure 12.4. When grade is over-estimated, this shows up in the distribution as a positive error—estimated grade is above the true grade. The vertical dimension records the frequency with which each error is made.

To simulate what happens to a particular producer who sells fed cattle only once a year, an "error" can be drawn at random from the error distribution shown in Figure 12.4. Taking 20 draws at random would simulate what would happen to a producer across 20 sales if we could assume the distribution of errors remained the same. It is, of course, possible to get 20 consecutive draws with positive errors—which means grades on our producer's cattle have been consistently over-estimated. And over-estimating grade means the producer is getting paid a price above the "true" price for his cattle. The opposite could also occur and price would be consistently below true value. Even if the particular producer is exposed to the distribution of errors shown in Figure 12.4, the level of pricing efficiency is affected by the errors. The producer does not know an error in estimating grade has been made and he is therefore faced with a pattern of prices and price differences that are difficult to relate to particular types of cattle. The inability to relate price levels and price differences to particular types of cattle translates into a low level of pricing efficiency.

Low levels of pricing efficiency over time can lead to higher production costs and higher costs of placing the product before the consumer than would be possible if the system had been motivated to adjust or change its

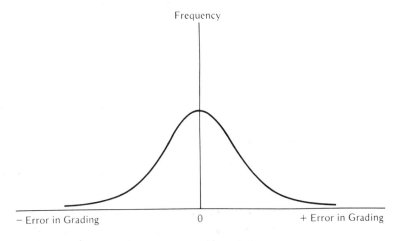

FIGURE 12.4   FREQUENCY DISTRIBUTION OF ERRORS IN ESTIMATING GRADE

production-marketing procedures. We can illustrate this by looking at simplified results of a simulation of the beef marketing system.

Table 12.4 records the type of cattle, the estimated profit per head, and the estimated cost of producing Choice grade beef at retail based on the simulation analysis referred to earlier.[8] More than pricing or technical efficiency is shown here. An elaborate model was developed to simulate production of calves of different types and carry them through the system to the retail level. At every level, such as the cattle feeding level, separate growth curves were estimated for the different breeds or types. The simulation eventually produced cattle of each breed-type with a unique set of slaughter weights, grades, yields of lean meat, and costs per lb. of producing retail cuts of Choice beef.

The cattle type shown for each stage is the type that would maximize returns or profits to that particular stage without concern for the profitability of the other stages. For example, when a replacement decision was made at the feedlot level, the optional type was ANAN (Angus-Angus), which matured at relatively light weights and allowed a quick turnover in the feedlot. At the packer and breeder stages, the results were predictable. The simulation suggests the larger cattle and larger carcasses because these

Table 12.4
Performance of a Simulated Beef Marketing System for Selected Organizational Structures

Market Structure	Profit in $ per Head ($)	Cost per lb. Beef[a] ($ per lb.)	Return on Total System Investment (%)	Cattle Type Preferred
Exchange Processes with Profits Maximized to				
Cow-Calf	11	NA	NA	Hereford-Angus
Feeding	77	.78	17	Angus
Slaughtering	5	.75	18	Simmental-Hereford
Fabricating	93	.75	18	Simmental-Hereford
Integrated System with No Exchange Processes	NA	.73	19	Charolais-Angus

[a] Cost of producing a lb. of retail cuts in the 1968–72 analysis period.

Source: Kenneth E. Nelson, *A System Analysis of Information and Communication in Beef Marketing*, Unpublished PhD Dissertation, Oklahoma State University, May 1976.

Table 12.5

Impact of a Restriction on Cattle Type on Performance of the Beef Marketing System for Selected Organizational Structures

Market Structure	Profit in $ per Head	Cost per lb. Beef[a]	Return on Total System Investment	Cattle Type Preferred
	($)	($ per lb.)	(%)	
Exchange Processes with Profits Maximized to				
Cow-Calf	11	NA	NA	Restricted
Feeding	31	.80	15	to Hereford-
Slaughtering	3	.85	13	Angus at
Fabricating	60	.83	13	all levels
Integrated System with No Exchange Processes	NA	.80	15	

[a]Cost of producing a lb. of retail cuts in the 1968–72 analysis period.

Source: Kenneth E. Nelson, *op. cit.*

would tend to keep the per lb. costs down. The "team solution" refers to the simulation of a vertically integrated structure. Preference is for the CHHE (Charolais-Hereford) and the cost of producing beef is lower than for other cattle types or organizational structures.

Table 12.5 provides an interesting set of data from this same analysis. There is always concern over the implications of failure to achieve relatively high levels of interstage coordination up and down through the system. One way to estimate the implication is simulation. The results in Table 12.5 show what would tend to happen if the rest of the system is forced to work with a particular type of cattle. Since this decision gets made at the cow-calf level, the type picked was the HEAN (Hereford-Angus), which was the optimal type for the cow-calf operator if no attention is paid to the needs of the rest of the system. Restricting the entire system to this type brought profits at the other stages well below the profits for the preferred type at each stage. Perhaps most important is the significant increase in the costs of producing lean beef. What these results suggest is that failure to achieve high levels of pricing efficiency has the potential to push the cost of the system up and decrease the level of technical efficiency that is achieved.

The potential for simulation is virtually unlimited. Training beyond the scope of this book is required to do sophisticated analysis. But being aware of the potential and the probability that we will see increased use of simulation as a marketing tool alerts marketing students to opportunities and encourages them to be aware of current and pending developments.

Summary

Market systems analysis is discussed in very simple terms in this chapter. It is an old adage that we must walk before we can run. As students of marketing, the first task is to understand what is needed to do system analysis.

The first need is simple but has proven difficult to accomplish. Before worrying about sophisticated analyses, we must learn first to take a systems orientation to our work and study. This means emphasizing the activities along the system's interfaces where the level of interstage coordination that is realized will be determined.

Once a system orientation is adopted, certain techniques can help. The mirror image survey procedure can be used to help isolate barriers to coordinated activity and provide a base to develop hypotheses that can be further analyzed and tested.

Among the analytical tools available are budgeting, linear programming, and simulation techniques.

Comparisons of system efficiency across types of information for given organizational structures highlight the importance of information and measure the implications of failure to adopt new technology. Measuring the efficiency of vertically integrated versus exchange systems gives an indication of both the economic pressures for vertical integration and the potentials of coordinated activity in an exchange system.

Systems analysis will be the "in" thing during the 1980s. As procedures and techniques develop, we will see a gradual shift in this direction by both the public and private analysts who do the marketing research. With some time lag to allow the output of the analysis to be disseminated and digested, we can hope to see some improvement in the performance of our food and fiber marketing systems.

Footnotes

1. Reference is to a research program conducted by Purcell and his associates at the Oklahoma Agricultural Experiment Station. The most concise description of the work is found in Wayne D. Purcell, "An Approach to Research on Vertical Coordination: The Beef System in Oklahoma," *Amer. J. of Agr. Econ.*, Vol. 55, February 1973.

2. This point is important. The individual cowman may be well informed but faces a challenge in finding or effecting a set of circumstances in which he can get paid a premium for superior feeder cattle. A parallel exists throughout the marketing system. The individual seller who knows the value of what he has may be frustrated in his efforts to sell effectively because the buyer has other sources who are not as well informed.

3. One of the biggest shortcomings of our efforts in research and analysis in recent years has been the failure to estimate such cost savings and how they might be distributed between the cooperators. Change might still be slow in coming but it is unlikely we will see concern about coordinated activity unless those involved are made aware of possible benefits.

4. In all candor, our marketing systems do not measure up very well here. At the production level, technology has helped usher in tremendous increases in the output per unit of inputs. Comparable progress in processing, distribution, packaging, etc. is not there. Part of the reason can be found in the prevailing institutions in the system. Labor unions are concerned about capital being used to displace labor and the adoption of new technology in packaging, canning, storing, or shipping is delayed. In addition, investment requirements and capital costs have increased rapidly in recent years. Processing has never been a highly profitable area of activity and the funds for research and development are not always available. Likewise, the huge investment of public funds in research at the producer level is not available in comparable magnitudes at other levels of the system.

5. There is no implication of suggesting or recommending vertical integration here. The hypothesis that moves to vertical integration will come at least partly because of the continued relatively low levels of pricing efficiency is not new. If the price mechanism cannot provide the degree of coordination progressive system participants want, they are likely to turn to other approaches.

6. These conclusions emerge in the analysis conducted by Rathwell and Purcell. A better level of understanding was demonstrated by stocker operators who deal directly with cattle feeders than by the cow-calf operators who tend to sell through auction markets. Refer to P. James Rathwell and Wayne D. Purcell, *Economic Implications of Conflict and Inconsistency in the Beef Marketing System: The Producer-Feeder Subsector,* Okla. Agr. Exp. Sta. Bul. B-704, Stillwater, October 1972.

7. For in-depth treatment of the cattle cycle, refer to Kendell Keith and Wayne D. Purcell, *The Beef Cycle of the 1970s: Analysis, Behavioral Dimension, Outlook and Projections,* Okla. Agr. Exp. Sta. Bul. B-721, Stillwater, March 1976.

8. The study referred to was conducted by Kenneth Nelson as part of a long-run research effort at the Oklahoma Agricultural Experiment Station. Refer to Kenneth E. Nelson, *A System Analysis of Information and Communication in Beef Marketing,* Unpublished PhD Dissertation, Okla. State Univ., 1976.

Questions

1. Select a product with which you are most familiar. Think about the market system for that commodity and focus your attention on a particular point of exchange. Describe the attitude that buyer and seller bring to their negotiations and write down the objective of each as you perceive what they are trying to do.

2. Assume you are a producer and feel you are not being paid a premium for what you know to be a superior product. What could you do to correct the situation? What are the obstacles to your plan?

3. Do you agree the continuing trend toward decentralized marketing will increase the level of pricing efficiency achieved by our marketing systems? Why or why not?

4. What is a marketing margin and how should it be used?

5. What is the "behavioral dimension" of a market system? Why is it becoming more important? Illustrate how the behavioral dimension has impact.

Selected References

Dunn, Terry L. and Wayne D. Purcell, *Economic Implications of Conflict and Inconsistency in the Beef Marketing System: The Feeder-Packer Subsector*, Okla. Agr. Exp. Sta. Bul. B-700, Stillwater, August 1972.

Farris, Donald E. and Raymond A. Dietrich, "Economics of Alternative Beef Production Systems and Locations," *Forage-Fed Beef: Production and Marketing Alternatives in the South*. Southern Cooperative Services Bulletin 220, June 1977.

Johnson, Ralph, *An Economic Evaluation of Alternative Marketing Methods for Fed Cattle*, Nebr. Agr. Exp. Sta. Bul. 520, Lincoln, 1972.

Nelson, Kenneth E., *A System Analysis of Information and Communication in Beef Marketing*, Unpublished PhD. Dissertation, Okla. State Univ., Stillwater, 1976.

Purcell, Wayne D., "An Approach to Research on Vertical Coordination: The Beef System in Oklahoma," *Amer. J. of Agri. Econ.*, Vol. 55, February 1973.

Rathwell, P. James and Wayne D. Purcell, *Economic Implications of Conflict and Inconsistency in the Beef Marketing System: The Producer-Feeder Subsector*, Agr. Exp. Sta. Bul. B-704, Stillwater, October 1972.

chapter thirteen

Market Strategies

The discussion to this point has included such topics as the operating environment, public policy, government programs, price and pricing processes, decision criteria, and analytical tools. This chapter will examine in more specific terms some ways this information can be used. Market strategies become the focal point of attention.

Any market strategy must start with an understanding of the consumer. We will start there and progress through such related topics as advertising, pricing policies, new product and new market development, interregional competition, and feasibility studies. These topics should help develop marketing strategies at the micro or individual firm level.

Increasingly, group action is becoming a "strategy" in the market place. A look at group action is included. The chapter concludes with brief coverage of the world market and international trade. No marketing strategy, from the level of the individual decision maker to the large and well organized group, can be called complete until it has recognized the increasing influence world trade has on our domestic markets.

Consumption, Consumer Behavior

The final objective of almost all marketing activity is to satisfy consumers' demands. Even if we concede the consumer's demand can be influenced by an aggressive advertising program, a basic fact remains—it is the consumer who casts a yes-no vote on the product-price combination offered at retail. It follows that we need to understand some of the basics of consumer behavior if marketing strategies are to be designed so they will work.

The theory of consumer demand is presented in texts dealing with microeconomic theory at the beginning, intermediate, and advanced levels. Here, some exposure to the concepts of utility, indifference curves, elasticity, demand, and demand shifters is assumed. Coverage of these concepts will be designed to illustrate their use and application. But first we need to describe the setting in which the marketing program must operate.

EXPENDITURES ON FOOD: SOME BASIC FACTS

For years, trade groups, politicians, and market analysts have quoted statistics that show the "percent of income spent on food" in the U.S. to be very low. The implicit position is that since food is such a bargain, the consumer should buy and keep his or her mouth shut! This perspective leads economists and advertisers to underestimating the importance of the consumer and consumer buying patterns.

The popular statistic so frequently quoted has varied in the 15 to 20 percent range in recent years.[1] It is calculated by dividing total expenditures on food by total income—and herein lies the problem. Like all arithmetic averages, the measure is subject to influence by extreme values. It treats the millionnaire and the pauper the same in terms of importance in the calculations and therefore fails to correctly represent any sector of the consuming public.

Table 13.1 provides data which clarify the picture. Using data on incomes by population groupings and the USDA's estimates of the cost of food for a typical family of four, we find that many families are spending 50 percent or more of their income on food. To these families expenditures on food are important. Significant changes in food prices put pressure on budgets and create very difficult adjustment problems.

The data in Table 13.1 are from the early 1970s and this time period was selected for a reason. During that period, food prices reversed a long-term trend and began to move up at a faster rate than the prices for non-food items. Figure 13.1 provides a picture of the relevant indices during the period within which the transition occurred. When the food index crossed the all-item index and moved rapidly higher, pressures were placed on budgets. Consumers pulled money from other areas to pay the food bill or cut back on the quality of their meal plans. Consumers screamed in an-

Table 13.1
Percent of Family Income Spent on Food by Income Levels 1966–75 [a]

Year	Families with Incomes Under $7,000		Families with Incomes $7,000–15,000	
	Percent of Families	Percent Income on Food	Percent of Families	Percent Income on Food
1966	45.4	44.5	45.3	17.7
1967	41.4	44.0	46.6	17.4
1968	36.9	44.7	48.4	17.7
1969	32.4	47.9	48.4	18.5
1970	31.0	49.6	46.7	19.1
1971	29.8	50.9	45.4	19.4
1972	26.8	52.4	42.9	20.1
1973	24.0	61.6	40.4	23.7
1974	21.5	68.0	38.0	26.6
1975	20.4	73.6	35.2	28.9

[a]Computed from *Statistical Abstract of the United States,* Bureau of the Census, Dept. of Commerce and *Family Economic Review,* Ag. Research Service, USDA. The percent of income spent on food is calculated by dividing the weighted average income for each income grouping into the yearly costs of food at home for a family of four based on the USDA's moderate cost meal plan.

guish, boycotts and demonstrations sprang up, and the political arena heard and reacted. Price ceilings were placed on prices of important foods in 1973.

Food prices *are* low in the U.S. relative to other developed countries. The percentage of incomes spent on food *is* low in the U.S.[2] And it is unquestionably true that the American farmer has done a fantastic job in increasing his productivity and providing for the American consumer and consumers around the world. But granting all this, we have to recognize some basic facts:

1. Many consumers spend substantial parts of their income for food. When food prices rise, the higher prices cause painful adjustments in consumers' buying patterns.

2. No matter what the level of food prices, consumers prefer them lower. The demand for food as a composite is highly inelastic—it is a necessity. Every dollar spent on food is a dollar that is not available to be used in improving the standard of living along other dimensions.

3. Consumers are selfish when it comes to protecting themselves. If the only way the standard of living of those producing and selling the product can improve is at the expense of the consumer, the consumer is not likely to be very sympathetic.

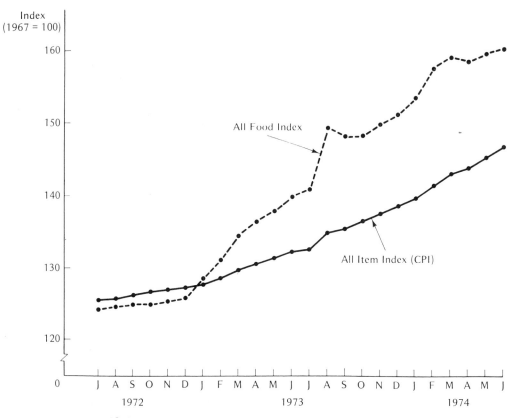

FIGURE 13.1 THE ALL-ITEM CONSUMER PRICE INDEX (CPI) AND THE ALL-FOOD
INDEX DURING A PERIOD OF TRANSITION, JULY 1972–JUNE 1974

4. Any seller of products or services to consumers must recognize the
    importance of understanding the consumer, must understand
    what motivates the decision to buy, and must appreciate the prob-
    lems the consumer is facing. Only then can a marketing program
    with its products and product attributes, its advertising message,
    and its pricing policies have a high probability of success.

PSYCHOLOGY OF CONSUMER BEHAVIOR

The study of consumer behavior is a study of applied psychology.
The consumer, every consumer, is first a psychological entity. Without
getting too deeply involved in the area, we need to look at some simple
dimensions of the consumer as a psychological being.

First and very importantly, the consumer is a creature of habit. The array of products in a particular consumer's basket is essentially stable over time. The same products, and the same brand names, are there week after week. After some initial experimentation each time a new product category is brought into the consumption pattern, the typical consumer settles into a comfortable routine. Brands that have been found acceptable are used a second, third, and fourth time. Each successful use contributes to what the psychology books refer to as "routinization"—and the particular brand becomes solidly entrenched in the consumption pattern.

Breaking consuming habits can be painful and traumatic. Deny the consumer his or her favorite brand and uncertainty edges in. Which brand will work? Which is the better buy? The experimentation process begins all over again. And the experimentation is costly in terms of time, the possibility of an unsatisfactory experience with the different product or service, and in the frustration that uncertainty always brings. It is from this resistance to change that we see a primary basis for product differentiation emerge. If the consumer can be influenced by an advertising effort so that the product or service is perceived as being better or superior, the battle is essentially won.

A second characteristic of the consumer's pattern of behavior is the differences in the attention paid to different products in the total buying pattern. Most of the difference can be explained by the frequency of purchase, the relative importance of the product category in the total consumption pattern, or some combination of the two.

In developing this point, it is useful to introduce the psychological concept of a threshold. In consumer behavior, both perception and reaction thresholds are important.

If price changes are the primary reasons for changing a consumption pattern, then it follows that the price changes must first be perceived by the consumer. There are two types of products for which a price change will be quickly perceived. They are products that are purchased frequently and products that are important in terms of the percentage of the total food budget they command. Sellers of products that meet one or both characteristics should be aware price changes will be quickly perceived. Figure 13.2 illustrates. If price has been stable at the level P_0 and increases to a level P_1, buyers will notice the change quickly for products such as bacon, sugar, milk, eggs, hamburger, round steak, bread, cheese, etc.—products purchased regularly that are not insignificant in terms of cost. A much larger price change might go unnoticed if the product is a frozen turkey, bulk ice cream, or some other product not purchased regularly. The same holds for salt, pepper, toothpicks, seasonings, or other products that do not require an important percentage of the food budget.

But perception of the price change does not mean the consumer will adjust his or her consumption pattern. Before a change will be made in the

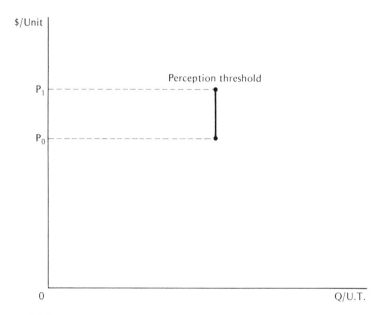

FIGURE 13.2   ILLUSTRATION OF A PERCEPTION THRESHOLD AFTER A PRICE
CHANGE FROM A FAMILIAR PRICE

consumption pattern, a reaction threshold must be violated—price must change enough that the consumer reacts. This can require a substantial price move beyond the perception threshold. Again, the degree of product differentiation becomes important. If the brand name has been effectively implanted in the mind of the consumer, price may increase significantly and many consumers will continue to buy the product.

Figure 13.3 pulls this area together. From a beginning and familiar price P_0, a move to P_1 might be required for a typical consumer to perceive a price increase. A move to P_2 could then be required to motivate a reaction and a change—and the seller "loses" this customer. Moving in the other direction, a price decrease to P_3 might be required for the typical consumer to perceive a change. Most consumers are more sensitive to price increases and a bigger price change might go unnoticed in the downward direction. But once the declining price is noticed, the reaction threshold might be very close—especially if this is a differentiated product. Therefore, the quantitative response to price declines below the reaction threshold can be quite large. But for price increases, the quantitative response across all consumers might be fairly small. Remember, change because of price increases involves searching for alternatives and disrupting the consumption pattern—a disturbing experience. But for price decreases, more of a favored product can be used, which is a rewarding experience to the buyer.

There is certainly no attempt here to reformulate the theory of consumer behavior. In the theory texts, we read about "elasticity" as the measure of quantitative response. But this is consistent with the concepts of threshold and reaction. Given enough time, most consumers will react to significant changes in price in either direction. In the long run, then, the quantitative response will be greater for a given change in price and demand is more elastic (or less inelastic). But in the short run, the seller can build a pricing program around the consumer's resistance to change.

A third dimension of interest is the way consumers react and eventually adjust to higher prices. Price increases in the important products, we have suggested, will be quickly perceived. The initial reaction can be volatile: vocal protests, demonstrations, calls for political action, boycotts, etc. But with the passage of time, the change is absorbed and a new era of stability emerges until price is changed again. What we see, therefore, as prices trend higher is a stair-step effect. Prices hold steady near a particular level because the retailer is aware of the disturbing effect of frequent price changes. Analysts talk about the "sticky" prices at retail and their failure to register short-run price changes at the farm or processing levels.[3] But when the price structure has moved upward and the higher prices show promise of being permanent, prices to consumers are increased. The increases are

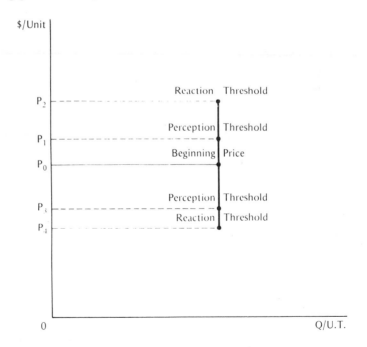

FIGURE 13.3 ILLUSTRATION OF PERCEPTION AND REACTION THRESHOLDS AFTER CHANGE FROM A BEGINNING PRICE

often in significant amounts as the retailers "catch up" with higher wholesale prices. Another round of anxiety is begun for the consumer. Eventually, things settle into an acceptable routine again at the higher price level.

Insofar as the psychology of consumer behavior is concerned, several key points to keep in mind in formulating a marketing strategy are:

1. Consumers do feel threatened during periods of rising food prices. Incomes may be higher but much of their income is committed to monthly payments on the house, car, or new stereo they bought after the last pay raise. Adjustments are difficult. The dollars to put into a higher food bill are difficult to find.

2. Consumers are creatures of habit. They dislike having their consumption patterns disrupted by changes in price. Making the adjustment is a traumatic experience. Anything the seller can do to smooth the transition is likely to improve his image with the buyer.

3. As a group, consumers will typically settle down and accept higher prices after a short-run period of agitation. Anything the seller can do to support the need for the change and offset the consumers' irritation will improve his position as a seller.

ECONOMIC PRINCIPLES AND CONSUMER BEHAVIOR

The psychological and all other dimensions of consumer purchasing patterns are reflected in the consumer's utility map. It is from the utility map that we must get an understanding of traditional economic measures such as elasticity.

The *price elasticity of demand* for a particular product measures the quantitative response to a price change at a given price level. What type of response there will be depends to a large extent on the product's utility as perceived by the consumer. A product with a favorable image, whether real or imagined, is likely to be elastic for decreases in price. Existing consumers will take more and the product, at a lower price, may move into the consumption pattern of new consumers who have a favorable attitude toward the product. In the discussion of the psychology of consumer behavior, we looked at the possibility that quantitative response to price increases will be less than for price decreases. But awareness of the level of price elasticity of demand, whatever level that might be, is important in formulating a marketing strategy and deciding on price levels. Let's look at why.

Cutting price makes no sense for commodities with an inelastic demand. The quantitative increase, in percentage terms, will be less than the percentage decrease in price. Total returns will fall. This suggests advertised price specials should be restricted to products with an elastic demand. This means products or services in favor with the consumer, products that require significant expenditures and thus make responding worthwhile, and/or products purchased frequently and regularly so that consumers will be familiar with price levels and recognize the "price special" as possibly a significant reduction in price.

Conversely, changing to a higher price makes no economic sense with an elastic demand. Total returns will fall because of a significant reduction in quantity taken. If charging a higher price is a strategy move, it should be preceded by attempts to differentiate the product and try to assure that for price increases demand is inelastic.

Prices trend up over time and the individual seller, the trade group advertising a product, and the system in its entirety are required to deal with the reality of periodic price increases. Knowledge of the consumer and how he or she tends to react to price changes is therefore important. Guidelines for pricing policies that relate to the price elasticity of demand are:

1. Given that price increases are inevitable and tend to be one-way changes, orient the marketing program and advertising message to minimize the adjustment problems of the consumer. Product differentiation will help but when this has reached its limit, understand the consumer will be upset and do all that is feasible to keep a positive image for pricing policies. When possible, focus attention on the stable or lower prices for a grade or product with an elastic demand. If you adopt a "take it or leave it attitude" with higher prices that must be charged, over time, consumers will "leave" it.

2. Be especially careful with advertising and pricing policies on products that are important to the consumer. A price special on beans will have little influence on the consumer. A price special and a favorable price image on an important commodity grouping such as the red meats can have significant influence. Keep the consumer coming by bolstering your price image for the products the consumer cares about.

3. For products in surplus supply, move the program toward a theme designed to make demand more elastic. Inform the customer about new ways to use the product. If price must come down because of periodic increases in supply, the price decline will be minimized if demand is more elastic or less inelastic.

Income elasticity is a very important barometer of the market and of consumer behavior. Technically, income elasticity refers to the percentage change in quantity taken in response to a given percentage change in income—with prices held constant. The success of any marketing program will be significantly influenced by the income elasticity of the product in question. Incomes have trended higher over time in real terms, which means purchasing power has increased. This is a potent demand shifter for products with positive and relatively large income elasticity coefficients. For such products an effective marketing program plan can have exciting results. But for the product or service with a coefficient near zero or negative, the possibilities are greatly reduced. Here, the marketing program will be battling to keep consumption levels from falling since the effect of rising incomes is to maintain or reduce demand.

In Chapter 6 (Table 6.1) we looked at income elasticity coefficients for some of the important food products. In general, per capita consumption increases over time for those products with positive and relatively large income elasticity coefficients. Per capita consumption declines or increases much more slowly when the income elasticity coefficient is positive and small or negative.

The theoretical relationship among income elasticity, consumption, and changes in consumption provides guidelines for the marketing program:

1. Tailor the product or service and the related marketing program to the market. If the income elasticity is known to be positive and relatively large, push the markets where incomes are growing rapidly. Present the product as an integral part of an improving standard of living so the consumer will want to move toward a higher level of consumption.

2. In marketing a product that has a small or negative income elasticity coefficient, focus on themes that offset the negative connotation the consumer brings to the product. As a rule, the income elasticity coefficient for products from the cereal grains is small. But a new image might be attached to the product by featuring it as a "natural" product or otherwise showing how it fits evolving life styles.

The concept of *cross elasticity* is another important part of the demand theory that shows an important relationship to consumer behavior. Cross elasticity refers to the change in quantity taken of one product in response to a change in the price of a related product. When the cross elasticity coefficient is positive, the products are substitutes. The larger the coefficient, the stronger the substitute relationship.

Strong substitutes come in clusters. In Table 6.2, we found that the red meats—beef and pork—are strong substitutes. Fish and poultry are weaker substitutes for beef and pork. The fresh fruits are substitutes for each other. If we go back to the utility base of consumption patterns, the products that fill a common need tend to substitute fairly easily for each other. But move out of this cluster of comparable products and the substitute relationship weakens. A more dramatic change in the consumption pattern would then be required to bring in a new product.

Awareness of these tendencies helps in putting together an effective marketing plan and pricing program. The negative reaction to price increases for a particular product can be countered if prices for an important substitute can be maintained or decreased. In a supply-demand framework, we see the interactions at work as a change in price disturbs the *ceteris paribus* conditions and shifts the demand for a related product. In a behavioral sense, the consumer reacts to the price change by shifting between products that fill a comparable role. When strong substitutes are available, the shifting will occur and this should be recognized in the pricing policy.

For products that are purchased regularly and that are significant in the budget but have no good substitutes, the situation is markedly different. Producers, processors, distributors, and sellers of beef and pork have seen periods of high prices come and go. Consumers complain but they usually still buy meat when prices stabilize. This is at least partly because of the availability of close substitutes. If pork is expensive, the consumer shifts to beef, mutton, fish, and poultry. When the price of pork declines, the shift is back toward pork. But the "damage" may be permanent when prices increase significantly for a particular product and no good substitutes exist. In the late 1970s, freeze damage in Brazil moved coffee prices to levels 2 or 3 times the prices consumers expected. Adjustments in consumption patterns were made; some coffee drinkers switched to tea, while others consumed less or no coffee at all. When the pressure on prices later subsided, some of the coffee customers were gone for good. Coffee has no effective substitute and permanent changes in the preference pattern resulted.

The messages are clear to those in charge of developing marketing programs and making pricing decisions:

1. Be careful with pricing decisions on products the consumers view as important but for which there are no effective substitutes. Raise prices on these products only when necessary. Higher prices mean a disruption of the consumer's routine, which can impose permanent damage on the consumer's image of the seller.

2. Identify products or groups of products that have positive and relatively large cross elasticity coefficients, and apply consistent pricing policies to these products. To the consumer, inconsistent pricing practices within the product group, which is a cluster of

substitutes, will prove disquieting. Variable pricing practices will also prevent shifting within the group and this shifting works to the advantage of the seller.

3. Be aware of the need to help the consumer make any adjustment. If the price of a product with strong substitutes must be increased, try to motivate a positive attitude by focusing attention on the stable or falling prices of the substitutes. If there are no effective substitutes and price must be increased, try to ease the pain of the major adjustment the consumer is facing by point-of-sale displays, volume discounts, etc.

Overall, an awareness of the basic dimensions of consumer behavior is an important ingredient in the successful marketing program. It complements the economic concepts with which we are familiar. The primary purpose of marketing activities is to coordinate production with the needs and demands of consumers. This will be difficult to accomplish if we don't understand the consumer and consumer behavior.

Advertising

The role and importance of advertising varies widely within our food and fiber marketing systems. At the farm level, we have noted the individual producer is a price taker. He faces a horizontal demand curve and advertising has no role to play in his plans. But producer trade groups are active in advertising and promotion. Financing is often a problem but there is widespread feeling among producers that they should participate in advertising efforts in an attempt to help themselves. At the other end of the continuum is the giant processing firm or retail chain that spends immense sums of money on advertising. Much of the effort is non-price competition instead of competition on a price basis. The value of huge expenditures on advertising is questioned by some analysts.

ROLE OF ADVERTISING

Just what role advertising should or does play in our economic system is, therefore, subject to considerable debate. Proponents point to the informational value of advertising. They expand this position into a claim that advertising is indispensable to a rapidly growing and complex society. Advertising, they argue, is an important catalyst to keep the economy growing and expanding.

But the opposition comes down hard on the other side. Opponents point to the billions of dollars spent by the large firms in highly concentrated industries and wonder about its value to society. If the expenditure by firm A is just to offset the impact of advertising by firm B, is there a net gain to anyone? And with the heavy expenditures on advertising comes product proliferation. A "new" or "improved" variety appears on the market that is essentially the same as the old product but with a new package and a new name. The opponents of advertising ask "who benefits?."[4]

We cannot solve the issue here but laying out a few generalizations should help:

1. Advertising expenditures by the individual firm will vary with the competitive environment within which the firm operates. The range is from no advertising by the firm under conditions approaching pure competition to extremely heavy expenditures by the monopolist trying to protect his position or the oligopolist who avoids competing on a price basis.

2. The benefits of advertising to introduce a new product that is essentially the same as the old are questionable. The same is true of the advertising by a firm to support several products that perform essentially the same function. An example is the breakfast ceral industry. Several cereals with the same product base—oats or wheat—are produced and advertised heavily. Some particular characteristic of the processing function is usually stressed in the advertising campaign ("puffed," for example) even though this feature has no influence on the nutritive value of the product.

3. Advertising is a very important factor in new product development. The risk of product failure is high and firms count on advertising to gain acceptance for the new product or service. We could argue less money would be spent on research and development if firms were denied the opportunity to accompany introduction of a new product with an extensive advertising campaign.

4. The purpose of advertising varies with the economic structure. A broad and general purpose is to increase demand. But another objective is to differentiate the product. In the highly concentrated industries where product differentiation is important, both increasing demand and making demand more inelastic are objectives. In the purely competitive industry, advertising by the trade group is designed to increase demand and to make demand more elastic.

PRINCIPLES OF ADVERTISING

In an economic setting where supply control is possible, the firm advertises to increase demand for its product and to differentiate that product in the eyes of the consumer. Figure 13.4 illustrates. Starting with a demand curve DD, the firm would like to shift demand to a schedule such as D'D'. Not only has demand increased but for a given quantity level, D'D' is more inelastic. Having accomplished this type of shift, the firm would then move along D'D' by controlling the quantity offered until it is operating in the elastic portion of the curve. Total revenue is increased.

Advertising by trade groups in production agriculture is also intended to increase demand. But at the industry level, demand is highly inelastic. When there is no effective control over supply, the related purpose of advertising may be to make demand more elastic. The explanation for such attempts lies in the behavior of industry supply.

For most major food and fiber products, year-to-year increases in supply are virtually automatic. Advances in technology and in production knowledge have enabled fewer producers to generate more product per unit of input. If the quantity produced is to trend higher, working to make demand more inelastic is a mistake. Total returns fall when supply increases with an inelastic demand.

When faced with autonomous increases in supply, the purely competitive industry will fare better if demand is more elastic (or less inelastic). Figure 13.5 shows why. If supply increases from S_1S_1 to S_5S_5 over a period

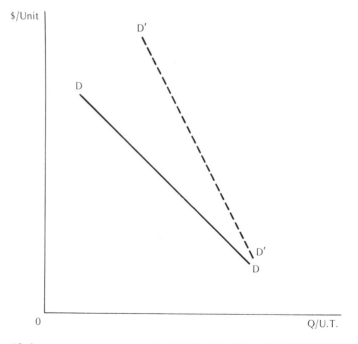

FIGURE 13.4 THE DESIRED IMPACT OF ADVERTISING IN AN ECONOMIC STRUCTURE WHERE SUPPLY CONTROL IS POSSIBLE

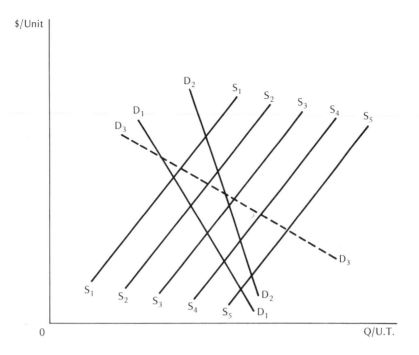

FIGURE 13.5   THE DESIRED IMPACT OF ADVERTISING IN AN ECONOMIC STRUC-
TURE WHERE AUTONOMOUS INCREASES IN SUPPLY ARE ANTICIPATED

of years, the industry will fare better if it is operating along D_3D_3 instead of
D_2D_2 or D_1D_1. The schedule D_1D_1 could be demand before advertising is
begun. A program of advertising that shifts the industry to D_2D_2 is not the
answer. While the total returns level will be higher with D_2D_2 for any
particular quantity, year-to-year increases in supply will come in the face of
an inelastic demand as the price that clears the market falls to lower levels.
The preferred position would be schedule D_3D_3, which is less inelastic
(perhaps elastic) at the lower price levels.

If making demand more elastic, or less inelastic, is a legitimate purpose of group advertising at the production level, the question then
evolves, "How can this be done?" Some of the more important possibilities
are considered as separate topics in this chapter. They include new product
development, introduction of a product to new markets, and specific pricing practices such as price discrimination.

Development of new uses for the product or the opening of new
markets serve essentially the same purpose. They take some of the supply
pressure off the existing market. Figure 13.6 illustrates. In the primary
market, call it market A, demand is highly inelastic in the lower price
levels. Increase supply and we know what happens—total returns fall. But

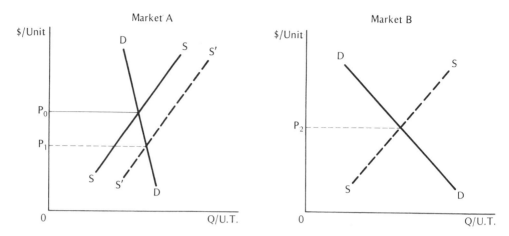

FIGURE 13.6   ILLUSTRATION OF THE IMPACT OF DIVERTING SUPPLY FROM A HIGHLY INELASTIC MARKET TO A SECONDARY MARKET WHERE DEMAND IS MORE ELASTIC OR LESS INELASTIC

what if this increase or part of this increased quantity can be absorbed in a new market? Market B, a secondary market, has now been opened up and some of the quantity can be moved here. With the new market the aggregate demand is increased, and increases in supply—if they come—can be absorbed at more favorable prices.

Often, a new use for the product is developed and this can open up new market possibilities. With the new use and/or new market may come the use of price discrimination if the markets can be kept separate and if the demand elasticities are significantly different. All of these possibilities depend on the success of the related advertising effort.

The question of how much money to spend on advertising is always difficult. Conceptually, the answer is straightforward. Estimate the response function to advertising, find the marginal response, and equate this marginal return with the marginal cost. But in practice the answer is not that easy. Quite often, there is no reliable estimate of the response function. Getting good estimates is difficult because of the many other factors that can influence sales volume or any other variable used to estimate the impact of advertising. But knowing what type of response the advertising program is getting is clearly important. Without attempting an exhaustive treatment of the subject, we will look at some possibilities.

The use of test markets is a common approach. Two or more markets are selected that present similar profiles in terms of income and education levels, ethnic groups, and other indicators of socio-economic status. Controlled levels of advertising are used in the various cities. Table 13.2 illustrates the nature of a possible set of results. Plotting sales against dollars spent on advertising in Figure 13.7 gives a picture of the response function.

This "test market" approach can be effective if the firm conducting the tests has control over price. If price varies between markets or within the test period in a particular market, it is very difficult to isolate what part of any change in sales is due to advertising and what part is due to the change in price. But there may be no acceptable alternatives. If the price changes are small or if the changes in price are similar in all markets, useful comparisons can be made.

Another approach is to build a model to explain variation in quantity sold or sales dollars and include advertising as an explanatory variable. The most common approach is to control the level of advertising expenditures and use a dummy variable approach to measure the impact. Assume, for example, we have the following model to explain sales in a particular market area:

$$Y = a + \beta_1 X_1 + \beta_2 X_2 + \beta_3 X_3 + \beta_4 X_4 + \beta_5 X_5 + e$$

where:

Y = sales per capita ($),
X_1 = price of product ($ per unit),
X_2 = average per capita disposable income in the market ($ per capita),
X_3 = price of the primary substitute product ($ per unit),
X_4 = education level of the average resident (years of school), and
X_5 = per capita expenditure on advertising ($).

Table 13.2
Expenditures on Advertising and
Dollar Sales per Capita in 10 Test Markets

Dollars Advertising	Sales
($ per capita)	($ per capita)
.40	$ 8.50
.45	10.25
.50	13.50
.55	14.75
.60	17.00
.65	17.25
.70	18.00
.75	18.00
.80	18.75
.85	18.25

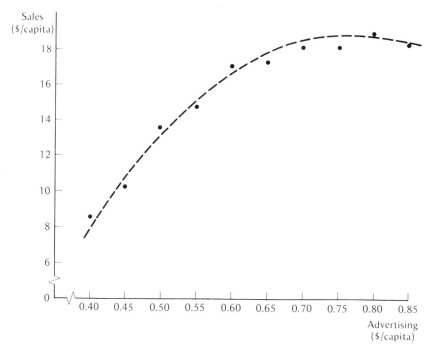

FIGURE 13.7   RESPONSE FUNCTION TO VARYING LEVELS OF ADVERTISING IN 10 HYPOTHETICAL TEST MARKETS

Given the model, the response to *added* dollars spent on advertising can be estimated via the following steps:

1. Increase the advertising expenditure periodically by a predetermined amount for a fixed period of time and then drop back to the original level. For example, advertising could be varied for alternate six-month periods from 10 cents per capita in the market area to 20 cents.

2. Introduce another variable, X_6, into the model. Let X_6 take the value 1 when the higher level of advertising is in effect, 0 when the normal or lower level is in effect.

3. When the test period is over, estimate the revised and expanded model. Test $\hat{\beta}_6$ for statistical significance. If it is significant, there is a basis for concluding the extra advertising expenditures have had an influence. The size of $\hat{\beta}_6$ can be used as a measure of the response to the additional expenditure.[5]

Whatever the measure employed, some means of estimating the value of advertising must be employed if intelligent decisions are to be made on how much to advertise. Given a measure, marginal analysis can then be employed. Dollars should be spent on advertising, subject to financial restraints, so long as the marginal return to the last unit of advertising is greater than the marginal cost of that last unit. The equimarginal principle also holds. Advertising dollars should be allocated across markets, or across products and markets, so that the marginal return from the last dollar spent is the same for all products and/or markets. In algebraic terms, this means the following equality holds:

$$\frac{\text{MV Adv } (Y_1)}{\text{MC } (Y_1)} = \frac{\text{MV Adv } (Y_2)}{\text{MC } (Y_2)} = \cdots = \frac{\text{MV Adv } (Y_n)}{\text{MC } (Y_n)}$$

where MV Adv (Y_1) = the marginal value of advertising in market (or product) Y_1, and

MC (Y_1) = the marginal cost of the advertising program in Y_1.

Before leaving the area of advertising, let's go back and review the area insofar as production agriculture is concerned. There is no advertising at the individual firm level. Any advertising that is done is at the aggregate level and usually seeks to increase demand. The advantages of making demand more elastic or less inelastic are not always recognized by the trade groups.

A number of problems are inherent to group advertising of food and fiber products. First, the possible response is constrained by the capacity of the consumer. This is especially true for foods. Any advertising effort by a trade group seeking to increase consumption of pork runs squarely into the problem of competition with the efforts of those promoting increased beef consumption. The two products are strong substitutes in consumption.

In a broad sense, all foods are substitutes. And this constrains the effectiveness of an advertising campaign for any one food. With the inherent difficulties in measuring response when neither supply nor price can be controlled, convincing producers they should help finance advertising has proven difficult for many trade groups.

The free rider problem is also very much in evidence. It is true that any benefits from advertising will accrue to all producers—participants and non-participants alike. Therefore, we see the tendency toward "let someone else pay" emerge.

Group efforts in some commodity areas have experienced problems because they bring a narrow perspective to the issue. Simply spending money on advertising is not the answer—and many producers are sharp enough to know it. A program to inform the metropolitan housewife about how tough it is "down on the farm" is not likely to help. She has her own problems and she has seen food costs rise relative to other products and services in recent years. What appears to be needed is a broad program that conducts the needed research and builds a base of understanding of the consumer. Short and long-run plans can then be tied to the current and projected pattern of consumer behavior. Such an approach puts an advertising program that carries a higher probability of success and lasting benefits in front of the consumer. Not all trade groups operate from such a perspective.

Approaches to Pricing

The pricing policy of the firm depends first on the competitive structure within which it operates. Within the restraints imposed by the competitive structure, pricing policy is a function of what the firm is trying to accomplish.

Alternative economic structures were discussed in Chapter 3 with emphasis on the implications to marketing decisions. Let's review briefly:

Pure competition: At the firm level, there is no pricing policy since the firm is a price taker. Each firm faces a horizontal (perfectly elastic) demand curve. Some form of group action is necessary if pricing policies are to be applied.

Monopolistic competition: Attempts to differentiate the product bring some slope to the demand curve facing the individual firm. There are many small firms, price competition is keen, the degree of product differentiation is usually minor, and the individual firm is limited by the competition in terms of what he can do with pricing policy.

Oligopoly: Each seller is large enough to influence the market. The exact demand curve facing each firm is a function of how competitors would react to a price change. Prices tend to be rigid. Frequent price changes are avoided to preclude the possibilities of "price wars." The pricing policy is largely one of stable prices. All firms may change prices under some type of price leadership arrangement when prices do change.

Monopoly: The monopoly firm faces the market or industry demand curve. In theory, the profit maximizing quantity is determined by applying the MC=MR criterion and price is then taken from the demand schedule for the particular quantity. But monopolists often have a "price policy." They may, for example, charge less than the price that would maximize profits in the short run to discourage new competition.

A widely used approach to pricing is *full cost* or *cost-plus* pricing. Costs of providing a particular product or service are estimated, some type of margin is added, and the price is set accordingly. The added margin is often a fixed percentage. For example, a 10 percent mark-up on an item costing $9.00 would mean a price of $9.90 to the buyer.

The cost-plus approach is a simple approach and this explains its popularity. There are advantages to simplicity. No particular skill is required once the cost is established. A clerk can apply a fixed percentage or per unit mark-up and price the product.

But the simplicity of the approach can prove costly in terms of opportunity costs. Applying the same mark-up to all product lines carries the implicit assumption price elasticity of demand for all product lines is the same—and we know this is not true. A product may well merit a special or individual pricing policy. The potentials of a sophisticated and successful advertising program to differentiate a particular product or product line may be wasted if a naive cost-plus approach to pricing is used. A major purpose of advertising by the individual firm is to make the demand for a product or brand more inelastic. But what if a cost-plus approach to pricing keeps the quantity above the profit maximizing level and possibly in the inelastic portion of the demand curve? Marginal revenue is negative at quantities for which demand is inelastic and no rational firm will operate here unless forced to do so by artificial controls.

The approach is improved by using variable mark-up procedures and bringing some judgment to the situation in deciding which products will sell with a higher mark-up. The nature of the demand for the product comes in here. In general, the higher mark-up will go on the products with the more inelastic demand.

An alternative to cost-plus pricing is to tie to marginal cost instead of average costs and practice *marginal cost pricing*. There are theoretical arguments in favor of such an approach. The marginal cost is effectively the cost of providing the last unit so why not price accordingly?

In industries with a high fixed-to-variable cost ratio, marginal cost pricing can lead to what has been labeled ruinous competition. In the railroad industry, for example, the fixed costs are relatively high. Rail companies have shown a tendency to compete for traffic by requesting Interstate Commerce Commission (ICC) approval for lower rates to battle barge and truck competition. In Figure 13.8, for example, the railroad would haul the product so long as the rate is above average variable cost (AVC). This approximates marginal cost pricing since the price (rate) is below average total cost (ATC). But hauling at rates below ATC to be competitive means long-run trouble for the railroads. Failure to cover ATC means not all fixed costs are being met. And when the fixed facilities wear out (lines, rolling stock, etc.), there is no pool of capital to permit their replacement.

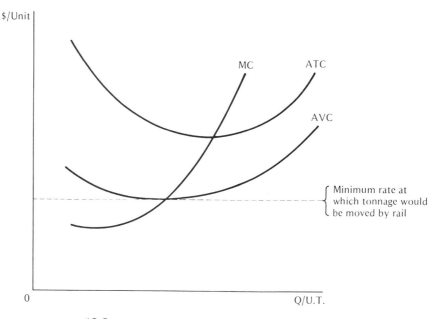

FIGURE 13.8 MARGINAL COST PRICING IN THE RAILROAD INDUSTRY

In other settings, marginal cost pricing is more practical. Consider the case of the processor who is processing and packing a brand name product under contract with a major retail chain. When the contractual obligation is met for the week, the processor may be able to package the product at very low variable costs and sell under a private label. Marginal cost pricing makes sense here since the fixed costs are covered in the contract with the chain. But these situations are not encountered that often. Marginal cost pricing is found most often in circumstances where intense competition is present or where the product must be moved because of a threat of spoilage or damage.[6]

The use of *loss leader pricing* is common in the retail food chains.[7] A particular product is advertised at a relatively low price, perhaps below cost (the "loss leader" idea), to attract customers into the store. The success of the pricing approach depends on the extent to which sales volume in other products is increased by bringing people into the store. Clearly, the product used as a "lead" must be one for which we would expect a large quantitative response to the advertised price decline. This is why the meats, especially hamburger and chicken, or the fresh fruits and vegetables are used. Demand at retail for these products may be elastic for price decreases.

A variation of the loss leader approach is often used in an attempt to capture new market territory. *Penetration pricing* refers to a pricing policy designed to enter a new market with low prices compared to the competition. Often, heavy expenditures on advertising will be used to "soften" the new market and increase early sales volume. Just how low the price is set or whether this approach will even be tried will depend on expectations as to what the competition will do.

When fear of competitors' reactions blocks the use of penetration pricing, some other approach must be tried. One possibility is to go to the other extreme and try what is often referred to as a *market skimming*. Here, the price is set *above* the competition with an objective of picking up a small but possibly profitable share of the market. We would expect to see heavy advertising expenditures in an attempt to differentiate the particular brand of the product. The success of the strategy will vary with the success of the advertising campaign in establishing brand differentiation and the strength of the competition.

Some form of *price discrimination* is often practiced. When there are two or more markets for essentially the same product such that (1) the markets can be kept separate, and (2) the price elasticity of demand in the markets is significantly different, total returns can be increased by practicing price discrimination.

The total output is decided using the familiar MR=MC criterion where MR is the sum of the marginal revenue functions in the two markets. Figure 13.9 illustrates. The profit maximizing quantity is OQ.

Quantity OQ is divided between the markets using the equimarginal principle. The quantity allocated to each market is controlled so that marginal revenue in market I is equal to marginal revenue in market II, and both are equal to the marginal revenue at the profit maximizing quantity OQ. Using this procedure, OQ_1 is sold in market I, OQ_2 in market II, and $OQ_1 + OQ_2 = OQ$. Figure 13.10 provides a graphical look at the solution. Price in market I is significantly higher than the price in market II. In general, price will be higher in the market with the less elastic or more inelastic demand. Price discrimination schemes are often started by developing a new market or new product use and diverting part of the volume from the original market.

The ideal situation occurs when price discrimination is possible, demand in the "old" market is inelastic, and demand is elastic in the new market. In this situation, taking product from the inelastic market will increase total revenue. Putting more product into the elastic market will also increase total revenue. In practice, however, both markets are often inelastic over many of the price-quantity possibilities. But price discrimination can still work. If the elasticities are sufficiently different that the gains are not offset by the transfer costs involved, total revenue across both markets can be increased by practicing price discrimination.

Examples of price discrimination are easy to find. The physician who charges patients different rates based on their income levels is an example. The "markets" are separated on the basis of income and socio-economic

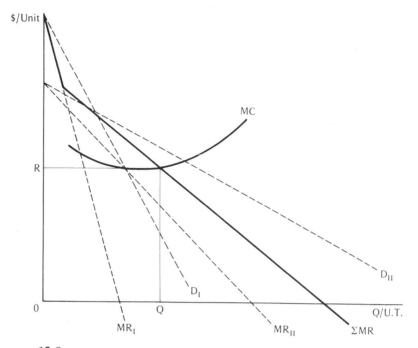

FIGURE 13.9   THE PROFIT MAXIMIZING QUANTITY WHEN PRODUCT IS SOLD IN TWO SEPARATE MARKETS

status. Appliances sold at one price level as a brand name product and sold at a lower price in the discount house under other names provides another example. In the international arena, with markets separated geographically, surplus product may be "dumped" on the more elastic market at almost any price when the demand in the producing country is highly inelastic and surpluses hang over the market.

Pricing in accordance with *what the market will bear* has connotations of both marginal cost pricing and price discrimination. Regulated carriers such as the railroads often practice price or rate discrimination when they compete for tonnage and price relatively low on the basis of the marginal cost of the haul. But for other products, especially products with a high per-unit value where the competition is less intense, the rates may be set as high as they can be set without running the risk of losing the business. The "what the market will bear" idea emerges.

There are no simple and reliable rules of thumb to make the pricing decision easy. Effective pricing requires work, study, and an understanding of the consumer. At a minimum, the pricing policy must be consistent with the competitive structure within which the product or service is being offered. Beyond this, it is wise to understand your competition, know how they will react, and to understand what you can and cannot do in the

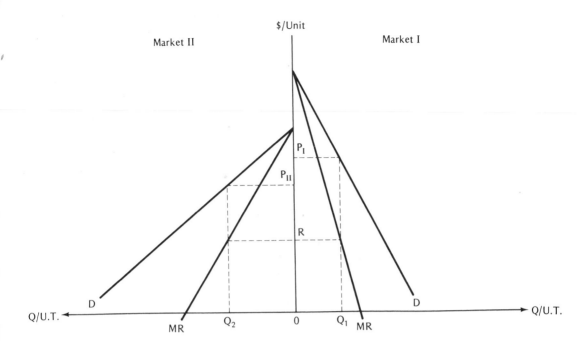

Market II

Market I

$/Unit

P_I

P_{II}

R

D

D

MR

MR

Q_2

0

Q_1

Q/U.T.

Q/U.T.

FIGURE 13.10   ALLOCATION OF QUANTITY PRODUCED BETWEEN TWO SEPARATE
MARKETS WHEN PRICE DISCRIMINATION IS EMPLOYED

marketplace. And then a simple rule should be followed—do develop a
policy! Don't drop back on a simple and easy cost-plus approach in a
market and with a product that offers potential. The long run economic
viability of the firm may rest in a very important fashion on the adequacy
and relevancy of the pricing policy.

New Product and Market Development

Development and introduction of new products involves new markets. If
no new market is involved in terms of geography, then a new consumer
clientele *is* involved in the existing geographical market areas. Advertising
and pricing policies are also important. Every topic discussed in this chapter provides background for our brief consideration of this topic area.

WHY NEW PRODUCTS?

Reasons for the often intense interest in development of new products vary with the nature of the industry, the type of product, and the
competitive structure within which the firm must operate. The oligopolist

who lives or dies with his ability to differentiate his products tries to keep a fresh product image before the consumer. The trade association for a farm commodity may be trying to find a less painful way of disposing of a chronic surplus.

In the breakfast cereal, detergent, paper product, cake mix, and to a lesser extent, the processed meats industry, a particular brand name often has a limited life in the marketplace. Figure 13.11 pictures what happens. The product is introduced, sales surge, reach a "saturation point," and start to decline. It is at this point the firm would like to have a "new" product ready for distribution.

The life cycle of a brand name shown in Figure 13.11 is related to the decay curve in advertising. When the advertising message ceases to "reach" the consumer, sales start to drop—and it is time for a new product and a new message. We will not debate the issue of whether the huge sums spent advertising a product that is new and different in name only is a worthwhile expenditure in terms of benefits to society. But the firms would argue they could not exist without an approach that allows them to supplement sales volume on established products by introducing a new product or brand name. Walk through a supermarket and count the number of different firms behind all the different soap products or behind all the many brands of cereal. New product development is a way of life in these industries.[8]

Motivations are different at the farm level. The trade group for the livestock, grain, or fiber sectors is usually concerned about a problem of

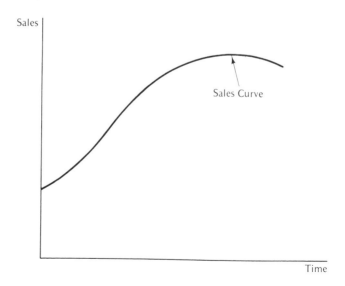

FIGURE 13.11   LIFE CYCLE OF A NEW PRODUCT

surplus production. Whether they recognize it or not, the basic purpose is to create a new market so price discrimination can be practiced. Consider what has been done with the potato. We have seen french fries, potato chips, instant potatoes, canned potatoes, a "pop up" product for the toaster, etc. All these are new products in that they serve a somewhat different clientele and/or a different purpose than the fresh potato. And without analysis to estimate the parameters, we can be reasonably sure the price elasticity of demand is less inelastic or even elastic for these uses compared to the highly inelastic demand for the fresh potato. Total revenues to the potato industry are increased by this process of diverting the product into new markets.

Frozen and canned orange juice, beef bacon, and cranapple juice are a few of the many other examples of new product development. For a product with a seasonal production pattern, the development of new product forms is especially important. Consider the plight of the orange producer if his only market was the fresh orange market where shelf life of the product is limited. There are other examples. Demand for whole turkeys, fresh or frozen, is highly seasonal but the production facilities are there year round. The turkey producer groups have not been particularly innovative in finding new markets but progress has been made. The rolled turkey roast can be frozen to extend shelf life and is consumed throughout the year. Turkey is packaged with TV dinners and other semi-prepared meals. Anything that can extend demand to a year-round basis will benefit producers whose fixed costs bring pressure for year-round production.

NEW PRODUCT IDEAS

The places from which new product ideas spring are many and varied. Sources such as the commodity trade group or the research and development department within a company are obvious. Generating new product ideas is their job. In the non-food products, some of the most innovative ideas come from workers in the assembly line. But potential from this source is limited in the foods to ideas on package design, the advertising message, or slight changes in the way the product is prepared.

Perhaps the most important source of all, the consumer, is also the most difficult to tap. After all it is the *consumer* that must be pleased. But the consumer is often a passive participant in the process and simply votes yes or no on the combination offered to him on the shelf or in the counter. If he or she has latent ideas that would prove useful, it is the market analyst's responsibility to uncover those ideas. Among the possible approaches are:

1. Generate a new product idea and test it in selected markets. This is a commonly used approach and brings the consumer in indirectly.

2. Use point-of-sale displays on existing products to solicit the consumers' ideas on new product forms, new uses for the product, etc.

3. Use personal interviews at the point of sale for similar products to get consumers' reactions to a new product form, a new product use, or to solicit suggestions on possibilities.

In the food and fiber products, the new product idea might require developing or adopting new technology. For example, the food products that have benefited from new "quick freeze" technology have moved into transportation channels and market outlets that otherwise were not possible. The rapid development of boxed beef in the late 1970s put the small outlet with limited storage facilities back on the delivery list of the large processor.

Advancement of technology in the spun protein fibers, especially from soybeans, ushered in the era of the synthetic or analog—and created new product forms. During periods of high ground beef prices, vegetable protein is used extensively in combination with the "natural" product. A blend of ground beef and vegetable protein provides an alternative to ground beef at a price 10 to 20 percent lower. Vegetable protein often constitutes 40 to 50 percent of the ground beef or sausage toppings for foods such as pizza. Manufacturers of the toppings like the lower cost of the vegetable protein, feel the topping has a more favorable appearance, and note quality control is easier to maintain.

The synthetic product is creating an increasingly important "new product" form. In general, it is competitive with the natural product. Examples not mentioned to this point (and their natural counterparts) include margarine (butter), dessert toppings (whipping cream), synthetic fibers (cotton, wool), vinyls (leather), and others of lesser concern. The synthetic product is most likely to be a factor when one or more of the following conditions are met:

1. The technology to approximate taste, texture, and other appeal-related dimensions of the natural product is available or can be developed;

2. The cost of the synthetic or natural-synthetic blend compares favorably with the cost of the natural product;

3. Shelf life or some other value-related attribute is improved by moving to the synthetic product or a synthetic-natural blend;

4. Production of the synthetic or blend is more suitable to mass production or assembly line techniques where high volume is important;

5. For comparable per unit profits or comparable returns on investment, the synthetic or blend can be priced below its competing
   natural product; and

6. Perhaps most important and more nearly a necessary condition,
   the consumer must accept the synthetic or blend product.

As a general rule, investment in facilities to produce the synthetic or product to be used in a blend will come when the outlook is favorable over a
long-run planning horizon. For example, investment in facilities to produce vegetable protein to be used as an extender with ground beef is most
likely to come when ground beef prices are high and expected to be high
for several years.

When the raw product is a blend, empirical research would be required to determine whether the relationship is one of substitution. To
illustrate, consider the case when the blend product is being produced and
sold significantly below hamburger or ground beef prices. Will the quantity
of ground beef sold decrease because of the competition? The answer depends on the price elasticity of demand for the blend product at retail and
the composition of the blend. If the demand for the blend product is elastic,
the quantity taken can be large enough to use more ground beef than
would be sold if the blend product were not available.

The new product and the new product idea can therefore take many
forms. An alert attitude and constant attention to consumption patterns are
essential if the potential from the new product idea is to be realized.

AN ANALYTICAL FRAMEWORK

Assuming a new product idea has been generated or a new market
area is being considered, the next question revolves around whether to go
ahead with introduction. The market analyst usually gets the job of answering this tough question and he needs a framework with which to
work.

The Bayesian framework fits this problem area very well. The
strategies are usually simple—introduce or don't introduce. The states of
nature can be as simple as alternative levels of consumer acceptance. The
entries in the payoff table will be a set of zeros for the "don't introduce"
strategy and estimated net returns for the different levels of acceptance for
the "introduce" strategy.

In many instances, the problem becomes more complex because the
reactions of competing firms must be taken into account. In this case,
which is the typical case for the firm operating under conditions of
oligopoly, the pricing policy used to introduce the new product becomes
very important. The ability to correctly anticipate reactions of competitors
may be even more important.

To illustrate, let's consider the situation facing a milk processor who is considering introducing milk in one gallon plastic containers in a new geographical area. Based on past experiences in other markets, some form of price cut will be needed to successfully enter the market. Market tests have demonstrated very limited consumer acceptance of the new container unless price is cut at least 10 cents per gallon. If the product is introduced, the decision is made to go in with a 10-cent price reduction after a month-long advertising program designed to "soften" the market.

Then comes the tough part—identifying the possible reactions of the competing firms and assigning the related probabilities of occurrence. This is a Bayesian problem and the basics are identified in Table 13.3. The three possible reactions are based on experiences in other markets—but that experience has been variable. One possibility (N_1) is that competitors will hold their price levels and rely on their brand name and consumer familiarity with their paper container. A second possibility (N_2) is that a partial price response will develop. This can take the form of reaction by part of the competing firms or price cuts to match only part of the lower price—such as a 5-cent cut. The third possibility (N_3) is that all competing firms will react by matching the lower price with a full 10-cent cut.

The entries in the payoff table reflect per gallon net returns for the first year of operation in the market. Cash flow needs are reflected in the costs.[9]

Probabilities are assigned the three states of nature after checking the files on reactions when entering other market areas and drawing on the experience of personnel in the research and market analysis departments. Visits are made to the market area to observe the prevailing price structure in the market, to watch the food ads for evidence of price competition, and to talk with managers of retail outlets. The probabilities assigned are as follows:

$$P(N_1) = .1$$
$$P(N_2) = .3$$
$$P(N_3) = .6$$

Applying these probabilities yields an expected value for strategy S_2 which is negative. The decision is made to stay out of this particular market with the plastic container and check other areas and other possibilities.

Distribution and Interregional Competition

With the advent of computerized techniques has come tremendous advances in decision making in product distribution. Techniques are available that allow the decision maker to minimize distribution costs, estimate

Table 13.3
Bayesian Approach to a Decision on Introducing a New Type of Container

	States of Nature		
	$N_1(.1)$	$N_2(.3)$	$N_3(.6)$
Strategies	Competitors Will Not Retaliate by Cutting Their Price	Competitors Will Cut Their Price by 5¢	Competitors Will Cut Their Price the Full 10¢
S_1: Do not introduce the new container	0	0	0
S_2: Introduce the new container	30¢	20¢	−40¢

$E(S_1)$: $= 0$
$E(S_2) = 30(.1) + 20(.3) - 40(.6) = -15¢$

the value of the product in one market region compared to others, and integrate several of the stages of economic activity in the marketing system. Coverage here will be restricted to the theory and what can be done with the techniques versus detailed examination of procedures.

LOCATION THEORY: BRIEFLY

In general, we expect price in a deficit area to be approximately equal to price in the surplus area plus transportation costs. Figure 13.12 illustrates. Market 1 has a surplus of product and a lower price than market 2. Without trade, prices in the two markets would be OP_1 and OP_2 respectively. If we subtract demand from supply in market 1 (the horizontal distance between the two curves), we get the excess supply curve shown in the bottom part of the figure. Note excess supply is zero at price OP_1. Subtracting supply from demand in market 2 (the horizontal distance between the two curves) gives excess demand for market 2.

The excess supply and excess demand curves intersect at price OP_3 and quantity OQ_1. If there were no transfer costs between the two regions, quantity $OQ_1 = ab = cd$ would be transferred from market 1 to market 2. Price would be OP_3 in both markets. The impact of transfer costs can be shown in several ways. One simple approach is to add the per unit transfer cost to the price at which the product is available in market 1. This shifts the excess supply curve for market 1 up parallel to the curve shown in the bottom portion of the figure. The quantity shipped is decreased since OQ_1

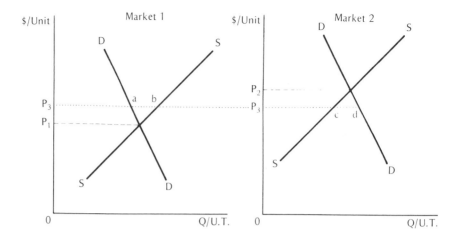

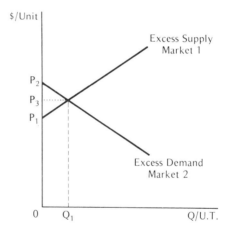

FIGURE 13.12   A TWO-MARKET EQUILIBRIUM POSITION BEFORE AND AFTER TRADE

is the amount shipped when transfer costs are zero. Prices in the two markets are no longer equal. If the slopes of the supply and demand curves in the two markets are equal (e.g., slope of demand in 1 = slope of demand in 2), the prices in the two markets will differ by the transfer costs. If the slopes are not equal, the price differences do not have to equal transfer costs.

To achieve real-world equilibrium positions comparable to that described in Figure 13.12 would require a market with no artificial restrictions on product flows. This requirement is seldom met. Lack of knowledge of needs in other areas, lack of adequate transportation facilities, differentials in highway taxes and load limits on commercial carriers across states, institutional barriers to flows such as labor union requirements—all these and other barriers prevent a nice, neat equilibrium. But the model is useful. Subject to such restraints, product *does* tend to flow from surplus to deficit regions until the price differentials approximate the transfer costs.

TRANSPORTATION MODELS

The simplest model with which we will deal is the transportation model. The problem is simple and straightforward. Given n supply points, m demand points, the available quantities, needs, and transportation costs, what transportation flow will minimize the costs?

Small problems of this type can be solved by hand. When there are as many as five or six supply and demand points, the use of a computerized routine is advised. The information needed will include:

1. Supplies available at each of the n supply points;

2. Demands or needs at each of the m demand points; and

3. The transfer cost between each supply-demand combination.

In algebraic terms, we have the following when looking at the general case:

$$\text{Minimize} \sum_{i=1}^{n} \sum_{j=1}^{m} X_{ij} C_{ij}$$

subject to $X_{ij} \geq 0$
$C_{ij} \geq 0$

where X_{ij} = quantity flowing from supply point i to demand point j, and
C_{ij} = transfer cost between supply point i and demand point j.

In practice, the problem is often set up with a related requirement that total supply = total demand. If this is not practical, a "warehousing activity" can be incorporated into the model with an appropriate cost to allow supply to temporarily exceed demand.

TRANSSHIPMENT MODELS

More recent advances in programming technology permitted development of the transshipment model. This model differs from the transportation model in that it allows the raw material to be processed. Examples include modeling work to estimate the least-cost flows of wheat and flour. The optimal solution shows flows of wheat from production areas to processing facilities and then the flow of flour to the final market area. In the livestock industry, transshipment models have been used to estimate the least-cost flow of feeder cattle jointly with the optimal location of feedlots, flows of live slaughter cattle, location of packing plants, and flows of dressed beef into final markets.

Data requirements are more extensive and more complex. Needed are the location and amounts of the original raw material, location and capacities of processing facilities, location and quantities demanded in the final markets, transfer costs for all flows and all product forms, etc. This is complex analysis but the joint treatment of the several stages of economic activity is to be desired if it can be accomplished given data availability.

SPATIAL EQUILIBRIUM MODELS

This model adds another dimension to the information in the optimal solution. Transportation is involved, product flows are involved, but estimates of the differentials in value (product price) relative to some selected base region are also provided. The price information is a valuable addition. To the firm considering moving into a new market area, information on how much more (or less) the product is worth in that new area can be important. Such information is also important to the long-run investment decision. Establishing a processing facility in an area where the product is worth less will mean trouble unless raw material costs are lower or other advantages come with the location.

To get price information into the optimal solution requires a significant addition to the information base that must be provided. Either a demand function, a supply function, or demand and supply elasticities must be provided for each identified region. This information is often not available and is always difficult to estimate because of problems in availability of appropriate data.

DATA NEEDS, ISSUES, INTERPRETATION

Brief attention to data needs, some basic assumptions underlying the models, and how the results should be interpreted and used will complete our coverage. This is a broad and complex area. More coverage can be found in the references listed at the end of this chapter.

Procedurally, the steps involved in setting up the models are as follows:

1. Divide the area to be covered, often the entire U.S., into supply regions and demand regions. Within each region, pick a supply point and a demand point. (They are often the same point but do not have to be.) In general, analysts work with states or groups of

states because the data are available in this form. States may be grouped into one multi-state region so long as the analyst feels there will be no flows within the large region that would significantly influence the optimal solution. The use of a single point to represent demand or supply points is obviously a restriction but this simplification is needed to estimate transfer costs.

2. Estimate the supply of, and demand for, the product for each region in terms of quantity. The supply-demand balance becomes important since flows will normally be from the surplus regions to the deficit regions. For analysis purposes, it is assumed all the supply is available in the supply point and all the demand is concentrated in the demand point. For the transshipment model, this must include all raw, intermediate, and finished products with which the study is concerned.

3. Gather or estimate the transfer costs from supply points to demand points. In most cases, judgment is used here and not all possible pairs are estimated. For example, shipment all the way across the U.S. is not likely so some of these can be eliminated. But be careful. We cannot assume a particular deficit region will be supplied from the surplus region that is closest because of the simultaneity in the flows. Truck rates are usually estimated with a function based on length of haul. Rail rates are regulated and must be acquired from a rail company, a primary user, or a transportation consultant. Rail rates are not always consistent with expectations nor are they linear with regard to distance. The rate from A to C may be higher than the rate from B to C even though A is farther from C. Care should be exercised to get *least-cost* rail rates. Barge rates are posted but the posted rates are often only places for negotiation to begin. They can be gathered by a survey or estimated using a cost function.

4. For the spatial equilibrium model, either a supply or demand function or elasticities are needed for each region. This allows price and changes in price to affect the optimal shipment pattern. In the transportation and transshipment models, price is not a factor. This means the implicit assumption is for constant price—and this means a perfectly elastic supply curve for all surplus products in the surplus regions and a perfectly elastic demand curve for all products needed in the deficit regions.

We see, therefore, that rather important assumptions are made. We see, too, that data can be a problem. Add the complexity of the process and we recognize cautions are in order in looking at the output from the models. Such analyses should be used as indicators of the patterns of interregional comparative advantage that prevail. If the optimal flows are different from real-world flows, do not expect the real-world pattern to change quickly. But if costs, production technology, and other factors that can influence the optimal patterns do not change dramatically, we will see real-world flows trend toward the optimal solution. It takes time.

Real-world confirmation can be seen in several commodity areas. In the wheat and flour industries, the models had suggested the processors would gravitate toward metropolitan areas, especially those served by barge transportation. We have seen this happen. The mills have moved out of the producing areas as their assets depreciated or became sufficiently obsolete to make moving feasible. Up through the 1950s and 1960s, the meat packers were concentrated in the Midwest in and around Chicago, Omaha, Sioux City, St. Louis, and other major central markets for live-stock. As the concentrated feeding areas began to develop in the Southwest, a gradual change began that has resulted in significant shifts in capacity out of the Midwest into the southwestern states. The analytical models both predicted and facilitated the transition. Analyses of the 1960s and 1970s gave optimal flows with locations in the Southwest and an ability to compete in the markets as distant as California and the New England states.

The references at the end of the chapter provide detailed coverage. It bears repeating that the results should be carefully interpreted. But it is also worth repeating that the general class of interregional models and the studies that have been completed since the 1940s have contributed to an interregional allocation and reallocation of resources, which makes our marketing and related distribution systems more efficient.

Feasibility Analyses

The big question in the feasibility analysis is the issue of *economic* feasibility. Will it make money? Will it be an economic success? And to get at the answers to these questions requires some sound and logical economic analysis.

The term "feasibility analysis" is broadly used. There are, however, a multitude of problems and questions that do require legitimate feasibility analyses—investment in a new facility in an existing location, a new facility in a new location, introducing a new product, going into a new market area, etc. Most of the important parts of feasibility analysis can be demonstrated by outlining the type of analysis required to evaluate investment in a new processing facility.

To establish a more definitive base, let's assume we are considering locating a new cattle slaughtering and breaking facility in the southwestern area of the U.S.: Texas, Oklahoma, New Mexico, Kansas, or Colorado. The steps required to analyze the feasibility of this prospective investment are:

1. Examine the industry trends;

2. Look at the current and evolving interregional pattern of comparative advantage;

3. Analyze the specific location being considered in terms of access to raw materials, cost of operating, and access to product markets; and

4. Conduct a cash flow analysis to check the adequacy of capital.

INDUSTRY TRENDS

The long-range outlook for the product is important. One approach is to examine and perhaps project the historical pattern. Insight is needed about why the trend has moved in a certain direction. If price is trending upward, for example, it is important to know whether this has been due primarily to an increase in demand or to a decrease in supply. Table 13.4 organizes the possibilities and provides a capsule interpretation of each. If the analysis shows demand has been increasing and pulling price higher, this is a very positive sign. But if the price improvement has been due to reductions in supply, this may be indicative of a cost-price squeeze that is forcing resources out of the industry. Higher prices from reduced supplies makes the proposed new investment look less promising. In looking at overall trends, therefore, deflate prices to get things in real terms and see which way prices are moving. But once the direction has been determined, look beyond the trend to see why prices are moving up or down.

Looking into the beef situation, the long-run trends are positive. Per capita consumption is trending higher as the supply of product increases over time. Cyclically induced increases, such as those that developed during the herd liquidation of the mid-1970s, were absorbed at lower real prices. But the long-run trend has seen increases in quantity taken at higher real prices—a sure sign demand is increasing.

INTERREGIONAL COMPARATIVE ADVANTAGE

The comparative advantage between regions changes over time, so it is important to get a reading on the direction of the changes. Moving processing capacity into a region where capacity is declining can be dangerous. Unless some special advantages exist at a particular location or there are economic reasons why this new operation could succeed where others have failed, the probability of economic success will be low.

Interregional flow models such as those described earlier in the chapter provide an excellent base of information. Least-cost flows from such a

Table 13.4
Price Trends, Economic Reasons, and Implications to the
New Investment Decision

Direction of Price Trend	*Reasons for Price Trend and Economic Significance*
Up	1. *Increasing demand relative to supply.* A positive sign for new investment. If long-run and sustained increases in demand are pulling prices up, prospects are favorable.
	2. *Decreasing supply relative to demand.* A negative sign for new investment. If prices are up because supply is not keeping pace, this could mean problems of excessive cost, lagging technology, or problems of raw material availability. The long-run prospects are not favorable. It is important that this is a long-run decrease in supply, not just a temporary shortage.
Down	1. *Decreasing demand relative to supply.* A negative sign for new investment. Existing capacity in the industry will be in use as long as price is above variable costs. If the demand continues weak, price could fall even lower before resources would be taken out of use. This is not a favorable setting for new investment.
	2. *Increasing supply relative to demand.* Length of run is important. If the price is falling because autonomous increases in supply are in excess of any strength in demand, the situation is likely to deteriorate even more. Price dips due to a short-run surge in supply can be corrected but if the trend is long run in nature, this is a most negative setting for new investment.

model show the direction in which the interregional pattern will tend to move assuming no major change in the forces that determine interregional comparative advantage. Figure 13.13 shows the type of map often used in presenting the optimal solution from a least-cost flow model. Other things equal, the new processing capacity should go to the areas that suggest economic viability.

In the beef business, the trend since the 1960s has been toward the major cattle feeding areas in the Southwest. Year-round feeding in large confinement lots began to develop in the panhandle areas of Texas and Oklahoma, eastern New Mexico and nearby areas in Kansas and Colorado. The trend continued through the 1970s. Among the important economic forces supporting the move were:

1. A surplus of feed grain in the sorghum producing areas of the Southwest;

2. Relatively inexpensive labor;

3. Transportation costs that favored the shipping of dressed beef from the areas of surplus grain as opposed to shipping the grain to feed cattle in other areas;

4. The availability of feeder cattle in the region to support cattle feeding activities; and

5. Developing technology in slaughtering, breaking, packaging, refrigeration, etc., which allowed the shipping of trimmed retail cuts as opposed to hanging carcasses containing low-value bone and fat.

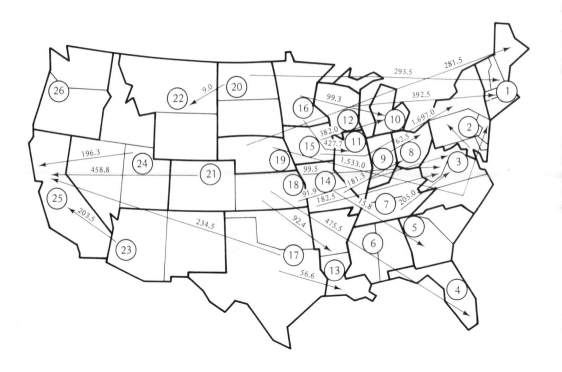

FIGURE 13.13   ESTIMATED LEAST-COST FLOWS OF DRESSED BEEF FOR 26 SUPPLY-DEMAND REGIONS IN THE U.S., 1975[a]

[a]The quantities shown are million lbs. shipped. For example, the least-cost solution shows 234.5 million lbs. moving from region 17 (Oklahoma and Texas) to region 25 (California).

Late in the 1970s some of the advantages in the Southwest were slowly disappearing. The surpluses of locally produced grain were eliminated as feedlot capacity climbed. Grain prices moved up to levels comparable on a corn equivalent basis to other major grain producing regions. Competition for feeder cattle squeezed the profit margins. But the region continued to show an upward trend in cattle fed both in absolute numbers and as a percent of all cattle fed in the U.S. In terms of regional comparisons, the Southwest shows a comparative advantage in cattle feeding and in processing.

INTRA-REGIONAL ANALYSIS

Within the region the important consideration is competition. Competition for the raw material—slaughter cattle—is to be avoided insofar as possible. But access to markets and competition among buyers is to be desired.

The first step in analyzing the competition is to locate the concentrated supplies of raw material and the other processors who will be competing for the available supplies. Figure 13.14 illustrates a simple but useful approach. The shaded areas show the areas with concentrated feeding

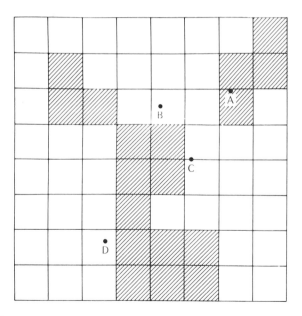

FIGURE 13.14   ILLUSTRATION OF A GEOGRAPHICAL GRID AS AN AID IN LOCATING AREAS OF RAW MATERIAL SUPPLY AND COMPETING PROCESSORS

activity. The points A, B, C, and D denote the locations of large competing processors. If the specific location within the region is truly variable, the best rule is to look for a location with concentrated feeding activity that has as little competition between processors as possible.

Figure 13.15 superimposes competitive circles on the grid. If each processor competes aggressively for cattle in a 50-mile radius of their plant location, there are areas in which processors will be in direct competition. These areas should be avoided if at all possible. Replace the grid with a map showing counties or other sub-state areas and the approach can be used to assess the situation in any region.

Access to markets is an essential ingredient of success. The plant must be able to compete in the consumer markets. Again, the interregional models can help. The optimal solution to a spatial equilibrium model gives an indication of the value of the product in various market areas compared to a base region. Adding an estimate of transportation costs to estimates of production costs indicates the market areas in which the plant could compete from a location within the southwestern region. Proximity to rail shipments, access to highways, and the condition of the railroads and highways should then be considered.

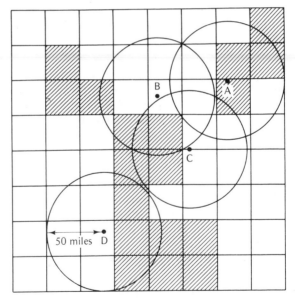

FIGURE 13.15 THE GEOGRAPHICAL GRID AND "COMPETITIVE CIRCLES" AS AIDS IN LOCATING AREAS OF INTENSE COMPETITION FOR RAW MATERIAL SUPPLIES

Many other variables are usually involved in comparing specific locations:

1. Taxes and the tax rate;

2. Availability of labor;

3. Availability and quality of schools;

4. Availability and quality of social services such as police and fire protection;

5. Attitude of the local community toward new industry;

6. Etc.

These variables must be considered on a case by case basis. Management personnel are usually moved into the area and the overall attractiveness of the community will affect their willingness to relocate. Some local governments try to entice new industry with tax incentives. Others present a largely negative attitude toward new industry. Some communities have a supply of labor that can be tapped, other communities do not. All these factors should be checked and used in selecting the final location.

CASH FLOW ANALYSIS

Once the decision is made on a specific location, the question of whether a new facility at that location will be profitable emerges. The next step, and a very important step, is to conduct a cash flow analysis.

At this point, accurate estimates of costs and realistic projections of selling prices are essential. The plant must be synthesized and "built" on paper. Company experience with costs in similar plants, engineering estimates, historical costs in similar plants adjusted for inflationary influences, or some other procedures can be used. Also needed are investment costs. Given the appropriate cost estimates, an estimate of the investment and production capital needs can then be generated and the necessary ingredients on the cost side of the cash flow picture are available.

The need for a cash flow analysis is apparent when we examine Figure 13.16. An outward flow of cash will begin immediately as new materials are purchased and labor is hired. Initially, there will be no cash inflow. Once the time lags associated with starting production and the normal pay period are spanned, an inflow of cash will begin but it may be sporadic at first. Some "down time" should be expected as the machinery and production lines are checked. Entry to markets, even for an established company, may not be smooth and easy. Typically, attempts will be made to

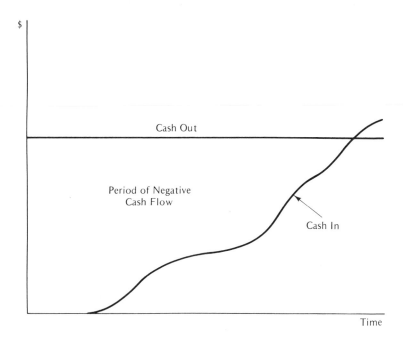

FIGURE 13.16   CASH FLOW PROBLEMS DURING THE EARLY DAYS OF A NEW
BUSINESS

enter new market areas from the new processing location. There will be
competition. Price specials, advertising, some type of penetration pricing,
or some combination of these and other market entry tactics will keep the
costs up early in the life of the new plant. Enough money must be bor-
rowed to cover the net outflow early and the cost of this money must be
brought back into the analysis in determining profitability.

After the cash-flow analysis is completed, it is then possible to look at
the volume of business required to break even. In Figure 13.17, the break-
even volume occurs at a level of OQ_1. If this level reflects a reasonable level
of operation as a percent of capacity, the decision may well be a "yes"
insofar as the new investment is concerned.

Group Action

Individual agricultural producers are price takers. As price takers, they
have no bargaining power and their possibilities in terms of superior marketing are limited to timing of sales, making decisions on when to hold and
when to sell, developing or adopting effective hedging decisions, etc.

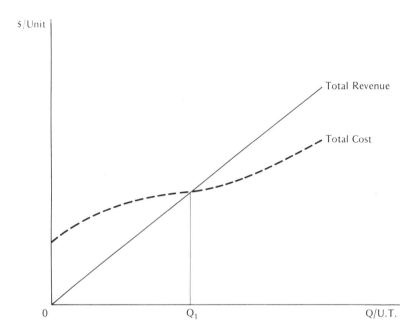

FIGURE 13.17   BREAK-EVEN VOLUME FOR A NEW BUSINESS

Against this backdrop there has long been a feeling that group activity would be the answer to the producer's problems of low prices, variable prices, or low incomes.

Shortly after the turn of the century farmers enthusiastically talked about group action. The Capper-Volstead Act of 1922 provided enabling legislation. Agricultural cooperatives were created and increased rapidly in number and relative importance during the 1920s and 1930s. Although there are many types of cooperatives, most have been designed to facilitate the members' efforts in buying inputs or in selling their farm products. Distinguishing features of the cooperatives include the patronage refund dimension that refunds returns over the cost of doing business to members and a degree of immunity from prosecution under the anti-trust laws that declare most types of group action to be illegal. Lauded as "the answer," cooperatives reached their peak in terms of numbers in the 1930s, but the number of active cooperatives has decreased since that time. Significant quantities of products are handled by the cooperatives but the cooperative has not reached the position of dominance as a form of group activity that many had expected and predicted.

The cooperative and any other type of group action where participation by the individual is voluntary is plagued by the "free rider" problem that we introduced earlier. Difficulty arises because the non-participating producer gets the same benefits, if there are benefits, as the producer who pays his way.[10]

Recognizing the inherent difficulties in voluntary group action by farmers is apparent in the report of the National Commission on Food Marketing released in 1966. After expressing doubt that producers, acting as individuals, would be able to coordinate their activities effectively with the rest of the system, the Commission recommended several alternatives that involved group action:

1. Legislation to protect the rights of producers to act as a group;

2. Extension of legislation to allow creation of marketing orders in more of the important crops; and

3. If all else failed, consider legislation to create a Federal Marketing Board.

The major developments since the mid-1960s were discussed in some detail in Chapter 4. Focusing on the implication to group action, the events can be briefly reviewed as follows:

1. Passage of the Agricultural Fair Practices Act of 1967. The act sets boundaries on the kinds of action a bargaining group can enter into, and protects the individual producer from discriminatory action by the processor or handler because the producer is a member of a bargaining group.

2. The "Sisk Bill" was introduced in 1971. It would have required the processor or handler to bargain "in good faith" with the producer bargaining association. The bill would have extended the legal base for marketing orders to the important food and fiber crops. The bill was never passed.

3. In the 1972–76 period, the attitude within the political arena fluctuated with the price levels. As prices of the food and feed grains increased, the enthusiasm for producer bargaining legislation waned. Late in the period, legislation was introduced to modify or repeal the Capper-Volstead Act but no action was taken.

4. By 1978 the pendulum was swinging back toward concern for producers. With the support of the Farm Bureau, the Farmers Union, the Grange, and other producer organizations, the National Agricultural Bargaining Act of 1978 was introduced by Senator Hart of Colorado and others. The bill did not pass but its introduction

suggested at least some reawakening of the interest of the early 1970s. The bill was similar to the Sisk Bill of 1971.

Having briefly described the background and current setting for group activity, let's look at some of the alternatives. Possible group actions to affect the economic position of producers include:

1. Influence the level or nature of product demand;

2. Influence the quality and/or quantity of product placed on the market;

3. Influence the efficiency with which the marketing function is performed;

4. Influence the competitive structure within which inputs are bought or the product is sold;

5. Influence the government in terms of programs and policies that affect producers' prices; and

6. Influence the orientation of producers toward the marketing system and marketing activities.

PRODUCT DEMAND

Most producer groups are active in trying to influence demand for their product. The primary objective is to increase demand for the product through advertising. If consumers can be influenced to buy more of a product, benefits will accrue to all producers who sell.

A second objective, to make demand at the aggregate level more elastic, receives less attention. As we noted earlier, more emphasis should probably be placed on this objective. Efforts to increase demand, if successful, push price up. This tends to motivate increased production, and pressure is placed on price again from increasing supplies. With no control over supply, expanding output in response to higher prices threatens the success of an advertising program.

If increases in supply *are* autonomous, changing the nature of aggregate demand to make it more elastic is important. If a new market can be opened up or a new use for the product found, the total demand across all uses or all markets is made more elastic (or less inelastic) at the lower price levels. This means the increases in supply do not push price as low.

It is worth repeating that the potential to increase demand for any food or fiber product is not that great. There are always good substitutes and expenditures on food and fibers do have a limit. The opportunity is restricted to what can be accomplished by pulling demand or buying power away from another food or fiber product.

QUANTITY, QUALITY OF PRODUCT SOLD

Without enabling legislation, the ability of producer groups to control quantity is limited. Some influence is exerted on the supply of regionally produced crops such as hops and celery but for the major grain and fiber crops, controlling supply is next to impossible. The NFO (National Farmers Organization) has attempted to gain control over supply by urging producers to sign contractual arrangements that turn decision making authority on marketing over to the NFO. Such efforts have met with limited success and do not appear to have exerted significant influence on price.

There are better chances of success where quality control is concerned. Whatever the product, processors and handlers want a consistent quality. Group activity to define quality standards and promote sorting, grading, and packaging to provide a more uniform quality has potential. Since many products are produced and sold in small, fragmented units, group efforts to allow commingling of the product can sometimes improve the quality, increase the size of the unit offered for sale, and thereby increase the value of the product to the processor. Marketing agreements to specify quality standards and handling procedures, though binding on only those who sign them, facilitate organization and quality control.

EFFICIENCY OF MARKETING

Group activities to increase marketing efficiency all revolve around an expanded and improved base of information. Both technical and pricing efficiency will typically increase when better information is available.

Technical efficiency is enhanced by putting together more viable units in terms of size and quality, by controlling the timing of product flows, and by eliminating duplication of handling and other services. A unit that is more consistent with the needs of the processor handler can mean a better price and a lower cost of marketing. In livestock, in cotton, in fresh fruits and vegetables, and in other commodity areas the cost per unit marketed goes down for larger units of consistent quality.

Timing is important because it affects the processor's cost of operation. The curve ATC in Figure 13.18 illustrates the cost of a particular function in the processing plant. It could be the packaging of bacon in a meat packing plant or the boxing of apples in an apple packing shed. We looked at costs and the need for coordination in Chapters 2 and 3. When we sketch in such a cost curve, we always implicitly assume an orderly and timely flow of product. But what if an adequate supply of hogs is not

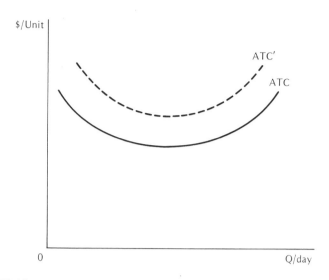

FIGURE 13.18   IMPACT OF DECREASED AVAILABILITY OF RAW MATERIAL ON
ATC OF A PROCESSING FUNCTION

available for a particular day? The ATC curve shifts to a curve such as ATC′
because the output for the day or week is down and the overhead costs are
spread over a smaller quantity. Technical efficiency is increased when the
product to be processed is available in a timely fashion. Producer groups
can help insure this is the case.

Duplication of handling is costly and inefficient. Livestock, especially
cattle, may be bought and sold five to 10 times before finally going to
slaughter. Some of this apparent duplication is necessary in completing the
assembly function and pulling together small, fragmented lots into units of
viable size. But at least part of the duplication of effort is due to lack of
information. When livestock or any food and fiber product is handled more
often than necessary, hauled further than necessary and in directions inconsistent with least-cost flows, or damaged in handling, the costs in terms
of inefficiency can reach significant levels. By providing more and better
information and making producers aware of alternative approaches to
marketing, producer groups could increase technical efficiency.

Well informed sellers can better decipher what the market is trying to
tell them. Better understanding of the messages inherent in price means a
higher level of pricing efficiency. Producer groups can help by providing
original information to participating producers, disseminating and/or interpreting information available from the USDA or other public agencies,
and pointing to opportunities available to producers. Since grades are an

important dimension of pricing efficiency, producer groups can provide input to the decision making process as revisions in grades are being considered. Any reduction in the time required to adjust production patterns and reallocate resources in line with changing consumer demand constitutes an increase in pricing efficiency.

THE COMPETITIVE STRUCTURE

We have given a great deal of attention to the competitive structure of agriculture in general and production agriculture in particular. That the individual producer is a price taker is well established. Producer groups can do little or nothing to change the overall competitive structure.[11] But they can be effective in influencing the level of competition in the local market where individual producers must sell.

Consider the situation where grain producers have a single elevator in their local area. The only alternative market is the elevator in a neighboring town 50 miles away. Under these conditions, the local elevator will get most of the grain so long as the local price is above that of the distant elevator minus transportation costs.

If a group of producers were to build an elevator, either as a cooperative or privately owned, the competition between the new elevator and the existing facility could change the local price structure. With competition, the manager of the established elevator might raise bid prices by accepting a cut in operating margin. With the competition, he might be motivated to improve his services by updating his equipment, offering market information to his clients, offering forward contracts to interested producers, etc. The cooperative, if it is set up as a cooperative elevator, might be offering the same price as the established elevator but the improvement in the overall price level can be significant.

We have seen other examples of producer groups taking steps that increase the level of competition. Cattle feeders who buy or build a meat packing plant provide themselves with an alternative outlet. Cotton producers who form a cooperative gin or buy a gin and operate it themselves have a chance to improve the level of competition in the market. Though the benefits are not always obvious, they can be substantial in the form of better prices for the product, improved quality or lower prices for inputs, improved services, or improved bargaining power when price negotiations begin.

GOVERNMENT ACTION

One of the most popular forms of group activity takes the form of lobbying efforts to influence government programs. Every major commodity has a national trade association that actively tries to mold government activities to benefit producers. Activities span a broad range and include attempts to promote the passage of legislation viewed as favorable, attempts to block legislation viewed as unfavorable, participation in government hearings to influence proposed legislation or pending changes in government programs, etc.

Several important farm associations cross commodity lines and boast members from coast to coast. The NFO emerged as a force in the 1960s. Prone to take a militant stand on issues, the NFO prefers to see the federal government stay out of agriculture and leave matters in the hands of industry groups.

The Farmers Union is an established group with a large membership. Objectives of this group emphasize soliciting help from the federal government. Government programs that guarantee farmers a certain percent of parity price would find favor with the Farmers Union. There is concern about the variabilities and possible inequities of a "free market" economy and there is a related belief the farmer deserves some protection from such variabilities.

A third important farm group is the Farm Bureau. More nearly supporters of a free market philosophy, the Farm Bureau opposes government intervention such as price ceilings, export embargoes, etc. But when government action does become a factor in the marketplace, the Bureau can then be expected to argue the government has an obligation to look after the welfare of the farm sector.

A newcomer to the scene is the American Agricultural Movement started in 1977 and 1978. Motivated by the losses during a severe cyclical liquidation of cattle and low wheat and feed grain prices, the loosely knit group launched a campaign based on visible protests, a nationwide "strike," visits to the USDA and Congressional representatives in Washington, and letter writing campaigns designed to influence government action. Although the impact would be difficult to measure, most analysts attribute at least part of the government action in 1977–78 to raise target prices, establish a long-range storage program to take wheat out of market channels, and enact legislation to loan money to farmers to the efforts of the group. The intensity of action has shown a relationship to price levels. As cattle prices moved higher following completion of the cyclical liquidation and grain prices moved up, the momentum of the movement diminished. But the concept is there. Producers now believe that by getting together in numbers, by demonstrating, and by putting pressure on the political representatives, they can exert influence.

KNOWLEDGE OF THE MARKETING SYSTEM

More of a long-run concept, this will be one of the last to be recognized as important by a producer group. But it *is* important. When producers don't see the total picture of the marketing system, it will be much more difficult for them to see the importance of coordinating their activities with the rest of the system. This was the concern of the Food Commission back in 1966 when they prefaced their recommendation for group action in the producer sector with the following observation:[12]

> Farmers as independent operators have not been able to coordinate quality improvement programs or to schedule more even flows of products to the extent demanded by today's food industry.

That comes out to be a rather harsh indictment of the farm sector but it was correct in 1966 and is basically correct today. Acting independently, the individual producer has a tough time establishing a set of circumstances that will reward him for trying to work with the rest of the system.

Let's look at some illustrations. The value of protein in wheat has long been recognized. But the individual producer who grows and harvests high protein wheat will get paid little or no premium unless the pricing mechanism is set up to pay for differentials in protein. And this will not happen unless a standardized set of grades has been established and is widely used in the industry. An association of wheat producers might get something done about the grades.

In the livestock industry, breeding and producing cattle that yield high ratios of lean meat to total carcass weight and reach an acceptable quality grade relatively early along their growth path has long been presented as important to the beef industry. But no grades were designed to get the message to the producer in terms of a premium for the better cattle prior to the 1960s. Then when the USDA introduced their dual grading proposal in 1962, it was opposed by livestock groups and breed associations because it eliminated conformation as a factor in determining quality grade. In 1965, the USDA introduced a separate yield grade and put conformation back in the formula to determine quality grade. But acceptance was slow in coming. It was in the mid-1970s, when the USDA moved to require both quality and yield grade if carcasses were graded, that yield grades came into use and started to appear in market news reports.

Granting the short-run adjustments can be troublesome, producers have a tendency to not look at the long-run possibilities. And here is where the group or trade association can help. From a vantage point that encourages looking at the broader picture, the association can take a longer range view. It has been the case over and over again that action that supplements the price mechanism has been required to effect needed adjustments. For example, the bacon-type hog arrived on the scene 20 years after widespread recognition of the needed change and after producer groups and packers moved in with sow and boar leasing programs, disseminated information on technology and breeding practices, and supplemented the pricing mechanism that had been slow to effect a change.

THE BASE FOR GROUP ACTION

Group activity and group bargaining will continue to receive attention. In earlier chapters, we raised doubts that new legislation to facilitate group action by agricultural producers would be passed. But the give and take will continue. In the meantime, the efforts with voluntary participation will meet with only limited success.

The framework for effective group bargaining is in the marketing order legislation of the 1930s. But with the exception of milk and peanuts, the legislation does not allow for market orders for the major food and fiber products. If we look at some of the things the enabling legislation allows, it will be easier to see why extension to other commodities is resisted:

1. Specify the quantity that may be marketed during a specified period;

2. Establish a pool to hold reserve or surplus product;

3. Limit marketings to a certain size or a certain specified quality; and

4. Allocate the quantity that can be bought by a particular processor or handler.

The federal legislation does not authorize production control but little imagination is required to see possibilities of controlling the quantity marketed. The volume marketed can be influenced by blocking shipment of inferior grades or by diverting product into the surplus pool. Opponents argue such moves constitute supply control and serve to raise prices. We are likely to see increased attention focused on the existing federal or state market orders for such products as milk, peanuts, potatoes, cherries, cranberries, and oranges. We are not likely to see legislation that would extend coverage to the grains, to livestock and to such important fiber crops as cotton. A marketing order is binding on all producers and handlers. An order, therefore, eliminates the free rider problem. Without legislation to permit broader use of market orders, the focus will still be on group efforts with voluntary participaton, and this means no dramatic shift in bargaining power toward producers in the near future.[13]

International Markets

The areas of international markets and international trade are broad and complex. But there is always interest in trade because (1) domestic industries seek protection against imports of competing products, and (2) trade groups present expanded exports as the answer to problems of surplus in our domestic markets. The two essentially inconsistent positions persist because they are presented by different groups with different interests.

The rationale of those seeking protection against imports is obvious. Shoes from Taiwan compete directly in the U.S. market. The same holds true of televisions and electronic items from Japan. Imports of palm oil upset the soybean producers in the U.S. because palm oil competes with soybean oil and puts pressure on soybean prices. In terms of the theory, we can see what is happening by thinking about the situation in a supply-demand context. When the competition is direct (shoes, TV's, autos) there is an increased supply of the general product category in U.S. markets and this tends to push price down. If the competition is indirect, such as with palm oil, it serves to decrease the demand for soybeans because of competition with soybean oil. Either way, the net result is downward pressure on prices in the U.S.

But international trade is a two-way street. Japan is an important buyer of corn, soybeans, and other farm products. Will Japan continue to buy if the U.S. places stringent controls on the importation of Japan's products? Can we reasonably expect to maintain significant barriers against imports without some retaliation on the part of other countries?

Without getting too deep into the policy-related issues, let's suggest several situations in which at least some control over imports would appear to be justified:

1. To protect a beginning industry in the U.S. In its beginning stages, any domestic industry is vulnerable to competition from imports. If the industry has a chance of being viable and of making a significant contribution to the economy later, some protection early in its development can be justified.

2. Import policies to protect domestic markets against dumping products at prices below costs have merit. We have seen dumping of goods consistent with price discrimination schemes many times in the world market. It can be a storable farm product such as wheat (the U.S. dumped its huge surpluses on the world market in the late 1960s) or an industrial good such as sheet steel from Japan. Dumping any product at prices below cost can be very disruptive to markets in countries on the receiving end and this justifies policy action.

3. Import policies designed to stabilize domestic prices and decrease cyclical moves in price that damage the stability of domestic industries have merit. Cyclical price problems in the livestock commodities, such as beef, are especially acute. The import policy in the U.S., established by legislation of 1964, sets quotas on the levels of beef imports. The quotas are tied to domestic beef production. This means more imports are allowed when domestic tonnage is swelled by cyclical liquidation of domestic herds. Rather than stabilizing prices, the import policy has accentuated the price

lows in slaughter cows and processing beef during periods of cyclical liquidation. If a policy on imports can be justified, then it appears the legislation should decrease allowable imports when domestic production increases and increase the imports allowed when domestic production decreases and prices rise. This would stabilize prices to consumers and decrease the impact of the cycle. Such legislation was passed by Congress in 1978 but was vetoed by President Carter because it also restricted his power to change the level of imports which are allowed.

The short-run effect of any move to restrict imports is to raise domestic prices. For a given level of demand in the domestic market, import restrictions set at levels that decrease imports will bring higher domestic prices. In the long run, the net impact is not so obvious. If the import policy promotes investment in an expanded domestic industry, domestic output might increase because of the import policy. Whether the quantity offered domestic consumers at a particular price will be less (or the price higher for a particular quantity) will depend on the cost of producing in the "protected" or "sheltered" domestic industry relative to other countries that would ship the product into the U.S. if allowed to do so.

Exports are extremely important to the U.S. agricultural industry. Prior to 1972, policies designed to support the price of agricultural crops, particularly the grain and fiber crops, required corollary control of production. U.S. prices did not move with the forces of world supply and demand, and exports were not large and were relatively stable from year to year. But changes in the world market in the early 1970s took the shackles off the farmer as export buying pushed prices well above support levels. Production increased dramatically. By the mid-1970s, we had seen our first corn crop of more than 6.0 billion bushels, record supplies of wheat of more than 3.0 billion bushels, record soybean crops, record levels of the crush in the oil and meal complex, etc. And with the growing size of the crops came growing importance of exports. A 2.0 billion bushel wheat crop is more than twice the domestic needs for food, seed, industrial and feed purposes. If the 1.0 billion bushels left after domestic demand is met is not exported, it ends up in storage in the U.S.—and prices fall under the pressure of increasing grain stocks. Table 13.5 provides a relevant picture. By comparing years in the 1960s with the years in the 1970s, we can see how the importance of exports has grown. So long as there are no artificial restraints in the market, the U.S. market and price levels are vulnerable to the weather in the USSR, in the People's Republic of China, and in other major importing countries.

With the potential, therefore, comes risk. If the U.S. farmer is to produce for the world market, this means he must also expose himself to the uncertainties of the world market. What is needed, therefore, is a

Table 13.5
Exports of Selected Products from the U.S., Calendar Years, 1964–77

Product Grouping

Year	Wheat and Products	Feed Grains and Products	Soybeans	Cotton	Meats and Products	Fats, Oils and Greases
			(1,000 metric tons)			
1964	23,234	16,914	5,702	1,139	203	1,407
65	19,770	21,725	6,196	825	150	1,027
66	24,797	25,186	6,687	782	141	907
67	19,090	20,245	7,169	864	147	1,106
68	18,222	19,482	8,014	841	162	1,103
69	14,036	17,232	8,469	521	196	988
1970	19,377	19,990	11,954	648	159	1,196
71	17,782	17,250	11,538	897	185	1,318
72	22,868	28,117	11,995	672	197	1,152
73	38,775	41,902	13,220	1,195	268	1,107
74	26,241	37,472	13,940	1,124	244	1,296
75	32,052	40,375	12,496	835	296	960
76	27,772	51,568	15,332	746	410	1,161
77	25,525	48,490	16,196	967	407	1,404

Source: *Foreign Agricultural Trade of the United States,* Economics, Statistics and Cooperatives Service, USDA, February 1978 and February 1975.

production and marketing strategy that will take advantage of the growth potential of the world market but which is designed to avoid the pitfalls of the uncertainties. A few guidelines are:

1. In making investment and production decisions, look at the long-run trend to establish expectations vs. the short-run moves in prices motivated by fluctuating export levels. Expanding the operation by buying land or new machinery when wheat prices jump up in one year is likely to create problems when prices move back down to their long-run trend level.

2. Look beyond the boundaries of the U.S. in seeking information upon which to base marketing decisions. The outcome of a decision to hold wheat, corn, or soybeans in storage may depend more on the condition of the soybean crop in Brazil, the wheat crop in Argentina, the weather in the USSR, or the level of world stocks than on any economic force within the boundaries of the U.S.

3. Be realistic in expectations of the export market and try to match production to world demand. In the beef industry, for example,

there is always much talk about expanding world markets for beef. Often, the question is raised as to why we can't export more high-value Choice and Prime cuts. But this is not the product that is in demand in the world market. With the exception of somewhat limited markets in Japan and Western Europe, other countries don't want our highly finished and marbled beef. But there *is* a world demand for our hides, edible offal, inedible offal, blood and bone meal, etc. There is reason to postulate that efforts to promote this type of product in the world market would be productive.

World trade is important and will become more important in the future. Policy positions and marketing strategies need to be developed at a realistic level, should give consistent treatment to our trading allies, and should be aimed at areas where the potential is real. If given a positive and progressive treatment by trade groups, analysts, and the policy makers, there is tremendous potential for our food and fiber marketing systems in the world trade arena.

Summary

Marketing strategies are important. The fact that a strategy has been formulated is a big step forward. Insight and understanding are gained during the process of accumulating and organizing information into some type of strategy or plan of action.

Most marketing strategies have to start with consideration of the consumer. It is important that we recognize this is important to *all* subsectors of the marketing system. The producer group cannot afford to fall back on the idea it is too far removed from the consumer.

The marketing agencies and middlemen between the producer and consumer simply contribute to the form utility that is begun at the producer level. Among the more important areas where understanding is needed are:

1. Many American families spend more than 50 percent of their income on food. Rapidly increasing food prices require significant and painful adjustments.

2. Consumers tend to be creatures of habit. They resist change in their buying routine until prices change enough to bring both recognition and reaction.

The importance of marketing strategies such as advertising, pricing policies, and new product development is a function of the competitive environment within which the marketing firm operates. At the production level, the individual firm faces a horizontal demand curve and does not advertise. Any efforts to influence demand are group efforts. Since demand at the producer level is a derived demand and the individual firm is a price taker, there is no "price policy" at the firm level.

In other subsystems, advertising and pricing policies are much more important. At the processing and retail levels, for example, the competitive structure often approximates oligopoly. Non-price forms of competition such as advertising are used to introduce a new product, gain access to a new market, or maintain established markets. Prices tend to be sticky and there is a tendency toward stable prices with infrequent price adjustments. When they come, the price changes are often market-wide changes by all firms.

The question of whether to make a new investment, introduce a new product, or enter a new market is often treated as a feasibility analysis. Costs are estimated and selling prices are projected to determine whether the proposed course of action will be profitable. When location is the issue, it is wise to look at the overall trends in demand and supply, changes in the interregional pattern of comparative advantage, and the location of raw material supplies relative to the location of competing buyers. Models showing least-cost interregional product flows can help.

Group action is becoming more important as a "marketing strategy." Efforts to influence policy decisions by organized producer groups are gathering momentum. These efforts are developing in an arena characterized by:

1. An "on again, off again" attitude in the legislative process toward the need for additional group bargaining legislation for agricultural producers. The trend is negative as the political arena increasingly responds to issues with a consumeristic orientation.

2. Apparently inconsistent positions by some groups. With international trade and the role of the U.S. in the world market becoming more important determinants of U.S. prices, we find trade groups opposing imports of raw materials and advocating expanded exports of finished products at the same time.

3. A need for better awareness of the total marketing system as the various groups develop their strategies and influence the actions of individual participants. The educational role should get more emphasis.

Volumes could be written on market strategies. This chapter attempts to deal with important topics. The references listed at the end of the chapter will provide more coverage for the interested reader.

Footnotes

1. The figure was at 22.2, 20.0, and 16.2 percent for 1950, 1960, and 1970, respectively. This downward trend was reversed and the trend apparently turned back up in the early 1970s.

2. In 1972, for example, the ratio of total expenditures on food to total disposable income had reached as low as .154—or 15.4 percent in the U.S. During that same year the percentages were 17.5 for Canada, 26.0 for Japan, 23.4 for France, 24.2 for Germany and 29.8 for the United Kingdom. Refer to V. James Rhodes, *The Agricultural Marketing System*, Grid Publishing, Columbus, 1978, p. 63.

3. Analysis of this area indicates it takes three to four months for most of the change at the wholesale level to be put into effect at retail. It is important to keep this in mind in analyzing prices. When prices at the producer or processing level are moving higher with stable or increasing supply, it is tempting to conclude that demand at retail must be very strong. But it is often because the price increases have not been "passed through" to the retail level. The apparent strength in demand may disappear when the price changes are made at retail.

4. The National Commission on Food Marketing was very negative with regard to spending huge sums of money on advertising to "puff" a product. The Commission was especially critical of the breakfast cereal industry. With very high levels of seller concentration, the breakfast cereal industry tends to avoid price competition, spend heavily on advertising, and bombard the market with "new" products very similar to existing products.

5. The dummy variable is also called the 0–1 variable when used this way. Testing the significance of $\hat{\beta}_6$ is testing to see whether the presence of the 20-cent level of expenditures made a difference in sales. The situation is complicated by the tendency for any response to advertising expenditures to be lagged—that is, to come in the time period *after* the added expenditure. More complex models are available to estimate the lag.

6. To illustrate, assume flour mill A is making a serious effort to enter a market previously dominated by mills B, C, and D by offering a low "introductory" price for its brand of all-purpose flour. Mills B, C, or D might practice "marginal cost pricing," lower their prices, attempt to thwart the efforts of A in the short run, and discourage firm A from staying in the market.

7. Pricing below cost or below cost plus some fixed percent is illegal in many states. When competitors have tried to block a particular firm or store from pricing below cost and offering an effective loss leader, it has been amazingly difficult to determine costs.

8. The firms would prefer to be able to eliminate this tendency toward a limited product life. In practice, what we often see are new ideas, new approaches, and new brand names around a product base that is stable over time. Ford Motor Company survived the Edsel because the Ford, Lincoln, and Mercury cars were there. Kellogg puts many cereals on the supermarket shelf but the old faithfuls like corn flakes are there to provide an element of stability to sales revenues.

9. The payoff table figures can include a discounting factor to reflect the inherent risk of error in this type of analysis. The mortality rate on new products and new package designs varies by product grouping but is generally quite high—above 40 percent. An element of protection can be incorporated into the payoff values by such discounting and leave the assigned probabilities consistent with estimates based on surveys, etc.

10. There are exceptions. The successes of a bargaining cooperative may extend only to cooperative members if a contract with favorable returns is negotiated with a handler. When monies are needed, when supply control is being considered, or when voluntary commitment of production to a quality control program is needed, the free rider problem is there. Benefits accrue to all producers, not just to those who participate.

11. Not all authors or analysts would agree. Some have argued the cooperative move is a way to change the structure of the agricultural sector. Perhaps it is more logical to suggest cooperatives have the potential, through organization and group activity, to provide a type of countervailing power when dealing with processors and handlers. Given good organization and majority participation, this could change the structure as measured by the concentration of sellers in production agriculture. The growth of AMPI, the giant coop in milk distribution during the early 1970s, certainly changed the balance of power in the milk market. But AMPI has been subjected to vigorous attempts at prosecution under the antitrust laws. Whether the experience and growth of AMPI under the sanctions of Capper-Volstead would be allowed again is certainly questionable.

12. National Commission on Food Marketing, *Food From Farmer to Consumer*, U.S. Govt. Printing Office, Washington, June 1966, p. 110.

13. Look for more emphasis on collecting monies to finance advertising, consumer education, market analysis, development of new markets

(including foreign markets), and lobbying efforts to influence legislation. A popular approach will be check-off programs that collect money at each major pricing point in the marketing system. A national referendum was held in 1977 to create such a program for the beef marketing system but it failed to get the needed two-thirds vote of all registered voters. But in 1978, an amendment was being tacked on to another legislative bill to allow approval of the referendum with a simple majority vote. These approaches to financing group efforts will become familiar in future years and span most of the major commodities.

Questions

1. Statistics show an increasing percentage of consumers' incomes go to meet fixed monthly obligations (mortgage payments, insurance, television payment, etc.). Could this increasing percentage be a factor in consumers' tendency to be upset and vocal over rising food prices? Explain.

2. Most references list "make demand more inelastic" as an objective of the advertising program of the firm that faces a sloping demand curve for its product or services. But theory shows us marginal revenue is negative in the inelastic portion of the demand curve and a firm would never knowingly operate at such a level. Explain this apparent contradiction and indicate what the firm actually does if it succeeds in making demand more inelastic.

3. List and discuss pros and cons of marginal cost pricing.

4. Do you agree we are likely to see more group action by agricultural producer groups in the future? If no, why not? If yes, what will the groups be trying to do? What *should* they be trying to do?

5. Argue the positive on the following debate topic:

   Resolved, that U.S. food and fiber production-marketing systems will be hurt by increased exposure to the world market and policy steps should therefore be taken to protect the U.S. from the pressures of world market developments and changing prices.

Selected References

Backman, Jules, *Advertising and Competition*. New York, N.Y.: New York Univ. Press, 1967.

Blakley, Leo V., "Domestic Food Costs," *Amer. J. of Agr. Econ.*, Vol. 56, December 1974.

Clarkson, Geoffrey P. E., *The Theory of Consumer Demand: A Critical Appraisal*. Englewood Cliffs, N.J.: Prentice-Hall, 1963.

Driscoll, J. L. and M. N. Leath, *Optimum Flows for Wheat, Feed Grain and Soybeans*, Mkt. and Trans. Sit. MTS-188, USDA, February 1973.

King, William R., *Quantitative Analysis for Marketing Management*. New York, N.Y.: McGraw-Hill, 1967.

McCoy, John H., *Livestock and Meat Marketing*. Westport, Conn.: AVI Publishing Co., 1972.

Padberg, D. I., "Emerging Effectiveness of Competition and the Need for Consumer Protection," *Amer. J. of Agr. Econ.*, Vol. 57, February 1975.

Rhodes, V. James, *The Agricultural Marketing System*. Columbus, Ohio: Grid Publishing, 1978.

Torgerson, Randall, "A Critique of Bargaining Efforts in Agriculture," *Proceedings: 20th National Conference of Bargaining and Marketing Cooperatives*, Washington, D.C.: USDA, 1976.

part six

Current Issues and a Look Ahead

The best way to deal with the unexpected is to be prepared. Developments of the 1970s, many of which will continue into the 1980s, have brought risk to the markets. With risk comes potential. But to tap that potential, the individual must be prepared.

Look ahead to higher food and fiber prices, even more volatile prices, increased involvement of the federal government in the markets, and increased world trade. And look ahead to a need for more time and sophistication in making marketing decisions. Better understanding of the implications of the economic environment in which the market system and the individual firm operate will be needed. But so will an increased awareness of the types of policies we will see and increased proficiency with the decision models and tools necessary to handle the high levels of uncertainty.

Part VI takes a look at the forces now at work in the market and then looks ahead to what we will see evolve. Given these developments, attention is paid to the research and educational programs that will be required to cope with the problems and bring increased efficiency to our food and fiber marketing systems. In a simple sense, the objective is to help the student, teacher, and analyst be prepared for the future.

chapter fourteen

Developing Trends, Issues in Marketing

Marketing systems are constantly changing. The important issues and problems at any one point along the time continuum lose some of their urgency with the passage of time as solutions are found and adjustments are made. But the individual decision maker cannot afford to wait when the problem of today threatens survival of his business. Society loses if the solution or adjustment is slow in coming. In this chapter, we will look at some of the issues that are important as we move to the decade of the 1980s and reflect on the probable implications of the developing trends.

Changing Economic and Organizational Structures

Decision makers from top to bottom in our food and fiber market systems are becoming aware of the realities of the economic and political environment within which they operate. The change is likely to become especially apparent at the producer level. Increasingly, producers are aware of their position as price takers and frustrated by the confines of an economic structure that restricts them to that role. In the age of a better informed and more enlightened producer, the individual will be increasingly interested in group activity to put pressure on the policy makers in Washington. Trade associations will be stronger, and agricultural people will give more support to groups such as the American Agricultural Movement, which crosses commodity lines and currently attracts a wide following.

Allegiance to the group effort will come and go with price levels. When prices are up or moving up, there will be less concern. When prices are down or falling, the enthusiasm to "do something" will increase. Because many producers believe Congressional action during the 1977–78 period to raise target prices for grain and establish set-aside and reserve programs was at least partly due to the agitation by producers, they will be encouraged to try again.

Increased understanding by decision makers throughout the system of the environment within which they operate will bring other changes. Impatient with the slowness with which the price mechanism works, moves toward increased levels of vertical integration will be seen for some commodities. Better understanding of the total system and developing awareness of the possibilities from coordinated activity will promote contractual arrangements and related attempts to increase the stability of quality and quantity flows. But to the extent these approaches fail, we are likely to see a slow but persistent trend toward vertical integration. More sophisticated analyses of the total marketing systems are expected to provide better measures of the costs of the lack of coordination and this will tend to prompt consideration of vertical integration as an alternative.

The trend toward a decentralized market structure will continue. Important advances will be made in grading and in the communication process used to expedite buying and selling. As the ability to accurately describe the product improves, moves toward electronic auctions and other means of buying and selling on the basis of description versus visual inspection will increase. In commodity areas such as in livestock, where exact product description is more difficult, an increasing percentage of the product will be sold on a carcass basis to eliminate the need to estimate dressing percentage, weight, grade, and other value-related characteristics in live weight sales.

What we see developing are gradual changes in organizational structure and in the mode of operation that are being prompted by demands and actions of an enlightened decision maker. Pricing efficiency will be sharpened. Technical efficiency will increase due to adoption of new technology, increased competition at many levels of the system, and increased awareness of the cost-saving implications of coordinated activity. A blend of improved operational procedure based on progressive approaches to exchange and vertically integrated operations will develop. The entire marketing system for most commodities should be more efficient.[1]

Changes In Public Policy

Projecting the policy developments and trends of the 1970s suggests the general tendency will be toward increased government involvement in the marketplace and a policy position that reflects a consumeristic orientation. The 1970s witnessed the move of the U.S. into world grain markets, volatile prices in most food and fiber products, consumer boycotts, peacetime price controls, export embargoes, and a swing toward increased concern about food prices. Underlying these visible developments was a change in the political arena. There was a noticeable decline in support of legislation to facilitate bargaining by agricultural producer groups. Group bargaining legislation introduced with high hopes early in the decade lost its support when grain prices moved sharply higher in the wake of heavy buying by the USSR. With the higher prices and the activities of large cooperatives in the dairy sector came increased concern over group actions. Attacks emerged against the Capper-Volstead Act. From the political arena have come charges that the enabling legislation for cooperatives is an umbrella of protection for monopolistic actions. Others point to the efforts of some agri-business firms to organize as a cooperative and thus gain a measure of protection against prosecution under the antitrust laws. Bargaining legislation is not likely to pass through a Congress with these issues and concerns on its mind.[2]

The price controls and export embargoes of the early 1970s grew out of concern over food prices. Given the makeup of our food and fiber systems and the nature of consumer demand, this concern over food prices will not be temporary. Across all foods, roughly 40 percent of consumers' food dollars goes back to the producing sector. The other 60 percent goes to the marketing agencies and middlemen who provide the services being demanded by the modern consumer. With rapidly increasing costs of labor, packaging, refrigeration, and transportation, we can expect the cost of the middlemen's services to increase. Costs of inputs—land, equipment, labor, oil and gas, fertilizers, herbicides, etc.—will continue to push higher at the farm level. Over the long run, these increased costs must be covered or resources will move out of production. Either way, food prices will be pushed up by the increasing costs. Add the influence of a rapidly increasing demand in the developed and developing countries and it is difficult to see anything but a significant upward trend in food prices.

Consumer groups are increasingly vocal about food prices and the political arena is prone to listen. Early in the 1970s, the government asked for all-out production from farmers to help feed a hungry world. Over-production of wheat and food grains in the 1976–78 period pushed grain prices to levels that were only 50–60 percent of many estimates of production cost. The cow-calf operator survived the five-year period of persistent losses from 1973 through 1977 by borrowing on the equity in his land. Many had to refinance. Some did not survive the cyclical liquidation and were forced to liquidate their cow herd and other assets. But by mid-1978, less than one year after the bottom of the cyclical price trough had apparently been reached, the headlines were pointing to rising food prices and concerns of consumers. The talk in Washington was about rising beef prices. The administration responded by increasing the quotas on beef imports by 200 million pounds. The psychological shock to the market brought a $14 per cwt. break in live cattle futures between May 22 and June 29.[3]

During the decade of the 70s production agricultural lost much of its political clout in Congress. Prior to the 70s, representatives and senators with seniority from the farming states had held key committee positions in the House and Senate. Their positions brought political power to the farm sector far in excess of what it could wield on the basis of numbers. But the decade of the 1970s saw retirement of some of the committee chairmen. On some committees new leaders were voted in by a committee membership that demonstrated increasing concern for the consumer sector. The agriculture committees in both the Senate and House had become a politician's graveyard during the days of support prices and huge surpluses in the 1950s and 1960s. But positions on these committees are now being eagerly sought by congressmen interested in food prices—and most are from the urban and industrial states.

Paralleling these developments was the emergence of the energy crisis. Balance of trade deficits mounted and the policy makers were acutely aware of the importance of agricultural products in our export and trade picture. This awareness was reflected in policy decisions. As wheat and feed grain prices trended lower into the late 1970s, both the Congress and Administration demonstrated a willingness to extend a subsidy to agriculture. But this was done by setting a target price and paying farmers directly for the difference between the target price and the market price for the first five months of the crop year (or between the target price and the loan price if the loan price exceeded the five-month average). The target price did not place a direct floor under market prices. This allowed the price to move with the world price and keep the U.S. in the world market. Without the sales of agricultural products, the record deficits in the balance of trade would have been even worse.

Against this background we can expect the key provisions of the policy that we carry into the 1980s to be characterized by the following:

1. There will be a reluctance to consider legislation or programs that increase the bargaining power of agricultural groups. A watchful eye will be kept on cooperatives to make sure monopolistic tendencies do not develop. We can expect to see court rulings that give less flexibility in terms of actions that will not be considered a violation of the antitrust statutes. A hard-line attitude will be taken by legislators and the courts, toward agri-business firms or non-producer groups who seek to qualify for cooperative status under Capper-Volstead.

2. Food supplies and food prices will be of primary concern. Some type of reserve program to keep the stocks of food and feed grains above nominal levels will receive continuing attention. If active export buying threatens the adequacy of domestic supplies, we can expect to see policies designed to evoke voluntary restraints by the buying countries. If this fails, export embargoes will be considered. With the concern over food supplies, food prices and the balance of payment problem, there will be a tendency to relax restrictions on imports of food products.

3. During periods of relatively high inflation, discussion of price ceilings or price controls will emerge. Although most analysts will agree the price ceilings of 1973 were disruptive and contributed to price volatility in the years after 1973, not everyone on the Washington scene would agree. If a period of sharply higher food prices brings on consumer agitation and boycotts, the political arena might well act—or overreact—again. Efforts by producer groups and trade associations to increase understanding of the cyclical nature of agricultural production within the political arena will be stepped up because they fear direct price controls will be considered.

4. Within broad limits, the policy will leave agriculture in general and production agriculture in particular exposed to the market. If prices push unusually high, price ceilings or export embargoes will be considered. The other side of the coin will be a factor. Prices will have to fall to levels low enough to threaten the economic viability of the production sector of agriculture before much help will be forthcoming. Even then, the assistance will tend to take the form of a direct subsidy rather than interference with the market price. The dual needs of relatively low-priced food to keep the consumers happy, and prices low enough to compete in the world market, will block moves back toward policies that support price at a certain percent of parity and keep them above world prices.[4]

Private Versus Public Activity

There will be a gradual but persistent trend away from public and toward private involvement in the areas of market analysis, information dissemination, and market news. Criticism of government activities in this area plus the perpetual problem of money on which to operate will take its toll. Changes in recent years have been toward providing less, not more, information. The market analyst who has seen data series disappear is keenly aware of this problem.

To illustrate, let's turn to the livestock sector. If we use price volatility as a gauge of the need for planning information, the livestock industry needs *more* information, not less. In the pork industry, the basic information for planning purposes comes in the form of the USDA's quarterly *Hogs and Pigs* report. Three months is a long time to wait for an indication of what is going on in terms of brood sow herd expansion, farrowing plans, and the number of market hogs on farms. Few alternative sources of information are broad enough in application to be of help. The market drifts with little direction between the reports and then, quite frequently, a shock emerges when the report is released. A solid case could be built for more reports, not fewer. But there was serious discussion in the mid-1970s about cutting back to two reports because of USDA budget problems. In late 1978, the number of weight groupings included in the report was decreased.

In the cattle sector, a cutback almost materialized. Since the early 1960s, the USDA has published quarterly cattle on feed reports that cover the important cattle feeding states. The number of states included has decreased over time. Throughout the 1970s, this has been a 23-state report. A monthly series that covered the six primary feeding states was started in the 1960s. The states included initially were Texas, Nebraska, Iowa, Colorado, California, and Arizona. As feeding activity in the southwestern states increased, Kansas was added in 1972 and the monthly report became a seven-state report. Then in mid-1978, came an announcement Iowa would be dropped. A cut in the operating budget was given as the reason by USDA officials. Protests from the industry and from livestock producer groups in Iowa brought a reversal of the decision. The problem will emerge again, however.

The picture is not all negative. Access to pertinent data relating to the food and feed grains is improving. Information on world stocks, crops in other countries, weather, and trade activity is better than ever. Some of the added effort in these areas has come because of public reaction. The USSR's wheat purchases in 1972 ushered in a public concern over the adequacy of domestic stocks of grain. In response, the USDA began issuing its now popular *Agricultural Supply and Demand Estimates* after every major crop production and grain stocks report. Presented in a convenient balance sheet format, this report is widely used and widely watched.

The same price volatility that has prompted criticism of USDA activities has given the private concern an opportunity. All major crops and livestock producers went through rough times in the first half of the 1970s. From those difficult periods has come a decision maker who has changed in several significant ways:

1. He is much more aware of the need to develop a marketing strategy, to come to grips with the situation and to make a marketing decision. This means he spends more time as a market analyst and this requires information.

2. Awareness of the commodity futures markets and the potential of hedging programs has been increased. During the periods of sharp price breaks, the decision maker looked for new tools and ways to help himself. Futures markets received more attention and many of the private and commercial market advisory services stressed information on futures trade and advisory positions on hedging.

3. With every year that passes, the individual producer is managing a larger and more sophisticated operation. As a decision maker, the individual is better informed, is better educated, and is a better manager. The potential in the marketing decision area is being more clearly recognized.

The producer will increasingly turn to private sources for planning, market analysis, and advice. Subscription fees vary with the service but may be less than $100 per year for a weekly market letter. Most commodity brokerage firms distribute weekly or periodic outlook and market analysis materials free to clients or potential clients. Producers appear to feel more comfortable with a private service because they feel, rightly or wrongly, the service is truly interested in the welfare of the producers. But the role of the USDA will be critically important for many years to come. It is the USDA that collects the data and makes it available for use. Collection of original data by the private services is in the embryo stage and will grow slowly. Most of the planning information (acreages, stocks, cattle on feed, cattle inventory numbers, sows farrowed, etc.) will come from the USDA while the private services will interpret and perhaps supplement USDA's reports with surveys of their own. To the extent new and original information is made available in the private sector, it is more likely to come through the sponsorship of a national trade association (National Corn Growers, National Cattlemens Association, etc.) than through the private advisory services.

In the market news area, less help from the private sector is likely to be forthcoming. A tremendous investment in facilities and manpower would be required and the urgency is not there. The market news activities of the USDA's Federal-State program have not felt the criticism that has been directed at the more nearly long-run planning information reported by the Crop Reporting Board. At the producer level, where dissemination to many interested parties is needed, the activity is likely to be left to the USDA. Higher up in the system, private reports will be more prevalent. Trade in the meats at the wholesale or carcass level and in wheat, flour, and other products at the processor and miller level will continue to use both private and public reports.

A significant trend toward more private involvement in analysis of markets and prices is underway. Historically, the role of analysis and outlook had been left to the USDA and the land grant universities. But this is changing. The needs will simply be beyond the capacity of the traditional publicly supported efforts. Producers in particular are starting to recognize the need and potential for market analysis. Too, they are realizing the processor or handler to whom they sell is always well informed. Since most producers lack the time, training, and inclination to do all the needed analysis on their own, they will buy the services and expertise from private and commercial advisory services. Trade associations, brokerage firms, private consulting firms, and market advisory services are all collecting a pool of analytical talent. The area is likely to become competitive, which will be an advantage to the producer in terms of better services and lower costs.

It is in the area of research, especially basic research, that the private sector continues to lag. The benefits of basic research are long run in nature and are difficult to see. For example, trade groups are slow to recognize the need for research in the areas of consumer psychology and consumer behavior. Yet, there is concern in the private sector and in trade associations over the effectiveness of advertising and informational programs sponsored by the trade group. The same paradox exists in other areas. The plea to "do something" about the price cycles is heard. But these and other measures require a base of research information if the trade association is to be effective. The connection has not always been made, the recognition of the importance of research is not there, and the willingness to help finance research lags behind apparent needs. The burden of basic and long-run research will continue to rest primarily with the USDA and with the universities.[5]

Impact Of The World Market

Since 1972, the policy position in the U.S. has left American agriculture exposed to the world market. With that exposure comes related exposure to the risks associated with weather, to the ups and downs of developing economies, and to the policy decisions of other countries of the world. In a few short years, trade has been opened up with the People's Republic of China (PRC) and moved to a more significant level with the USSR. A policy decision by officials in the USSR to enter the world market and buy to offset their poor grain crop in 1972 has had immense implications to American agriculture. The European Common Market remains essentially "closed" to U.S. exports because of their protectionist policies but the PRC, the Eastern Europe countries, and the USSR have joined Japan, Mexico, and other traditional customers to push export demand for U.S. products higher.

Neither the agricultural sector nor the policy makers handled the situation very well after the first wave of export buying in 1972. Wheat prices felt the direct impact and jumped to record levels. Fueled by another price surge in 1975 when the USSR suffered through another short crop, actions were taken by wheat producers that implicitly assumed $5.00 wheat was here to stay. With the official policy allowing and even encouraging the expansion, production pushed to record levels and the wheat producer was quickly in trouble. Exposure to the variabilities of the world market was a primary causal factor.

The trouble spilled over into corn as corn production pushed above 6.0 billion bushels for the first time in history. Barley, oats, grain sorghum and, to a lesser extent, soybeans, went along for the ride. Cotton production increased as planted acreage increased in response to a strong export demand. Prices were forced below $50 a bale in 1977 and below most estimates of the production cost.

At least part of the difficulty stems from the way the trading process was handled. In the USSR, trade negotiations are handled by official representatives. But their bargaining counterparts in the U.S. have been representatives of private exporting firms. Even if the U.S. firm is concerned about dwindling domestic stocks, it has not had access to information about the private sales efforts of competing export firms. When all the 1972 sales were added, the stocks of wheat and, to a lesser extent, feed grains were pulled to unusually low levels. Among policy moves made to correct this situation was the "reporting plan" instigated by the federal government, which requires U.S. firms to announce their sales and, in the case of large-volume sales, clear the sale with the appropriate federal agency. Still later, the U.S. entered a long-term agreement with the USSR specifying a range of yearly volumes within which the USSR would be expected to operate. To buy more than the upper end of the range requires approval by the U.S. government.

The most costly mistakes made during the early years of involvement in the world market were made at the producer level. Decisions to buy land and/or machinery in the aftermath of the USSR purchases were not always sound decisions. A long-run commitment was made on the basis of a short-run surge in price. This topic has been treated in other chapters but the importance of making long-run decisions only on long-run price expectations that have sound anaytical support deserves emphasis. In particular, taking action on the strength of export buying by one country is dangerous. Examination of data reporting world trade activity indicates the USSR was a net importer of significant volumes of wheat only twice between 1960 and 1978. The two years were 1972 and 1975. We would expect the USSR to be a heavy buyer only when weather or other problems mean a shortfall in her crop. Long-range decisions by producers in the U.S. should not be made on the basis of strong export buying that will be sporadic in nature.

Still better information is needed on world levels of production, stocks, and trade activity. The traditional ways of reporting in the U.S. have not focused attention on world-level variables and economic forces. But the weather in the PRC can have a significant influence on grain, rice, and soybean markets in the U.S. Both the USDA and the private advisory services will be expanding their coverage of existing data and developing new ways, such as aerial photography, to supplement on-site inspection of crop conditions in key countries around the world. The necessity of staying in tune with world markets increases the difficulty of the task facing the decision maker and also increases the probability he will be paying an advisory service for assistance.

The Changing Role of Price

Price is the focal point of attention in the marketplace. In an exchange economy, price is charged with the task of coordinating activities, guiding production, and allocating resources. It is a herculean task and as the marketing systems become more complex, price will need help.

The role of price has changed with the move to decentralized markets. Trade in the terminal markets once set the price levels for livestock. In the 1950s and early 1960s, traders in other markets would mark time and await the first word from the Chicago yards before a price level and trend was established. Soybean prices around the country were tied to Decatur, Illinois. Wheat prices were set by the local mill and vegetable prices were set at the local cannery or processor. Prices were tied to a central market or local collecting point. But times have changed. The Chicago livestock yards are extinct. Wheat, corn, and soybean prices are determined by subtracting a basis from a futures quote. Most vegetables are produced under contract with processors. Broiler production is integrated and the only visible cash price is at the retail level.

The centralized markets were characterized by physical proximity of buyer and seller. With the move to decentralized markets has come an increase in the importance of terms of trade other than price. Weighing conditions for livestock, moisture discounts in the grains, protein premiums in wheat, and quality specifications on fruits and vegetables may be more significant than price. Price is still important but it is part of a total package. Cattle are sold weighed at the feedlot with a four percent shrink. Beef carcasses are quoted by weight ranges and yield grade. Wheat is not just wheat but No. 2 Hard Red Winter, ordinary protein. With the need for specificity in trade and in the reporting of trade activity, price is supplemented by increasingly sophisticated descriptive terminology.

With the move to decentralized markets have come new approaches to pricing and price discovery. Where price was once determined by competitive bidding of buyers, it is now increasingly tied to some specific market indicator. This practice is called formula pricing and has been a source of concern for many market analysts. In Chapter 6, we noted that questions are being raised as to what percentage of the total trade volume can be tied to a particular market report before the report is determining rather than reporting price. Does at least part of the trade have to be on a "competitive bid" basis or be negotiated by buyer and seller to insure the price is a representative price? What price is *the* correct price on any particular day? These and related questions still have not been answered.

As the competitive bidding and negotiation dimensions of price discovery diminish in importance, it appears the role of price is becoming more passive. We have to remember that price for agricultural products is a derived price. Increased awareness of this and increased understanding of the interrelations between stages of our marketing systems is moving price toward a role of registering the net result of economic activity. To illustrate, the soybean crusher does not move into the market and bid a price for beans without reason. Given the price at which he can sell soybean oil and soybean meal and given his operating margin, he can calculate what he can afford to pay for beans. The cotton gin calculates an offer price in the same fashion. The wheat elevator ties his bid to a futures quote. The breaker of beef carcasses bids for carcasses given knowledge of his costs, losses during breaking, and prices of the primal and subprimal cuts he will sell. Given time for the impact to be registered in the derived prices, an increase in operating costs for the processor or handler will mean a lower bid to the producer. At times price appears to be more a residual and a reflector of other activity than a causal factor—especially in the short run.

Forward pricing schemes and hedging programs influence the role of price. The truck farmer who forward contracts his vegetable crop with a processor for a particular price will complete the production process with little or no interest in price changes. His fertilizer, cultivation, irrigation, harvesting, and packaging decisions will not be significantly affected by price within the production year. The corn farmer who has hedged his stored corn crop will not necessarily be influenced to pull corn out of storage by a declining price. Theoretically, a declining price would encourage use of corn and discourage holding it in storage. But the hedged corn will be at least partially immune. Changes in the basis, the relationship between cash and futures, not just changes in cash price might be required to encourage selling the cash product.

In vertically integrated structures, there are no visible prices because there are only product transfers from stage to stage internal to the organization. There are no price quotes for live broilers, for example, because there is no market for live broilers. The industry is almost totally integrated and decisions to adjust production levels are made on the basis of the prices of broilers at retail. Prices in the dairy market are administered prices based on a calculating formula and a program to divert surplus milk into secondary uses away from the fluid market.

In an exchange economy, price will always be important. But price does not always behave the way the theory texts say it should—especially in agriculture. The trend toward various forms of administered and contractual price arrangements will continue as decision makers at all levels seek refuge from the problems of volatile prices. The nature and level of economic activity will increasingly be determined by a combination of price and related considerations that grow from increased awareness of the economic environment, public policy, the world market, and a better understanding of the rules for economic success in an increasingly complex market system.[6]

Summary

The decade of the 1980s will be a combination of the old and the new. Many of the changes and trends that have been started or were accentuated in the 1970s will extend into the next five to 10 years. But new influences will also be seen, some of which we cannot even visualize yet.

Although the picture will vary by commodities, we will see a gradual but persistent tendency toward vertical integration. Much of the motivation will come from the economic incentives provided by the opportunity to coordinate economic functions and to gain a measure of protection from the price volatility that plagued most markets in the late 1970s. Increasing costs of transportation and increasing charges for marketing will bring concern about the multiple selling and handling of many agricultural products, and this will mean the integrating of at least two functions.

Public policy will tend to be oriented toward the consuming public. Food and fiber prices will be determined largely in the marketplace. The concern over rising food prices and the need to keep prices at a level that will compete in the world market will largely preclude price supports above the equilibrium level.

We can expect to see increased activity by the private concern in market analysis, in the collection and dissemination of news and information, and in the role of educator of the decision maker. More producers are aware of the dangers and potentials of the market. The next "wave" of adoption by agricultural producers may well be in the area of marketing strategies and decision models. The long-range research efforts will be left to the universities and to the USDA.

Price and the manner in which price is discovered will receive a great deal of attention. In 1978, we saw Congressional hearings on price reporting in the meat business. More concern over formula pricing will emerge. Most references with a copyright of 1970 or later are debating the pros and cons of formula pricing, administered pricing, committee pricing, and other non-traditional approaches to price discovery.

Perhaps the most important development of the 1980s will take the form of a dramatic increase in the time and attention paid to the marketing decision. The U.S. economy is exposed to the world. U.S. agriculture is an important part of world trade. Prices will be volatile because we will be exposed to weather, pest and disease problems around the world. The percentage of decision makers who use, not just watch, the futures markets will increase dramatically. There will be more agitation about the role of futures trade. An upper echelon of decision makers who are well informed and who will become more sophisticated as market analysts will create a knowledge and ability gap between themselves and the rank and file producer who lags in adoption of new procedures. This gap in knowledge will be unavoidably accentuated by the market advisory services that will reach a broader audience but whose members will still be a fairly small percentage of the total and will be the more progressive decision makers. The markets and marketing will be exciting—and challenging.

Footnotes

1. We should guard against being too optimistic. Some of the positive trends of the 1970s have been a long time in coming. In Chapter 15, brief attention is paid to the needed changes in research, in the educational process, in public policy, and in public services that have impact on our marketing systems. If progress is not made in these areas, progress toward more efficient marketing systems will be slowed.

2. But that does not mean bargaining legislation will not be introduced. Enthusiasm dropped off in the mid-1970s with the price recovery in the grains but the lower prices in 1977 and 1978 rekindled the fires. The National Agricultural Bargaining Act of 1978, introduced by senators from the farm states, was essentially a rehash of the 1971 Sisk Bill. It is politically wise for the senators and representatives from the farm states to introduce such legislation even if the chances of its passing are slim.

3. The concern for long-run implications in such actions as these is conspicuous in its absence. Cyclical patterns in production and prices, we have discovered, are largely a function of expectations. The announcement on imports came during a period when market analysts were expressing alarm at the extent to which the cow herd had been liquidated. Expectations dimmed with the announcement—and a new surge of liquidation followed. Beef prices will be higher in the 1980s because the import announcement reduced the potential for beef production in the 1980s. This topic will be treated again in Chapter 15 in building a case for more enlightened public policy.

4. The concept of parity or parity prices has received little attention to this point. Demands for parity price are still heard from some producer groups. Parity means equal. The parity price for wheat is the price that gives wheat the same purchasing power relative to prices of other products that it had in the 1910–14 base period. In the late 1970s, wheat price at 100 percent of parity would be well over $5.00 per bu. The concept largely ignores the impact of cost-reducing technology, mechanization, improved varieties, and other advances across the years. For many commodities, a competitive return on investments in production will be earned at prices well below parity price. We are not likely to see the concept of parity included in future policies directed toward the agricultural sector.

5. Overall, the development we are seeing in the private sector is en-

couraging. Efforts by the private advisory services to educate their subscribers and to keep them informed on market developments will help. Many decision makers will attach more credibility to the efforts of the advisory service than to the efforts of governmental agencies. This should mean a larger percentage who are aware of what is going on in the markets.

6.   No area will be more important than the area of prices. Price and price expectations are always the crux of the marketing decision. That is why so much attention in this book has been paid to price and ways to handle price risk.

Questions

1. What are the pros and cons of moves toward vertically integrated market structures?

2. Select a commodity with which you are most familiar. Within a supply-demand framework, analyze the implications of a price ceiling at retail below the equilibrium price.

3. In what sense is the price volatility we are seeing in the markets creating an opportunity for the private market advisory services? Explain and list the type of services you feel the advisory service should provide.

4. If you were an agricultural producer who was poorly informed in terms of prices and what is going on in the markets, would you prefer to sell your product direct or through an auction market? Why?

5. Why is it important that the individual producer be aware of crop conditions around the world?

Selected References

Breimyer, Harold F., *Economics of the Product Markets of Agriculture.* Ames, Iowa: Iowa State University Press, 1976.

Collins, Norman R., "Changing Role of Price in Agricultural Marketings," *J. of Farm Econ.*, Vol. 41, August 1959.

Forker, Olan D., "Agricultural Prices in the 1970s: How Will Value be Established?" *Southern J. Agr. Econ.*, Vol. 6, July 1974.

Rogers, George B., "Pricing Systems and Agricultural Marketing Research," *Agr. Econ. Res.*, ERS, USDA, January 1970.

Shaffer, James D., "Changing Orientations of Marketing Research," *Am. J. Agr. Econ.*, Vol. 50, December 1968.

chapter fifteen

Needs for More Effective Marketing Systems

This book has been written with an underlying concern for better understanding of the dimensions that make the composite of our marketing activities a system. When appropriate, attention has been focused on the interstage activities as determinants of the level of vertical coordination that is achieved by the system. The need for increased attention to the total system has been recognized for many years but we will move to the 1980s with little progress having been made.

Several complementary developments will be necessary to move our marketing systems to a higher plane of technical and pricing efficiency for any given level of technology. In this chapter, we look at what would be required and offer a combination of hypotheses and suggestions that might benefit the student, market analyst, and decision maker.

A Revised Research Orientation

Progress in moving our research orientation toward more concern for the total system has been and continues to be slow. The fault here rests primarily with the research community. Recognizing the need by a few professionals has not been enough. To change requires adjustment, reorganization, and, in some cases, going back to the books to get exposure to the analytical skills needed to do effective systems research. The changes have not been made partly because of the perceived difficulty in making the change and partly because there has been no pressure for change coming from the industry and its trade groups. We should not be surprised at this lack of pressure. If the research community waits for pressure from the industry before changing the subtle dimensions of its research orientation, it will be too late for the change to make a significant contribution. The problems, difficulties, and inefficiencies will be acute before the industry presses for change in the research community. By that time, the researcher will be analyzing the impact of economic forces that are at work and that are largely irreversible, instead of offering information that contributes to the knowledge base and guides the direction of change in our marketing systems.

The change required for more productive research orientation is not as great as many researchers have perceived. The first and most important step is simply an increased awareness of the nature of the marketing system. Before we worry about highly sophisticated analyses in terms of quantitative rigor, we must first understand the internal workings of the market system. Said another way, we have to identify and understand the interrelationships before we can quantify them.

Basically, in what ways does the body of marketing research appear to be deficient? Three areas that can be identified are:

1. The research methodology has tended to ignore the activities along the interfaces of the marketing system. The emphasis has often been on activity at a particular level as if it were independent of the rest of the system. The question is one of the value of research which, in the process of trying to increase efficiency of activity at one level, generates operations at that particular level that do not "fit" the rest of the system. An example is found in the critical attack on the research community by Hightower in his *Hard Tomatoes, Hard Times*.[1] To mechanically harvest tomatoes, Hightower says the research community generated a variety with a "tough" skin that could tolerate the mechanical handling. But it was not, in the opinion of many, a very desirable product at the consumer level. The first deficiency, then, is simply one of an orientation that appears to pay too little attention to the interstage interrelations and to the importance of interstage coordination. The work by Mighell and Jones was an exception but there has been little follow-through after they presented their conceptual framework.[2]

2. Related, the research output has not provided measures of the implications to the marketing system, to system participants, or to

society of the continued failure to move to a higher level of vertical coordination. Much of the research appears to have implicitly assumed coordination is a zero-sum game. There has been little or no concern over how the benefits of coordination would be distributed within the system simply because there has been little recognition and measurement of the benefits. And before change is likely at the individual participant level, that decision maker must be shown the implications of change and how he would fare if he changed his mode of operation.

3. The marketing research community has tended to back away from taking what we could call a conditional normative approach. During the 1950s and 1960s, marketing research was being handled by a professional group characterized by a relatively conservative approach. Other areas such as resource economics and economic development looked more appealing to the newly trained and younger researcher who tended to be a bit more liberal in his or her thinking. The situation changed somewhat in the 1970s but the majority of researchers stuck with the traditional so-called "positive" approach of measuring the implications of changes that have already occurred. Few were willing to take a position such as, "If these are the goals, then here is the way to get there" or "If these changes are made, then these will be the economic implications." This is a loose interpretation of the conditional normative approach to research but it illustrates the point that needs to be made in this area.

Part of the research community will change as we move to the 1980s. The pattern is being set. The market analyst will either keep up with the needs of the industry in his program of applied research or he will be left standing as the decision maker turns to the private advisory and information services. The market analyst can still be productive with a program of basic research or in applied work that lags comfortably behind the needs of the top-notch decision makers. The need to keep up is there, however, and he will have missed a real opportunity to serve his profession and his clientele.[3]

Changes in the Educational Effort

Even if all the needed research and analysis is done, there will need to be change in how this information is disseminated. In the classroom, in the extension session, in the regional conference, and in the adult education course there is a need to develop a more rigorous analytical framework and then a follow-through for application.

On several occasions in early chapters, the importance of understanding the competitive structure within which the decision maker is operating has been stressed. If everyone associated with marketing understood this one concept, some problems that plague production agriculture would disappear. At a minimum, there would be better understanding of what to expect in terms of a macro or aggregate response to a short-run increase in price. The reaction of the decision maker who decides the higher prices are short-run in nature will be limited to the supply response that is possible given the fixed resources—and this is important. Part (a) of Figure 15.1 illustrates the response when no change in the cost structure is involved. Part (b) shows the response when new resources (land, machinery, storage equipment, etc.) are brought in as part of the response. The cost structure shifts, usually up, and the producer who reacts this way is in trouble when the price later falls. As we have stressed, a response to higher prices that involves moving up the short-run marginal cost curve is theoretically

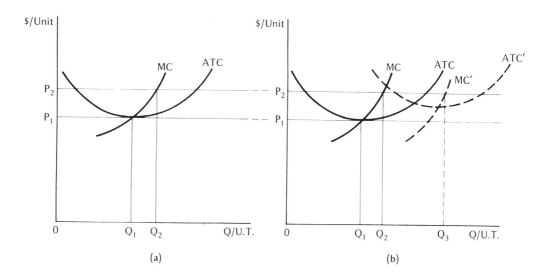

FIGURE 15.1   DEMONSTRATION OF THE COST IMPLICATIONS OF BRINGING IN NEW RESOURCES IN RESPONSE TO A HIGHER PRODUCT PRICE[a]

[a]In part (a), the response is from OQ_1 to OQ_2 when price moves up to OP_2. The cost structure does not change and, if price subsequently falls, no new resources have been brought into production. In part (b), an identical firm responds by bringing in new resources and the quantitative response is to OQ_3. The cost structure shifts and, if price falls, losses would be incurred at a higher price than would be the case for the firm represented in part (a) of the figure.

sound. It is the response that involves changing the cost structure that is not theoretically sound if the stronger prices do appear to be only in the short run.

This point is simple and important. Do the students who leave the B.S. programs in Agricultural Economics really understand the concept? How about the operating farmer? Have we found ways to get this basic concept into extension programs? Are we really coming to grips with the root of the problem when we sympathize with the producer when prices break and do whatever is possible in helping him ease the pain by making better hold-sell or hedging decisions?

Other concepts are equally important. For decades, farmers have talked about "merchandising" their product. At countless meetings an attempt is made by some producer to draw parallels with the steel or auto industry and then he asks the inevitable question, "Why don't we price our product the way they do?" And how many times have we seen resulting actions that reflect a failure to understand that, in the short run, price of agricultural products can and will fall below the cost of production? Both the question and the lack of understanding spring from a common base— total ignorance of the type of economic structure in production agriculture.

Much of what is needed, therefore, is understanding of some basic economic facts of life. But that understanding will be neither quick nor easy to get. Part of the problem is a lack of resources. The university teacher can do only so much to assure he is "getting through" when he is looking at class sizes consistently in the 80 to 120 range. And, unfortunately, some classes are taught by teachers whose only reason for being in the front of the lecture hall is because they were assigned the course by the administrator. But in spite of these barriers there are excellent university teachers who are excited about their work, who are involved in it as researchers, market analysts, or extension specialists, and who find ways to overcome the numbers barrier and motivate students.

But the resources are thin. At most land grant universities, the number of extension specialists to handle the marketing area for all commodities ranges from zero to three. The number of researchers is comparable and many of these carry heavy teaching loads. The job is simply too big to expect overnight success from the limited resources.

Increasingly, however, it appears the task is going to be left at least partly to the private concerns and advisory services. Companies who have long been interested in financing and otherwise facilitating the dissemination of technical information and know-how on production are recognizing the need for help in the marketing area. Moves to finance seminars, short courses, weekly or monthly market letters, and similar efforts are a step in the right direction.

The decade of the 1980s will see tremendous advances in the decision maker's level of understanding in our food and fiber marketing systems. If developing patterns continue and persist, a significant minority among producers will move to a more sophisticated level of awareness and understanding of markets, prices, and marketing strategies. The knowledge gap between this minority and the remaining majority of the producers is likely to widen but this could turn out to be a healthy development in the long run. As innovators and early adopters of advanced knowledge and more sophisticated tools, the more progressive element will set an example, and, through competition, may force increased concern by the masses of producers. Given what we have seen in the 1970s, it is difficult to shake the feeling that the producers as decision makers are ready and would be receptive. The big question is whether the educational push will be there.[4]

A More Enlightened Public Policy

Earlier, an entire chapter was devoted to discussion of public policy. The treatment there was primarily descriptive and focused on "what is" and the general impact of the prevailing policy. The theme was again noted in Chapter 14 with discussion of the type of policy we are likely to see in the 1980s. But a more consistent and enlightened policy is needed to allow, perhaps promote, progressive growth and more efficient marketing systems.

We can start with the perennial problem of a farm policy. Producers always seem to be holding decisions in limbo, waiting action on a farm policy. Even granting the slowness with which bills move through Congress, there is little excuse for uncertainty that the delays have often created. Actions by producers are taken not because of the inherent uncertainty of the marketplace but because of the uncertainty with regard to policy.

The complexity of the federal bureaucracy often presents problems and leads to seemingly inconsistent positions by different arms of the federal government. In the early 1970s, the beef industry was being criticized for not expanding beef production. As we have seen in earlier chapters, the criticism was invalid. Herds were being built at an almost frantic pace and beef production was imminent. But at the same time the criticism was being levied, the use of diethylstilbestrol (DES) in cattle feedlot rations was being banned by the Food and Drug Administration (FDA). Most analysts had estimated a 10 to 15 percent increase in gain from a given feed intake using DES in the rations. This position by the FDA was later declared illegal by the courts on the grounds no adequate public hearings were held. Still later, the ban on usage was reinstated and the on-again off-again approach to policy was a disruptive influence to the industry. Actions by the Environmental Protection Agency (EPA) toward more stringent rules on pollution have proven costly to feedlots and to packing plants. Moves by the EPA to outlaw certain pesticides and herbicides have required adjustments. For several years, the pork belly and hog and cattle markets have been treated to periodic "scares" on the issue of using nitrites as a preservative for bacon and processed meats.

The regulations may well be needed. But certain conditions should be met in handling these issues:

1. A significant need should be shown to exist and supported by a substantial volume of scientific evidence;

2. Public officials should be encouraged to refrain from releasing public comments until the facts have been reviewed and a decision has been made on what official action will be taken; and

3. Subject to the severity of the need, an orderly adjustment process should be planned and enough time should be allowed for the new adjustments.

Policy positions should be based on solid analysis and, once developed, should be followed to their prescribed conclusion. In the early 1970s, production controls were lifted from most major food, feed, and fiber crops and the explicit message to the American farmer was to "produce for a hungry world." But the policy makers issued no warning of what would happen if overproduction became a problem. There were no official guidelines in terms of how much wheat, corn, cotton, soybeans, and all the other crops could be moved into the domestic and world markets without significant reductions in price. But the most obvious inconsistency came about one year later when a policy move placed an embargo on the shipment of soybeans to Japan. This denied the American producer access to the markets for which he had been encouraged to produce. Such moves are extremely disruptive to markets and do much to weaken the credibility of any governmental program.

Perhaps most importantly, those in charge of making policy should accept the responsibility of being better informed. Capable market analysts and competent economists are in the USDA, on the staffs of Congressional representatives, and in the land grant universities. But their expertise is often not called upon until after the fact. How much analysis was completed to estimate the impact of the price ceilings on food in 1973 before they were imposed? The market analyst who from an objective perspective would have argued prior to the price ceilings that the net impact would be positive was difficult or impossible to find. Many vocally opposed the move. After the embargo on soybeans to Japan, that important customer of ours attempted immediately to negotiate a long-range commitment from Brazil. Were such long-run implications of the embargo considered before it was placed? The lack of dialogue between the federal agency, industry, and the research community before a policy move is made may be an important reason why there is so much dialogue to defend and justify the policy *after* the fact.

Part of the problem is that policy makers are often guided by the politician's need for a short-run boost to his image. Doing something to hold down food prices is a natural image builder. But the consumer has to live with the long-run implications. We can close this plea for a more enlightened policy with the example discussed earlier. In June of 1978, the administration relaxed import restrictions on beef and allowed an additional 200 million pounds to enter the U.S. during the remainder of 1978. The increase is not that large and amounts to less than the tonnage from three days slaughter in the U.S. But the psychological shock to the market was tremendous. Prices of live cattle futures, carcass beef, and all classes of live cattle fell before, during, and after the announcement. The retail price of beef declined by a much smaller percentage and then turned higher again.

In terms of short-run impact, we could argue the retail price averaged less during the rest of 1978 than the average which would have been seen without the action on imports. But more significant long-run implications could be listed:

1. The price volatility during the period of speculation on what would be done hurt the chances of attracting investor capital into cattle feeding, and

2. The still fragile frame of mind of the cow-calf operators took a giant step backwards toward the negative attitude that had lingered during the 1974–77 period.

This second development was and is critically important. If the cyclical liquidation is to stop, it always happens when the attitude of the cow-calf operator changes toward the positive. The cow that is sent to slaughter in 1978 is not there to contribute to the calf crop in 1979—or 1980 or 1982. Cow slaughter in the first half of 1978 exceeded the predictions of most analysts. During the April–June quarter, it actually exceeded the heavy slaughter of April–June 1977.[5]

Better Supporting Services

In a very real sense, any marketing system is a communication system. The subject of pricing efficiency has been discussed many times in this book. It deserves repeated mention because it is so important. Whether the system is doing the right thing in terms of what is being produced and how it will be handled next year, or several years into the future, will be directly related to the level of pricing efficiency being achieved today. High levels of pricing efficiency are synonymous with effective communication up and down through the market system and between consumer and producer.

One of the primary enemies of pricing efficiency is price variability. To help cut down on the magnitude of price variability, we need better awareness of the present and probable levels of supply and demand. The uninformed and naive critic cries for less governmental activity in reporting basic information series. But as we have argued in earlier chapters, this would work to accentuate, not reduce, price variability. Prices move when they react to new information on the apparent or probable levels of supply and demand. Whether it comes from the private sector or from state and federal agencies, we need *more* information, not less. An entire quarter passes before decision makers get an update of the situation in the swine industry. During the planning season, information on acreages to be seeded to various crops is critically important. But for the important spring-planted crops, the normal pattern is to publish planting intentions as of January 1 and April 1. The first estimate of actual plantings is then released in late June. The two-month "gaps" are a long time and much can change during those periods. Decisions are made on the varying output of the rumor mill, on the tendency of the producer to generalize for the entire U.S. based on what he sees in his immediate locality, and to largely inadequate personal reports and private surveys.

The futures market gets misused in many ways but an additional and potentially very legitimate use of futures gets no attention. Since the level of futures prices reacts and usually overreacts to the government report that is a surprise to the trade, perhaps the frequency with which we see dramatic moves in futures prices—up or down—in response to periodic reports should be used as an indication of the need for more frequent reports. After all, the reaction would not be so dramatic unless enough time had passed to allow the scenario being developed by the report and the scenario in the collective mind of the trade to drift apart. Again, we can point to the quarterly *Hogs and Pigs* reports to illustrate. During the period March 1977 through June 1978, four of the five quarterly reports were "bullish surprises" with prices trading sharply higher after the reports.

Nothing is more critical to the level of pricing efficiency achieved than the set of grades and related descriptive terminology used. In discussing this area earlier, mention was made of the need for grades that would receive consistent interpretation up and down through the system, which have actually been used by the trade and which categorized all of the significant, recognizable differences in product value. The USDA has responsibilities in administering the existing grades and suggesting changes when changes are needed. It is important that the grades employed be based on attributes that can be recognized at the price negotiation points in the system and be brought into the pricing process. And since the USDA has responsibility for providing the grading services, it is important that all users and potential users be informed concerning the grades, how they are determined, and what product attributes they are designed to identify.

If the official grades identify important value-related product attributes, then it follows that grades should play a prominent role in market news efforts to report trade activity. Moves to higher levels of pricing efficiency can be blocked by failure to consistently and persistently use the grades in market news messages. Progressive moves in theory don't quite measure up in practice unless an effort is made to get the grades introduced and part of the common practice in the trade. If high protein wheat is more valuable, then it is obviously important that any price premium paid for the higher level of protein gets reported and made visible to all buyers and sellers. The same need is there for grade A eggs, U.S. No. 1 potatoes, No. 2 yellow soybeans, U.S. No. 1 hogs, Choice slaughter steers, utility grade slaughter cows, or any other product where the grades reflect recognizable and significant value differentials.

Problems persist in the livestock industry. After efforts toward change throughout the 1960s and 1970s, grades for carcass beef and live cattle incorporated yield grades as a measure of the ratio of lean cuts to total carcass weight. But the Market News Service was slow to get the "yield grade" into market messages. When it was included, the message often quoted a price range for Choice 2–4 (meaning Choice quality grade with yield grade from 2 to 4) when reporting live cattle. This did not help in terms of getting more specificity into the message since 90–95 percent of fed cattle would be in the 2–4 yield grade range. And with the sporadic reporting and equally sporadic usage came a problem the textbooks did not predict. At the carcass level, prices tend to get quoted for yield grade 3, the predominant grade. Yield grade 4 tends to move at a discount but the trade reports real problems in moving a yield grade 2 at a premium to the yield grade 3. But it is here that stability and persistence will pay off. Market analysts generally agree the advent of yield grades has significant long-run potential in increasing the level of pricing efficiency in the beef marketing system.

Difficulties have also arisen in the grains. The People's Republic of China represents a huge pool of potential export buying. But the PRC tends to favor wheat from other producing countries because of an alleged lack of consistent quality in U.S. wheat. Some trade participants argue that testing procedures for high-protein wheat are not adequate. Sales are reported for only two levels—ordinary and high-protein wheat.

In the feed grains, users talk about the differences in quality of grain sorghum. Some cattle feedlots have developed their own testing procedures before they will accept shipments of grain sorghum. Whether related to varieties or some other variable, there appears to be significant differences in quality that are not stated in the price reporting efforts. As always, it takes a recognizable price premium or discount to get the message to producers. This is next to impossible to accomplish unless an adequate set of grades is available.

What is needed in the grading and in the market news area is a progressive and enlightened attitude—and it has not always been there. Pressure from the trade was required to move the Federal-State Market News Service into reporting direct trade in addition to the traditional reporting activities at the central markets. Reporting volumes of trade has been equally slow in coming even though awareness of the trade volume on which a price report is based is obviously important. The Market News Service is in the communication business and anything to meet the requisites of effective communication and to promote accurate interpretation of the message being transmitted should be encouraged.

Summary

In a sense, this entire chapter is a summary of the textbook. It deals with some of the perceived inadequacies and looks at some of the needs for more progressive and better informed marketing processes.

A change in research orientation is first in importance. We need to stop paying lip service to the need for systems analysis, and actually conduct more systems research. Without progress along these lines, we will not know which organizational structure will feel the pressures to change, which structure is more efficient in terms of basic measures of technical and pricing efficiency, and how the system participant will fare under the different alternatives.

If the research and analyses get conducted, then they need to be disseminated to a better informed decision maker who is not an economic illiterate. More attention should be placed on teaching the basic economic facts of life in our campus classrooms, extension meetings, and adult education groups. How can we expect the decision maker to cope if he or she does not understand the economic environment and how it makes an impact on the individual firm? Help is likely to be coming from the private analysis group or market advisory service because decision makers, especially agricultural producers, are going to insist on more help and the universities and governmental agencies will not have the resources to meet the need.

Much progress could be made toward a more enlightened public policy and more effective services from governmental agencies. Policy prescriptions should obviously be released in a timely fashion and before all the flexibility is gone from the producer's decision model. All policies should be based on sound analysis but the need is especially important for policies such as price controls, export embargoes, and the relaxing of import requirements that directly affect the performance of the system. The need for long-run consideration of policy moves *before they are made* is obviously important but appears to get overlooked when short-run political expediency is the motivating force behind the policy or policy change.

Footnotes

1. Reference is to Jim Hightower, *Hard Tomatoes, Hard Times*, Schenkman Publishing Co., Cambridge, Mass., 1973. Hightower's book is a report of the Agribusiness Accountability Project, a non-profit research organization funded by private grants. The report is critical of the land grant universities and claims the universities have "sold out" rural America by the aid and assistance that has been given the agribusiness complex.

2. Mighell, Ronald L. and Lawrence A. Jones, *Vertical Coordination in Agriculture*, Agr. Econ. Rep. No. 19, ERS, USDA, February 1963. This was a forward-looking publication which made a significant contribution to the conceptual framework insofar as vertical coordination is concerned. It is now out of print but copies should be available in the documents section of most university libraries. It is worth digging out.

3. This point was apparent during the writing and review periods of this manuscript. The rather extensive coverage of price and the commodity futures markets was considered to be "too much" by most reviewers. It may turn out that they were right. But it appears that price, price risk, trade in commodity futures, and hedging strategies will occupy much time of the analyst and teacher over the next 10 years. If this proves correct, then even more extensive coverage of these topic areas will be needed.

4. Discussion of the limited public resources reinforces the conviction that the educational push will come from the private sector—if it comes at all. The pace is quickening in this area. Private market advisory services are conducting seminars on market outlook, marketing strategies, analysis of commodity futures charts, hedging, how to get and handle credit, management strategies, and other topics. Attendance is typically good with top producers from 15–20 states often at particular meetings. It is these producers who will lead the way as decision makers in future years.

5. Developments such as these are frustrating to the market analyst. Theoretical support for moves to artificially disrupt the market processes is not there. Empirical analysis of past attempts to exert influence by price controls, control over exports, etc., offers little to support such actions. Any positive impact in the short run is typically overwhelmed by the negative implications over the longer planning horizon. But the decisions continue to be made and actions are taken on the basis of short-run considerations.

Questions

1. Do you think market economists should take a "conditional normative" approach in their analyses? Why or why not?

2. Assume you were restricted to three basic economic concepts that you could get across to those making decisions in our food and fiber marketing systems. State the three you would choose and justify your choices.

3. Pick a policy decision with which you are most familiar that had impact on the agricultural sector. Within a supply-demand framework, try to analyze the short- and long-run impact on price. (Define "short run" as within the production year, "long run" as across 2 or more production years.)

4. Write down all the arguments you can in support of the need for more, not less, planning and market information.

5. What possible problems could develop when a decision maker uses a market news message that reports price but gives no indication of the volume of trade on which the price is based?

Selected References

Alderson, Wroe, *Marketing Behavior and Executive Action.* Homewood, Ill.: Richard D. Irwin, 1959.

Buchanan, James M., "A Future for 'Agricultural Economics'?" *Amer. J. Agr. Econ.*, Vol. 51, December 1969.

Hightower, Jim, *Hard Tomatoes, Hard Times.* Cambridge, Mass.: Schenkman Publishing Co., 1973.

National Commission on Food Marketing, *Food From Farmer to Consumer.* Washington, D.C.: U.S. Govt. Printing Office, 1966.

Shaffer, James D., "Changing Orientations of Marketing Research," *Amer. J. Agr. Econ.*, Vol. 50, December 1968.

Index

DATE D